Screen Nazis

WISCONSIN FILM STUDIES

Patrick McGilligan
*Series Editor*

# SCREEN NAZIS

## Cinema, History, and Democracy

Sabine Hake

The University of Wisconsin Press

The University of Wisconsin Press
1930 Monroe Street, 3rd Floor
Madison, Wisconsin 53711-2059
uwpress.wisc.edu

3 Henrietta Street
London WC2E 8LU, England
eurospanbookstore.com

Printed in the United States of America

Library of Congress Cataloging-in-Publication Data

Hake, Sabine, 1956–
Screen Nazis : cinema, history, and democracy / Sabine Hake.
p.    cm.—(Wisconsin film studies)
Includes bibliographical references and index.
ISBN 978-0-299-28714-6 (pbk.: alk. paper)
ISBN 978-0-299-28713-9 (e-book)
1. Nazis in motion pictures.
2. National socialism in motion pictures.
I. Title.   II. Series: Wisconsin film studies.
PN1995.9.N36H343       2012
791.43´658—dc23
2011043917

# Contents

# Illustrations

# Acknowledgments

All book projects are the product of conversations and debates; this one is no exception. During the five years of working on this project, I was able to present parts and versions to interested audiences at the University of Leeds, the University of New Mexico, the University of Washington, the University of North Texas, Hebrew University, the University of Southampton, SUNY Binghamton, the University of Arizona, the University of Kentucky, McGill University, the University of Texas at San Antonio, the University of Houston, the University of Wisconsin at Madison, Duke University, Georgia State University, the University of Maryland, FU Berlin, and the University of Geneva. I thank Paul Cooke, Susanne Baackmann, Sabine Wilke, Erica Nelson, Ofer Ashkenazi, Tim Bergfelder, Ingeborg Majer O'Sickey, Barbara Kosta, Harald Höbusch, Peter Gölz, Nancy Membrez, Hildegard Glass, Henning Wrage, William Donahue, Joe Perry, Peter Beicken, Bernhard Groß, and Margrit Tröhler for inviting me to share my findings with receptive audiences.

The Department of Germanic Studies at the University of Texas at Austin has been very supportive of my research; a special thanks to the department chair, Peter Hess. Colleagues in the Film Studies group have provided a productive work environment, especially Janet Staiger, friend and collaborator. Katie Arens and Kirsten Cather made useful suggestions for chapter 4; David Crew generously agreed to read the entire manuscript and offered constructive suggestions for final revisions. Marc Silberman, Erica Carter, Lutz Koepnick, and Gerd Gemünden have supported this project in various ways; I am deeply in their debt. I am grateful to Gregory Maertz for sharing his art historical expertise, David Prindle for giving feedback on the politics of 1940s Hollywood, Ann Morey for telling me what to cut from the chapter on West German film, Raymond O'Brian for introducing me to obscure British anti-Nazi films, Marcia Landy and Paola Bonifazio for contributing their expertise on Italian film, Marc Silberman and Paul Cooke for reviewing the chapter on the East German antifascist film, and Vladimir Padunov and Andrew Chapman for helping with hard-to-find Soviet materials. I appreciate the insights by the participants of the "Film and the Political" workshop at Rice University, especially Carsten Strathausen und Martin Blumenthal-Barby. The suggestions by members of the writing group at the National Humanities Center, and James Philipp and Leslie Tuttle in particular, helped me improve the introduction; Barbara McCloskey with her probing questions motivated me to make last-minute changes. Chapter 6 would not have been possible without the help of Daniel Jessen Greenfield (for Danish and Norwegian), Bradley Boovy (for Dutch), and Michael Gott (for French). Thank you to my students at the University of Texas and Rice University for allowing me to test some of the book's arguments on them; I truly appreciate Michael DeMarco for offering me feedback from an undergraduate's perspective. His input has given me hope that this book will not only be of interest to scholars in film studies, history, and German studies but might also prove suitable for teaching upper-division undergraduate and graduate courses.

Some parts of the book have appeared in earlier versions, and I am grateful to the publishers for granting their permission to use the material here. Parts of chapter 3 have been published as "Political Affect in the Antifascist Films of Frank Beyer and Konrad Wolf," in *Screening War: New Perspectives on German Suffering*, edited by Marc Silberman and Paul Cooke (Rochester: Camden House, 2010), 102–22. Some ideas for chapter 4 were first presented in "Art and Exploitation: On the Fascist Imaginary in 1970s Italian Cinema," in *Studies in European Cinema* 7.1 (2010): 11–21. An early version of chapter 7 appears as "Entombing the Nazi Past: On *Downfall* and Historicism," in *Hitler—Films from Germany*, edited by Karolin Machtans and Martin A. Ruehl (New York: Palgrave MacMillan, 2012, 81–119). And a German translation of an even earlier version of chapter 7 was published as "Raus aus dem Bunker: Über *Der Untergang* und die Ästhetisierung der NS-Vergangenheit," translated by Martin Kley, in *Nach-Bilder des Holocaust*, edited by Inge Stephan and Alexandra Tacke (Cologne: Böhlau, 2007), 1–34.

Several individuals were essential in bringing the manuscript to publication. Raphael Kadushin, my editor at the University of Wisconsin Press, was an enthusiastic supporter from the start. I thank the two anonymous readers for their incredibly generous reviews. Karen Carroll at the National Humanities Center provided amazing copyediting before the manuscript was submitted to the University of Wisconsin Press, and Barb Wojhoski gave it a final polish. At the press, Sheila McMahon expertly saw the manuscript to its next stage. The timely completion of this project would not have been possible without the generous support of a Humanities Research Center Fellowship at Rice University, a Josephus Daniels Fellowship at the National Humanities Center, a University of Texas Humanities Research Award, and, throughout the last years, the Texas Chair of German Literature and Culture. A publication subvention grant by President William C. Powers Jr. of the University of Texas at Austin paid for copyright permissions.

For everything else, I thank the love of my life, Fred Nutt.

Screen Nazis

# Introduction

I am the bad conscience of democratic systems.

Heinz Schubert as Adolf Hitler in

*Hitler—Ein Film aus Deutschland* (*Hitler: A Film from Germany,*

Hans-Jürgen Syberberg, 1981)

How can we make sense of the seemingly unending stream of feature films about the Third Reich? What causes the almost compulsive preoccupation with "sexy Nazis" and "nasty Nazis" in popular culture? And what are the emotional sources and aesthetic effects of this continuing fascination with Nazi leaders, rituals, and symbols? At regular intervals, film critics have expressed their puzzlement but failed to come up with compelling answers. Confronted with this "startling phenomenon of our times," one film journalist in 1978 observed, "Hitler and the Nazi era have been erupting on our cinema screens."[1] Declaring 1999 the year of the Nazi, another critic asked: "Why are today's film-makers so desperate to confront Nazism?"[2] And yet another decade later, in the midst of the 2009 Oscar season, reviewers once again spoke of "Nazi overload" and complained: "Nazis, Nazis, everywhere."[3]

Neither the history of the Third Reich nor its difficult legacies can explain the strange affinities between film and fascism or account for the deflationary economy of signs and significations that sustain their mutual instrumentalization—a dynamic acknowledged in the convergence of Nazism and fascism in the

3

popular imagination and the prevailing use in political debates of fascism as a generic rather than a historical term.[4] Fascist Italy, Francoist Spain, and Vichy France have been the subject of numerous films in their respective countries. But none of these regimes has achieved the kind of global recognizability enjoyed by what I call the fascist imaginary in postfascist cinema, that is, the feelings, attitudes, and beliefs by nonfascists about Nazism/fascism as a historical period, political ideology, form of dictatorship, and social, cultural, and aesthetic phenomenon. For reasons that will be presented in this introduction, the fascination with fascism is inseparable from its long history and unique status as a filmic fantasy. Neither narrative analysis nor thematic criticism can fully explain the underlying dynamics of attraction and revulsion; that is why our attention must turn to the specific feelings, emotions, and affects produced by, and projected onto, the fascist spectacle. Similarly, the history of the Third Reich and the place of fascism in the mass politics of the twentieth century are important but not sufficient to explain the iconic status of the Nazis in postwar popular culture and political debate—reason enough to focus on its contemporary meanings and significatory functions.[5]

Answering the questions posed by the exasperated reviewers quoted earlier requires a fundamental reconsideration of the terms that have guided scholarly engagement with these films until now, especially in the German context of *Vergangenheitsbewältigung* (coming to terms with the past) and its emphasis on national narratives and historical legacies. Above all, it calls for a closer look at the fascist imaginary as a signifying system whose primary function is to give expression not to our relationship to the past but to something else: present and often urgent concerns about democratic subjectivity, defined here as an essential part of civil society and public life and a particular set of attachments and identifications. In other words, the central perspective through which to analyze the fascist imaginary in postfascist cinema is not the historical but the political. And the main category through which to gain new insights into fascism's enduring attractions is that of affect, to be defined for now as the ability of feature films to affect someone or something and to produce affects beyond contents and meanings.[6]

This book is the first, in any language, to offer a comprehensive historical overview of, and a new theoretical approach to, the large number of European and American films about the Third Reich made since the beginning of World War II. From the Hollywood anti-Nazi films of the 1940s to the European resistance films produced in the last decade, from Italian Naziploitation films of the 1970s to international blockbusters such as *Inglourious Basterds* (2009), filmic representations of Nazism/fascism have provided a projection screen for the problems of postwar democracies and the contested status of ideology in the postfascist period. In seven roughly chronological chapters, I reconstruct this interrelatedness of fascist past and postfascist present through the historical contexts in which these films were originally made and seen. At the same time, through close attention to the role of affect in film, I analyze the antagonistic structure that makes the fascist imaginary the absolute other of the democratic imaginary, with both terms to be understood as two competing and evolving sets of feelings, attitudes, and beliefs about government, society, community, nation, and, most importantly, the individual as the founding site of democratic subjectivity. The historically developed and nationally specific relationship between film and fascism, once defined in these terms, offers a rich source for analyzing the mutual instrumentalization of history and politics through its textual, intertextual, and contextual manifestations and for considering its far-reaching consequences for contemporary mass culture and democratic societies.

The formative principle of "us" versus "them" that constitutes the relationship between democracy and fascism will be examined through what I describe as political affects, the discourses that sustain the fascist imaginary—that is, the fantasies about fascists (i.e., Nazis) by nonfascists—from the perspective of postfascism. A product of the cinemas of Germany, the United States, and the European countries most affected by the Nazis' racist policies and military wars, the fascist imaginary thrives on an endlessly repeated process of demarcation and externalization, a process reconstructed best through the changing conditions of film production and reception and the intense emotional reactions generated by what for audiences today are familiar, perhaps all too familiar, historical figures and events. In the films discussed in this book, the name of this outer limit, this dangerous enemy, and this absolute other is fascism. Yet as a first indication of the semiotic slippage between fascist and Nazi shared by all these films, the look of the fascist imaginary in postfascist cinema is invariably that of the Third Reich. The interplay of identities and identifications within the diegesis—that is, the fictional world of the film—is essential to analyzing this process, but so are the forms of typization, embodiment, and performance and the formal conventions and aesthetic interventions that establish correspondences between two affective economies, the filmic and the political, and their respective systems of signs and significations.

The thematic focus on the quintessential modern dictatorship and the highly standardized, if not clichéd, representation of its leaders, institutions, and organizations suggest that the films about the Third Reich, despite the inevitable methodological problems, can be described as something akin to a genre, a genre made up of historically and nationally distinct subgenres or series. Belonging to the large and unwieldy category of the historical film—that is, feature films about actual historical figures and events or fictional stories set against an authentic historical background—most films chosen for the seven chapters share key elements such as an identifiable time and place (i.e., Europe, 1933–45), a limited group of protagonists, familiar story lines, and recurring themes and motifs. In accordance with the rules of classical narrative, these films introduce the main characters within a larger social and political context, develop their personal stories against the backdrop of momentous historic events (e.g., war, occupation, genocide), and use these filmic conventions to examine the relationship between individual and society, subject and state, citizen and nation, and so forth.

Made over a period of seventy years and an integral part of both the history of film and the history of feelings about fascism, the films borrow key elements from melodrama, comedy, biopic, horror, thriller, and film noir; share important characteristics with the World War II film and Holocaust film; and draw on realist, documentary, modernist, and postmodernist styles. Furthermore, they reflect fundamental changes in the conditions of film production, exhibition, and reception since the war years and incorporate a wide range of filmic formats and styles beyond mainstream cinema (e.g., art films, exploitation films) as well as a great variety of production models beyond the Hollywood studio system (e.g., European coproductions, independent productions, state-subsidized productions). The films rely heavily on the historical research, intertextual references, and media synergies that have fueled the fascist imaginary from the beginning and made it an important part of larger debates about the future of the past in the age of mediality, visuality, and specularity. But most importantly, the filmic representation of the Third Reich is inseparable from the political conflicts and debates that inform the imaginary relationship between fascism and democracy at a particular time and place and, from the perspective of today, gives access to the changing meanings of the political since the end of World War II.

There is no doubt that the historical film serves as an important source of information and entertainment, but it also is a powerful tool of subjectification, that is, of interpellating individuals as political subjects. Film scholars and historians agree on three closely related points: The filmic representation of specific historical periods, figures, and events changes with their changing political functions (e.g., as legitimizing narratives of nation) and scholarly interpretations (e.g., in relation to questions of agency and causality) and, for that reason, must be treated as historical in and of itself. Second, the historical film, according to Robert Burgoyne, plays a pivotal role in shedding light on contemporary problems, for "by reenacting the past in the present, the historical film brings the past into dialogue with the present."[7] Finally, historical films, far from trivializing or falsifying history, provide compelling solutions to the challenges (e.g., in relation to the production of collective memory) of what Robert Rosenstone calls "looking at the past in a postliterate age" and are inseparable from the history of audiovisual media.[8]

What scholars have not yet considered in greater detail are the ways in which history offers a conduit to the political in the broadest sense, that is, its institutions, procedures, conventions, identifications, and forms of engagement. What has also escaped scholarly attention thus far are the affective dimensions of the historical film and their contribution not only to the meaning of history and memory but also to the aestheticization and medialization of politics. To evoke two metaphors often used to describe the filmic medium, the historical film may function like a mirror and a window, but increasingly it also functions like a telescope and a kaleidoscope, and one of the problems thus brought into the space of historical and political representation is that of textuality, contextuality, and intertextuality and their respective affective economies, that is, the production of perceptions, emotions, and sensations within the signification systems and discourse networks associated with the cinema.

Rather than define this heterogeneous corpus of films through normative definitions that assume a stable relationship between signifier and signified, I propose to use the significatory excess associated with Nazism/fascism to examine how democracy acquires an emotional vocabulary or affective habitus through confrontation with its enemy—which also means its suppressed self. This dynamic reflects several paradigm shifts in the status of the historical referent over the past seventy years: from the Third Reich as a political and military threat during the war years to the competing definitions of Nazism/fascism in the ideological confrontations of the cold war to its transformation in the 1970s into what Michel Foucault famously called a "floating signifier."[9] In an era of disappearing referentials (i.e., in the age of the simulacrum), "history is our lost referential, that is to say our myth on the screen," concluded Jean Baudrillard at the time.[10] Continuing in the discourses of heritage prevalent since the 1990s, this momentous shift from referentiality (i.e., that the films are "about" the Third Reich) to indexicality (i.e., that the films refer to something else) attests to fundamental changes in the basic terms of filmic, historical, and political representation since the historical defeat of the Third Reich. Precisely by complicating the relationship between film and history, the films made since the 1970s have sharpened our awareness of the political as an affective intensity that assumes form through identifications and attachments while reproducing the kind of radical ambiguity, the absence of stable, innate meanings that, in the words of Ernesto Laclau, makes democracy a floating or empty signifier as well.[11]

The conversion of fascism into an empty signifier and the impossibility of controlling such semiotic excess through ethical or aesthetic strictures must be seen in the context of two larger developments: the emergence of poststructuralism as a new epistemological and aesthetic paradigm and the decline of communism or socialism as a valid alternative to capitalist liberal democracies. Indicative of a broader crisis of referentiality, postmodernism profoundly changed the terms of historical representation: from narrative to spectacle, from authenticity to performativity, and from belief in the real to the pleasures of simulation. However, the "return of history as film," to quote German studies scholar Anton Kaes, did not just produce highly mediated forms of engagement with the Nazi past.[12] Above all, it announced the disappearance of the ideological master narratives first diagnosed in the crisis of Marxism and, according to Alain Badiou, a contributing factor in the much discussed crisis of the political today. The process culminated in the fall of the Berlin Wall in 1989 and the ensuing collapse of the Soviet Union and the Eastern Bloc in 1991, a moment celebrated by some commentators at the time as the beginning of the era of postideology. These events, in turn, contributed to the second major paradigm shift in the filmic representation of the Third Reich, namely, the historicization of the past, the proliferation of heritage culture, and what, in a variation on Kaes's phrase, might be called the return of politics as history. Once again, the fascist imaginary is being marshaled in order to confront what Chantal Mouffe and others describe as a crisis of liberal democracy and its connections to the postpolitical as a politics of managed interests and administered differences beyond the antagonisms associated with ideology in the traditional sense.

Furthermore, the remarkable filmic productivity surrounding fascism as an empty signifier is inseparable from the term's inflationary use in public debates since the 1970s. During the heyday of the cold war, the choice of terminology—Nazism or fascism, anti-Nazism or antifascism—reflected insurmountable ideological differences and stood for dangerous political confrontations. With the profound changes in the location of the political brought about by the events of 1968 and, later, of 1989–91, these terms have become virtually synonymous with totalitarianism, militarism, antisemitism, right-wing extremism, and ultranationalism. Hans Magnus Enzensberger's assertion that "fascism is repugnant not because the Germans practiced it, but because it is possible everywhere"[13] early on announced its suitability as a convenient weapon of political denunciation. Neo-Nazism, neofascism, cryptofascism, and Islamo-fascism: these are only some of the neologisms coined to describe anything opposed (or accused of being opposed) to democratic principles and practices. In many cases, such polemics are closely tied to feelings of fear, loathing, and a considerable dose of paranoia on the side of the self-declared defenders of democracy.[14] This phenomenon is largely limited to the United States and the nations of Western Europe, the countries most involved in the making of the postwar settlement and most invested in promoting a specific kind of liberal democracy; as we will see, the discourse of antifascism in the Eastern Bloc countries functioned according to very different principles. Yet in all cases, the intense emotions generated by, or attributed to, fascism are closely linked to persistent anxieties surrounding the weakness of democratic institutions and practices and, even more troubling today, the renewed appeal of ideologies that mobilize racial, ethnic, religious, and national differences in an effort to revive old or invent new enmities.

Feelings, emotions, and, in the broadest sense, affects, three terms to be defined in greater detail in the next section of this introduction, play an important role in the construction of democratic subjectivities and the filmic imagination of politics and the political. These notoriously elusive sensations or intensities facilitate the mutual articulation of past and present in the historical film and make possible the presentation/representation of the historical as the political, and vice versa. Most historical films rely on stories about individuals to show the reality—and imagine the possibility—of political experiences. Their heavy reliance on emotions and affects as sites of ideological interpellation allow us to move beyond the binaries of public versus private, personal versus political, and individual versus collective inscribed in classical narrative and to conceptualize democratic subjectivity in terms not part of a conventional rights-based definition of democracy. By shifting the focus of analysis from the representation of history to the history of a representation, we can take advantage of the largely untapped potential of the historical film as a laboratory of emotions and an "archive of feelings" about the political in the broadest sense and about democracy in its various postwar manifestations.[15] These feelings might be related to experiences of, or in, society, community, nation, democracy, and public life. But most importantly, the structure of sympathies and antipathies at the center of classical narrative places the individual in relation to "the people," that elusive category regularly evoked in social utopias and political rhetorics but available to filmic representation only in particular manifestations, that is, as individuals—a point of great relevance to the historical film given its double focus on individuals' complicated relationship to power and the profound effects of public events on private lives.

There are many reasons for approaching the large and unwieldy group of films about the Third Reich from the perspective of political affects; some of them even involve the ideology of Nazism. The twentieth century has been the century of film and the kind of mass mobilizations that gave rise to fascist movements as well as modern democracies. Both forms of addressing, conceiving, and engaging "the people" rely heavily on emotions in creating forms of political engagement and attachment. The emotions engendered by film have been used throughout its history to build and maintain support for dictatorial regimes and their oppressive policies, a connection examined extensively by studies on film and propaganda. Yet the same strategies—of course, employed more subtly—can be found in the stories, sounds, and images created to defend and promote democracy. The historical attempts to harness the power of emotions for political movements and ideologies and the repeated failures to establish another kind of politics based on reason and rationality have not increased suspicion about the reliance in politics on what might be called technologies of emotion. On the contrary, the proliferation of new media and communication technologies has dramatically increased the possibilities, both in the imagining of political alternatives and in the promotion of emotion as a substitute for ideology. The consequences for cinema and for society are nowhere more apparent than at the outer limit of the political in the democratic imaginary: the spectacle of fascist rule and its embodiment in the overdetermined figure of the Nazi.

The inherent abstractness of democracy, as both a form of government and a way of life, has posed a considerable challenge to filmmakers because of its lack of compelling myths and symbols and the resultant difficulty of sustaining democratic commitments through fictional scenarios and imagined identities. Defined in the most basic sense as government of, by, and for the people (to reference Lincoln's Gettysburg Address), democracy does not translate easily into the formal registers of classical narrative, given the latter's emphasis on individual experiences and psychological explanations. Not surprisingly, democracy's foundational narratives are often depicted through the more familiar and highly codified narratives of nation, with the nation-state hailed as the originator and protector of democratic rights and freedoms. As a result, democratic subjectivity in the cinema remains inextricably tied to the discourses of nationalism and patriotism and their established range of emotions: love of the fatherland, a sense of belonging, feelings of loyalty and pride, but also more problematic, complicated ones such as hubris, resentment, guilt, and shame. For the same reasons, democratic subjectivity is heavily dependent on a filmic genre that functions like a veritable laboratory, archive, and museum of its triumphs and defeats: the historical film. No other genre is better suited to show the struggles for liberty and equality in their appropriately epic scales, and no genre (with the exception perhaps of the political thriller) is quite as successful in locating the nature of the political in conflicts and confrontations. The films about the Third Reich combine both perspectives in almost ideal-typical ways: through their conflation of the personal and the political in the shared language of affect and through their definition of the political as the relationship between friends and enemies. Of course, the enemy-friend distinction is not the only form of representing democracy in the cinema, and the historical film is only one of several genres through which political questions can be addressed directly. However, for reasons that should become clear in the following pages, the us-versus-them structure is a particularly effective way of presenting historical events and aligning them with broader political questions.

The current debate on the crisis of democracy among political theorists and the growing attention in cultural studies to the role of emotion in political life suggest that the time has come to take a closer look at the political affects organized by the cinema and, specifically, by one subset of the historical film: films about the Third Reich. One way of approaching this heterogeneous body of work is to recognize the films' shared reliance on the friend-enemy distinction as their central narrative structure and principle of character engagement, a connection that, as political theorists Chantal Mouffe, Ernesto Laclau, and others would argue, is not coincidental. According to Carl Schmitt, the controversial German political theorist of the 1920s and 1930s and an important interlocutor for many thinkers currently writing on the crisis of democracy, the opposition between friend and enemy marks the foundation of the political and informs the opposition between good and evil in the moral sphere, and between beautiful and ugly in the aesthetic sphere.[16] Yet whereas the real enemy for Schmitt is a legitimate opponent who is fought according to established rules, the absolute enemy comes to represent the other that, once designated as non-human, must be defeated and eliminated.

As the real enemy, to continue the analogy from the perspective of post-fascism, the Nazis after 1933 destroyed the remaining vestiges of democracy developed during the Weimar Republic and forced democracies elsewhere to defend their core political values in a series of political confrontations that culminated in World War II.[17] Yet as the absolute enemy, fascism in the cinema has since also come to represent that which exists outside the symbolic order, a provocation to democracy as felt commitment and lived experience and a threat to the mechanisms of inclusion and exclusion that sustain both, hence the frequent association of the fascist spectacle with fear, horror, and revulsion and its close affinity with the aesthetics of the grotesque. Through the fictional confrontation with both types of enemies, the inherent contradictions of democracy between freedom and unity, equality and liberty, and self-interest and the common good are temporarily forgotten or resolved. At the same time, the exposure to fascism, its spectacle of power and violence and its cult of folk and community, brings into sharp relief the weaknesses of the democratic system, including its highly formalized process of representative government and co-determination, and calls into question its underlying assumptions, a process analyzed best through the affective investments—the identifications, projections, and embodiments—that define the relationship between democracy and its absolute other, fascism.

What does the friend-enemy distinction add to our discussion of the enduring fascination with fascism in the cinema, and popular cultural more generally? Many scholars until now have followed Susan Sontag and her influential 1974 essay "Fascinating Fascism" by assuming a libidinal economy of domination and submission at the heart of such incessant fantasy production.[18] Relying heavily on psychoanalytic theories, these explanations usually conclude with Freud (e.g., in *Totem and Taboo*) that the dynamics of attraction and repulsion set into motion by the Nazis is the expression of the fundamental ambivalence at the core of all emotions and the driving force behind the endless projections that, both figuratively and literally, guarantee their eternal afterlife on the movie screens. However, such a psychoanalytic, if not anthropological, approach is too broad to explain historical contingencies and fails to account for the specifically political meanings of the postfascist imaginary. Its amalgam of fantasies, insights, pleasures, and attitudes mediates between the social and the individual and partakes in the conscious and the unconscious but cannot be reduced to either one of them. (The same reservations might apply to speculations about a so-called Nazi myth and its appropriation by contemporary culture that focus on "the fashion by which National Socialism constitutes itself, with or without the use of myths, in a dimension, for a function, and with a self-assurance that all three can be properly termed mythic."[19])

Here Schmitt's attempt to define the political by emphasizing what distinguishes it from the social and the cultural and his insistence on the centrality of antagonism to political life and, by extension, political imaginaries go a long way in providing a model of mediation between two systems of representation: politics and cinema. Moreover, the fact that Schmitt developed the friend-enemy distinction in the last years of the Weimar Republic as part of a larger critique of liberal democracy and used related concepts such as the state of exception to legitimate the Nazi ascent to power establishes a productive correspondence on the level of political theory between fascist and postfascist imaginaries that cannot be dismissed simply on the basis of such problematic genealogies. At the core of "fascinating fascism," then, we find the kind of ambivalences not reducible to the problem of desire (or myth) but in fact analyzable in relation to the history of postwar democracy and its crises.

More specifically, the filmic representation of the personal and the political can be used to illustrate the discursive function of fascism as a signifier of the inherent contradictions of postwar democracies. In most films, fascism is associated with excessive control over public and private life, whereas democracy—which almost always refers to liberal democracy—stands for the protection of private life from state supervision and interference. Yet seen from another perspective, that of fascist attractions, the fascist spectacle also promises to reconcile the personal and the political, thus putting an end to feelings of modern alienation and social anomie. In this version, democracy may promote individual self-realization but at the expense of social cohesion and economic equality. To rephrase these two alternatives and their false binaries in ideology-critical terms, in fascism the political is personalized, institutionalizing forms of community and collectivity that, at least according to theories of totalitarianism, return to the screen in the communist antifascist films. Meanwhile, liberal democracies, as cultural theorist Andrea Slane rightly observes, achieve a false compromise between the personal and the political as they purport to defend the primacy of the private sphere but in fact end up depoliticizing domestic problems.[20]

To further complicate matters, the much-discussed problems of democracy today—and the resonance of these problems in the fascist imaginary in postfascist cinema—are brought about by two adversaries: a clearly defined, external enemy of democracy, called tyranny or dictatorship, and a more insidious phenomenon, "the evil quite simply called democratic life," which Jacques Rancière describes as the relentless promotion of individual rights and demands as a result of which citizens eventually become indifferent to the necessary sacrifices in the name of the common good.[21] Addressing a similar problematic, Mouffe speaks of a democratic paradox, the "tension between an individualistic rights-based notion of citizenship, and civic republicanism, with its emphasis on communitarian political participation."[22] It is precisely this evil called democratic life that, in the films about the Third Reich, gives rise to the specter of evil personified by the Nazis and that accounts for the enduring power of fascist attractions. But it is also against this strange democratic paradox that the private individual is introduced and validated as the embodiment of democratic subjectivity.

The main function of the underlying process of demarcation and externalization, that is, of abjection, is to overcome the inherent abstractness of democracy—what Claude Lefort calls disembodied power—and, through the prevailing patterns of identification and forms of embodiment in narrative cinema, establish the contours of democratic subjectivity through what it is not and what it can never be.[23] Once understood in this way, the us-versus-them distinction organized by the films allows us to reconstruct the antagonistic structures that (re)produce democratic subjectivity in confrontation with its historical and universal enemy. It gives us an organizing principle through which to trace this dynamic into the more fluid and ambiguous constellations of the postwar years and to consider the role of historical film more generally in the production of political affects. Materials for analyzing filmic constructions of democratic subjectivity through the lens of enmities—which also means through strong emotions and affects—can be found in a wide range of sources: the filmic production of antipathies in the films themselves, the heated debates surrounding the films, and the larger political antagonisms to which they refer or for which they are claimed.

Democracy in the selected films may appear as an abstraction that only becomes visible, audible, and palpable through its difference from the specter and spectacle of fascism. But this does not mean that we cannot identify any discerning features—especially once we move beyond a formal definition of democracy based on the structures and procedures created to carry out the will of the people. A further step in developing such an approach, beyond the personal-political binary discussed earlier, is to take advantage of the distinction made in current political theory between politics and the political, with the latter exceeding the narrow meaning of politics as calculated tactics, rhetorical strategies, and institutional practices and moving toward the elusive affective economies found at its margins.[24] Accordingly, Mouffe defines politics as "the ensemble of practices, discourses and institutions which seek to establish a certain order and organize human existence" and the political more broadly as "the dimension of antagonism that is an ever present possibility in all human society."[25] The political, in other words, demarcates the discursive space in which politics takes place, a space that includes reason and emotion and encompasses conscious and unconscious processes. Thus the goal cannot be to eliminate what Mouffe refers to as passions—already considered by Aristotle an essential part of organizing the *demos* (people) and sustaining the *polis* (city or citizenship)—but must be to integrate what is in fact an essential part of the political process. For democracy, this means to make productive use of disagreements and resentments and to transform the antagonisms unavoidable in pluralistic societies into what she calls agonistic pluralism. The cinema, and the historical film in particular, is one place in contemporary media society where these alternatives of antagonism and agonism can be articulated and the modalities of democratic subjectivity be tested precisely through the exposure to enmity in its most extreme form.

Enmity—the distinction between "us" and "them"—is the main organizing principle by which democracy in the films about the Third Reich asserts its superiority as a form of sociability and governmentality and defines the terms that have come to represent it in the popular imagination, namely, liberty, equality, justice, and (especially in the Hollywood/American context) the individual pursuit of happiness. The production of enmity always operates on two very different levels, with the moral and political binaries established by the narrative not always replicated in the forms of character engagement and spectatorial pleasure. On the level of narrative, we are drawn into fictional worlds organized around a core antagonism: between a state, society, and culture identified as fascist and represented by stereotypical, barely articulated characters and a group of fully developed individuals associated with democracy as a way of life, a state of mind, and, most importantly, a set of feelings. As a rule, the intersection of public and private spheres in these films marks the boundary where this confrontation takes place. Similarly, personal relationships and psychological conflicts usually define the terms under which the historical is translated into the political.

Meanwhile, on the level of identifications, we enter a universe structured around a primary emotion shared by most main protagonists and audiences: their hatred of the Nazis, whether as the real enemy (e.g., during times of war), the absolute enemy (e.g., as the embodiment of evil), or the enemy we "love to hate" (e.g., in its various postmodern permutations). All other emotions assume form and must be evaluated in relation to this initial identification of the enemy, which then becomes the first step in the making of democratic subjectivity. To begin with the feelings experienced by the defenders of democracy, they usually respond with fear or anger to the threat to the private sphere posed by Nazi ideology and the Nazi state. These primary emotions provide the basis on which various forms of alignment between protagonists and spectators become possible (e.g., righteous indignation, the humiliation of defeat, the desire for revenge). Equally important to the affective economy of the friend-enemy distinction are the more intimate emotions such as love, kindness, empathy, trust, and compassion that, by being distinguishing traits of nonfascists (exception: *Downfall*), confirm the political significance of the seemingly apolitical. Among the characters, feelings of disgust, shame, and guilt predominate whenever clear lines of demarcation cannot be established or maintained any longer. In the more recent films, such emotional ambiguity sometimes gives way to forms of detachment on the side of audiences who either question the need for antagonism altogether or compensate for its lack with nostalgia for the clear binaries once provided by ideologies. Wherever the narratives fail to provide positive figures of identification (e.g., in the films discussed in chapters 4 and 6), their absence is more than compensated for through the audience's negative reactions to the Nazis in the diegesis. In other words, even the exclusive focus on the enemies creates a relationship on the level of spectatorship and reception that reproduces the antagonistic structures constitutive of democratic subjectivity.

Whether through dramatic or comical modes, conventional or innovative styles, and narrative or identificatory strategies, the films about the Third Reich set up an antagonistic relationship between democracy, with its insistence on liberty, equality, individual rights, and rule of law, and fascism, with its promises of social unity, collective agency, and a transfigured world. This antagonism gives rise both to the world of the film and to the film as a work of art. All three elements—the diegesis, the text, and the context—are equally important to the definition of "us" versus "them" and the assertion of an irreconcilable difference between friends and enemies. Notwithstanding the sense of clarity with which this difference is proclaimed, the friend-enemy distinction shares important characteristics with the relationship between self and other and its manifestation in the master-slave dialectic first analyzed by Hegel as the basis of political consciousness and, ultimately, the nation-state. Both stand for an acute awareness of power relations that cannot be absorbed into culturalist celebrations of difference as plural and contingent. Through the dynamics of self and other, the films similarly reveal the absolute enemy as a function of the self and acknowledge the enduring power of fascist attractions: in the rituals of submission and domination, the cult of order and discipline, the exclusionary models of community, and the aestheticization of everyday life.

On the one hand, the films' affective economies bear witness to a deeply seated frustration with the perceived ineffectiveness of democratic institutions and the messiness of democratic life. This frustration finds expression in the sense of transgression at the heart of any engagement with the fascist imaginary, whether as an object of fascination, horror, or disgust. These, in turn, point to a central prohibition in the democratic imaginary that assumes the inherent superiority and greater desirability of democracy in comparison to other forms of government; in the words of Badiou: "It is forbidden, as it were, not to be a democrat."[26] On the other, by responding—again on the level of emotions—to the provocation of fascism as an affective regime or intensity, the films offer preliminary answers to a number of pressing questions: How does one desire democracy? How do we connect it to compelling images and stories? How can we imbue it with meaningful messages and experiences? And, most crucially, how do we produce democratic subjectivity through enduring attachments, engagements, identifications, and the conceptual terrain marked by political affects and the politics of affect—questions to be addressed through a more detailed discussion of affect in the next section.

During the first decades of cinema, theorists and critics extolled the new medium as a quintessential democratic medium, made for a homogenized mass audience beyond social, ethnic, and national differences and part of a "vernacular modernism" through which the divisions between high and low culture could finally be overcome.[27] Identified with an equally compelling counternarrative, the Nazis were the first political movement to use film in the mobilization of mass emotions, including those directed at the elimination of democratic institutions and the eradication of a racialized other. Both kinds of films, those made during and after the Third Reich, arrive at their respective perspectives on democracy by aligning public and private emotions within the imaginary coordinates of the body politic. Identities and identifications become politicized through their inscription in the grand narratives of community, society, nation, folk, and state. In each case, enmity provides the organizing principle for narrative structures and dramatic constellations. And in the same way that Nazi propaganda films highlight the failures of democratic institutions, the films about the Nazi dictatorship promote democratic values such as equality, liberty, rule of law, divisions of powers, and, above all, individualism. However, with one significant difference: whereas Goebbels famously declared that he wanted the Nazis marching on the streets, and not on the screens, filmmakers since the 1940s have kept them on the screens so that they, to complete the analogy, do not show up on the streets.[28] Similarly, whereas the head of the Nazi culture industry considered the introduction of Nazis as fictional characters undesirable, filmmakers since then have fully embraced the Nazis' status as a media phenomenon and today see their ubiquity as an essential part of the politics and economics of images in popular cinema as well as art cinema.

Understanding this strange division of labor and its strategic articulation across the fascist-postfascist divide requires us to take a closer look at the two terms that constitute the book's central argument, "political" and "affect." The previous section discussed the conditions under which fascism emerged as an empty signifier in the making of democratic subjectivity and through which film came to rely on the friend-enemy distinction in producing political alliances and allegiances. As we have seen, these processes involve three kinds of identification: identification of the enemies of democracy, identification with the protagonists as democratic subjects, and identification with (liberal) democracy as the only legitimate political system. Yet how are these identifications translated into the generic conventions and thematic registers of the historical film? How exactly do the films mobilize emotions in the making of democratic subjectivities? And in what ways are empathy, sympathy, and antipathy central to demarcating the treacherous terrain shared by the political and the historical? As should be clear by now, satisfying answers are not to be found by looking at the filmic representation of the institutions, procedures, and rights (e.g., independent judiciary, free elections, right to privacy) that distinguish liberal democracies from other forms of government. Instead we must focus on the identificatory patterns, aesthetic sensibilities, intertextual references, and contextual meanings that produce democratic subjectivity in the encounter with fascism as its absolute other. Facilitating this process, affect functions as a form of engagement that includes not only emotion but also cognition and intention, that mediates between the visceral and the rational, and that establishes homologies between the aesthetic and the ideological.

We cannot reconstruct these processes without reference to two very different lines of inquiry: cognitive film theories on the structure of affect and emotion in the narrative film and cultural studies theories on "public feelings," "ordinary affects," and "intimate publics" in contemporary culture and society.[29] In both contexts, "feeling," "emotion," and "affect" are sometimes used interchangeably, and definitions of affect—if given at all—vary considerably according to the respective disciplinary or theoretical framework. Cognitive film theorists have developed analytical models that help us move beyond simplistic understandings of character identification and narrative point of view and equally undifferentiated notions of fantasy and pleasure in psychoanalytically inspired screen theory.[30] Concentrating on the spectator's relationship to fictional characters, they tend to emphasize the beneficial aspects of identification rather than the problematic ones examined by psychoanalytic film theory and apparatus theory. For my purposes, their focus on character engagement will be especially useful in evaluating the filmic resonances of sociopsychological theories of fascism, but their systematic approach to identification will be equally relevant for understanding the role of character engagement in cognitive processes, including those involved in forming political points of view.

Meanwhile, affect theory and its connections to cultural studies and feminist and queer theory has played an important role in assessing the contribution of feelings, emotions, and affects to ongoing transformations of the public sphere.[31] "Feelings are *personal* and *biographical*, emotions are *social*, and affects are *prepersonal*"—this is how one scholar, perhaps too neatly, summarizes the differences among these terms.[32] Implicit in such a definition is a conception of affect as noncognitive, nonintentional, nonrepresentational, and nonsubjective that manifests itself above all in the corporal—what John Protovi calls the somatic—and that, in the films under discussion, finds expression in fear, terror, and disgust, those bodily experiences of abjection identified earlier with the fascist other.[33] Most important for our purposes is the understanding of affect as a prepersonal phenomenon sharply distinguished from emotion with its subjective and intersubjective qualities and better suited to account for the aesthetic experiences and physical sensations associated with "fascinating fascism."

My previous comments on the fascist imaginary should make it easy to identify the limitations of cognitive film theory and affect theory for an analysis of historical films based on clear ideological differences and informed in equal measure by the cognitive, affective, aesthetic, and discursive processes required to produce/reproduce these differences. Cognitive film theory has little to say about specific affects in the context of political ideologies (e.g., nationalism) and, given its emphasis on close textual analysis, is ill-suited to trace the movement of affects from texts to contexts (e.g., in the process of reception) or account for historical contingencies (e.g., in relation to cinema as a public sphere). Meanwhile, some variants of affect theory exhibit such an aversion to questions of signification and cognition (and such a penchant for theoretical obtuseness) that they offer only limited insights into textual practices with a clear investment in the production of meanings and have no critical vocabulary to distinguish among the different archives of feelings presented by films from different historical periods and national cinemas.

By turning to the films themselves to develop a better understanding of affect, this book pursues a theoretically more modest project. Instead of treating affect as an intensity that exceeds (if not eliminates) all distinctions among texts, media, subjectivities, and publics, I examine the functioning of affect in a particular audiovisual medium, namely, film, and, more specifically, a subset of the historical film. And rather than conceptualizing affect as a general or universal category, I approach its elusive effects through its association with a particular set of meanings associated with the political. It is precisely through the specificity of the material examined that we are then able to analyze the relationship between the historical and the political and reconstruct the dynamics of fascist and democratic subjectivity. And it is within these clearly defined parameters that the focus on political affect allows us to identify the competing interests and conflicting positions that, in fact, sustain the fascist imaginary as an affective force and do so in ways that contradict the rhetoric of democracy and politics under the conditions of postideology.

This point has been made most forcefully by cultural theorist Brian Massumi, who uses affect and its resonances in contemporary culture as a way of identifying "ideological effects by non-ideological means." His conclusion that "affect holds a key to rethinking postmodern power after ideology" concedes that ideology may no longer provide a master narrative.[34] But it remains a powerful and perhaps more virulent presence—a point not always shared by those who theorize affect in opposition to cognition and signification and, as a consequence, no longer can, or want to, imagine the political in terms of disagreement and struggle. Identified with a decidedly political genealogy, the affective economies in the films under discussion are therefore not dissimilar to what Louis Althusser some time ago called interpellation, a process by which individuals are turned into subjects and placed within ideology, that is, "the imaginary relationship of individuals to their real conditions of existence."[35] For in the same way that ideology cannot be reduced to the problem of misrecognition/recognition and representation/misrepresentation, affect cannot be divorced from cognition and signification, reason enough not to separate discussions of affect from theories of ideology.

Making use of the important distinction between emotions and affects but refraining from a more sustained theoretical discussion of its implications for the study of film in general, I will henceforth refer to emotions and, occasionally, feelings whenever I describe the characters' experiences and behaviors in the narrative but will limit the term "affect" to the power of film, as a fictional construct and aesthetic phenomenon, to produce democratic subjectivities through the antagonistic, if not dialectic, terms inscribed in the friend-enemy distinction. Such an expanded notion of affect is especially important for situating the films about the Third Reich in their historical contexts and for uncovering their ideological projects beyond the level of narrative contents and manifest meanings. Treating affect as a corporal, emotional, cognitive, and aesthetic phenomenon forces us to recognize the importance of our intense engagement with these films to the making of democratic subjectivities and to appreciate the role of aesthetic mediations in definitions of the political that cannot be subsumed under the physical-psychological, rational-emotional, and public-private binaries outlined earlier. Moreover, conceptualizing affect as a category irreducible to texts or contexts allows us to establish a connection between two seemingly distinct spheres: the affective regimes linking films and audiences and the world of democratic institutions, structures, and practices.

The affective dimensions of the enemy-friend distinction are in full evidence already on the level of characterization and character engagement. Both reproduce a core contradiction in the genre as a whole, the terrifying power of Nazism as a dictatorial system and the weakness of individual Nazis as fully developed characters. The real Nazis consolidated their rule by making the state of exception what Giorgio Agamben calls a paradigm of government, a permanent condition exemplified by the camp as its most extreme manifestation.[36] In the diegesis, the Nazis' primary role is to personify the monopoly of violence and the power over life and death associated with the totalitarian state, to perform the suspension of the rule of law and its replacement by total surveillance, and to embody the elimination of all boundaries separating private from public life. Confirming their status as absolute enemies, they remain identified with a complete lack of emotion—to be precise, the power to affect (i.e., someone or something) but not to be affected. All their attention is focused on the expansion and preservation of power; all their desires are channeled into its rituals and hierarchies. If the filmic spectacle of the Third Reich stands for any utopian project at all, it is precisely this possibility to assert one's will or have none at all and to be free of all obligations or entirely bound by duties. In acting out the possibility of a life outside consensus or compromise, the Nazis on the screen allow us to control and preserve the threat of their otherness; therein lies the enduring appeal of those we "love to hate."

At the same time, the Nazis rarely acquire the status of fully developed characters; they appear primarily as stereotypical villains, clichéd madmen, and voiceless, faceless extras. Their lack of psychological interiority, their inability to learn and change, and their unwillingness to acknowledge the other as other find foremost expression in their exclusion from what, according to the films, creates and sustains democracies: a rich, complex, and satisfying personal life. Consequently, the main protagonists—the anti-Nazis, antifascists, and nonfascists—assert their narrative agency and prove their democratic credentials through that which, according to the ideology of liberal democracy, exists outside the sphere of the political. Inextricably linked to the assertion of individual free will and the pursuit of happiness, democratic subjectivity thus finds its most convincing manifestation in the defense of love and marriage, the involvement in families and communities, and the adherence to moral values and ethical principles in everyday life. Under these conditions, political affects develop not out of specific convictions and opinions but through the relationships between characters and the spectator's engagement with them. In what ways aesthetic experiences are an essential part of what has previously been called affective interpellation will become even clearer through a brief look at specific affective intensities shared by the films under discussion.

Three recurring features can be identified: the films' heavy reliance on the melodramatic mode, their preoccupation with the problem of masculinity, and the importance of spectatorship and reception to the actualization of their meanings. First: In highlighting democracy's strengths and shortcomings, the fascist imaginary establishes homologies between the emotions represented in the diegesis and the affects produced by the films, that is, the world in which the films are produced and consumed. The paradigmatic stories of occupation, oppression, and resistance find a privileged register in the melodramatic mode that, according to film scholar Linda Williams, establishes clear moral binaries of virtue and vice, makes Manichean distinctions between good and evil, and relies heavily on visual spectacle, performative excess, and an almost visceral mode of address that far exceeds the boundaries of melodrama as a genre.[37] Often contained within dramatic sequences of pain and suffering and accompanied by somber music that conveys affect in its purest form, the melodramatic mode portrays individuals and, by extension, the people as victims of the larger forces of history. The main themes in the filmic representation of Nazism/fascism—the crisis of masculinity, the sexualization of power, and the aestheticization of violence—all fall under its purview and become part of the equation of the political with victimization. The heavy reliance on the melodramatic mode even in comedies and war films confirms its effectiveness in staging historical conflicts and struggles and in translating national traumas into the more intimate registers of personal relationships. Similarly, the prevalence of what Williams describes as realistic effects operating in the service of melodramatic affects points to a shared commitment on the level of representations to the mimetic conventions codified by classical narrative cinema and the "authentic" reproductions attributed to the historical film. Most importantly, the remarkable adaptability of the melodramatic mode bears witness to what she describes as the unique status of cinema as a democratic mass medium, drawing on the popular traditions and delivering the emotional rewards that previously inspired literary scholar Peter Brooks's description of "melodrama as radically democratic, making its representations clear and legible to everyone."[38]

To move on to the second recurring feature, the affective mapping of democratic subjectivity depends heavily on gender as a central category in the staging of the friend-enemy distinction. The implications are most apparent in the affirmation of traditional masculinity as the most important mediator between personal and political life and the assertion of male heterosexuality as the most powerful defense against political perversions. Fascism, by contrast, is regularly associated with defective masculinities (i.e., too much, as in machismo, or too little, as in effeminacy), deviant sexualities (i.e., promiscuous, perverse, or homosexual), and dysfunctional personalities (i.e., too submissive or too dominant). In other words, and rather paradoxically, democracy in these films is equated with the fantasies of normalcy mobilized by the Nazis against the alleged moral degeneracy of the Weimar Republic: traditional masculinity, normative heterosexuality, and national community, that ubiquitous last instance of authority known in democratic societies as "the people." But in the films, it is the private individual rather than the racial community who becomes the site of negotiation where everything "queer," in the sense of different or other, must be denounced and excluded as fascist and where traditional gender roles and family values and a popular/populist conception of the people can be affirmed as inherently democratic.

To conclude with the third feature, the question of spectatorship and reception is central to tracing political affects beyond the films as texts and analyzing their aesthetic manifestations in the larger context defined by intentions (e.g., of directors and producers), interpretations (e.g., by reviewers and scholars), and implications (e.g., for the film industry and definitions of national history). From the propagandistic goals of the Hollywood anti-Nazi films to the controversial domestic reception of *Der Untergang* (*Downfall*, Oliver Hirschbiegel, 2004), films about the Third Reich have always relied more than other examples of the historical film on the additional meanings produced in the intense public engagement with this history.[39] Often valued and remembered more for the way they generate responses and mobilize audiences, they are a perfect illustration of the distinction made in film studies between spectatorship and reception. Spectatorship typically refers to the processes and techniques—from formal elements such as point of view to the psychological and physiological dimensions of looking—that allow a spectator to make sense of, and take pleasure in, a particular film. Reception extends this process into cinema as a public sphere—a perspective emphasized in the chapter outline presented in the next section.

Always historicize," insists Fredric Jameson.[40] To historicize in this case means to trace the changing constellations of film and fascism since the war and postwar years and to assess their discursive function in defining the enemy, the absolute other of democracy, as part of larger political constellations. To historicize means to treat the emotions and affects created by historical narratives as an important part of the production of democratic subjectivities and the management of fascist attractions. This process can be traced through the films' contribution to definitions of history, memory, and heritage; their connection to larger debates about national identity, liberal democracy, and public life; their role in redefining the relationship between the personal and the political; and their participation in the aestheticization of politics and the medialization of history. In other words, to historicize means to reconstruct the conditions under which fascism turned from signified into signifier and became identified with the project of democracy and the crisis of the political. It ultimately means to reconstruct, through textual and contextual analysis, how fascism—in the disguise of the Nazis—emerged as one of the privileged sites in mainstream cinema for the production of political affects. Again the comparison to film historical precursors—in this case, *From Caligari to Hitler* (1947), Siegfried Kracauer's influential study on prefascist tendencies in Weimar cinema—is useful precisely in articulating the differences. Kracauer uses psychoanalytic categories to analyze the role of fantasies in the psychological (i.e., Oedipalized) emplotment of social conflicts and political crises.[41] Through thematic readings of the popular genres that constitute Weimar-era cinema, he seeks to understand the rise of Nazism and, more generally, to examine the ways in which films reflect the mentality of a particular nation, its hidden dispositions. The postfascist imaginary, which is predicated on the convergence of fantasy and politics achieved after 1933, represents the other side of Kracauer's teleological construction, namely, a continuing process of "acting out" and "working through" that, if we want to stay within a Freudian framework, reveals the films made since 1945 as a paradigmatic case of cinema, history, and trauma. However, such a psychological approach to film's manifest contents and latent meanings does not explain the contextual functions and intertextual effects unique to the historical film. Thus rather than examining how films reflect political mentalities, this study focuses on how they articulate, transform, and produce them through the cognitive, affective, and aesthetic dimensions of what this study calls political affects; the transnational rather than national(ist) nature of the postfascist imaginary is an integral part of such processes.

We can distinguish three periods in the ongoing transformation of the postfascist imaginary: the post-1945 period (1945–68), during which Nazism/fascism served as a stand-in for the antidemocratic other, communism (in the West) and capitalism (in the East); the post-1968 period (1968–89), which, under the influence of the poststructuralist critique of the master narratives and Enlightenment rationality, brought a confrontation with fascism's erotic and aesthetic attractions; and the post-1989 period (1989–present), which, partly in response to the forces of globalization and the weakening of the nation-state, has contributed to the historicization of the Nazi past and its enlistment in new postpolitical configurations, including nostalgia for the politics of clear enmities. The paradigm shifts marked by 1968 and 1989 align this almost uncanny hyperproductivity with important political developments and events: the freezes and thaws of the cold war, the student movement and sexual revolution, the fall of communism and the Berlin Wall, and European unification and the advent of globalization and neoliberalism. Confirming the inextricable link between politics and aesthetics that has sustained the relationship between film and fascism from the start, these historical markers can furthermore be used to identify significant changes in the modes of historical representation: classical realist or socialist realist styles in the 1950s and early 1960s, modernist and documentary styles in the 1960s and 1970s, postmodern or retro styles since the 1980s, and historicist or heritage styles since the 1990s. This aestheticization is repeatedly thematized in the films' self-reflexive commentaries, through the inclusion of audiovisual material from the Third Reich, the many films about filmmaking in the Third Reich, and/or the pervasiveness of intertextual references that acknowledge the status of fascism as a media-produced fantasy.

"The history of our images of fascism is, among other things, the history of our growing doubts about the present," writes critic Georg Seeßlen, but it also is the history of our desire for images and stories of democracy and the kind of identifications that make possible a relationship to politics and the political in the broader sense.[42] Consequently, reading the films as a sustained engagement not with the Nazi past but with the problems of postwar democracy requires a radical departure from prevailing approaches structured around thematically oriented readings, organized within national cinema frameworks, and based primarily on quality films (e.g., art films, blockbusters). A thus-defined revisionist project involves three methodological interventions. First, close textual readings that analyze generic conventions, formal strategies, and authorial styles may be well suited for studies that focus on questions of historical narration, but they reveal little about the contemporary fantasies and desires that are brought to bear on these narratives. Political affects develop primarily in the relationship between films and audiences, and between films and earlier films. They emerge out of the interplay of textual, contextual, and intertextual effects. And they acquire their meanings precisely within the larger discourses that constitute the political at a particular historical conjuncture. In acknowledgment of these connections, the individual chapters are organized around highly contextualized readings that situate the films within the political, social, economic, cultural, theoretical, and ideological constellations of postfascist cinema and society.

Second, though deeply invested in fantasies of nation and nationalism, the fascist imaginary has always been a transnational phenomenon and, for that reason alone, cannot be understood within the confines of national cinema. Whereas the enormous literary productivity that has defined the German and Austrian projects of coming to terms with the Nazi past may be productively evaluated in a national framework, the German films about the Third Reich require a comparative approach to film as an international mass medium and a global commodity.[43] Such a comparative approach guards against reductive readings and opens up our analysis to the interplay of convention, innovation, and appropriation unique to genre cinema in general. It brings out the specificities of the fascist imaginary in different national cinemas without automatically reducing that difference to the logic of the referent, that is, the history of Nazism, Fascism, anti-Nazism, or antifascism in a particular country. Moreover, a comparative approach allows us to locate the function of fascism as an empty signifier in the modes of competition, imitation, and differentiation that have always defined the relationship between Hollywood and Europe. Last but not least, only sufficient consideration of the broader aesthetic trends in postwar cinema and the specific political problems in individual countries can account for the ways in which films about the Third Reich invariably reproduce the dominant discourses of the political in 1940s America, 1950s West Germany, 1960s East Germany, 1970s Italy, and so forth.

Third, against the prevailing tendency to concentrate only on quality films and big-budget productions, this study approaches the dialectics of art and exploitation as an integral part of the fascist imaginary in postfascist cinema. The goal is not simply to present a more complete picture but to shed light on the structural affinity between the fascist imaginary as a media-produced fantasy and the inflationary use of signs and significations that allow specific topoi to circulate in vastly different aesthetic registers. Previous studies have focused on prestige productions that serve largely self-legitimizing functions in defining national identities, or they have privileged art films that use formal innovation to challenge hegemonic accounts of national history and heritage. What has been ignored in the process are the middlebrow productions and low-budget films that have contributed significantly to the devaluation of fascism as a historical referent and paved the way for its transformation into an empty signifier. Even though my selection still favors the more successful and influential films, I make an effort throughout to acknowledge the margins of filmmaking where so much of the fascination with "sexy Nazis" and "nasty Nazis" has in fact found an aesthetic and erotic outlet.

All book projects require careful selections and difficult choices. In consideration of the dialogic structure that makes the fascist imaginary primarily a German-American affair, the majority of films are either German or American, with the remainder produced in the European countries most affected by the cataclysm of the Holocaust and the carnage of World War II. Regrettably, the limited availability of subtitled Soviet/Russian and East European films has prevented an adequate discussion of films from the former Eastern Bloc countries and their very different conception of fascism and democracy. The filmic representation of Hitler, the subject of two recent anthologies, will only be discussed to the degree that it is relevant to larger questions of embodiment and performativity.[44] Limitations of space made it necessary to concentrate on feature films and not consider documentaries and television features. Given the focus on film, I also decided not to include potentially illuminating comparisons to the fascist imaginary in literature, theater, art, and exhibition culture, the subject of an ever-growing body of scholarship in German studies. Films about the legacies of the Third Reich in postwar political institutions and family histories could have provided much supporting evidence for my argument about democratic subjectivity but would have made the scope of the project unmanageable.[45] The same might be said about those productions, often associated with horror, that perform fascism's eternal recurrence through bodies imagined as monstrous and indestructible: neither dead nor alive, a product of cloning, breeding, and other mad-science experiments, and featured in alternate histories that envision different outcomes for world history.[46] The films presented in this study in fact serve an analogous function by at once excluding, demonizing, and reintroducing the political in its most monstrous embodiment in fascism—what German film scholar Eric Rentschler calls the Nazi undead.[47]

Representing a different kind of boundary, the thematic overlaps with the Holocaust film and the World War II film have sharpened my understanding of the specific role of affect in articulating the larger historical and political questions addressed by these three types of historical films.[48] Significantly, all of them share a strong investment in the melodramatic as a privileged mode for asserting the relevance of the past for the present; the same might be said about the role of masculinity and the importance of reception. Through their differences, they have brought into relief the uniqueness of the fascist imaginary as a function of the democratic imaginary, whether in relation to the promise of "never again" associated with Holocaust narratives or the mythification of World War II as the "last great war." Yet whereas the Holocaust films take the perspective of the victims, often using empathy to reflect on the complications of memory and postmemory or to probe the aesthetic and ethical limits of representation, the films about the Third Reich are primarily concerned with individual acts of resistance, accommodation, and subordination in the confrontation with state-sanctioned power and violence. And whereas the war films maintain a clear emphasis on action and suspense, the films discussed in this book foreground dramatic conflicts and psychological complications.

Proceeding more or less chronologically, the seven chapters offer highly contextualized readings of feature films from the 1940s to the present. Comprising both well-known and unjustly neglected films, big-budget and low-budget productions, and examples of art and exploitation cinema, this highly diverse group presents us with a veritable archive of feelings about democracy created in the encounter with fascism, its horrors, dangers, and attractions. In line with the larger methodological framework outlined earlier, each chapter develops its contextualized readings from a slightly different perspective, including production history, reception history, film authorship, and questions of performance, spectatorship, and intertextuality. The first three chapters, which cover the 1940s, 1950s, and 1960s, situate the films firmly within the discourses of anti-Nazism during World War II and of antifascism/anticommunism during the cold war. Reflecting the emergence of fascism as an empty signifier during the 1970s, the fourth chapter breaks with this chronological structure and begins a more thematic exploration of fascism and sexuality; similar problematics— related to the fascist aesthetics, the ethics of resistance, and the politics of historicization—are laid out in the last three chapters, which cover the period from the 1990s to the present. As a consequence of the disappearance of the ideological master narratives, the clear friend-enemy distinction of the 1950s and 1960s is absorbed into more complicated constellations that seem to marginalize democratic subjectivity—or relegate it entirely to the terms of spectatorship and reception.

Focusing on Hollywood as an industry and institution, chapter 1 locates the beginnings of the fascist imaginary in the anti-Nazi films made between 1939 and 1945 in support of the United States' entry into the war and, later, the war effort. The series that started with *Confessions of a Nazi Spy* (1939) established the antagonistic structure, especially pronounced in the stories set in the United States, through which filmmakers were able to counter the political and military threat of Nazism and build support for American democracy and its core values. Classical Hollywood defined the stereotypical Nazi characters and basic narrative patterns that would henceforth dominate filmic representations through forms of embodiment and modes of character engagement. As will be shown, this unprecedented politicization of film culture in confrontation with an external enemy had profound consequences for the relationship between film and politics during and after the war. Two films, *Watch on the Rhine* (1943) and *The Stranger* (1948), will be analyzed as representative of the two prevailing strategies, namely, the mechanisms of externalization known from propaganda films, which separate the other from the self and maintain clear distinctions, and the more unsettling scenarios of invasion and contamination in the noir aesthetic, which signal the arrival of the dreaded other, the enemy of democracy, as an integral part of the body politic.

Chapter 2 follows the difficult transition from Nazi to anti-Nazi in the first West German films about the resistance in the officer corps and examines its contribution to the process of postwar democratization and coming to terms with the past. Closely associated with the culture of the Federal Republic, they include *Canaris* (*Canaris: Master Spy*, 1954), *Des Teufels General* (*The Devil's General*, 1955), and two films about the 20 July assassination attempt on Hitler, *Es geschah am 20. Juli* (*It Happened on July 20th*, 1955) and *Der 20. Juli* (*The Plot to Assassinate Hitler*, 1955). As I argue, the films about Admiral Canaris, Ernst Udet, and Count Stauffenberg served to familiarize West German audiences with the history of the resistance movement, rehabilitate the officers as national heroes, and provide a space for emerging democratic attitudes as well as residual fascist attachments. These contradictory affects will be analyzed within the political and ideological divisions of the cold war and the search for an alternative, uniquely German genealogy of the political based on traditional masculinity and the culture of Prussianism.

Also concerned with the German perspective, chapter 3 discusses the crisis of antifascism in several films made by the state-owned DEFA studio during the 1960s and 1970s. Whereas the first part introduces the filmic conventions that contributed to the establishment of antifascism as the founding myth of the German Democratic Republic, the second part analyzes its critical revisions in the work of Frank Beyer and Konrad Wolf: Beyer's *Fünf Patronenhülsen* (*Five Cartridges*, 1960) and *Nackt unter Wölfen* (*Naked among Wolves*, 1963) and Wolf's *Ich war neunzehn* (*I Was Nineteen*, 1968) and *Mama, ich lebe* (*Mama, I'm Alive*, 1977). The reenactment of the antifascist narrative is marked by ambivalence, with the films at once exploring formal alternatives to socialist realism and classical narrative in dialogue with the European New Waves and confirming their commitment to socialism as the only valid alternative to fascism and its postwar legacies. The resultant production of what the chapter calls antifascist melancholia will be examined through a comparative reading of two very different directorial styles, Beyer's neorealist style and Wolf's documentary style. The performance of masculinity again plays a key role in the enactment of ambivalence and facilitates its opening toward a different kind of democracy associated with socialist identities and subjectivities.

The Italian films of the 1970s allow me in chapter 4 to confront desires and pleasures entirely missing from cold war representations of Nazism/fascism and articulated most provocatively at the intersection of sexuality and violence. The displacement of politics into sexualized scenarios of domination and submission and its surprisingly similar filmic treatment in the registers of art and exploitation will be examined as part of a larger crisis in the European Left in the aftermath of 1968 and a first indication of more-fundamental shifts in the fascist imaginary diagnosed by Baudrillard through the notion of retro style and captured by Sontag in the famous phrase "fascinating fascism." Focusing in particular on horror, aversion, and disgust as key elements in the ideological exorcism performed on, and through, the body of Nazism, I pursue this connection in three controversial auteurist films, Luchino Visconti's *La caduta degli dei* (*The Damned*, 1969), Liliana Cavani's *Il portiere di notte* (*The Night Porter*, 1974), and Lina Wertmüller's *Pasqualino settebellezze* (*Seven Beauties*, 1975), as well as the cheaply made pornographic films known as Naziploitation that bring the scenarios of abjection associated with fascism to their most extreme conclusion.

Chapter 5 addresses the equally complicated relationship between fascism and aesthetics first examined by Walter Benjamin in his comments on the aestheticization of politics and revisited in two very different films from the two sides of the post–cold war divide, Aleksandr Sokurov's *Molokh* (*Moloch*, 1999) and Quentin Tarantino's *Inglourious Basterds* (2009). Focusing on intertextuality as an essential feature of the fascist imaginary, my comparative reading reconstructs the directors' extensive engagement with fascist iconographies and their underlying affective economies in a three-part fashion: an analysis of Sokurov's and Tarantino's use of intertextuality in reconstructing fascism as a postmodern simulacrum and testing its broader implications in the affective registers of elegy and parody, respectively; a reconsideration of the aestheticization of politics thesis in the context of postfascism and postmodernism; and a discussion of the function of self-referentiality in films about filmmaking in the Third Reich.

Relying on reception as yet another way of accessing the connections between fascist imaginary and democratic subjectivity, chapter 6 investigates the validation of violence as a political means in recent European films about the Nazi occupation. The Dutch *Zwartboek* (*Black Book*, 2006), the Danish *Flammen & Citronen* (*Flame & Citron*, 2008), and the Norwegian *Max Manus* (*Max Manus: Man of War*, 2008) all address themselves to domestic audiences as they celebrate political violence as the foundation of a postideological identity politics and postnational patriotism; the French *L'armée du crime* (*Army of Crime*, 2009) responds to the same problematic by calling for a new leftist politics of international and multiethnic solidarity. As evidenced by the films' extensive reception in newspapers, magazines, and Internet discussion groups, the resistance narrative in all cases functions as a conduit in two very different political scenarios: the defense of freedom and democracy in the European tradition, and the hallucination of new kinds of dangerous enemies. As evidenced by the frequent comparisons between anti-Nazi resistance and contemporary terrorism, the films sometimes end up serving as a projection screen for growing anxieties about European unification, globalization, and mass migration that make violence an attractive form of imagining antagonism in the postpolitical age.

Finally, chapter 7 takes a close reading of *Der Untergang* (*Downfall*, 2004) to assess the shift in postunification cinema from the dominant West German mode in speaking about the Third Reich—coming to terms with the past—to the historicist strategies that today aim at a normalization of that past. The Bernd Eichinger production, I argue, redefines the postfascist imaginary in full accordance with the marketing of Nazism as a media phenomenon—qualities that account for the film's success as an international blockbuster but also explain its contribution to the creation of a different public sphere dominated by heritage and event culture. The heated debates surrounding the production also partake in ongoing transformations of the political in liberal democratic societies and thus allow me to consider again the relevance of the coupling of film and fascism to the making of democratic subjectivity, whether in the diegesis or the public sphere. Like the countless other films about the Third Reich made since World War II, *Downfall* thus offers a useful case study for analyzing these little understood and crucially important processes of affective and ideological interpellation and arriving at a better understanding of the role of emotion and affect in the historical film and their contribution to the ever-changing definitions of the political.

# 1

# Democracy in Action

## The Hollywood Anti-Nazi Films of the 1940s

> Those babies are strictly no good from way down deep.
> They're no bunch of petty racketeers trying to muscle in
> on some small territory. They want to move in wholesale,
> take over the whole country. [Let's] kick 'em right in the
> swastika.
>
> Humphrey Bogart as Gloves Donahue in
> *All through the Night* (Vincent Sherman, 1941)

Memo to screenwriter: "Hitler box office poison. Revise story." This is how Klaus Mann, son of the famous novelist, imagined discussions in Hollywood back offices shortly before the United States' entry into the war on 7 December 1941.[1] However, neither his mocking depiction of a film industry unwilling to take on political subject matter nor his profound distaste for a group of films dismissed as worthless and ineffectual can invalidate the fact that between 1939 and 1946 Hollywood studios made approximately 180 feature-length films known as anti-Nazi films; that these films fundamentally changed the relationship between entertainment and politics prevalent in genre cinema; and that these wartime productions introduced the stereotypical characters, narrative

32

structures, and identificatory patterns that would henceforth dominate the filmic representation of screen Nazis.[2]

In the larger context of this study, the Hollywood anti-Nazi films allow us to consider the conditions under which the Nazis became the absolute enemy in the friend-enemy distinction constitutive of democratic subjectivity. The coupling of film and fascism as an integral part of such affective and ideological interpellations cannot be examined outside the principles of standardization and serialization that distinguished the classical Hollywood mode of production, including in its approach to mobilizing emotions. On the following pages, I reconstruct this historical constellation in a three-part fashion: a general definition of the anti-Nazi film as both a typical Hollywood product and a new kind of political propaganda; a brief overview of the politicization of the Hollywood community after the arrival of the European exiles and émigrés; and based on three examples, a more detailed discussion of the forms of character engagement used to convey to contemporary audiences what it meant to be an American, and, within the logic of these films, a democrat. In relation to the fascist imaginary in postfascist cinema, the purpose of this first chapter is likewise threefold, namely, to define a filmic topos that, from the beginning, was highly politicized in its conditions of production and reception, equally concerned with national and international perspectives, and inextricably bound up with the generic conventions and identificatory patterns of classical narrative cinema.

On the most basic level, the anti-Nazi films represent Hollywood's response to what the Nazis in 1933 had announced as a fundamental new approach to politics as a series of tightly scripted media events and highly emotional mass experiences.[3] These mirroring effects connecting films by and about the Nazis became an integral part of the emergent iconography of anti-Nazism. With the help of a large and distinguished group of actors, directors, and screenwriters, many of them German-speaking exiles and émigrés, Hollywood ended up emulating Babelsberg, the famous Ufa studio, in several significant ways: through the recruitment of modern mass media in ideological warfare, the enlistment of classical narrative for propagandistic purposes, and the reliance on national stereotypes in identifying an external enemy. Analyzing the anti-Nazi films therefore requires a closer look at the multiple connections between the first media dictatorship and the most powerful film industry, a connection defined by hidden patterns of influence, mutual dependencies, and surprising correspondences. As the most visible manifestation of such uncanny effects, the antagonistic figures of Nazi and anti-Nazi became the central organizing principle in the self-representation of American democracy during World War II.

Yet these figures could not have performed this pivotal function without the audience's emotional involvement through what is commonly referred to as identification and what Murray Smith, in discussing character engagement, calls recognition, alignment, and allegiance. Given their historically contingent nature and politically overdetermined function, these forms of engagement will prove to be key to our understanding of the central role of cinema in the affective politics of modern democracies and their complicated relationship with fascism as a transnational media invention.

It was from the Nazi culture industry and the refugees from the German-speaking stage and screen that the anti-Nazi films acquired the constitutive elements of the Third Reich as a cinematic fantasy, a production so all-encompassing that historian Scott Spector has wondered: "Was the Third Reich movie-made?"[4] Of course, it was, but also by Hollywood. Starting with Leni Riefenstahl's Nuremberg party rally film *Triumph des Willens* (*Triumph of the Will*, 1935), the countless instructional films, cultural films, and newsreels produced under Propaganda Minister Joseph Goebbels and widely shown in American motion-picture theaters until 1939 provided Hollywood with an extensive audiovisual archive out of which to create a compelling image of the political and military enemy. The resultant process of appropriation and reinscription began with the uniforms, rituals, and props necessary for fashioning the "typical" Nazi; continued in the fictional recreation of what might be called the aesthetics of totalitarianism; and culminated in the enlistment of older iconographies of German nationalism, authoritarianism, and militarism in establishing fascism as the absolute other of twentieth-century democratic (i.e., US-American) politics.

Nazi cinema has been the subject of numerous studies, while the anti-Nazi films have not attracted much critical attention. With production values closer to B pictures, they do not fit easily into the self-image of Hollywood as a dream factory manufacturing skillfully made, beautiful illusions. Major stars, from Joan Crawford and Bette Davis to James Stewart and John Wayne, were cast as resistance fighters, but these roles have not been considered part of their screen personas or filmographies. Aside from *Casablanca* (Michael Curtiz, 1942) and *Notorious* (Alfred Hitchcock, 1946), both of which reduce historical events to a mere backdrop for romantic love stories, none of the films has achieved the status of a classic, a result primarily of their precarious position between entertainment and propaganda. Yet unlike other marginal sensibilities that, like film noir, have since been reclaimed as part of a counter-Hollywood, the anti-Nazi films remain haunted by their rhetorical excess, an unwelcome reminder that classical narrative is inextricably linked to ideological inscriptions and that even genre cinema can serve openly propagandistic purposes.

In the only existing German-language monograph on the topic, Jan-Christopher Horak rightfully highlights the contribution of what he calls "propagandistic entertainment films" to the establishment of US postwar hegemony.[5] The meaning of democracy in the anti-Nazi film, he argues, is established through a series of binaries, with Nazism always identified with the second, negative position: liberalism versus totalitarianism, individualism versus communalism, humanism versus collectivism, freedom of speech versus censorship, religion versus ideology, love versus sexuality, monogamy versus promiscuity, and, ultimately, life versus death.[6] Through the representation of Nazism as both antidemocratic and anti-American, "America" is constituted as a discursive subject that appears to exist outside all ideologies. However, the fictional confrontation with the enemies of democracy at the time not only allowed audiences to form emotional attachments to the abstract principles of freedom and equality, as Horak shows, but also prepared them to acknowledge conflict and contradiction as an integral part of political life, an important lesson for the postwar period. Even more important, the emotional rewards provided by classical narrative accustomed audiences to the reliance of film and politics on the production of affects that would become more pronounced with the mediazation of politics after the war. To return to the Klaus Mann quote at the beginning of the chapter, the anti-Nazi films may not have been very successful as propaganda vehicles during World War II, but they laid the foundation for the postfascist imaginary shared by Hollywood and European cinema and marked the starting point for the seemingly unstoppable filmic productivity surrounding the Third Reich as the absolute other of liberal democracy.

Anti-Nazi films are, at their core, films about democracy and its others. The mobilization of affects made them part of democracy in action; through specific strategies of interpellation, audiences were to be turned into citizens. Yet what conditions made their production possible, and what factors played a role in their reception? What were their political goals, artistic influences, and intellectual debts? In order to fully appreciate the films' interventionist stance, we must begin with the diagnosis of isolationism as the dominant position in US-American politics and cultural life throughout much of the 1930s and acknowledge their contribution to the gradual dismantling of the Wilsonian neutrality stance during the presidency of Franklin Delano Roosevelt. Even after the German annexation of Austria in 1938 and the invasion of Poland in 1939, American attitudes toward the Third Reich and views of the situation in Europe remained deeply divided between isolationists and interventionists. The nativist arguments advanced by the proponents of a virulently anti-immigrant, anti-urban, and (often) antisemitic Americanism spoke to a deeply ingrained tradition of noninvolvement in international affairs and an attendant unwillingness to match the United States' growing economic power with a corresponding political and military presence on the world stage. The anti-Nazi films signaled a radical departure from such isolationist positions as they reenvisioned twentieth-century America in an international context—with allies and enemies and a renewed sense of manifest destiny.

The film series began in 1939 as part of broader initiatives intent on enlightening audiences about the Third Reich and calling for the United States' entry into the war. Production ceased after 1945, with anti-Nazi themes continuing in the Hollywood rubble films and World War II films and with the wartime emphasis on civic duty and patriotic spirit replaced by affirmations of American cultural, political, and economic hegemony. One of the first American newsreels about the Third Reich, the March of Time's 1938 *Inside Nazi Germany*, still had to justify its critical perspective on the Third Reich. Likewise, the first anti-Nazi film, Anatole Litvak's *Confessions of a Nazi Spy* (1939), encountered considerable opposition in Hollywood and Washington. Announcing very difficult priorities after Pearl Harbor, the famous *Why We Fight* series, made under the direction of Frank Capra, already included two films with a German focus, *Prelude to War* (1942) and *The Nazis Strike* (1943). With production peaking in 1942–44, the anti-Nazi films played an important role in the enlistment of all media and cultural practices in the war effort. But as the last productions completed after 1945 make clear, their discursive function did not remain limited to the identification of a real enemy. A much more elusive threat, what Schmitt calls the absolute enemy, would continue to haunt the postwar imagination in the form of internal dangers and domestic crises.

Any attempt at a clear-cut definition of what—partly because of the short time period—never amounted to a genre in its own right is further complicated by the films' diverse moods and styles. Many anti-Nazi films are easily identifiable as propaganda films through their use of real or staged newsreel sequences, the inclusion of montage sequences and voice-over commentaries, and the preference for stereotypical characters, simplistic binaries, and highly didactic tones. Beyond that, the realist styles and documentary aesthetic in the government-sponsored films have little in common with the hyperbole, garishness, and crudeness of the cheap Poverty Row productions. *Confessions of a Nazi Spy* marks the beginning of what could be called a series, but the endpoint is more ambiguous, given the gradual change from anti-Nazi to denazification rhetoric in rubble films such as *The Master Race* (Herbert Biberman, 1944) or war tribunal films such as *None Shall Escape* (André de Todt, 1944) and the almost unperceivable transition from antifascism to anticommunism in *Berlin*

*Express* (Jacques Tourneur, 1948) as the master narrative of the cold war. This ideological realignment can be seen in a noticeable shift from the well-founded reasons for suspicion in the Nazi espionage films to the pervasive sense of fear and paranoia in noir classics such as Orson Welles's *The Stranger* (1946).

The range of genres that provided the anti-Nazi films with their formulaic story lines is indeed considerable: from family dramas such as *Mortal Storm* (Frank Borzage, 1940), gangster films such as *All through the Night* (Vincent Sherman, 1941), spy thrillers such as *The House on 92nd Street* (Henry Hathaway, 1945), romantic comedies such as *Once upon a Honeymoon* (Leo McCarey, 1942), and military instructional films such as *Resisting Enemy Interrogation* (Bernard Vorhaus, 1944), to two critically acclaimed comedies of mistaken identity involving Hitler and his doubles, Charlie Chaplin's *The Great Dictator* (1942) and Ernst Lubitsch's *To Be or Not to Be* (1942). Whereas the beginnings of the Holocaust film can be traced back to Fred Zinnemann's *The Seventh Cross* (1942), the overlaps with the war film are evident in Alfred Hitchcock's *Lifeboat* (1944). Nazis appeared in the most improbable contexts, including in a contribution to the *Invisible Man* series, *Invisible Agent* (Edwin L. Marin, 1942), and the *Tarzan* series, *Tarzan Triumphs* (Wilhelm Thiele, 1943). While sharing many thematic preoccupations with the small but significant number of British anti-Nazi films, beginning with the defense of the real and imaginary borders of the homeland, the Hollywood anti-Nazi films ultimately pursued a very different ideological project that was inseparable from the belief in American exceptionalism.[7]

Occasionally the choice of humor, satire, or parody ended up being problematic as the military situation in Europe changed, resulting in sharp attacks on *To Be or Not to Be* for its mocking portrayal of Nazis as bad actors and on *Once upon a Honeymoon* for its use of a concentration camp as the setting for a screwball comedy. The transgressive function of humor is most evident in the filmic representation of Hitler, which, given the primary focus on American democracy, remained limited to B pictures (exception: *The Great Dictator*). As psychopathology became the dominant narrative mode for explaining the Führer phenomenon, mockery and ridicule emerged as the preferred form of political denunciation. Accordingly, designated Hitler actor Robert (Bobby) Watson, in *Hitler, Dead or Alive* (Nick Grinde, 1942), plays the Führer as someone whose entire sense of self is dependent on his mustache. Similarly, in *The Hitler Gang* (John Farrow, 1944), he portrays him as a paranoid madman whose worldview is based in insecurity and resentment. Slapstick elements also predominate in *The Devil with Hitler* (Gordon Douglas, 1942) and *Natzy Nuisance* (Glen Tryon, 1943).[8] Animated shorts proved to be especially suited for the kind of political satire that envisioned Hitler as a wolf in *The Blitz Wolf* (Tex Avery, 1942) and a duck

Donald Duck in *Der Führer's Face*

in *The Ducktators* (Norman McCabe, 1942). Even the Disney studio contributed two popular anti-Nazi cartoons: *Der Führer's Face* (1942), with Donald Duck as a frantic Nazi armament worker, and *Education for Death* (1943), about the making of a typical Nazi follower. Yet whereas Disney's Donald Duck still awakens from what turns out to be only a bad dream to embrace the Statue of Liberty in his bedroom, a rather dour-looking Mickey Mouse makes a surprise appearance as the airplane emblem chosen by the pilots of the infamous Legion Condor during its 1936 bombing raids against Republican Spain.[9]

Because of such a wide range of genres, modes, and styles, identifying basic narrative patterns may initially seem difficult or even unproductive. Nonetheless, given the centrality of spatial fantasies to the fictional encounter between Nazis and anti-Nazis, four kinds of stories can be distinguished based on their settings: in the Third Reich, in neighboring countries invaded by the Nazis, in transitional places promising escape from Europe, and in the United States itself; all examples discussed in the chapter's third part fall into the last category. The films set in the Third Reich either attempt a psychopathology of its leaders, with *Women in Bondage* (Steve Sekely, 1943) and *Enemy of Women* (Alfred Zeisler, 1944) emphasizing the sexual aspects, or they retell the rise of Nazism through the experiences of ordinary citizens, as is done in *Hitler, Beast of Berlin* (Sam Newfield, 1939) and *Mortal Storm*. Frequently, German Americans serve to demonstrate the insidious effects of political indoctrination, with *Hitler's Children* (Edward Dmytryk, 1943) relying on the nature-versus-nurture argument to refute essentialist arguments about German national character. By contrast, Czechoslovakia, Austria, France, and Norway are chosen as the preferred locations for heroic stories of resistance that sometimes involve secret alliances, even dalliances, between female civilians in the resistance and undercover military men from the United States or Britain. Three films alone were made about

Lidice, site of the 1942 massacre ordered by the Nazis as punishment for the assassination of Reich Protector Reinhard Heydrich: *Hangmen Also Die* (Fritz Lang, 1943), *Hitler's Madman* (Douglas Sirk, 1943), and *Hostages* (Frank Tuttle, 1943). Finally, many stories of exile take their protagonists to the edges of Europe, to Marseille, Lisbon, Casablanca, and Istanbul, where various groups compete for narrative agency: German and American espionage agents, refugees desperately trying to secure a passage to North or South America, and corrupt local officials profiting from the political, military, and humanitarian crisis in Europe. *Casablanca* and two inferior imitations, *Passage to Marseille* (Michael Curtiz, 1944) and *The Conspirators* (Jean Negulesco, 1944), exemplify this exoticizing form of spatial emplotment.

The stories set in the United States, in turn, involve three kinds of protagonists: federal agents and policemen (e.g., *Confessions of a Nazi Spy*), espionage agents and fifth columnists (e.g., *The House on 92nd Street*), and average Americans such as the ones portrayed in *Watch on the Rhine* (Herman Shumlin, 1943), *Tomorrow the World!* (Leslie Fenton, 1944), and the previously mentioned *The Stranger*. At times, the dramatic confrontations involve German Americans who must work through their divided loyalties and prove their allegiance to their new homeland, most often by going undercover as Nazi spies in the service of the FBI; a good example is *They Came to Blow Up America* (Edward Ludwig, 1944). At other times, the democratic commitments of native-born Americans are put to the test in cautionary tales about worldly women with untrustworthy friends and questionable lifestyles, like those showcased in *Espionage Agent* (Lloyd Bacon, 1939) and *Madame Spy* (Roy William Neill, 1942). Not surprising in light of the pervasiveness of antisemitism at the time, the anti-Nazi films rarely address the persecution of Jews in Nazi Germany. Only two films feature American Jews as protagonists, *Address Unknown* (William Cameron Menzies, 1944) and *Margin for Error* (Otto Preminger, 1943). Even the refugee stories set in Europe mention the characters' Jewishness only in passing; the exceptions include *Mortal Storm* and *Hotel Berlin* (Peter Godfrey, 1945).[10] Hyphenated identities and cosmopolitan sensibilities are downplayed in favor of a distinctly American identity beyond ethnicity and nationality. The ultimate goal is the transformation of all citizens, whether native or foreign born, into what one character in *Spy Ship* (B. Reeves Eason, 1942) calls "square, honest Americans." The process of assimilation necessary to acquire this new identity is set into motion through the fight against the Nazis as the absolute other of American democracy; the result is a unified democratic subject based on the values of freedom, equality, and individualism.

Within these parameters, the Nazis serve two closely related functions: as antagonists to the psychologically developed main characters (usually Americans) and as catalysts in the affirmation of democratic attitudes, mentalities, behaviors, and beliefs. This structure requires that the Nazis—whether as supporting characters or anonymous extras—be reduced to a few easily identifiable and immutable traits. In the conception of the villains, externalized conflicts predominate over the internal struggles that, in the classic Lukácsian definition, make a character the embodiment of competing historical forces and social contradictions; such complexities are typically reserved for the leading protagonists. The anti-Nazis' status as characters and the Nazis' status as types, to use a distinction made by film scholar Richard Dyer, facilitate forms of engagement that, through the distribution of sympathies and antipathies, align individualism with democracy. If, as Dyer asserts, "the role of stereotypes is to make visible the invisible," their primary purpose in the anti-Nazi film is to create, strengthen, and promote democratic values through confrontation with the historical enemy.[11] But instead of depicting Nazi dictatorship and American democracy as two opposing forms of government or political ideologies, the anti-Nazi films, through the use of stereotypes, end up equating Nazism with ideology as such: deviant, deficient, and dangerous. Meanwhile, the denunciation of ideology as psychopathology establishes American democracy as presumably unmarked in terms of race and gender and hence normal and normative. As a result, the threat of ideology is displaced into essentialized terms and the possibility of contamination between normal and abnormal minimized, a convenient strategy of othering analyzed at the time by Siegfried Kracauer in a critical article on Hollywood's use of national stereotypes.[12]

Beyond serving such propagandistic aims, the stereotypical Nazis—virtually all of them are male—illustrate well the contradictory functions of stereotypes as condensed forms of knowledge and experience; as expressions of ethnic, social, and sexual prejudices; and as performances of public sentiment and popular opinion. Each stereotype is identified with a particular body type and set of gestures, movements, and facial expressions. Based on established acting conventions, the Nazi's social status and political stance manifest themselves in the smallest details: how he enters a room, walks down the stairs, sits at his desk, answers the telephone, wears his uniforms, puts on his gloves, smokes a cigarette, talks to subordinates, flirts with women, and so forth. Moreover, each stereotype is identified with a specific emotional register (e.g., arrogance, brutality, subservience) and primary affect (e.g., anger, fear, lust) that grant access to the psychopathology of power and establish the other against which the life-affirming attitudes and beliefs associated with democratic subjectivity are presented. This connection is nowhere more apparent than in the equation of Nazism with deficient masculinity and deviant sexuality, a pattern that

Sig Ruman in *To Be or Not to Be*          Conrad Veidt in *Casablanca*

continues throughout the postwar years (e.g., in the Italian Naziploitation films) and that allows the spectator at once to partake in, and guard against, fascist attractions.[13]

Four basic stereotypes, all defined through their position within the power structure, can be identified: the party member, the officer, the sympathizer, and the collaborator. Usually limited to supporting roles, the party member, typically an SA (Sturmabteilung) man, SS (Schutzstaffel) man, or Gestapo agent, personifies the hierarchical structure and institutional violence of the regime in almost grotesque ways. As performed by German émigré actor Sig Ruman in several films, he is usually lower class, uneducated, eager to take orders, and willing to follow without questions; he is the ideal subordinate. Often short, pudgy, and balding, this type compensates for his physical shortcomings with excessive brutality. His authoritarianism hides a weak, not fully formed personality, dependent on the surrogate identities acquired in the humiliation and mistreatment of others. In accordance with sociopsychological theories of fascism developed at the time, such characteristics are introduced to show his lower-class position or rather the discrepancy between social status and social ambition that is typical of authoritarian, highly stratified societies; more middle-class versions of this type are often depicted as cold, cynical desk murderers. In all cases, this type is an entirely negative figure, the object of intense aversions in the diegesis and a preferred object of loathing or ridicule by the spectator.

The second stereotype is the only one who appears in leading roles: the Nazi officer, embodied to perfection by the tall, lean, elegant, and sexually alluring Conrad Veidt, the German-born actor best known for playing Major Strasser in *Casablanca*. Pointing to entirely unexplored patterns of influence that link Hollywood and Leningrad, the same type can be found in the Soviet

Francis Lederer in *Confessions of a Nazi Spy*          Peter Lorre in *All through the Night*

antifascist films of the 1940s.[14] Often a member of the aristocracy and a propo-
nent of high culture, this officer is a tragic figure torn between honor and
duty, obligation and conviction, with his internal conflicts hidden by his emotional reserve and sense of social propriety. Exploring such conflicts, *Nazi Agent*
(Jules Dassin, 1942) presents Veidt in a double role as German American twin
brothers, with the good American killing the Nazi sympathizer and assuming
his identity to uncover Nazi espionage activities in the United States. Yet even
though the latter invites empathetic responses, he remains a figure from the
past: a representative of Old Europe and ultimately not suited for democracy.
Unlike the malleable Hitler Youth from *Tomorrow the World!*, he cannot be saved.

The third stereotype, the sympathizer, is attracted to the movement because of experiences of downward mobility and social marginalization not in-
frequently connected to his immigrant status. As played by the Czech-born
Francis Lederer in *Confessions of a Nazi Spy*, the sympathizer is young, male, and
impoverished, but with petit bourgeois aspirations. His financial problems fill
him with frustration and resentment, and his nagging wife undermines his
sense of masculinity; thus he escapes into the fantasies of racial superiority
offered by American Nazi agitators. Although the character's evolution from
army deserter to embezzler to espionage agent is explained as the result of a
narcissistic personality disorder, the nuanced performance by Lederer leaves
room for compassionate feelings toward ordinary people who, as victims of the
Great Depression and its lingering effects, turn to mass movements not because
of strong political convictions but because of a pervasive sense of alienation,
isolation, and disempowerment.

The fourth type, the collaborator, uses the Nazi regime solely to his personal advantage. As played by the enigmatic Peter Lorre, an Austro-Hungarian
Jew, he is a wanderer between worlds, a man without a country, family, or

community; his ethnic ambiguity is closely tied to sexual ambiguity. Often a refugee or émigré without papers, he lives in hotels and other transitional places where he survives on shady business deals. As the quintessential stranger, the collaborator knows everyone but always stands alone; he appears at the center of dramatic events but resists emotional attachments and political commitments. Too vulnerable to act according to moral principles, he moves between all fronts, but because of his intimate knowledge of the mechanisms of power, he sometimes becomes an ally in American undercover operations. Precisely because he is a figure of suspicion, the collaborator invites more complicated forms of engagement as he forces the naive Americans in the diegesis (and, presumably, the audience) to accept the difficulty of adhering to rigid moral standards in the fight against the Nazis.

Through these four basic stereotypes and the forms of character engagement discussed in the third part of this chapter, the anti-Nazi films affirm freedom and democracy as core American values worthy of being defended in public and private life. The agitational character of the films is most apparent in the direct appeals with which filmmakers warn the moviegoing public about the Nazi threat at home and abroad and outline the dangers of nonaction. Time and again protagonists articulate this rhetorical position, often with a direct look into the camera. In *Espionage Agent*, a State Department briefing concludes with the sobering warning: "If America, lacking the protective laws it needs, is drawn into another war, it will be because of those human ostriches who keep their heads buried in the sand." Frequently, the developments in Europe are presented as part of a larger threat to the liberties protected by the Bill of Rights. The preamble to *Hitler, Beast of Berlin* includes a dedication to "all who believe that the flaming torch of liberty will at some future day disperse the doom that has darkened half the world." After Pearl Harbor, such comments become more belligerent, but again with a clear understanding of Hitler as the personification of broader antidemocratic—that is, anti-American—tendencies. The question posed by one of the shipwrecked in *Lifeboat* about whether to "throw the Nazi off the boat" speaks precisely to this sense of a growing threat and is answered with an unambiguous "yes": "We can't treat them as human beings. You got to exterminate them." In *The Hitler Gang*, too, US agents promise to "purge the world of Hitler and his gang" and "eliminate German militarism and all that it [stands] for." Confidence in an American victory is both ubiquitous and obligatory. A federal agent in *Madame Spy* defiantly declares: "We are going to win this war. . . . America is awake."

In support of this military and political project, the victims of Nazi aggression frequently call upon the United States to become a defender of democracies

Poster for *The Hitler Gang*

Poster for *None Shall Escape*,
courtesy Sony Pictures

worldwide. At the ending of *Hitler's Madman*, the occupied Czechs speak directly to the American audience: "Keep your country free of the enemy! Catch him! Do not wait!" In *Hostages*, a Czech woman evokes the populist language of the US Constitution's "We, the people" to call for a united front against fascism and totalitarianism: "We believe in people. If we didn't, what would be there to fight for?" And as the Jewish barber pretending to be Adenoid Hynkel, Chaplin in *The Great Dictator* passionately implores the defenders of humanity: "In the name of democracy, let us all unite."

Notwithstanding such appeals to international solidarity, the ultimate goal of the anti-Nazi films remained the forceful affirmation of American values. Nowhere is this more apparent than in the films that use Nazi children to prove the superiority of liberal democracy, not least through its belief in the reformability of all human beings. Two examples may suffice to illustrate this point. In *Tomorrow the World!*, an obnoxious Hitler Youth called Emil arrives in small-town America and soon tyrannizes his entire host family.[15] A bully without self-awareness, he makes antisemitic, sexist, and racist remarks at school, fights with other boys, assaults his host sister, and is almost arrested by the police. Fortunately, his host's Jewish fiancée recognizes his cold fanaticism as a sign of trauma—the imprisonment and public denunciation of his father by the Nazis—and initiates the first steps toward healing when she gives him license to shed tears and show himself as a true human being, that is, someone who supports democracy. His new American father summarizes the lesson to be learned in the following way: "Anytime anybody tells you anything, you've got to ask why. That's the difference between us and the Nazis."

Similarly, *Hitler's Children* uses the story of two childhood sweethearts grow-ing up in Nazi Germany, a German boy born in America and an American girl born in Germany, to assert the primacy of nurture over nature in developing an autonomous self and a sense of civic responsibility.[16] Inoculated against Nazi ideology through her experience of romantic love (and, by implication, norma-tive heterosexuality), the young woman resists induction into the Bund deutscher Mädel and confinement in a Lebensborn home for single mothers and bravely endures sadistic flagellation by a member of the SS. In the end, love triumphs over ideology and, despite the young couple's sacrificial death, the question "Can we stop Hitler's children before it's too late?" will be answered in the affirmative—because American democracy has rediscovered its core values in confrontation with its greatest enemy, the Nazis.

For the Hollywood majors, the anti-Nazi film marked a significant break with industry practices and required a temporary departure from established aesthetic and artistic models. While Warner Bros. decided early on to join in the fight against the Nazis, Metro-Goldwyn-Mayer and 20th Century Fox did not want to jeopardize their trade relations with the Reich and lose access to lucrative European markets.[17] Poverty Row studios Monogram and Republic rushed in to satisfy the growing demand, thereby also establishing the close connection between Nazis and exploitation that, most noticeable in the sexualization of power, would continue to haunt the postfascist imaginary; in fact, some critics during that time cited prurient interests as an added attraction of the anti-Nazi film.[18] The ensuing division of labor between the majors and Poverty Row re-flected official Hollywood doctrine about the incommensurability of classical narrative with the visceral pleasures served by exploitation and the techniques of persuasion known as propaganda. The politicization of cinema, the argu-ment went, not only compromised the global marketability of Hollywood films but also opened the doors to a decidedly European definition of politically com-mitted art and a film aesthetic inspired by social realism and Soviet-style mon-tage. Their ideological foundations, in turn, posed a serious threat to basic assumptions about filmic narrative and social reality, a point indirectly confirmed by the anti-Nazi film's difficulty in representing collective agency. Klaus Mann's identification of a constitutive tension between the personalized view of fas-cism in the narrative and the actual politics of depersonalization in the Third Reich refers precisely to this problem when he concludes, "What we see is the misfortune of a family, not the terrific drama of a people or a continent."[19]

In developing compelling modes of address, filmmakers profited from new studies on propaganda offered by emerging new disciplines such as communi-cation studies. Most scholars agreed on the importance of using modern mass media to advertise democratic principles and ideas to a citizenry increasingly dependent on audiovisual representations in forming political opinions, attitudes, and beliefs. In fact, one of the discipline's founding fathers, Harold Lasswell, developed a mass-based model of reception that assumed the full realization of a film's propagandistic intentions by a largely passive, uncritical audience. He concluded that in modern society, propaganda had to function as "the new hammer and anvil of social solidarity" and help to preserve a sense of social cohesion against "the idolatry of the individual [which] passes for the official religion of democracy."[20] Dire pronouncements about the future of American democracy further added to the heightened significance ascribed to mass media as a new public sphere and declared the motion-picture theater the most important venue for raising political awareness.

However, already a series of Rockefeller Foundation–funded research projects on the effectiveness of wartime propaganda, including the *Why We Fight* series, pointed out the limits of such ambitions. In his contribution, sociologist Paul Lazarsfeld questioned the existence of the homogeneous audience presupposed by Lasswell and instead emphasized the role of social stratification and differentiation in the actualization of filmic meanings.[21] Along similar lines, Kracauer, like Lazarsfeld a scholar in exile, approached the inherent tension between depiction and suggestion in the propaganda film through the double optics of Babelsberg and Hollywood and raised concerns especially relevant for the democratic credentials of the anti-Nazi film and its postwar reincarnations. For if "totalitarian propaganda endeavored to supplant a reality based on the acknowledgment of individual values," he insisted, "propaganda for democracy had to do the opposite, namely to validate and celebrate the individual."[22]

The production and reception history of *Confessions of a Nazi Spy* illustrates well the various arguments over the politicization of filmmaking prior to the United States' entry into the war.[23] Openly propagandistic in subject matter and mode of address, the Warner production documents the activities of the German American Bund and the efforts of the FBI under J. Edgar Hoover to uncover Nazi spy rings in the United States. Inspired by the actual case of a New York–based group that was exposed in 1938 by special agent Leon Turrou, the project was taken on by Harry Warner as part of his active involvement in the Hollywood Anti-Nazi League and his deep concern, as an Orthodox Jew, about the Third Reich's antisemitic policies. Then again, *Confessions of a Nazi Spy* was also a typical Warner production modeled on the studio's critically acclaimed gangster films and their potent mix of crime, action, and suspense. "I hope to do for the persecuted victims of Germany—Jews and Germans—what we did for law and order with *Public Enemy*," Jack Warner declared proudly.[24]

Because of its equation of Nazism with gangsterism, *Confessions of a Nazi Spy* encountered numerous problems before and after its Beverly Hills premiere on 27 April 1939. The Breen Office, which had been enforcing the Production Code since 1934, required several rewrites in line with the "national feelings clause," which demanded respectful treatment of the history and culture of other nations.[25] Reactions from the State Department were mixed because of concerns about the film's negative effect on diplomatic relations with Nazi Germany, a fear confirmed by official protest notes by the German embassy in Washington and the influential German consul in Los Angeles, Georg Gyssling. And indeed, *Confessions of a Nazi Spy* could not be shown in several European and Latin American countries and contributed to the end of the highly profitable German-American film trade; in 1940 Goebbels announced a ban on all Hollywood film imports, and even Paramount and Metro-Goldwyn-Mayer were forced to close their Berlin-based German subsidiaries.[26]

*Confessions of a Nazi Spy* made a modest profit for Harry and Jack Warner, who would continue to produce anti-Nazi films throughout the war years; the studio rereleased the film in 1940 with additional news footage.[27] A poster declaring the film a must-see for every patriotic American reads: "The picture that will open the eyes of 130,000,000 Americans! Over there, they wouldn't allow you to see this picture. But this, Thank Heaven, is America—where pictures like this can be made and seen and cheered." Reviews were mostly positive, despite concerns about Hollywood's sudden foray into foreign politics and complaints about the detached documentary style and incendiary montage sequences. The National Board of Review of Motion Pictures chose the film as the best picture of the year in recognition of its "artistic merit and importance" (*New York Times*, 25 December 1939). Rather predictably, the trade press emphasized the film's political and historical relevance. "Decades from now what's happening may be seen in perspective. And the historians will certainly take note of this daring frank broadside from a picture company," wrote *Variety* (3 May 1939). Some film critics were less enthusiastic, with Frank S. Nugent's damning conclusion, "Hitler won't like it; neither will Goebbels; frankly, we were not too favorably impressed either" (*New York Times*, 29 April 1939) applicable to the majority of anti-Nazi films.[28]

The reception of *Confessions of a Nazi Spy* established a pattern for the entire series: some commercial successes but often only as the first film in a double feature; mixed responses in the trade press, with critics citing audiences' lack of interest in the subject before 1941 and problems with films made obsolete by military developments after 1941; and divided opinions in the German exile press, with reviewers appreciating the growing attention to the Nazi threat but dismayed about the films' low artistic quality and insufficient differentiation between Germans and Nazis. This did not stop pro-Nazi groups from organizing protests in several cities with sizable German American communities. A motion-picture theater burned down in Milwaukee, several reels of the film were stolen from a theater in New Mexico, and the Bund filed a series of temporary injunctions in federal court. Homegrown demagogues such as the right-wing Father Coughlin railed against a Judeo-Bolshevist conspiracy and attacked Harry Warner as a Jewish propagandist. Meanwhile, the isolationist politician Burton Wheeler of the America First Committee cast suspicion on the many foreigners working in Hollywood. Responding to growing anti-foreigner sentiments, the congressional Nye-Clark Committee in 1941 was briefly charged with investigating "Hollywood warmongering" before the enlistment of film in the war effort became official policy and an expression of true patriotism. In a humorous comment on the intended popular reception of the anti-Nazi film, in *Margin for Error*, a Jewish New York cop even takes the pretty housekeeper of the German consul to a screening of *Confessions of a Nazi Spy*; naturally, she falls in love with him.

One of the goals of *Confessions of a Nazi Spy* was to draw attention to the activities of the German American Bund and its leader Fritz Kuhn, the so-called American Führer from 1936 to 1939.[29] Through mass rallies, public lectures, and recreational activities, the Bundists had established themselves as a significant presence in immigrant communities in Cincinnati, Chicago, Milwaukee, and the Yorkville neighborhood of Manhattan. However, the footage of the 1939 Pro-America rally at Madison Square Garden, with twenty thousand people in attendance, gives an exaggerated picture of their actual influence. Like neo-Nazi groups today, the Bund and its allied organizations remained a fringe phenomenon, unable to stop the forces of integration and assimilation. Their official purpose was to unify the large group of German Americans and overcome negative attitudes toward Germans in the aftermath of World War I; less openly acknowledged goals included the promotion of Nazi ideology under the motto "Tomorrow the World Is Ours." In fact, the House Committee on Un-American Activities (later renamed the House Un-American Activities Committee, HUAC) was originally founded in 1934 to investigate the involvement of German Americans in Nazi activities. After years of inactivity, it resumed its work in 1947, with anticommunism declared the new threat to American democracy and Hollywood now vilified as a hotbed of communist subversion.[30] But while anticommunism during the cold war fueled an atmosphere of paranoia and mass hysteria closely identified with the name of Senator

Joe McCarthy, anti-Nazism during the 1930s never acquired the same affective charge because of the conflicting news about the Third Reich circulating in US mass media and the complicated relationship between Germans and Americans in cultural and political life.

The United States' entry into the war fundamentally changed the debates on film and politics and resulted in a rare alignment between the interests of the film industry and the federal government. The Roosevelt administration in 1942 created the Bureau of Motion Pictures (BMP) in the Office of War Information (OWI) to coordinate propaganda efforts during the war but with potential foreign policy applications for the postwar period. OWI guidelines instructed filmmakers to educate and entertain the citizens and show them "what [Americans were] fighting for, the American way of life."[31] In response, producer Walter Wanger promised "to inspire the American people with fervor about American life." "Democracy," he concluded, "must be clothed with ringing affirmations; it must be imbued with a virile and aggressive mass spirit."[32] Although most film professionals had little interest in making this "mass spirit" the foundation of a new film style, even seemingly personal pursuits and private desires—foremost those related to romantic love and family life— would henceforth be closely aligned with the self-representation of American democracy.

Not surprisingly, this historical moment gave rise to new political initiatives and alliances within the Hollywood community. A loosely organized group of film professionals, the Anti-Nazi League had been founded in 1937 by liberals, moderates, and communists in a broad popular-front alliance against fascism; Anatole Litvak and John Wexley, who adapted the story of *Confessions of a Nazi Spy* to the screen, were members of the league and active in various leftist groups. The Anti-Nazi League eventually became part of what historian Michael Denning suggestively calls a cultural front: a diverse group of film professionals, especially screenwriters, leftist New York intellectuals, and émigré actors and directors who introduced political subject matter with the expectation of more long-term changes in the aesthetic possibilities and social functions of cinema.[33] They worked together in a spirit of political critique that, in its left-wing version, found expression in Max Horkheimer's often cited remark from the period, "Whoever is not willing to talk about capitalism should also keep quiet about fascism."[34] Unfortunately, the dream of radical political critique proved short-lived. The Nazi-Soviet Non-Aggression Pact of 1939, which to many contemporary observers showed fascism and communism as two comparable totalitarian regimes, marked the beginning of the end for the broad leftist alliance that would become the target of paranoid projections during the Red Scare of the 1950s. The US entry into the war, finally, brought a realignment of forces described by historian Saverino Giovacchini as a renationalization of political positions, with the internationalist Anti-Nazi League replaced by the ethnically based European Film Fund and with film production henceforth consumed with "the 'politicization' of ethnic identities, and the 'ethnicization' of political ones."[35]

Film scholars have described wartime Hollywood as a unique moment in the history of American film, and some of their conclusions are highly relevant to our discussion of the anti-Nazi film as the founding site of the postfascist imaginary. Thomas Doherty, for instance, argues that the war fundamentally changed the function of entertainment, opening up traditional genres to more serious subject matter and allowing political topics to appear in fictional formats.[36] Focusing on the relationship between narrative and ideology, Dana Polan speaks of the 1940s as "a moment that is trying to hold different grids— different ways of representing—together in a single, volatile space," which in this case means "the grid of war and peace, of a successful war, successful peace, and a successful transition from one to the other."[37] In the tension between power and paranoia that characterizes this transition, Polan concludes, we can see the workings of narrative as ideological strategy, developed to achieve a "compromise position between the two poles of utopian disavowal and active aggression."[38]

Two groups in particular, the Hollywood Europeans and the Hollywood New Yorkers, contributed to the filmic confrontation with Nazism under the conditions of what Giovacchini perceptively calls democratic modernism. To be understood as a particular social, intellectual, and aesthetic constellation, democratic modernism refers to an aesthetic middle ground, beyond high and low culture, in which the old distinctions between realism and modernism, or escapism and activism, dissolve and an overly homogeneous national culture opens up to other cultures without losing its sense of coherence. As part of this process, the introduction of social realism into mainstream cinema and the resultant politicization of entertainment must be seen both as a response to the crisis of European culture and democracy and as an attempt to make productive use of the difference between European and American perspectives, including in the overdetermined function of the discourse of "the people" in staging the ideological confrontation between fascism and democracy as a populist/popular narrative.

Playing a central role in this process, the émigrés, according to Giovacchini, had experienced a highly compromised discourse of *Volk* (nation or people) that, given its exclusionary function, stood in stark contrast to the inclusionary American discourse of the people as an interclass phenomenon and, to a degree, an experience of belonging beyond race and ethnicity.[39] In the films, this difference manifests itself in the confrontation between the stereotypical Nazi as the representative of a degenerate *Volk* and the ideal-typical American as the representative of a healthy people. In more subtle ways, the anti-Nazi film also allowed some émigré directors to introduce the question of class into American contexts. Whereas Nazi sympathizers are presented as petit bourgeois—that is, through their precarious position between classes—Nazi officials and party members are associated with either the upper or the lower classes. By contrast, their American antagonists are all part of a large and homogenous middle class that, because of the implicit promise of social mobility, presumably makes them immune to totalitarian tendencies. Last but not least, the Europeans brought to the anti-Nazi film an acute awareness of the interrelatedness of narrative and ideology and the difficulties of reconciling artistic innovation with mass appeal. For Giovacchini, the failure of the historical avant-gardes in the face of fascism led to a renewed appreciation for affect—its strong sensations and identifications—as an instrument of political mobilization, whether in the context of Brechtian experiments with epic montage or in the reclamation of Aristotelian mimesis and catharsis. The collaboration of Bertolt Brecht and John Wexley on the screenplay for Lang's *Hangmen Also Die* bears witness to this utopian project of combining modernist and popular elements and, despite the well-documented problems, offers a model for reconciling emotion and critique.

What roles did the German-speaking exiles and émigrés play in the return to nationalist sentiments and the resultant universalization of American values during the later war years? "Complicated" and "conflicted" are the terms best suited to describe their contribution. Working as directors, actors, screenwriters, composers, or cameramen, they were part of a well-documented history of German immigration that, during the 1920s, had brought Ernst Lubitsch and Friedrich Wilhelm Murnau to Hollywood and prompted studio executives to extend invitations to Marlene Dietrich and, later, Fritz Lang. After the United States' entry into the war, European-born directors felt a special obligation to lend their talents to the propaganda effort, as Chaplin did in *The Great Dictator*, Lubitsch in *To Be or Not to Be*, Hitchcock in *Saboteur* (1942) and *Lifeboat*, and, most famously and controversially, Lang in *Hangmen Also Die*.[40] Meanwhile, screen adaptations of literary works by Erich Maria Remarque for *So Ends Our Night* (John Cromwell, 1941), Stefan Heym for *Hostages*, Anna Seghers for *The Seventh Cross*, and Vicki Baum for *Hotel Berlin* underscored the close connection between literary fame and political commitment and aligned the fight against the Nazis with the defense of European high culture and Western humanism.

The emigration waves after 1938–39 brought large numbers of actors from the German-speaking stage and screen to Hollywood and, in some cases, to the work of the cultural front. Many saw the anti-Nazi film as an integral part of their involvement with the Anti-Nazi League and, when it was dissolved in 1942, the European Film Fund, a refugee aid organization. For others, participation was primarily driven by financial needs and professional considerations. Because of their strong accents, the new arrivals from Germany, Austria, Czechoslovakia, Hungary, and Poland were almost exclusively cast as Nazis. Conrad Veidt, Fritz Kortner, Albert Bassermann, Paul Henreid, Peter Lorre, and Francis Lederer often appeared in leading roles, whereas the more clichéd supporting roles were reserved for Sig Ruman, Wolfgang Zilzer, Reinhold Schünzel, Martin Kosleck, Hans Heinrich von Twardowski, and others. Some actors were too embarrassed to be listed in the credits or wrote dismissively about the dreaded "accent roles" in their memoirs. But in all cases, it was the constructive tension between caricature and mimicry especially in the performances by Jewish actors that gave rise to the physiognomy of the "typical" Nazi and that is perhaps described best as political drag, to appropriate a term from theater scholar Katrin Sieg.[41] The tragic ironies behind such performances are acknowledged in the telling anecdote, attributed to writer Walter Slezak, that if students of history in two hundred years were to ask their teachers what the Nazis looked like, they might turn to Hollywood films from the period—only to be faced with an almost exclusively Jewish group.[42]

Just as the Hollywood community was deeply divided over the politicization of filmmaking, the exiles and émigrés engaged in heated debates on the future of Germany and the national character of the Germans. Disagreements over the causes of Nazism and the best approach to postwar denazification came into sharp relief during the 1943 Hollywood Writers' Mobilization Congress at UCLA, with the implications for the anti-Nazi film most apparent in the exiles' complaints about lacking distinctions between Germans and Nazis. The purpose of the meeting had been to counter statements by conservatives such as Emil Ludwig, who had spoken of an innate German disposition toward obedience, pedantry, and arrogance that would complicate attempts at postwar democratization. Thomas Mann, the self-appointed representative of a better Germany in the United States, similarly noted the difficulty of separating Nazism from Germanness, arguing, "There are *not* two Germanies, a good one and a bad one. . . . Wicked Germany is merely good Germany gone astray, good Germany in misfortune, in guilt, and in ruin."[43] Whereas Mann took the

long view and pointed to the tradition of German inwardness as a major cause
for the prevalence of antidemocratic sentiment, the left-leaning Lion Feuchtwanger limited his comments to recent political developments and placed most
of the blame for Nazism on the aristocrats, generals, and industrialists who had
supported them.[44]

The conservative defense of individualism as a weapon against fascist mass
movements and homegrown mob rule, on the one hand, and the leftist call for
international solidarity and new forms of sociability, on the other, can be found
in several books by émigré scholars that, in all likelihood, were known to the
screenwriters and directors involved in the making of anti-Nazi films. Most
scholars acknowledged the difficulty of mobilizing mass support for abstract
principles such as liberty or equality and saw the survival of democracy as
closely tied to the ability of mass media to imbue politics with strong emotions.
However, by treating the Third Reich as a symptom of the rise of the modern
masses, they also identified this politics of emotions with fascism and used their
own aversion to massification, which was rooted in bourgeois fear, elitist disdain, and deep pessimism about the future, to warn about the dire consequences for liberal democracies.

Concerned about the dangers allegedly emanating from these homogenized masses and the troubling rise of what philosopher Max Scheler called a
"democracy of emotion" (*Stimmungsdemokratie*), sociologist Karl Mannheim
insisted on the need for both "planning for democracy" (by political elites) and
"planning for freedom" (by nonconformist artists). The economist Emil Lederer,
cofounder of the University in Exile at the New School, evoked the "threat of a
classless society" posed by the totalitarian state and declared the fascist eleva-
tion of crowds as a surrogate for society and its creation of a political system
based on institutionalized masses to be the central problem facing all modern
democracies. Radically expanding the scope of investigation and introducing a
Marxist perspective, Theodor W. Adorno and Max Horkheimer, the main
representatives of the Frankfurt School, analyzed these developments as part of
a dialectic of Enlightenment that, rather than fulfilling the ideals of humanism,
brought forth the barbarism of fascism and now threatened to erode the foundations of democracy through the rise of what they called the culture industry
and a totally administered world. In *Behemoth* (1943), the first comprehensive
analysis of the Third Reich, political scientist Franz Neumann paid special attention to the Nazis' systematic use of disorder and lawlessness in establishing a
"totalitarian monopolistic capitalism" but admonished his readers that, in the
struggle against Nazism, "the process of democratization in England and the
United States be not sacrificed but that it be encouraged to progress."[45]

How did the anti-Nazi films engage with these scholarly contributions and intellectual debates? As I have shown, by means of stereotyping and, closely related, character engagement. If it is true, as anthropologist Margaret Mead argued during the war, that we can identify a distinct democratic character structure, we should also be able to define a corresponding fascist character structure, such as the anthropologically determined one described as incurable German paranoia and megalomania by a little-known psychiatrist named Richard M. Brickner or the socially constructed one based on the so-called F-scale (F for fascism) examined by Adorno and others in their influential studies on the authoritarian personality.[46] Affirming the close connection between constructions of the political in scientific knowledge and popular opinion, the anti-Nazi films presented audiences with textbook examples of how to confront F-scale traits such as authoritarian aggression, servility, and cynicism through an allegedly innate American love of freedom, belief in equality, and respect for others. Moreover, the films offered highly moralistic lessons on how to defeat totalitarian societies ruled by terror, violence, and paranoid contagion and to counter their false promises of community through reeducation for democracy American style. These calls for greater political awareness in the United States and the reliance on character engagement to achieve this goal will be analyzed in the three case studies that make up the last part of this chapter.

As we have seen, the anti-Nazi films rely heavily on stereotypes and the binaries of friend and enemy organized through them. The sympathies and antipathies structuring the relationships among characters and those between characters and spectators, in turn, are central to the production of political affects, the kinds of feelings, emotions, and aesthetic pleasures mobilized in the affirmation of "American" values such as freedom, equality, and democracy. In analyzing this process of ideological and affective interpellation, it might be useful to draw upon the previously mentioned distinction among recognition, alliance, and allegiance proposed by Murray Smith. Recognition, the most basic one, refers to the construction of the character "as an individuated and continuous human agent" and encompasses the cognitive processes shared by all protagonists, including the stereotypical Nazis. Alignment refers to "the way a film gives us access to the actions, thoughts, and feelings of characters," especially the main protagonists—in this case, the Americans.[47] Made possible through point of view, spectator alignment allows the audience to follow a character throughout the narrative, with all the attendant cognitive and emotional challenges and rewards. According to Smith, this process entails various possible constellations, from congruence, incongruence, movement from congruence to incongruence to ambiguous or conflicted congruence, and distanced observation. The most powerful form of engagement, allegiance, involves "the way a film attempts to marshal our sympathies for or against the various characters in the world of the fiction" and frequently includes the kind of moral evaluation that, in this case, sustains the all-important distinction between friends and enemies.[48]

In a thus proposed "structure of sympathy," alignment and allegiance are not necessarily coextensive; allegiance for Smith has a stronger moral component and is best described as a basic affective structure rather than a particular response to characters. These elements are especially pronounced in what he calls the Manichean moral structure of good versus evil prevalent in the agitational film—the anti-Nazi film certainly fits that category—and the kind of rhetorical strategies and iconographic motifs analyzed in this first part of this chapter.[49] In all cases, the Americans, as the main protagonists in both the diegesis and the auditorium, perform the important narrative function of providing, through their interactions with the Nazis, what Smith calls moral centering and moral resolution and what, to finally turn to the question of the political, closely resembles the process of ideological interpellation, including through the translation of political into moral categories.

The stories set in the United States perform these functions by relying on two basic narrative structures and their respective affective modes: the investigative mode, with its emphasis on rational analysis, in the male-dominated espionage stories; and the melodramatic mode, with its emphasis on emotions, in the female-dominated conversion stories. Both kinds of films confirm the importance of characters as, in the words of film philosopher Noël Carroll, "the most integral factor in establishing the spectator's moral perspective on the action."[50] And despite their different generic models, both kinds of films rely on the melodramatic mode identified in the introduction as an essential part of the democratic imaginary and draw upon the sentiment and sentimentality of patriotism to align anti-Nazi with pro-American positions. But whereas the first persuade us that we can and should trust the government, the second one locates trust—an important political affect—and its lack entirely in the private sphere.

The espionage stories aim at what is presented as an impartial account of the serious threat to American democracy, focusing in particular on Nazi espionage in the United States; their strategy is critical detachment and their goal political education. Direct confrontation with the political enemy is considered enough to convince audiences of the need for immediate action; the belief in the power of knowledge—that is, in the Enlightenment project—is still very much intact. Stylistically, the espionage stories stand out through the use of newsreel footage in fictional contexts, voice-over narratives and flashback structures, and a preference for conventional realist styles. The result is a comprehensible, calculable world in which government employees fight the nation's enemies through well-established procedures and systematic analyses: decoding secret letters, observing suspects, searching apartments, interviewing witnesses; in short, by collecting and interpreting evidence. The real heroes in the espionage stories are federal agents, policemen, and state attorneys; they personify the principles of rationality, objectivity, and factuality and stand for the rule of law as the foundation of liberal democracy. Edward G. Robinson, who plays a federal agent in *Confessions of a Nazi Spy* and *The Stranger*, represents the prototype: intelligent, restrained, unassuming, meticulous, and guided by a clear sense of moral purpose. In both films, he functions as a defender of freedom and democracy and a stand-in for the narrator as he quietly assumes control over the narrative in the course of the investigation.

*Confessions of a Nazi Spy*, the first film to rely on documentary styles in the defense of democracy, features extensive news footage about the German annexation of Austria, the invasion of Czechoslovakia, and the attacks on Poland, Belgium, Norway, France, and the Netherlands; it also includes several staged scenes depicting mass rallies, public speeches, and the Horst Wessel camp for Nazi youth organized by the Bund under the leadership of Dr. Karl Kassel (a reference to Fritz Kuhn). The close attention to Nazi rhetoric implies that a strong anti-Nazi movement can only develop through direct confrontation with the threat to America emanating from Europe. Accordingly, the flashback structure, which shows the positive outcome of this confrontation in the espionage trial, sets up a dialogic structure in which statements by Nazi leaders and their American followers are juxtaposed with sequences that disprove their grandiose claims and reveal their true personal motives.

The main weapon mobilized against totalitarian ideologies is individualism, both as an instrument of critique that reduces political positions to individual solutions and as a model of explanation that locates liberal democracy outside ideology. Introducing the requisite binaries of evaluation, the commentator in the montage sequence describes the Third Reich as "a new fascist society based on the devout worship of the Aryan superman, a new fascist culture imbued with the glorification of conquest and war, a fascist system of life where every man, woman, and child must think alike, speak like, and do alike." The New York sequences that follow, however, unmask the Nazis as morally deficient characters who rely on political rhetoric to compensate for personal pathologies: delusions of grandeur and an extramarital affair in the case of Dr. Kassel,

 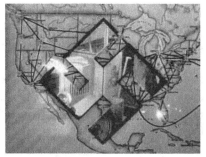

Montage sequence in *Confessions of a Nazi Spy*     Montage sequence in *Confessions of a Nazi Spy*

and an inferiority complex and inability to provide for his family in the case of Kurt Schneider.

To give two examples for the displacement of the political into the personal and its subsequent enlistment in the self-assertion of American democracy: During a meeting with Nazi espionage agents, the Goebbels character asserts, "The new Americanism is a formless iron that we will beat into another new swastika," a reference to the isolationist America Now movement and attempts by the Bund to attract discontented Americans with their antidemocratic rhetoric. The narrative immediately disproves these outrageous claims as it shows the successful investigation methods and interrogation techniques used by federal agent Edward Renard (French for fox) in the FBI's fight against Nazi spies in the United States. And, in response to Goebbels's sneering characterization of "the strongest remaining democracy, America," the prosecutor at the espionage trial declares triumphantly: "America is not just one of the remaining democracies. . . . America is democracy." The closing sequence confirms this point and validates the political allegiances formed through the film. At a neighborhood diner, on the day of the verdict, the federal agent and the prosecutor meet for coffee. Watching the newspaper boy and the other customers discuss the trial, both agree that the Nazis wouldn't "have much luck in this country" because, in the words of one of them: "This ain't Europe. We'll show them." The melody of "America, the Beautiful" on the soundtrack implies that their trust in the people is not misplaced, that "allegiance to the flag of the United States and the Republic for which it stands" is stronger than ever, not least through the powerful emotions elicited by this familiar song.

In contrast to the espionage stories, the conversion stories rely explicitly on melodramatic effects and focus on problems in love, marriage, and family life to interpellate their viewing subjects into liberal democracy. Being an American in these films means commitment to the nation but also belief in the essential goodness of all human beings. According to this logic, German Americans must prove themselves as true patriots, apolitical Americans must learn about foreign policy, and even gangsters must show loyalty to their country. Applying these new rules of democracy in action means shedding one's political ignorance or naïveté and showing caution and vigilance in dealing with strangers, foreigners, and other suspicious individuals. Most importantly, becoming a democrat means realizing one's full potential as an individual: in love for the right man or woman, in love of family, and in love of country. To make this point, most conversion stories take the Nazi threat straight into the American home, to communities from Washington, DC, to Harper, Connecticut. But in their living rooms and bedrooms, rational methods no longer work; in the production sites of intimacy and sociability, the fight against fascism can be won only through an acute awareness of the elusiveness of desire and the power of emotions.

No film makes this argument more forcefully than the Warner production *Watch on the Rhine*. Based on the eponymous 1941 play by Lillian Hellman and adapted to the screen by Dashiell Hammett, *Watch on the Rhine* is the only anti-Nazi film that refers explicitly to the antifascist struggle and promotes a popular-front position. As their leftist authors make unmistakably clear, Americans have to change their attitudes and behaviors. They can no longer afford a position of splendid isolation; they need to think and act politically and start to build international alliances in the fight against war and oppression. These points are developed through the encounter of two families and the implicit making of a third one. All the narrative strands come together through the daughter of a prominent Washington family who returns home with her German husband and three children after many years spent in Europe. As played by Bette Davis, Sara is a typical steel magnolia—strong, proud, and committed to her man, but seventeen years as the wife of a resistance fighter have made her weary and anxious. Hungarian-born Paul Lukas plays her husband, Kurt Müller, as a quiet, cautious, and thoughtful man who nurses an old wound from the Spanish Civil War. "I fight against fascism. That is my trade," he announces to his puzzled in-laws, placing himself in the tradition of political martyrs who live and profess in the tradition of Luther: "Here I stand, so help me God." Together with their well-mannered, highly educated, and politically precocious children, the couple arrives in a capital seemingly stuck in colonial times.

The poker game at the German embassy in
*Watch on the Rhine*

Yet, as the sequence at the German embassy shows, Washington has in fact profoundly changed. A highly symbolic poker game introduces the main players in what is staged as a clandestine assault on American democracy. The men assembled include three familiar stereotypes: the officer (here, the German military attaché), the collaborator (here, the Romanian count), and the party member, a Gestapo man called "butcher boy," who deals the cards and offers his blunt assessment of the players' selfish motivations. Significantly, the Gestapo man is the only one dressed casually, whereas the others wear uniform or tails. Hiding in a backroom in the embassy, he vows to fight "those who hate us" and control "those who want to work for us." The latter group includes three new types of collaborators, Americans all, who serve to illustrate the anti-fascist theory of a close alliance between fascism and capitalism evoked in Sara's description of the Nazis as people "who stand on the shoulders of the most powerful people in the world." These collaborators include a newspaper publisher who is only interested in power, a businessman who is always looking for deals, and the quintessential silent observer who, in the Gestapo man's words, might be a secret agent or an intellectual. "Perhaps he is a member of the underground anti-Nazi movement," quips the cynical military attaché. "Perhaps he is even Max Freitag . . . the legendary hero of the underground movement." Of course, it is in fact a close associate of Freitag who has just arrived in the capital with his American-born wife. And in the highly didactic format favored by Hellman and Hammett, it is the intellectual, the silent observer at the poker table who, as a stand-in for the audience, is called upon to make the change from apolitical private citizen to political activist and become an ally of the real-life Kurts and Saras in their brave fight against fascism.

Paul Lukas, Lucile Watson, Donald Woods,
and Bette Davis in *Watch on the Rhine*

The events in *Watch on the Rhine* unfold through a series of conversations between two very different families, the politicized European family and the apolitical American family. The problem of fascism is consequently approached from two perspectives: that of Sara, the returning daughter, whose view of America is one of estrangement, and that of her mother and brother, who try to make sense of the political views of their European visitors. Most of the learning is done by Sara's family of origin, whose status and wealth are on full display in their antebellum estate, complete with black servants and assorted houseguests, including the Romanian count and Nazi informer who will later try to extort money from Kurt. The matriarch is a stereotypical southern belle, a superficial, talkative, and flirtatious woman unaware of the troubles of the world but with her heart in the right place. "The world has changed, Mama, and some of the people in it are dangerous," Sara tells her clueless mother, Fanny. Her husband, Kurt, puts it more diplomatically: "Fanny and David are Americans. They do not understand our world. And if they are fortunate, they never will." After tense exchanges with her daughter, an extortion attempt, and a killing in her own house, this pillar of Washington society finds herself profoundly changed. "We've been shaken out of the magnolias," she remarks self-critically at the end of the film. The same could be said about Sara's brother, David, a privileged and sheltered young man who works in his father's old law firm—friendly, naive, and a real mama's boy. Throughout much of the film, he passively stands on the sidelines and observes, without strong desires and opinions of his own. Only the machinations of the count propel him to act on his innate sense of fairness; they also allow him to assert his masculinity and admit his love for the count's pretty wife. "We will be in for trouble," even he realizes toward the end.

As the closing sequence suggests, David and Sara will lay the foundation of a more cosmopolitan America both rooted in its history and open to the world: Sara by fighting for the antifascist cause in the United States after Kurt goes back to Germany and thereby providing a better life for her children and David by marrying the count's wife and, this being the implication, serving his country in the coming war. These new American families will be different from the old ones. Through the figures of the anti-Nazi and the Nazi collaborator, they have come in contact with the friends and enemies of democracy and rediscovered their strength of conviction. However, this opening toward the world, toward greater political awareness and international involvement, requires that the two foreigners—both representatives of Old Europe—be eliminated from a narrative that cannot accept moral compromise or the possibility of defeat. With a sangfroid worthy of a Gestapo or KGB agent, Kurt kills the extortionist, which is one reason why some critics have called *Watch on the Rhine* a Stalinist film.[51] And this violent act requires that he return to Germany to resume work in the underground movement, far away from the American experiment in democracy.

Whereas *Confessions of a Nazi Spy* in 1939 presents the Nazi threat as a counterintelligence problem to be solved by federal agencies, and *Watch on the Rhine* in 1943 insists on building a stronger democracy by politicizing the American people, *The Stranger* in 1946 follows a fugitive Nazi to a small town in Connecticut to demonstrate the inherent limitations of both approaches. It is there that the threat of ideology—fascist and, later, communist—becomes the organizing principle behind the new constellations of "power and paranoia" (Polan) emerging in postwar America. Based on a story by Russian-born Victor Trivas, with Orson Welles directing and appearing in the title role, this early film noir approaches the threat of fascism through the quintessential figure of the stranger. An external threat, a foreign presence, has invaded the lives, fantasies, and desires of ordinary people, its destabilizing effect captured brilliantly in the haunting lush score by Max Steiner. Nothing distinguishes Charles Rankin alias Franz Kindler, one of the men responsible for the Holocaust, from the WASP population of Harper, where he teaches history at the Harper School for Boys—nothing except his strangeness. What, then, does it mean when Mary, the pretty daughter of a Supreme Court judge played by popular ingénue Loretta Young, falls in love with this unrepentant Nazi, when she endures his increasingly erratic behavior, and when she stands by him even after having been shown Holocaust atrocity films by the FBI agent hot on his trail? And what does it say about the affective politics of the late anti-Nazi film when the heroine at one point can be heard screaming incredulously: "My Charles is not a Nazi! . . . It's a lie!"

*The Stranger* revisits the terrain established by *Confessions of a Nazi Spy* and—with Edward G. Robinson once again representing the voice of reason—takes account of the loss of political innocence in the intervening years. The story starts out at the Allied War Crimes Commission, where the officials assembled decide to let a Nazi criminal escape in order to lead them to a more important one still in hiding. "This obscenity must be destroyed," declares Robinson. Nazi and Nazi hunter arrive in Harper on the day of Charles and Mary's wedding. In this picturesque small New England town, complete with white church steeple and quaint town square, the world is still intact, untouched by the carnage of World War II. Like Washington, Harper stands for a uniquely American way of life. Here to be a young man means playing sports, whistling after girls, and going fishing with friends, in short, being, like Mary's brother, Noah, a clean-cut American kid.

But Welles's noir aesthetic, his expressive use of shadows, skewed angles, and distorted close-ups, suggests that evil has invaded this idyllic, peaceful place. Its presence can be glimpsed in the shifty eyes, threatening poses, and increasingly panicked behavior of the Nazi in hiding—portrayed with dramatic flair by Welles—but it also makes an appearance in the lined face and weary eyes of the man from the Allied War Commission, played with quiet intensity by Robinson. As is often the case in film noir, it is the woman who, in this case as unknowing victim, facilitates the blurring of boundaries between good and evil. More specifically, it is female desire that produces the fatal lapse of judgment from which Mary can be rescued only through the shared efforts of three American men: the federal agent, her brother, and her father. Close to a mental breakdown after Charles's confession of two murders and racked by feelings of guilt and shame, Mary follows him to the church tower in her nightgown, prepared to shoot the man who has destroyed her dreams of wedded bliss.

As is clear from the beginning, Charles is an unrepentant Nazi and proud of his perfect cover. "I'll stay here until the day when we strike again," he tells an old associate before he kills him. During a discussion with the FBI agent about the situation in postwar Germany, he unwittingly gives an indication of his grandiosity and self-hatred: "The German sees himself as the innocent victim of world envy and hate, conspired against and sat upon by inferior people's inferior nations. He cannot admit to error, much less to wrongdoing. Not the German. . . . For the German, the Messiah is not the Prince of Peace . . . but another Hitler." His conclusion: "The basic principles of freedom and equality never have and never will take root in Germany." To Robinson's question of what he is advocating, he has only one answer: "Annihilation." In line with the psychoanalytic references used by Welles throughout the film, Charles's true

Orson Welles and Loretta Young in *The*    Orson Welles in *The Stranger*
*Stranger*

Nazi identity reveals itself in such unguarded moments: when he refuses to consider Karl Marx a German because he was Jewish or when he absentmindedly
draws a swastika on a telephone notepad. In his last minutes on the clock tower,
he uses the standard Nazi excuse when confronted with his guilt, pleading, "I
followed orders. I only did my duty. . . . I am not a criminal." Tellingly, it is in
the glockenspiel, whose mechanism he restores with obsessive meticulousness,
that he meets a gruesome end: shot at by his wife in a murderous rage but killed
by the extended sword of the angel of justice. At least in that moment, in the
fight with a symbolic devil, the foundations of democracy are still intact. However, as the woman's bad romantic choices suggest, the stabilizing role of
heterosexual love and middle-class marriage as the foundation of American
democracy can no longer be guaranteed.

The threat posed by American women unwittingly marrying Nazi men, a
scenario first seen in *I Married a Nazi*, released under the title *The Man I Married*
(Irving Pichel, 1940), continued unabated after the war, now with anticommunist references, in *I Married a Communist*, which reached movie theaters as *The
Woman on Pier 13* (Robert Stevenson, 1949).[52] As evidenced by these title changes,
the displacement of political enmities into marital problems and the subsequent
erasure of ideology from dramatic conflicts capture in almost symptomatic
form the representational strategies of a group of films situated uneasily between
entertainment and politics.

To conclude: A closer look at the Hollywood anti-Nazi films confirms that
fascism functioned as a floating signifier already by 1946, organizing the divisions between friend and enemy, native and stranger, and self and other necessary to the production of democratic subjectivity. Moreover, the seemingly
effortless shift from the popular-front rhetoric before the entry of the United

States into World War II to the rhetoric of totalitarianism during the cold war suggests that fascism continued to play a key role in the assertion of American postwar hegemony. This shift from real enemy to absolute enemy and the underlying significatory and affective realignments confirm how, in the words of Mouffe, all politics is agonistic and, under certain circumstances, antagonistic. The anti-Nazi films and their cold war successors demonstrate that, in her words, "the dimension of antagonism [is] . . . constitutive of human societies." The films subsequently allow us to analyze the filmic construction of antagonism in visual, narrative, and performative terms. Moreover, in their strategies of exclusion and modes of abjection, the affirmations of individualism and patriotism bring into sharp relief the failure of liberal democracy to integrate struggle and disagreement. Rather than recognizing real difference, liberal democracy according to Mouffe displaces these irruptions of real conflict into the specter of the other and creates stories in which "politics [is] played out in the moral register."[53] The fascist imaginary may thus give contours to the democratic imaginary; yet what is being defined as democratic is not some universal celebration of freedom, equality, individual rights, and rule of law but a specific kind of liberal democracy whose ideological underpinnings are inscribed in the personal narratives that come to stand in for the people as the absent subject of democracy.

In capturing this overdetermined function of fascism in the democratic imaginary and the production of political affects, we may want to close with an unlikely commentator, Georgi Dimitrov, the main advocate of antifascism as popular-front strategy, who declared at the 1935 Seventh World Congress of the Communist International, "It is a peculiarity of the development of American fascism that at the present stage it comes forward principally in the guise of an opposition to fascism, which it accuses of being an 'un-American' trend imported from abroad."[54] His equation of American democracy and fascism could be dismissed as mere communist polemic if it did not return in a very similar argument by a member of the faculty of Yale Divinity School who in 1938 asserted, "When and if fascism comes to America, it will not be labeled 'made in Germany'; it will not be marked with a swastika; it will not be even called fascism; it will be called, of course, 'Americanism.'"[55] In the same year, the author of a book on Nazi Germany issued the following warning to his readers: "If Fascism comes to America, it will come in the name of American Democracy and its advent will be hastened by a refusal to apply to our own problems the insight gained from an objective study of German Fascism."[56]

Since the war years, later generations have offered their own variations of the famous apocryphal statement attributed to, among others, Sinclair Lewis:

"When fascism comes to America, it will be wrapped in the flag and carrying a cross." Using this quote as a segue to the next two chapters, the follow-up questions must logically be: When America came to Germany after 1945, what were the ideological constellations that gave fascism new meaning in the confrontation of East and West Germany and, by extension, the United States and the Soviet Union? How did Nazi stereotypes change when they were evoked as the absolute other in the German context? What emotions were produced and mobilized by postwar films about the anti-Nazi or antifascist resistance? And most importantly for the broader questions addressed in this book, how did these films resolve the persistent problem of desiring democracy, whether liberal or socialist?

# 2

---

# Resistance to the Resistance

## Denazification and Democratization
## in 1950s West German Cinema

There is a difference between a German and a Nazi!

Susan Cummins as Helga Schiller in *Verboten!*

(Sam Fuller, 1959)

In one of the earliest films made in Germany after the war, programmatically titled *Film ohne Titel* (*Film without a Name*, Rudolf Jugert, 1948), a film director, an actor, and a writer meet to brainstorm about the future of German cinema. They agree on what they do not want: no rubble film (*Trümmerfilm*) about destroyed cities, no returnee drama (*Heimkehrerfilm*) about traumatized men, no fraternization comedy about unfaithful women, and, "above all, no anti-Nazi film," insists the actor played by former Ufa heartthrob Willy Fritsch. "That would indeed be inconsiderate," responds the writer sarcastically. But inconsiderate toward whom? Postwar audiences trying to forget traumatic experiences? The professionals starting to rebuild the German film industry? The Americans who created the anti-Nazi film as a form of propaganda? Or to introduce yet another possibility, insincere and hypocritical in light of the strong continuities in the film industry before and after 1945, the residual

66

emotional attachments by many Germans to Nazism and Hitler, the wide-spread resistance to Allied denazification efforts, and the ideological divisions of the emerging cold war?

Less than a decade after this fictional exchange, the first West German films about the Third Reich appeared in motion-picture theaters: *Canaris* (*Canaris: Master Spy*, Alfred Weidenmann, 1954), *Des Teufels General* (*The Devil's General*, Helmut Käutner, 1955), and two films about the failed assassination attempt on Hitler, *Es geschah am 20. Juli* (*It Happened on July 20th*, Georg Wilhelm Pabst, 1955) and *Der 20. Juli* (*The Plot to Assassinate Hitler*, Falk Harnack, 1955).[1] These films contributed to intense public debates on the legacies of the Nazi past, the question of German guilt, and the resistance in the military. In the context of this study, they also attest to the audience's complicated attitudes toward Nazism and reveal with particular clarity their difficulties in accepting, embracing, and desiring democracy, processes that, because of their historically specific nature, cannot be explained through psychoanalytic models of identification and spectatorship. Ranging from sympathy and admiration to suspicion and disdain, the audience's feelings about the men of the resistance point to a much greater ambivalence about democracy than is often assumed in historical accounts of the role of cinema in postwar democratization efforts, including those initiated by the Americans in the first years after the war. As my analysis suggests, these forms of character engagement reinscribe the contradictions of denazification, an Allied-led initiative to remove former Nazi party members from public institutions and political life and to counteract the lingering effects of Nazi ideology through education for democracy American style, which invariably meant Americanization in the broadest sense.[2]

Preserved in the constitutive tension between narrative meaning and affective surplus, the spectatorial ambivalences organized by the first West German films about the resistance allow me on the following pages to retrace the shift from Nazi to anti-Nazi as the primary figure of German self-identification. This means identifying the moment when the Nazis lost their status as real enemies and became absolute enemies, the excluded other that, according to Schmitt, returned to the political imaginary as an aspect of the self. We cannot analyze these affective realignments without considering the beginning of the cold war after the founding of the two German states in 1949—the Bundesrepublik Deutschland (Federal Republic of Germany, FRG) in the West and the Deutsche Demokratische Republik (German Democratic Republic, GDR) in the East—and without taking into account the transatlantic alliance that helped transform West Germany under Chancellor Konrad Adenauer into a liberal democracy, free-market economy, and modern consumer society.[3] These geopolitical constellations produced the homologies between the rhetoric of anti-Nazism and the politics of anticommunism through which a divided Germany became the main battleground in the cold war and West Germany a premier showcase of postwar Americanization. In the accompanying search for new images and stories, the close but not always harmonious relationship between Hollywood and Washington in bringing democratic subjectivity to the legal successor state of the Third Reich must not be underestimated, but neither should the continuities of German film history and antidemocratic thought — in short, the attachments to Nazism as both an ideology and an affective intensity. The confrontation between capitalism and communism as two competing worldviews and spheres of influence made the stories of anti-Nazi/antifascist resistance, and the ideological difference inscribed in these two terms, an essential part of cold war culture and society. Within this oppositional logic, the American and West German films promoted the individual as the basis of liberal democracy, whereas the East German films established the collective as the foundation of (democratic) socialism. Under such conditions, the definition of the enemy — the Nazis, the anti-Nazis, the communists, or the American occupiers — remained a site of contestation.

On the divided screens of postwar Germany, the disagreement over the best kind of government produced competing histories of political resistance: opposition within the officer corps during World War II in the West and communist resistance during the Weimar Republic and the Third Reich in the East. The celebration of liberal democracy in West Germany was achieved through the conflation of Nazism and communism under the heading of totalitarianism, whereas the building of socialism in East Germany became closely identified with antifascism and its equation of fascism and capitalism.[4] Yet the theory of totalitarianism, developed during the 1950s by Hannah Arendt and others, did much more than give political legitimacy to conservative arguments that posited Nazism and communism as two equally dangerous enemies of democracy.[5] In the words of historian Frank Biess, totalitarianism in the guise of anticommunism was also described as "a psychological force that threatened to destroy the moral and personal integrity of the individual."[6] It legitimated a mechanism of displacement that allowed West Germans retrospectively to see themselves as the victims of Nazism.

The management of emotional ambivalence in the early West German resistance films can be reconstructed through the emotions projected on, and channeled through, a familiar figure, the military officer. While the Hollywood anti-Nazi films introduced him to show the Germans' potential for rehabilitation, his filmic representation in the West German films elicited more complicated responses. To return to a distinction made by Murray Smith, the officer in the latter functions as a figure of sympathetic and empathetic identification, but neither form of engagement is unambiguous or uncontested. Sympathy, Smith observes, requires comprehension of the narrative situation and cognitive processing of the character's emotions, followed by an appropriate emotional response by the spectator.[7] Unlike empathy, which only calls for the recognition of similar experiences of human suffering, sympathy is based on, and often results in, shared values and beliefs. In the films under discussion, postwar audiences are invited to feel empathy with the members of the resistance, their professional dilemmas as military officers and their personal struggles as men fearing discovery and arrest. However, because of their association with political failure and military defeat, these men cannot be portrayed as wholly sympathetic figures. The assumption of shared values and beliefs is reserved for the supporting characters, the young officers—friends, in Schmittian terminology—who are destined to become the citizens of a more democratic Germany. By contrast, the title characters must be eliminated as enemies: products of an authoritarian past and its antidemocratic traditions.

The performance of masculinity and its relationship to nation, history, and democracy is key to these concurrent processes of rejection and acceptance. As embodiments of what Raya Morag calls posttraumatic masculinity, a gendered and sexualized representation of traumatic experiences typically found in national cinemas in the aftermath of war, the officers reenact Germany's military and political defeat and reinscribe the experience of that defeat in their performances of resistance as simultaneously heroic and shameful, extraordinary and deviant.[8] In other words, they function as objects of contradictory identifications and projections, including the desire for punishing the men of the resistance as traitors to the fatherland and containing their threat to the spectators' residual attachment to Nazism through specific strategies of othering. As a result, the dominant political affect embodied by the men of the resistance is not love of democracy but resistance to democratization.

Analyzing the filmic representation of the resistance invariably brings us to those transformative or decisive moments when the habitus of resistance takes hold of the officer's body and reveals the processes of incorporation and expulsion through which the affective transfer from Nazism to anti-Nazism as a site of political identifications is to occur for contemporary audiences. In all films, these moments are captured in dramatic close-ups of the officer's face, his eyes directed upward, to the heavens, or fixed onto some point in the distance, accepting the consequences of his decisions but also addressing those who come after him; chiaroscuro lighting and dramatic and elegiac music suggest inner

O. E. Hasse in *Canaris*                    Curd Jürgens in *The Devil's General*

turmoil. Affirming the close-up as the central locus of affect in the cinema, a connection acknowledged by Gilles Deleuze in his notion of affection-image, these moments corroborate the importance of male melodrama to the spectator's ideological and affective interpellation into postwar democracy.[9]

The men thus positioned at the precipice of democratic consciousness are respected military leaders and controversial historical figures: Admiral Wilhelm Canaris, head of the Abwehr, or military intelligence; flying ace and Luftwaffe General Ernst Udet (Harras in the film); and Claus Schenk Graf von Stauffenberg, a colonel in the Wehrmacht and key figure in the failed 20 July 1944 assassination attempt on Hitler. The contradictions in their lives and the heroism of their deaths make them perfect embodiments of the German resistance during the Third Reich and the German resistance to postwar democratization. For comparative purposes and as a preview of the next chapter on the East German antifascist film, we might want to include Ernst Thälmann—first chairman of the KPD (Kommunistische Partei Deutschlands, Communist Party of Germany), inmate of the Buchenwald concentration camp, and celebrated hero of the working class—in order to better understand the films' shared ideological projects and aesthetic debts in the postwar reenactment of German suffering and sacrifice and the main characters' very different roles in the divided iconographies of anti-Nazism and antifascism.

The close-ups capture conversion experiences in the sense that Canaris, Harras, and Stauffenberg have just made a decision—to join the resistance—that breaks with their self-perception as loyal German officers and in the sense that the recourse to an identifiable Ufa style preserves the tension between the commitments and attachments associated with the modifiers "Nazi" and "anti-Nazi." Expressing the underlying tension in aesthetic terms, these close-ups facilitate the transformation of physical reality into abstract principles and, for

*Above left*: Bernhard Wicki in *It Happened on July 20th*

*Above right*: Wolfgang Preiss in *The Plot to Assassinate Hitler*

Günther Simon in the second part of the *Ernst Thälmann* epic

our purposes, offer a revealing example of the making of political affects through empathetic identification and stylistic excess. Presenting anti-Nazism as an act of self-sacrifice, they draw upon a uniquely Christian iconography and distinctly German tradition that equates political consciousness with psychological inwardness. For Canaris and Harras/Udet, these transformations occur as they look out of windows seemingly lost in deep thought, with the glass functioning quite literally as a medium of self-reflection and the window cross as a poignant symbol of their guilt and atonement. In a similar scene of quiet contemplation, Stauffenberg visits a small country church before his flight to the Wolf's Lair, reaffirming a belief in the identity of God and nation that also inspires his last words, "Long live our sacred Germany!," in the Bendlerblock.

Even though Thälmann, the quintessential antifascist, has no need for such last-minute conversions, the second part of Kurt Maetzig's monumental two-part epic, *Ernst Thälmann: Führer seiner Klasse* (Ernst Thälmann, leader of his class, 1955), concludes with a very similar moment of transfiguration that has the Communist Party leader leave his prison cell and walk calmly toward his execution. Once again political allegory takes hold of the filmic image as the actual setting gives way to a gigantic red flag waving in the wind, confirmation that his struggle will be taken up by the working class as the true agent of History, the revolutionary masses whose voices can already be heard in the triumphant chorus praising his name. Relying on the same melodramatic mode found in the close-ups of Canaris, Harras/Udet, and Stauffenberg, the postfascist imaginary comes into being through an aestheticization of sacrifice in which individual and collective thus become one in a shared experience of the political sublime, that which escapes representation but is recognizable in its significance. In this moment of semiotic surplus, the hero's gaze once again aims offscreen, toward a future yet to be realized while his body is transformed into the image of an idea: the idea of resistance. Physical reality recedes and gives way to political allegory; this is how the death of Canaris, Stauffenberg, and Thälmann satisfies the need for atonement and sets the next generation free to put into practice the lessons to be learned from the past.

Equally significant, all the films rely on the formal conventions of the World War II film and the so-called genius film in showing the character's acceptance of his imminent death as an act of martyrdom, with the narrow framing denoting detachment from the mundane concerns of the world and the high-contrast lighting and emphasis on the eyes suggesting spiritual connections and eternal meanings. The focus on individual heroism references both Hollywood and Babelsberg in the reliance on filmic means as conduits to the affective politics of anti-Nazism/antifascism. On the one hand, these close-ups recall the final shot of Field Marshal Rommel in *The Desert Fox* (Henry Hathaway, 1951), with his face superimposed over clouds and his gaze directed upward as the voice-over proclaims him to be a true hero who paid the ultimate price for saving his country from Hitler—compelling evidence of the degree to which the postfascist perspective on fascism was from the beginning influenced by Hollywood. On the other hand, these moments of symbolic transubstantiation refer back to Ufa's big-production genius films, films about great men—writers, architects, composers, scientists, and so forth—whose sacrifices in the service of German culture and nation made them ideal figures of masochistic identification and nationalist myth-building during the Third Reich.

In all cases, the main protagonist's precarious position between power and knowledge is articulated through the tension between looking and being looked at that identifies him at once as the subject and the object of the postfascist gaze. However, the precise meaning of such overdetermined images can be reconstructed only through further historical contextualization. In the West, the Christian symbolism in conversion stories that turn sinners into martyrs became an essential part of the displacement of political conflicts into the existential humanism shared by the intellectual and cultural elites and the ruling conservative Christian Democrats, the CDU (Christlich Demokratische Union). In the Thälmann film, the staging of the Communist Party leader's death served very different functions, namely, the celebration of the party as all-knowing and all-powerful by the nomenklatura and the cultural establishment, but it relied on surprisingly similar filmic means to achieve this ideological effect.

Taking up lines of argumentation from the previous chapter, I approach the postwar production of democratic subjectivity from two perspectives: through a reconstruction of the larger historical constellations that implicate *Canaris, The Devil's General, It Happened on July 20th,* and *The Plot to Assassinate Hitler* in the process of coming to terms with the Nazi past and the cold war present and, second, through close attention to the formal elements—casting choices, performance styles, and modes of character engagement—that reproduce the contradictions in the transition to democratic subjectivity, including the residual attachments to nondemocratic traditions. The pivotal role of affects in over-coming old and forging new political attachments can best be analyzed through the aesthetically mediated forms of emotional excess and restraint in the diegesis or, to describe these alternatives in terms of character engagement, through the opposing strategies of emotional attachment and detachment.

The first West German films about the resistance clearly recognize emotion as an essential part of Nazi ideology and choose two very different approaches—comparable to the melodramatic and investigative modes in the Hollywood anti-Nazi films—to move beyond these problematic legacies. *Canaris* and *The Devil's General* produce a surfeit of emotion in the tradition of male melodrama in order to represent resistance as an internal conflict between duty and free will, state power and individual morality. In so doing, they depoliticize the re-sistance movement and translate the political into existential, humanistic terms. By contrast, the two Stauffenberg films rely on a realist aesthetic modeled on the docudrama in order to arrive at a presumably more objective representa-tion of the same conflict at the heart of democratic culture and civil society. Yet their chronological method comes at the expense of a complete bracketing of emotions as a political force.

The problem of masculinity plays a key role in all four films, whether in the conception of Nazi/anti-Nazi stereotypes, the performance of fascist/demo-cratic subjectivities, or the presentation of Germans as victims and perpetrators of the Nazi regime. The ideal of mature masculinity posits a political ethics based on individual conscience, personal responsibility, and public service against which all deviations from the norm are to be measured. Yet by expressing the confrontation of Nazi and anti-Nazi in gendered terms, masculinity—especially its excesses and failures—also becomes a symptom of the audience's continued attachment to the Third Reich and their resistance to the resistance, as it were; this is nowhere more apparent than in the different status attributed to political affects in the process of totalitarian seduction and democratic reeducation.

Ten years after the end of World War II, West German film producers agreed that the time had come to take on the story of the resistance and released four films in the course of one year: *Canaris, The Devil's General, It Happened on July 20th,* and *The Plot to Assassinate Hitler.* Yet the announcement in the summer of 1954 of two films in production in preparation for the tenth anniversary of the assassination attempt on Hitler resulted in unexpected problems and disputes. The legal battles over film titles and release dates, the competition over endorsements by family members, and the films' mixed critical reception are all well documented and, for our purposes, can alternatively be read as evidence of the problematic legacies of the Nazi past or the beginnings of a vibrant democratic culture of public debate. Among the three historical personalities chosen as figures of postwar identification, Stauffenberg today stands out as the most famous one. Yet at the time, the officers involved in the 20 July 1944 plot were still highly controversial figures, with occasional references to *Eidesbruch* (breaking one's oath) and *Hochverrat* (high treason) indicative of postwar audiences' continued belief in the Nazi state as legitimate and their resultant unwillingness to consider resistance other than in terms of loss of honor or dereliction of duty. By contrast, Udet and Canaris were popular heroes and greatly admired despite their professional failings and personal flaws. In fact, it was the commercial success of the film about Canaris that started the entire series and confirmed the close connection between the restoration of traditional masculinity and the culture of paternalism in Adenauer Germany. Similarly, it was the screen adaptation of *The Devil's General,* the 1946 Carl Zuckmayer drama modeled on the life of Udet and the most successful play on the postwar German stage, that made the greatest contribution to the remapping, via masochistic identification with its unwilling hero, of the emotional landscapes of Nazism and its aftereffects.

Like the Zuckmayer drama, which some critics dismissed as a *Mitläuferdrama* (fellow-traveler drama), *The Devil's General* and the other resistance films from the mid-1950s have not been viewed kindly by later generations of film scholars and, given their lack of a clear political position, have sometimes been read as typical products of a postwar culture of self-exculpation. Confirming later claims by the Mitscherlichs and others about Germans' residual emotional attachment to Nazism, controversies surrounded all four productions from the start, with epithets such as *Nestbeschmutzer* (people fouling their own nest) hurled at some of the professionals involved. Two types of producers were drawn to the topic of resistance: those with a personal interest such as suspected communists Walter Koppel and Gyula Trebitsch, whose Hamburg-based Real Film produced *The Devil's General*, and Holocaust survivor Artur Brauner, whose West Berlin–based CCC-Film produced *The Plot to Assassinate Hitler*, and those with limited resources and therefore nothing to lose, namely, the small Hamburg-based Fama-Film for *Canaris* and the equally unknown Munich-based Ariston Film for *It Happened on July 20th*. Aside from Falk Harnack, who through his brother Arvid had personal connections to the resistance, the directors selected for these projects could look back on successful careers during the Third Reich, with Georg Wilhelm Pabst still benefitting from his reputation as one of the leading figures of Weimar cinema and Helmut Käutner highly praised for his melancholy psychological dramas. Explaining his choice of the lesser-known and much younger Alfred Weidenmann as the director for *Canaris*, producer Friedrich Mainz described such aesthetic and ideological continuities as both necessary and desirable: "I need a man who is also familiar with the mindset of that time."[10]

The intense media attention, from reports about preproduction problems to comments about opening-night protests, attests to the films' complicated role in the self-representation of the young Federal Republic. To preempt negative publicity, the distributor of *Canaris* played down its political significance and marketed the film as the story of a good German Christian "whose human tragedy reflects the experience of millions of Germans."[11] And perhaps to avoid more controversy, two of the films opened in the mid-size city of Hannover: *Canaris* on 30 December 1954 and *The Devil's General* on 23 February 1955. The premiere of *It Happened on July 20th* took place in Munich on 19 June 1955, and its competitor *The Plot to Assassinate Hitler* premiered only two days later, in Frankfurt am Main on 21 June 1955. All these films received several film prizes for the actors and directors and so-called predicates awarded in combination with tax breaks—"valuable" for *The Devil's General* and *It Happened on July 20th*, "especially valuable" for *Canaris*, and a special prize "for the promotion of democratic ideas" in the case of *The Plot to Assassinate Hitler*. Benefitting from the star power of their male leads, *Canaris* and *The Devil's General* fared relatively well at the box office. By contrast, the two Stauffenberg films failed to reach a larger audience, presumably because of their reserved documentary style. Newspaper reviews remained decidedly mixed, with comments wavering between dutiful praise and open disapproval. Some critics' discomfort with Canaris's domestic arrangements and objections to Harras's hard drinking suggest that the men of the resistance served much more contradictory functions than merely completing the process of denazification.

Departures from facts (or their prevailing interpretation) are an inevitable part of historical narratives and often take the form of temporal compression, figurative condensation, and dramatic personification. However, the deletion of entire scenes and the addition of side stories can only be attributed to widespread concerns about audiences unwilling to have the motion-picture theater be turned into a political institution. Thus the screenwriters for *Canaris* added an espionage subplot, possibly under the influence of the screen adaptation of the Operation Cicero story in *Five Fingers* (Joseph Mankiewicz, 1951); the romantic side story in *The Plot to Assassinate Hitler* serves similar functions. Less harmless were extensive cuts made in response to official interventions after the films' theatrical releases. To give only two examples, the industry-run FSK (Freiwillige Selbstkontrolle, Voluntary Self-Regulation), at the request of the Foreign Office, asked the producers of *Canaris* to delete a newsreel sequence depicting the annexation of Austria because of concerns about negative reactions abroad. Similarly, the confrontation between Canaris and Schmidt-Lausitz at the end of *The Devil's General* was removed from later prints, resulting in the suppression of what would have been the most explicit critique of the Nazi regime in the cinema of the Adenauer era.[12]

In establishing the historical significance and political meaning of the resistance, all four films approach the Third Reich from the perspective of the last war years and through the conflation of the resistance with the military. Film scholars agree that these choices must be evaluated against the backdrop of the political rehabilitation of the Wehrmacht and the ideological confrontation with communism in the mid-1950s, a connection that requires a brief digression on the relationship between war and resistance narrative. Ten years after the end of World War II, with the last wave of *Spätheimkehrer* (late returnees) released from Soviet POW camps, the existence of the Iron Curtain required a clear commitment on both sides to the principles of military preparedness and *Wehrhaftigkeit* (pugnacity) in the ideological sense. The remilitarization of Germany began with the creation of the West German Bundeswehr (Federal Army) and West German membership in NATO (North Atlantic Treaty Organization) in 1955, and the establishment of the Warsaw Pact in 1955 and the East German Nationale Volksarmee (National People's Army) in 1956. The arguments for remilitarization in the defense of Western democracy and the fight against US imperialism, respectively, were part of larger debates on world peace, rearmament, and the threat of nuclear war that produced the purely symbolic East German Law for the Protection of Peace in 1950 and inspired the pacifist West German Easter Marches after 1958.

The specter of anticommunism contributed significantly to the exoneration of the Wehrmacht and the rehabilitation of its officers as exemplary, if deeply conflicted, men and, for that reason, all the more credible advocates for democracy. The narrative focus on the resistance among high-ranking officers, their status as representatives of the "other Germany," and the reduction of the central dramatic conflict to a classic military conflict between duty and conscience marginalized other forms of civilian resistance. The competing ideologies of communism and anticommunism, which necessitated the forced unification in 1946 of Communists and Social Democrats into the SED (Sozialistische Einheitspartei Deutschlands, Socialist Unity Party of Germany) in the East and the constitutional ban in 1956 of the KPD in the West, made it all the more important for West German filmmakers to clearly distinguish anti-Nazism from antifascism. Many of the asymmetries in the filmic representation of the Third Reich can be explained through these political exigencies: the focus on the military in the West and on the capitalists in the East, the suppression of the communist resistance in the West, and similar strategies of forgetting concerning the Protestant churches in the East.

For the most part, the problem of continuities in the West was bracketed, as were questions of historical agency and causality that could have been addressed through stories set during the late Weimar Republic or the early years of the Nazi regime. Instead, the first West German films about World War II must be seen in dialogue with the German reception of two famous Hollywood films: the failure of *Decision before Dawn* (Anatole Litvak, 1951), which featured two German prisoners of war turned American spies, and the success in 1952 of *The Desert Fox*, which romanticized the German officer as a tragic hero. Beginning with the influential *08/15* trilogy (Paul May, 1954–55), West German directors focused all their attention on the permanent state of exception brought about by war, thereby bracketing the realities of everyday life during the Third Reich and avoiding difficult questions about individual responsibilities and institutional structures. Moreover, the myth of the good German soldier allowed them to make the Nazis the reviled other of history, the true enemy of Germany, and the brutal oppressor of its people. As the following examples show, this affective displacement was achieved through the depoliticization of the military in the past and contributed to its repoliticization in the fight against communism in the present.

Immensely popular with audiences, the West German war films dealt with presumably universal themes such as individual courage and dignity, the military code of honor, and the joys of male camaraderie. Almost exclusively set on the eastern front, these cautionary tales of German suffering often did double duty as vehicles for anticommunist propaganda and theories of totalitarianism.[13]

Accordingly, the confrontation in *Der Arzt von Stalingrad* (*The Doctor of Stalingrad*, Géza von Radvány, 1958) between a German prisoner and the camp commandant in a Soviet POW camp uses the equation of Nazism and Stalinism to dispense with the problem of German guilt and turn all attention to the cold war: "Why weren't you a hero under Hitler?" asks the Russian. "Why aren't you one under Stalin now?" responds the German. Protagonists in other films give voice to the equally problematic equation (and belated justification) of the Nazi fight against Bolshevism with the American fight against communism. Thus *Nacht fiel über Gotenhafen* (*Darkness Fell on Gotenhafen*, Frank Wisbar, 1959), the first of several films about the sinking of the *Wilhelm Gustloff*, has a Nazi character promise, "Never again will a Bolshevik walk on German soil." Within the narrative logic of this virulently anticommunist film, the implicit reference to the Soviet occupation of the so-called Ostzone (Eastern Zone) raises the question of whether it would therefore be up to the Americans to complete the historical mission started by the Nazis and make Germany once again "communist-free." Based on the imaginary solutions offered in another Wisbar film, *Fabrik der Offiziere* (The officer factory, 1960), the answer would have to be an emphatic no. The only legitimate resistance during the Third Reich, both films suggest, could be found among national-conservative officers and, for that reason, the only defense of the "free West" against the threat of communism was to be sought in Christian conservatism and its ethos of individual and social morality.

In contrast to the clear distinction between bad Nazis and good soldiers in the war films, the resistance films organize their more complicated affective economies through the main protagonists' double position as traitors and patriots. On the one hand, the positive portrayal of the homosocial milieu in the military establishes the conditions for the historical rehabilitation of the officer corps and the promotion of the Bundeswehr as a pacifist, apolitical institution. On the other, the stylistic debts that locate these films in German film history reintroduce mentalities with a long history of attachment to authoritarianism. Thus the iconography of masculinity betrays the enduring influence of the soldierly types known from the Nazi war films and the Weimar-era Prussian films, whether in the cool conduct displayed by Stauffenberg or the fatherly authority exuded by Canaris. The films' intimate and occasionally claustrophobic settings are reminiscent of the 1920s chamber-play films and their sharp division between public and private spheres that legitimated social hierarchies already during the Weimar Republic. Meanwhile, the extensive discussions among the members of the resistance seem to prefigure a model of deliberative democracy that looks and sounds uncannily like that of the Bonn Republic. Perhaps it is in this sense of backward projection and secondary revision that we must also interpret one of Canaris's last utterances: "What a chance for those able to start all over again!"

As the resistance narrative is removed from contamination by the fascist politics of the masses, it becomes available to the exaltation of humanism as the foundation of a postfascist West German identity, reason enough to look more closely at the competing definitions of the political that inform the filmic representation of historical events. The negotiation of democratic and antidemocratic positions takes place on two levels: performance, especially the embodiment of the transition from Nazi to anti-Nazi, and intertextuality, especially the visualization, through works or art in the diegesis, of alternative forms of government. Significantly, the distinction between Nazi and anti-Nazi is achieved through recourse to the decidedly undemocratic iconography of Prussia and the equally problematic evocation of normative masculinity. Through these forms of mediation, the residual attachments to Nazism continuously jeopardize what, on the level of the narrative, appears like moral clarity and political resolve but what, on the level of affective engagements, returns in the subtle resentments directed against the main characters and what they represent: an opposition to Hitler that threatens the audience's narcissistic identification with Nazism. In accordance with the earlier distinction between emotional excess and restraint, these ambivalences are highlighted in the male melodrama of *Canaris* and *The Devil's General* and downplayed in the documentary style of *It Happened on July 20th* and *The Plot to Assassinate Hitler*.

Bringing with them the extrafilmic references organized through the star system, all the actors chosen to perform these affective realignments started their careers before 1945 but were not famous enough to compromise the performative reenactment of the resistance through their own work in the Nazi film industry. In casting *The Plot to Assassinate Hitler*, Brauner explicitly looked for male actors "whose faces [were] not too familiar"—that is, familiar from the films of the Third Reich.[14] Acting out the tension between a heroic masculinity associated with national greatness and military might and a postwar masculinity marked by trauma and loss, O. E. Hasse, Curd Jürgens, Bernhard Wicki, and Wolfgang Preiss became participants in the making of a transnational fascist imaginary based to a not insignificant degree on the traffic in male stars and national stereotypes between Hollywood and its West German counterparts.

These transnational connections, like the previously mentioned historical continuities, are inscribed in the actors' career trajectories before and after 1954–55. Prior to playing Canaris, O. E. Hasse, who, after years as a bit player in propaganda films, landed the title role in *The Devil's General* on the 1948 Berlin stage, appeared as a German colonel in Anatole Litvak's *Decision before Dawn*, as an unrepentant Nazi in *I Confess* (Alfred Hitchcock, 1953) as well as *Betrayed* (Gottfried Reinhardt, 1954), and as an army physician in the previously mentioned *The Doctor of Stalingrad*. Whereas Hasse's officers were calm, reserved, and highly cultured, Curd Jürgens, who had a background in operetta films, emphasized their vitality, strength, and sex appeal. He built an international career playing German officers in films like *The Enemy Below* (Dick Powell, 1957) and would continue to be cast as famous men caught between individual ambition and world politics, most famously in the screen adaptation of Stefan's Zweig's *Schachnovelle* (*Brainwashed*, Gerd Oswald, 1960) and the Wernher von Braun biopic *I Aim at the Stars* (J. Lee Thomson, 1960). Even character actors Wolfgang Preiss and Bernhard Wicki developed international reputations based on their filmic association with the Third Reich. Having started his career as the male lead's best friend in the propaganda vehicle *Die große Liebe* (*The Great Love*, Rolf Hansen, 1942), Preiss frequently appeared as a proud, honorable officer or a brutal, cynical Nazi. Meanwhile, brooding newcomer Wicki, somewhat miscast as the aristocratic officer in the competing Pabst production of the same year, would go on to direct the critically acclaimed antiwar film *Die Brücke* (*The Bridge*, 1959) and the German episodes in the World War II epic *The Longest Day* (1962).

The compelling performances by Hasse in *Canaris* and Jürgens in *The Devil's General* validate resistance as an act of individual heroism but undermine its usefulness as a new model of political ethics. In the same way that the Stauffenberg figure, through his lack of psychological interiority in both versions, blocks access to resistance as a political affect, the Canaris and Harras/Udet figures bring out its contradictions, a point that is crucial for uncovering the antidemocratic impulses behind the narrative rehabilitation of the Wehrmacht officers. Through the conception of the characters, the transition from compliance to resistance becomes associated with mature, patriarchal masculinity. However, the performative excess produced by Hasse and Jürgens draws upon a troubling tradition of equating political deviancy with sexual deviancy. As in the Hollywood anti-Nazi films and the Italian Naziploitation films discussed in chapter 4, this connection is made through the problem of masculinity: too little in the case of the effeminate hypochondriac Canaris and too much in the case of the philandering hedonist Harras/Udet. Rather revealingly, the Nazis are always portrayed as aggressively virile and conventionally heterosexual. In a complete reversal of the early Hollywood stereotype of the Nazi as sexually deviant, the anti-Nazi position now invites allusions to closeted homosexuality in

Canaris, who in fact was rumored to be gay, and compulsive heterosexuality in Harras/Udet, who was known for his heavy drinking and womanizing. The casting choices only added to such sexualized readings, with the openly gay Hasse tried and convicted in 1944 under Clause 175 criminalizing homosexuality and with Jürgens a favorite of the yellow press because of his five wives and countless affairs.[15] In the case of *Canaris*, such extrafilmic references might even give new meaning to the comment in one review that Hasse and the other actors in the film "deploy their personality to the fullest," perhaps by taking advantage of the epistemology of the closet.[16]

For the same reasons that the performance of masculinity allows the films simultaneously to honor and denounce the resistance, the self-reflexive use of political iconographies enables them to stage the confrontation between two political systems, totalitarianism and liberal democracy, without making a full commitment to the latter. Most troublesome, the presentation of what the men of the resistance are fighting for—presumably, a democratic Germany—is achieved through an almost compulsive evocation of Prussia, *the* historical model of a militaristic society and authoritarian state. In developing a usable political iconography for the Federal Republic, the films make a clear distinction between the idolatry surrounding Hitler and the representatives of the other, "true" Germany. Given the conservatism of the milieu depicted, this can only mean the Prussia of Frederick the Great, the Wars of Liberation against Napoleon, and the founding of the Second Reich under Bismarck.

In re-creating the look of the Third Reich on the screen, the West German resistance films follow the model of the Hollywood anti-Nazi films and rely heavily on paintings, photographs, sculptures, posters, and wartime newsreels. In a country where the public display of Nazi symbols is still forbidden, the many images of Hitler and other Nazi leaders make up for the dearth of swastikas due perhaps to concerns about their appearance even in a historical film; perhaps the focus on the Nazi leadership also reflects personality-based theories of Nazis favored at the time over social and economic explanations. In either case, the heavy dependence on mediations, and the implicit equation of politics with representation, points to an unwillingness on the side of the filmmakers to confront the Nazi system of terror and intimidation and examine the mechanisms of mass seduction and control directly. Himmler, Göring, and Hitler remain absent as dramatic characters and become visible or audible only metonymically: through the shadowy outlines of the Reichsmarschall's massive body behind a glass door and the close-up of the Reichsführer SS's beringed hand in *The Devil's General* and through the image of the Führer's hunched back and the sound of his familiar voice in *The Plot to Assassinate Hitler*.

Himmler's hand in *The Devil's General*      Hubert Lanziger's *The Standard Bearer* in *The Plot to Assassinate Hitler*

The scarcity of Nazis as developed characters is more than compensated for through their iconographic omnipresence, and the absence of any critical analysis of Nazi ideology is offset by open acknowledgment of its heavy dependence on visual effects. Weidenmann in *Canaris* and Harnack in *The Plot to Assassinate Hitler* repeatedly use Nazi newsreel footage, complete with original commentary, to surround the fictional scenes with an aura of historical authenticity. To what degree such practices allowed postwar audiences to nostalgically relive the war years remains a point of contestation in the scholarship.[17] Equally ambiguous in its spectatorial effects is the artwork placed strategically to evoke Nazism as a particular aesthetic and worldview. The selections suggest a totalitarian system of embodied/disembodied power but are also available to more problematic forms of recognition on the side of audiences familiar with some of these works through Nazi-era publications and the Greater German Art Exhibitions. To give a few examples, in *The Devil's General*, a copy of Ferdinand Hodler's well-known 1910 work *The Woodcutter* adorns the offices of the SS. *The Plot to Assassinate Hitler* offers a veritable museum of Nazi art, including a version of Hubert Lanzinger's famous 1938 allegorical painting of *The Standard Bearer* depicting the Führer as a Teutonic knight. The film also features an equally well-known 1936 Hitler bust by Jan Thorak and kitschy Nazi knick-knacks. The sets of *Canaris* and *The Devil's General*, too, contain numerous portraits of Hitler, including a 1938 Franz Triebsch portrait, that are placed strategically to comment on the title characters' changing views on the regime.

While the Nazi leaders surround themselves with images of Hitler simultaneously to assert their power and signal their subservience, the members of the resistance plot the regime's overthrow under the eyes of historical personalities distinguished precisely by their lack of democratic commitments. Evoking a

Curd Jürgens next to a Bismarck portrait in *The Devil's General*

Maximilian Schell next to a Frederick the Great portrait in *The Plot to Assassinate Hitler*

very different political heritage, *The Devil's General* at one point has Harras standing next to a portrait of Bismarck. Similarly, the plans for a coup d'état and, later, tyrannicide in *The Plot to Assassinate Hitler* are finalized in a drawing room filled with paintings and etchings depicting Frederick the Great, Carl von Clausewitz, Yorck von Wartenburg, and other lesser-known Prussian generals. (The fact that, fifty years later, *Downfall* depicts Hitler in front of the famous Frederick the Great portrait by Anton Graff points to the continuing relevance of Prussianism as a political myth.) The central place of these eminent Prussians in the conservative vision of a new Germany in 1955 is confirmed through the reading of an Ernst Moritz Arndt quote by an unidentified member of the Kreisau Circle intended to provide inspiration for their moral battle against Hitler (i.e., as a latter-day Napoleon) and, by extension, for a unified Germany (i.e., against the GDR). Through these intertextual references, Prussia is offered up as an alternative history of German nation and statehood and a perfect model for postwar masculinity, sociability, and governmentality. An object of intense nostalgia, it comes to stand in for the good continuities of nationalism, authoritarianism, and militarism. And in the context of postwar Americanization, it allows West German audiences to imagine a political culture untainted by the abuses of power during the Third Reich and untouched by the leveling effects of American mass democracy.

Having introduced the four resistance films as part of the same ideological constellation, I will use the next two sections to focus more specifically on the forms of character engagement that establish a relationship to the resistance and, through the production of sympathies and antipathies, to the Third Reich. As in the Hollywood anti-Nazi films with their alternately melodramatic and

documentary modes, we can distinguish two approaches: emotional attachment in *Canaris* and *The Devil's General* and emotional detachment in *It Happened
on July 20th* and *The Plot to Assassinate Hitler*. The conventions of the melodrama
grant access to the psychology of conformity, resignation, and commitment. By
contrast, the conventions of the docudrama promise an objective account of
the sequence of events. In both cases, the function of emotion on the level of
characterization must be located within the larger aesthetic and ideological constellations associated with political affect. While the mode of detachment re-
affirms the linkage between political resistance and traditional masculinity, the
mode of attachment makes possible the exploration of different, if not deviant,
sensibilities, a connection most obvious in *Canaris*, but this rare opening toward
a politics of desire also lays the ground for the process of abjection by which the
failed opposition to Hitler can be expelled from the body politic.

Known as a conservative and a nationalist, Admiral Canaris, to begin with
the film that started the series, was anything but a rebel. Admitting to a pessi-
mistic worldview, he at one point in the film describes himself as a "notorious
doomsayer." Why did Weidenmann choose such an unheroic character? The
answer lies in his usefulness in embodying the contradictory public feelings surrounding the leaders of the resistance while at the same time offering an acceptable, nonthreatening model of patriotism for the postwar years, a point
openly acknowledged in the film's subtitle, *Ein Leben für Deutschland* (A life for
Germany). A Christian perspective on history as a narrative of guilt and redemption guides Canaris's passive responses to political events after 1935 and
explains his continuing hesitation to take action. His decision to join the resistance group around General Beck is captured in the previously mentioned decisive moment at the window. The 1939 Munich Accord thwarts their plans to
prevent the outbreak of war and, with it, the fall of Germany. "Operation Gol-
gotha" is how the admiral refers to the coming catastrophe symbolized by the
shadow of a crucifix looming over the scene. After the invasion of France, he
asks in growing despair, "Why should I continue serving a cause I don't believe
in?" Instead of joining another group, he confesses to a friend, "I no longer believe that supporting actors like you and I can play fate. That chance is lost."
The impending military defeat after 1942 finally gives Canaris the courage to
establish contact with the Allies through a neutral emissary. However, his unwillingness to accept an unconditional surrender for Germany prevents him
from taking the last step and becoming what he calls a traitor to his country.

Canaris's troubling passivity cannot be understood apart from the film's
surprisingly frank treatment of his homosexuality. On the surface, Canaris, to
use German studies scholar Erica Carter's apt phrase, is one of the many "men

O. E. Hasse and uncredited actor in *Canaris*     O. E. Hasse and Martin Held in *Canaris*

in cardigans" who, whether as politicians or entrepreneurs, populated West German cinema as stand-ins for Chancellor Adenauer, eager to emulate his aura of patriarchal authority and provincial modesty.[18] Yet these allusions are immediately undercut by Hasse's openly queer performance of the role. Canaris may be a loner and aesthete prone to doubt, resignation, and melancholy; he is also unmistakably presented as gay, a fact first noted by Carter. Thus he not only plays a double role as a spymaster and member of the resistance, but he also applies the same skills of deception to his own life in the closet. His strongest public expressions of affection are reserved for two dachshunds that command his full attention in the opening scene—"Where are my dogs?" he apprehensively asks his aide—and that run after the Gestapo car taking him to the Flossenbürg concentration camp in the final scene. Yet his private desires, too, are acknowledged in many moments of blissful domesticity with a mysterious neighbor and a surprisingly casual physical intimacy with his subordinates.

This intimate relationship with the neighbor is central to the film's denunciation of Canaris as a member of the resistance and, more specifically, a movement doomed to fail. The specter of queerness first appears when the admiral is shown cooking enchiladas con carne for his friends and said neighbor, a pianist by the name of Dannhoff; neither the character nor the actor are listed in the credits. A later scene captures an evening of quiet domesticity and casual intimacy, with Canaris reading files and Dannhoff playing Brahms; their tender exchange of glances suggests that they are indeed a couple. From then on, all intrusions of politics into the admiral's private life take place in his living room. After his dismissal, Canaris can be seen playing solitaire and listening to his friend's improvisations on the piano. Reports of the failed assassination attempt find the two men at home in gardening clothes. The last goodbye, with Canaris in full military attire awaiting arrest by the Gestapo, brings an open confession of homosexual love, Dannhoff's "You don't know what our friendship has always meant to me." Yet once again, in the interest of the closet, it is the dogs that express what cannot be openly acknowledged. Carter perceptively reads the film's final scene in terms of "a spectatorial ambivalence toward the military body in democracy, an experience of its failure to embody classical military values (patriarchal order, security, discipline) and of the fragility therefore of the soldier citizen as an object of postwar popular desire."[19]

The function of Canaris as the embodiment of such ambiguities is developed further through his relationship with Heydrich, an old friend and former protégé turned deadly enemy, and to Colonel Holl, his subordinate officer and a member of the resistance. As played by Martin Held, Heydrich is cynical, smooth, elegant, and cruel—the personification of "cool conduct" but without the demonic qualities that would allow him to stand out as the embodiment of evil.[20] Their differences are most evident in their physical habitus: whereas Hasse moves slowly and tentatively, Held is dynamic and assertive, with a loud and clear voice. In a conversation with Canaris, Heydrich speaks of shared values but complains, "You never fully understood our worldview." Whereas the confrontations with Heydrich show Canaris and his dilemmas in an almost sympathetic light, his disagreements with Holl highlight his shortcomings as the representative of an older generation firmly committed to the authoritarian state and its representatives. As the personification of the younger generation and their future leadership role in the Federal Republic, Holl (played by Preiss) thus stands in for a third perspective within the narrative: admiration for Canaris as a military hero and frustration with his inability to carry out the "liberating deed." In the context of the times, precisely this willingness to compromise makes Holl the perfect model for the principles of *innere Führung* (inner leadership) and *Staatsbürger in Uniform* (citizen in uniform) through which the Bundeswehr sought to overcome the bad legacies of Prussian militarism and authoritarianism and integrate the new army into the postwar democratic state.

Like *Canaris*, *The Devil's General* introduces the resistance narrative and, by extension, the relationship to Nazism through the problem of masculinity. But in this case, the man in question is an aging general with a drinking problem and a weakness for twenty-one-year-old women. "Prussian sentimental" is how Harras describes his personality: gruff and tender, sarcastic and compassionate, full of self-pity and self-hatred. His towering body in various stages of intoxication suggests an old-fashioned masculinity no longer in control, with his status as reluctant hero reproducing the transition from Nazi to anti-Nazi outlined earlier. His association with what historian Ulrike Weckel calls limited ambiguity opens up a space for the spectator to at once admire and detest his stance of individual opposition; but it also closes off any opportunity for historical analysis and displaces all political struggles into the terms of individual character and morality.[21]

Venerated as a people's general, in the words of Schmidt-Lausitz, and admired by men and women for his independence of mind, Harras has little in common with the aristocratic officers, fanatical ideologues, or opportunistic businessmen who, in this film, make up the power elites of the Third Reich. "I am a flier," he declares, seduced by the professional opportunities and willing to make the required compromises. At the same time, Harras is a compulsive womanizer and self-loathing drunk, with his drinking serving two important functions: it justifies his impaired sense of judgment in collaborating with the Nazi regime and explains his readiness to sacrifice his life as a final assertion of his free will. His condition of lack—his deviancy—is established through his failure to have a wife and family, a source of deep personal regret, and, closely related, his failure to hold firm convictions and beliefs. At one point he confesses to the widow of a subordinate officer: "The best in this little bit of life is faith [*Glaube*]," with the ambiguity of the term—Nazi ideology or faith in the religious sense—clearly intended. For his lack of political commitment, his being "nobody's enemy, nobody's friend, always sitting on the fence," Harras atones with his suicide. To postwar audiences, these shortcomings make him a figure of abjection who, like the Nazis, has no place in the new culture of democracy. Even the promise of true love embodied by the young, innocent Diddo cannot prevent his necessary expulsion from the narrative.

As in *Canaris*, the unstable patterns of character engagement are organized through Harras's relationship with two men: the engineer Oderbruch and the SS man Schmidt-Lausitz. Oderbruch, the man responsible for sabotaging the planes, represents Harras's alter ego and brings about his redemption. In the final sequence, he becomes the general's conscience when he declares that "evil in the world does not exist because of those who do evil; it exists through those who tolerate evil." To Harras's question about how he arrived at this point of view, Oderbruch responds: "One day I started feeling ashamed of being a German. That so much injustice was being committed in the name of the people, thus also in my name." His moral denunciation of Harras for the sin of inaction represents the most explicit critique of the political and military elites of the Third Reich and the most compelling example of the postwar subsumation of politics under ethics: "I was only able to slow things down, but you functioned like a lubricant. . . . Your hesitation, your compliance, your collaboration are responsible for the demise of millions of innocent people."

As played by Viktor de Kowa, Schmidt-Lausitz—like Heydrich in *Canaris*—is the quintessential embodiment of bad politics and bad ideology: cold, calculating, and interested only in preserving the Nazi state. His role as the main representative of its rule of terror and intimidation is on full display in a missing scene toward the end where he threatens Harras to either deliver to him the man responsible for the sabotage of the planes or to face removal from all his positions. Reacting with barely controlled rage to the SS man's empty talk about duty and fatherland, Harras points to a propaganda poster in the room and spells out what he sees as its debased meaning under the Nazis: "What did you say? Fatherland [*Vaterland*]? What do you mean with that? *V* like people's court [*Volksgerichtshof*]? *A* like hanging [*Aufhängen*]? *T* like death [*Tod*]? *E* like shooting [*Erschiessen*]? *R* like racial persecution [*Rassenverfolgung*]? *L* like camp [*Lager*]? Auschwitz, Neuengamme, Dachau? See, that's how we today spell fatherland in Germany!" Schmidt-Lausitz's continuing threat to the project of postwar democratization is even more apparent in the way that de Kowa performs fascism: through his uncanny confidence and preternatural calm, his virile strength and authority, his clear sense of meaning and purpose, and, above all, his complete lack of doubt, inhibition, and indecision. It is precisely in this utopian promise of existing outside feelings, of affecting situations but not being affected, that we must locate one of the main reasons for such projections. The power of the fictional Schmitz-Lausitz, like that of the historical Heydrich in *Canaris*, resides in promising solutions to what democracy invariably fails to deliver: strong identifications, clear antagonisms, stable hierarchies, and liberation from the burdens of free will.

Against these totalitarian utopias, *Canaris* and *The Devil's General* mobilize the power of sympathy and empathy, key components in the making of democratic subjectivity and its humanistic redefinition during the 1950s. In the case of *Canaris*, the general's love of his dogs in the opening sequence introduces him as a likable character, an impression confirmed by his paternal concern for the well-being of his subordinates; his friendship with the neighbor further strengthens the underlying belief in the right to private happiness shared by characters and spectators. The more the film, through Hasse's nuanced acting style, grants access to his internal conflicts, the more Canaris becomes a figure of empathetic identification, a connection first tested in the conversion scene described earlier. However, the surfeit of empathy toward the end is also the main reason for what must be the audience's growing frustration with a powerful man paralyzed by doubt and fear.

In *The Devil's General*, this dynamic unfolds in very similar ways. Here the initial impression of Harras is one of strength and independence, but the sense of admiration conveyed through the supporting characters' points of view is soon undercut by displays of personal shortcomings. Small acts of kindness, from his willingness to help a Jewish couple in hiding to his encouraging words for a disillusioned pilot, increase our awareness of his inner struggles. Even initial irritation over his macho bravado eventually gives way to deeper understanding because of his genuine feelings for Diddo. Harras's anguished response to his imprisonment and interrogation by Schmidt-Lausitz firmly establishes him as a figure of empathetic identification, especially as it brings him face to face with the truth about Nazism (quite literally, in the scene in front of the mirror). However, in the moment that he begins to act decisively and reject the compromises that made possible his military career, he, like Canaris, becomes a tragic figure, a figure that needs to be sacrificed to the grand narratives of history and the contemporary demands of politics.

The two films discussed thus far shed light on the contradictory feelings of guilt, shame, resignation, and contempt that haunt their characters even in, or rather because of, their close association with the resistance. Through the crisis of masculinity—closeted homosexuality in *Canaris* and compulsive heterosexuality in *The Devil's General*—and through the affective registers of male melodrama, both films grant access to the attractions of fascism as a spectacle of strength even in defeat. By contrast, *It Happened on July 20th* and *The Plot to Assassinate Hitler* rely on a restrained documentary style with voice-over commentary to guard against such troublesome emotional investments. Whereas Hasse and Jürgens add layers of attraction through their status as famous stars, Preuss and Wicki disappear entirely behind the historical character. The bracketing of Stauffenberg's private life (and that of his associates) may have been necessary because of filed injunctions during preproduction by the widows of the conspirators, veterans' associations, and national conservative groups. But in the filmmakers' accommodation to such pressures, we can also detect a different conception of political life founded on the avoidance of personal charisma as a mobilizing force. Their strategy for establishing a relationship between past and present is to prohibit any kind of interiority, prevent any form of identification, and preclude any interpretative instability by telling a so-called true story based on facts. In other words, the goal is to counter the psychological appeal of fascism with the affective constraints on the political process favored during the Adenauer era, beginning with the emphasis on sobriety, modesty, and self-effacement.

Much has been written about the differences between the two versions of the Stauffenberg story: the focus on a single day in *It Happened on July 20th* and its embeddedness in a longer narrative in *The Plot to Assassinate Hitler*; the privileging of the military and political elites by Pabst and the inclusion of the middle and working classes by Harnack, and, to add an amusing detail, the correct

wearing by Wicki of Stauffenberg's eye patch on the left side and its misplace-
ment by Preiss on the right side.[22] These differences continue in the directors'
surprisingly subjective approaches to what was promoted as an objective account of Operation Valkyrie. Pabst, who had just completed the Austrian–West
German coproduction *Der letzte Akt* (*The Last Ten Days*, 1955) about Hitler's last
days in the bunker, resorted to familiar cold war rhetoric in framing the
conspirators' initial discussion about unconditional surrender, with one of the
men warning, "The Americans should know that once the East [i.e., the Soviet
Union] invades Germany, Europe is lost." By contrast, Harnack—a sympathizer of the White Rose resistance group, cofounder of the East German Antifascist Committee "Free Germany," and acclaimed DEFA filmmaker until official disputes over the Arnold Zweig adaptation *Das Beil von Wandsbek* (*The Axe of
Wandsbek*, 1951)—emphasized the working-class resistance through the addition
of a subplot probably suggested by his screenwriter and former Brecht collaborator Günter Weisenborn.

Both Stauffenberg films revolve around the "liberating deed" as a legitimate act of tyrannicide but distinguish their cold war politics of action from
Schmittian decisionism, that is, the conferral of political and moral legitimacy
based on the mere fact that a decision has been made. Moreover, through the
lengthy discussions among the men of the resistance, both films assert their belief
in the deliberative process as the foundation of postwar democracy. Beyond this
shared emphasis on communicative acts, however, the construction of political
identities and the presentation of political motivations could not be more different. In *It Happened on July 20th*, the main goal of the officers is clear: to put an
end to Hitler's rule of terror, if necessary by sacrificing a few innocent lives, and
to rescue what is left of German honor and renown in the world. The key terms
through which the men justify their actions are "conscience," "duty," and
"honor," terms that enlist the myth of Prussia in the proposed return to a Christian worldview. Forced to choose between their military oath of loyalty and
their moral conscience, the conspirators opt for the latter and, from then on,
prepare themselves to face a court-martial, the verdict of history, and the Last
Judgment. These religious associations are confirmed in a somber ending that
calls on contemporary audiences to prove themselves worthy of such sacrifices
through their commitment to a Christian Democratic understanding of politics
and the polity. "Millions of men, women, and children would still have to lose
their lives. Now it is up to us to ensure that they did not give their lives in vain,"
declares the voice-over, retroactively making all Germans coconspirators of the
resistance.

*The Plot to Assassinate Hitler* ends with a similar reference to God, who "knows that [their] insurrection was an act of conscience, the elimination of lawless tyranny and the protection of the honor of the German name." Yet here such statements serve a more critical goal, a reassessment of the meaning of the political in the past and the present. Through the habitus of emotional detachment, Harnack enlists the men of the resistance in a critical reevaluation of the Prussian heritage evident already in their tense discussions about the most appropriate form of provisional government. Carl-Friedrich Goerdeler, the designated head of state, favors a social monarchy, while another participant, a member of the Kreisau Circle, vaguely calls for a new ethics in politics; clearly marked as an outsider, the representative of the labor unions proposes socialist democracy as a possible model. In prefiguring the postwar years, such discussions may be read as an expression of the director's concern over the official commitment to democracy and the nostalgic attachment to authoritarianism embodied by Adenauer.

The same sense of disagreement and ambiguity troubles the characters' self-perception as political actors. Stauffenberg's old teacher insists that "soldiers are not supposed to be involved in politics," yet his escort officer asks indignantly: "Are we only marionettes in the hands of the powerful?" Stauffenberg finds a preliminary answer in the village church where he seeks absolution before flying off to the Wolfsschanze. As the setting for the decisive moment discussed earlier, this brief scene juxtaposes medium shots of the altar and three crosses and increasingly closer shots of Stauffenberg's face, with the subsequent montage sequence of war and destruction offering moral justification for his coming actions. The making of what might be called militant Christianity is achieved through the acoustic transition from Bach organ music via dissonant sounds to the nationalistic "Watch on the Rhine" song over snapshots of air raids, bombed cities, and defeated armies on the eastern front. Through the unusually dramatic presentation of the scene, Harnack suggests that Christian faith continues to exert considerable power as a political program for the present. However, it remains unclear what role the conspirators' geopolitical visions for Germany after Hitler play in this context. Alluding to old ideas about *Mitteleuropa* (Central Europe), Stauffenberg at one point speaks of "a new life between East and West in line with our interests," with the conflation of Germany and the resistance movement clearly intended. Yet by setting out to "eliminate totalitarianism and reintroduce the rule of law," his group ends up with a political program that translates the historical context of World War II into the contemporary context of the cold war.

Two concepts have dominated public debates during the postwar period and profoundly affected the critical reception of the first West German films about the Third Reich as a historical period and political legacy: *Stunde Null* (zero hour) and *Vergangenheitsbewältigung* (coming to terms with the past); no discussion of the first resistance films would be complete without some consideration of this larger discursive configuration. Extensively studied, these concepts give us privileged access to the affective economies of postwar cinema and its competing modes of internalization and externalization, emotionalization and rationalization. In order to extricate the films' contradictory identifications from the retrospective logic imposed on them, we need to resist prevailing readings that, in accordance with the interpretative logic suggested by these two concepts, approach the films exclusively through the lens of history, memory, and trauma rather than through the political conflicts of the times.

Suggesting a complete break, the notion of the zero hour provided occupiers and occupied with a convenient myth of new beginnings.[23] For the Western Allies, the zero hour was closely identified with the four *D*'s: demilitarization, denazification, decentralization, and democratization, with the last category soon to emerge as the most contested ground in the cold war confrontation between a parliamentary democracy and a communist one-party state. For the Germans embarking on the monumental task of reconstruction, the myth facilitated a return to the incomplete project of democratization and modernization presumably interrupted by the Third Reich and a reaffirmation of the values of Western humanism and the principles of the Enlightenment sacrificed to the exigencies of war and genocide. By emphasizing historical discontinuity, Germans for a brief moment could imagine post-1945 Germany as a clean slate on which to project dreams of a politically neutral and truly democratic country mediating between East and West. With the cold war, the Nazi past (rather predictably) returned with a vengeance, but in the form of a very contemporary struggle over competing definitions of democratic subjectivity, historical agency, and national identity that found expression in the parallel trajectories of anti-Nazism in the West and antifascism in the East.

Acknowledging the burdens of historical continuity, the notion of coming to terms with the past similarly came with a complex set of political rhetorics, public rituals, and therapeutic techniques—but this time for creating the conditions of economic reconstruction and integrating (West) Germany into the group of Western democracies.[24] The various meanings attributed to this much-studied term extend from the assumption of collective guilt after 1945 to repeated calls after 1989 for a normalization of the German past, a development to be examined in greater detail in chapter 7. The term was introduced around 1955 and then repeatedly used by President Theodor Heuss to describe the political and moral responsibilities of the Federal Republic as the legal successor state of the Third Reich. At the time, it opened up a discursive space for recognizing the interrelatedness of past and present and acknowledging the difficulties of building a democratic society on the institutional, ideological, and sociopsychological foundations of Nazism. The distinct mentality of the Adenauer era—the determination, confidence, and belief in the project of reconstruction that made possible the "economic miracle" and the patterns of denial and forgetting that resulted from the trauma of loss and defeat in World War II—is preserved in the competing discourses of continuity and discontinuity and their reproduction in the split political imaginary of the Federal Republic.

Questions of continuity and discontinuity also preoccupied the political scientists and philosophers who analyzed the failures of the Weimar Republic and considered their long-term implications for the Federal Republic. Their shared insistence on a strong civil society as the best protection against a future dictatorship, whether fascist or communist, is relevant not only for a better understanding of the new emotional attachments that were created in the process of coming to terms with the past, but they also shed light on the pivotal role of Prussia and the military in the highly ambivalent resistance narratives discussed in the previous pages. Setting the tone, the influential historian Friedrich Meinecke identified the legacies of Prussian militarism and the weakness of the middle class as contributing factors in the rise of National Socialism.[25] Similarly, the philosopher Helmuth Plessner pointed to the late development of democratic institutions in the German nation-state and its foundation on an essentialist notion of *Volk* rather than abstract ideas such as freedom and equality. The Lutheran tradition of inwardness as the main form of individual self-realization and the resultant separation of private and public spheres featured prominently in his analysis of the shortcomings of German civil society and public life.[26]

Postwar democratization required a fundamental rethinking of the category of the political, a process that began with its subsumation during the 1950s under the ethical categories introduced together with the guilt question and that continued with its expansion through the acknowledgment of marginalized voices and forgotten perspectives under the influence of the radical political movements of the 1960s. The goal in all cases was to find an alternative to the spectacle of the masses, the cult of community, and the aesthetics of war and violence associated with the Third Reich. Once again, the implications for the films under discussion are most obvious in the reaffirmation of the individual as the basis of a new political ethics. In *The Question of German Guilt*, philosopher

Karl Jaspers distinguished among criminal, moral, and metaphysical guilt, with collective guilt being limited to the political realm and atoned for through a postwar culture of moral responsibility and democratic renewal.[27] Searching for an alternative to the agonistic model of the political in Schmitt and its bracketing in the existential humanism of Jaspers, political scientist Dolf Sternberger, at the beginning of the 1960s, redefined the political with a view toward peace as "the ultimate political category," presenting an argument for a forceful pacifism that can be understood only through its difference from the mobilization of the masses in war and genocide during the Third Reich.[28] Finally, the beginnings of yet another understanding of the political can be located in the work of political scientist Wolfgang Abendroth—the doctoral adviser of Jürgen Habermas—who was the first to consider an alternative history of political affects identified with working-class subjectivity that allows us to understand better the radical alterity within postwar culture of the Thälmann figure and the antifascist film.[29]

Aware of the interrelatedness of history, memory, trauma, and affect, philosophers and cultural critics early on recognized the emotional work of coming to terms with the past, drawing heavily on Freud's writings on mourning and melancholia to distinguish, in sometimes problematic ways, between productive and unproductive ways of achieving democratic subjectivity. Already in 1954, Theodor W. Adorno in his famous lecture "The Meaning of Working through the Past?" commented on the half-hearted support for democracy among West Germans and described "the survival of National Socialism *within* democracy to be potentially more menacing than the survival of fascist tendencies *against* democracy."[30] Similarly, Alexander and Margarete Mitscherlich's influential study *The Inability to Mourn* diagnosed the Germans' inability to mourn the loss of Hitler and interpreted the resultant narcissistic crisis as a major reason for the failures of postwar democratization.[31] Both of these critical interventions relied on psychoanalytic models of repression and traditional notions of masculinity to analyze seemingly inappropriate affective responses in the self-representation of West German culture and society, Adorno by speaking of "intense affects where they are hardly warranted by the situation" and "absence of affect in the face of the gravest matters," and the Mitscherlichs by pointing out the affective blockages shared by fascist and democratic imaginaries.

The concept of coming to terms with, or working through, the Nazi past has sometimes allowed subsequent generations of scholars to reduce the complexities of postwar culture to an ongoing struggle between remembering and forgetting that presumably haunted all postwar literature, film, art, and public debate and cast everything under the spell of the Third Reich. Yet as cultural historian Aleida Assmann reminds us, we can talk about amnesia not in absolute terms but only as a process of selective memory and commemoration. The shift from collective memory to cultural memory that defines historical representation is inseparable from the politics of history and its changing functions from the 1950s to the 1990s.[32] This process is most apparent in the discursive competition among, and mutual instrumentalization of, three pasts—the Third Reich, World War II, and the immediate postwar period—and their respective roles in the rewriting of the resistance narrative. The systematic bracketing of Nazism as a political ideology and form of government and the exclusive focus on the war and postwar years involved much-analyzed political rationales as well as less-studied popular attitudes. Speaking to the latter, historian Michael Geyer has shown that the majority of West Germans during the 1950s retained a positive image of the Third Reich and, notwithstanding the hardships on the front and the home front, considered 1945–51 to have been the worst years of their lives.[33] Other questionnaires from the period confirm that a sizable number continued to see the men of the resistance as traitors who betrayed their oath of allegiance to the Führer. Thus, instead of automatically equating the resistance narratives with a critique of Nazism, we must pay closer attention to how they in fact reconcile the need to expunge the political legacies of the past with the desire to hold on to specific emotions, dispositions, and attitudes marked as fascist, a point confirmed by the films' contradictory politics of affect.

Recent studies on the relative openness of political debates immediately after the war and the surprising wealth of early literary representations of the Third Reich and World War II have thoroughly discredited the repression theory, canonized in the post-1968 period, that placed the postwar years under the sign of total amnesia and willful forgetting. No longer dismissing the production of an entire decade as escapist entertainment, film scholars, too, now read the films of the 1950s as equally marked by expressive eruptions of traumatic memories and compulsive reenactments of political attachments. In one of the first studies on the subject, Wolfgang Becker and Norbert Schöll in fact examine how the West German films locate in the Nazi past (or project onto it) specific experiences, attitudes, and feelings in order to rescue them, to make them usable for the present and the future. More specifically, by equating political subject and object, and by conflating ruler and ruled, these films, in their view, depict subservience and opportunism in the Third Reich as a voluntary service to humanity and, hence, a political model for the future.[34] Taking a similar approach, the resistance films confront their audiences with two kinds of enemies: the Nazis and the anti-Nazis, with the position of friends reserved for the younger officers and their allies. Distinguished by an unsettling preoccupation with honor, duty, and sacrifice, these films leave the affective structures of Nazism—its patterns of engagement as well as its strategies of detachment—surprisingly intact and, through their contradictory or ambiguous qualities, prove ideally suited for the reenlistment of political affects in the ideological confrontations of the cold war.

By mobilizing fascist imaginaries in postfascist conflicts, the mid-1950s marked a pivotal moment in the making of West German democracy, a moment that integrated national and transnational perspectives and produced often unexpected intertextual and contextual effects: not only through the discourses on German masculinity shared by Hollywood anti-Nazi films and West German resistance films but also through the less predictable similarities operating across the cold war divide—reason enough to conclude with a preview of the same problematic from the East German perspective. After all, in the same way that 20 July 1944 allowed West Germans to work through their contradictory attitudes about the so-called right of resistance, the *Widerstandsrecht* added to the Basic Law in 1968, 27 February 1933, the day of the Reichstag fire, allowed East Germans to celebrate the communist resistance as a historical legacy and political model and portray themselves as the original antifascists. In a strange mirroring effect, the two West German films about Stauffenberg thus found their equivalent in the East German preoccupation with the Reichstag fire trial and the charges against Bulgarian communist leader Georgi Dimitrov; the best-known film about the trial is *Der Teufelskreis* (The vicious circle, Carl Balhaus, 1956). The association of the myth of resistance with Dimitrov and Stauffenberg, respectively, in turn produced two prevailing narratives in postfascist cinema, with the former reaching its most heroic moments before World War II and the latter substituting a military crisis for a political conflict.

At first glance, the representation of the Third Reich in the West and East German films and its enlistment in the making of democratic and socialist subjectivity could not be more different.[35] But as we will see in chapter 3, both cinemas developed their relationship to Nazism/fascism through a series of antagonisms that extended from the initial division of Germany to the two political blocs emerging during the cold war. West German filmmakers relied on the myth of Prussia to reconcile antidemocratic traditions with the requirements of postwar democracy. By contrast, their East German colleagues enlisted communist martyr figures to perform the logical unfolding of history toward communism as its ultimate destiny. Whereas the former explained the Third Reich as a historical aberration, the latter located political agency in social classes, not individuals, and analyzed fascism as part of a far-reaching critique of capitalism. Not surprisingly, their films offered very different strategies for dealing with the legacies of Nazism/fascism: individualism and collectivism. The narrative trajectory in the West revolved around a totalitarian past to be overcome through the establishment of liberal democracy, whereas the same trajectory in the East pointed toward a future only guaranteed by socialism. In both cases, the representation of the resistance ultimately failed to break free of the aesthetic of the Ufa genius film and its impossible position between the fascist celebration of German character and strength and the (Christian) cult of suffering and the (socialist) cult of sacrifice. The dominant political fantasy remained that of the leader figure who sacrifices himself for the nation and the people.

These historical conditions produced the affective constellations that aligned the German films about the Third Reich with the cold war project of interpellating subjects, of producing citizens for the GDR and the FRG. In the West, the prevailing sense was one of victimization, first of the Germans by the Nazis, and then of the West Germans by the Soviets, and, at least in the eyes of conservatives, by the Americans. In the East, two historical scenarios of encirclement were superimposed on each other, that of the communists by the Nazis before 1945 and of the East Germans by the West Germans and the Americans after 1945. Through such projections, the stage was set for the enlistment, from the late 1940s to the early 1960s, of American, West German, and East German films about the Third Reich in the ideological confrontations of the cold war. But such political pressures also made necessary and possible the ongoing reassessment of antifascism as the foundational myth of the GDR in the 1960s and 1970s, which will be examined in the next chapter.

# 3

# Melancholy Antifascism

## The East German Antifascist Films
## of the 1960s and 1970s

> There is no greater crime than refusing to fight where the
> situation demands it.
>
> Closing words of *Professor Mamlock* (Konrad Wolf, 1961)

Antifascism occupied a central place in the affective economy of the German
Democratic Republic, but it also remains one of the clearest indicators of the
deterioration of socialism into a hegemonic discourse and antidemocratic practice.[1] The withering away of antifascism and, by extension, of socialism cannot
be fully understood without consideration of what Raymond Williams describes as structures of feeling—that which at once exceeds and sustains ideology, "not feeling against thought, but thought as felt and feeling as thought."[2]
This process is captured in two symptomatic scenes from Hans-Joachim
Kunert's *Die Abenteuer der Werner Holt* (*The Adventures of Werner Holt*, 1964), a controversial adaptation of the eponymous antifascist classic written by Dieter
Noll, and from Heiner Carow's *Die Russen kommen* (The Russians are coming,
1968/1987), a bleak antiwar film immediately banned upon completion and re-
released nineteen years later. The respective scenes revolve around young men

Klaus-Peter Thiele in *The Adventures of Werner Holt*        Klaus-Peter Thiele in *The Adventures of Werner Holt*

seduced by fascism but no longer saved by the prosthetic identities offered by antifascism. In both films, the familiar heroic narrative of political resistance has been invaded by the overwhelming sense of paralysis, loss, and defeat experienced on the battlefields of World War II. And in both cases, the camera repeatedly arrests the flow of the narrative to explore youthful faces marked by shock and disbelief, faces that register the failure of the antifascist narrative to provide emotional sustenance and political meaning and that subsequently serve as conduits to the hidden history of what I call melancholy antifascism.

The first face belongs to Werner Holt (Klaus-Peter Thiele), whose sullen, pensive gaze marks a radical break with the expressive physiognomy of antifascist heroes in the tradition of East German character actors Erwin Geschonneck and Armin Mueller-Stahl. By highlighting his sense of indecision and detachment, director Kunert portrays Holt as someone without strong commitments, which in the context of the late 1960s must be read as a clear commentary on the waning attachment to socialism among the generation of East Germans born after the war. Time and again we see him sitting in a bunker on the eastern front, establishing radio contact with other units, and, in extensive flashbacks, revisiting the personal and political choices that brought him to this point. Unable to share his friend Gilbert Wolzow's unwavering belief in National Socialism, he at one point admits: "I wished I were a fanatic. All this pondering and brooding is destroying me." This remarkable confession explains his yearning for the existential certainties promised by fascism, but for reasons relevant to my later discussion, it also announces his unsuitability for the alternatives offered by antifascism; unlike in the two-part novel, the Werner Holt of the film no longer experiences the promised "arrival in socialism" (*Ankunft im Sozialismus*).

The second face belongs to fifteen-year-old Günter, a *Flakhelfer* (antiaircraft auxiliary) on the eastern front near Stettin during the last days of the war. Arrested because of his involvement in the killing of a forced laborer and detained in the same cell as the policeman responsible for the crime, the adolescent suffers a mental breakdown. He erupts into hysterical laughter, incapable of comprehending the reality of the German defeat and the enormity of his disillusionment. Once again, the close-up of his face suggests that the victory over fascism does not result automatically in the triumph of antifascism as a liberating narrative. The robotic tone with which a Russian soldier (in English!) later declares, "Fascism is a crime. All fascists are criminals," indirectly confirms this fear. The demonization of fascism fails to undo the trauma caused by the loss of illusions and to overcome the speechlessness that in this film and others remains the most troubling legacy of fascism—a legacy alluded to in Günter's earlier plea that "all of this must have some meaning."

"Could it be that everything was in vain?" asks an equally desperate Werner Holt as he faces the approaching Soviet tanks, his presumed liberators. What are we to make of a narrative point of view that, in a radical break with DEFA conventions, presents the Germans as victims and the Soviets as intruders? What is the significance of traumatized protagonists looking for some validation of their experiences during the Third Reich? How are we to interpret the refusal of Kunert and Carow to engage the familiar ideological oppositions and liberatory scenarios and concentrate on the psychic devastations of war instead? And how are these representations of World War II indicative of a broader crisis in the antifascist narrative and its role in the making of socialist subjectivity? In what follows, I attempt to answer these questions by analyzing the affective economies of the antifascist film in a three-part fashion: first, by tracing the emergence after 1945 of this most important genre of East German cinema; second, by assessing its aesthetic revision, critical deconstruction, and ideological reinscription during the 1960s and 1970s; and third, by diagnosing its political reclamation by Frank Beyer and Konrad Wolf through a comparative reading organized around melancholy as a specific political affect.

Rather than choosing films that are openly critical of the ossified structures and normative effects of the antifascist myth, this chapter focuses on well-known directors who, despite everything, insist on its relevance to the self-understanding of GDR culture and society. The convergence of the antifascist narrative with the war narrative played a key role in this revisionist process and produced two very different approaches that are central to the discursive reconfigurations during the 1960s and remain relevant to the ongoing debate on antifascism and its legacies: Frank Beyer's antifascist classics *Fünf Patronenhülsen* (*Five Cartridges*,

1960) and *Nackt unter Wölfen* (*Naked among Wolves*, 1963), and Konrad Wolf's autobiographical World War II films *Ich war neunzehn* (*I Was Nineteen*, 1968) and *Mama, ich lebe* (*Mama, I'm Alive*, 1977).[3]

A comparative reading of their work allows me to consider the role of the war narrative in realigning the antifascist narrative with the hegemonic perspective of the communist movement (in the case of Beyer) or the Soviet Army (in the case of Wolf); to discuss the contribution of formal innovation in reinscribing the antifascist myth (in the case of Beyer) or deconstructing it (in the case of Wolf); and to assess the function of masculinity in validating the figure of the antifascist leader (in the case of Beyer) or exploring new forms of male subjectivity (in the case of Wolf). In relation to the larger questions addressed in this book, the antifascist films are especially relevant for two reasons: their promotion of socialism/communism as the only historical alternative to fascism and liberal democracy and their contribution to the political legitimation of the country, the party, and the state that relied so extensively on antifascism as an ideological fantasy. Since the GDR was founded in the spirit of "antifascist-democratic transformation," the state's failure to establish democratic structures and processes was bound to leave behind symptoms of crisis in the antifascist narrative. As a sustained reflection on attachment and loss, melancholy emerged as one of the privileged registers through which to express a thus-defined legitimation crisis in aesthetic and affective terms and to partake in a very different process of coming to terms with the past, namely, through the legacies of antifascism and socialism.

In critical assessments of DEFA (Deutsche Film Aktiengesellschaft) and its contribution to German film history, one fact seems undisputable: the centrality of the antifascist film to the DEFA legacy.[4] The hundred-plus films of this type produced by the state-owned studio between 1946 and 1989, most scholars agree, captured the artistic ambitions, political commitments, and filmic sensibilities of this major socialist cinema in almost ideal-typical form. As the large number of DEFA coproductions devoted to antifascist subject matter confirms, they also played a key role in the building of a transnational socialist imaginary based on international solidarity and economic cooperation.[5] Part of the larger discourse of antifascism in literature, theater, visual arts, and official memory culture, the antifascist films established a foundational narrative for "the first socialist state on German soil," to cite the GDR constitution, and supplied a rich source of identifications, attachments, and affiliations for its citizens. Moreover, through their historical belatedness, the antifascist stories bestowed legitimacy on an increasingly autocratic party leadership during the freezes and thaws of the cold war and, over the course of forty years, functioned as a depository for the expectations, disappointments, and regrets associated with the project of "real existing socialism," a phrase introduced in the 1970s to defend the reality of socialism against the obstinacy of socialist utopias.

The antifascist films cannot be fully understood without at least a few comments about the broader meaning of antifascism as foundational myth and state doctrine and about its steady decline, its reduction to an empty public ritual, after the building of the Berlin Wall on 13 August 1961.[6] Antifascism universalized the Nazi threat, as is evident in the linguistic shift from Nazism to fascism, and made its specific history part of the global confrontation between communism and capitalism. Based on the official definition by Dimitrov of fascism as "the open terrorist dictatorship of the most reactionary, most chauvinistic, and most imperialist elements of finance capital," the antifascist doctrine allowed the East Germans after 1945 to side with the victors and conceive of the end of World War II as a moment of liberation rather than defeat.[7] Organizing a series of antagonisms that recall the friend-enemy distinction, antifascism after the war became synonymous with anticapitalism, anti-imperialism, and anti-Americanism and acquired quasi-religious status in the creation of a GDR cultural heritage and socialist public sphere. As an integrative myth, antifascism supplied the new workers' and peasants' state with a ready-made past and future. Through its moralistic stories of courage, conviction, and commitment, it relieved the first generation of GDR citizens of the necessity of dealing with German guilt and shame, confronting the trauma of war and expulsion, and recognizing the continuities between the Third Reich and the GDR. By identifying with the Soviet Union, GDR citizens were able to turn military defeat into a moment of (self-)liberation and to externalize the Nazis as that absolute other henceforth identified with the Federal Republic. Moreover, antifascism established a political model for coming to terms with the past in which the inability to mourn the loss of Hitler as love object could be bracketed, if only temporarily, through the identification with Stalin, the narcissistic wound of defeat healed through overidentification with a new political order, and the trauma of war forgotten through the frenzy of postwar reconstruction and the building of socialism. Last but not least, antifascism continuously reaffirmed the reasons for the division of Germany by locating the origins and legacies of fascism in West Germany and affirming the working class as the true agent of history in the Marxist sense.

The early antifascist films contributed to the making of the first generation of GDR citizens by assigning them a position in the history of class struggles that was prescriptive as well as interventionist, commemorative as well as anticipatory.[8] A limited number of story lines were established during the 1950s: the founding of the KPD and the growing Nazi threat in the late Weimar Republic; the systematic and brutal elimination of the political opposition after 1933; and, last but not least, the close ties between National Socialists and the representatives of big business and finance capital. Relying on familiar oppositions (e.g., capitalism vs. communism, nationalism vs. internationalism, individualism vs. collectivism), filmmakers created a distinct social typology and political iconography around the paternal figure of the antifascist hero and what he embodied: the Communist Party. The films presented the Third Reich and World War II as necessary phases, or crisis moments, in the defeat of capitalism and the triumph of communism, with antisemitism and the Holocaust usually treated as complicating factors. From this teleological perspective, the GDR could be conceived as the ultimate other of fascism and its legacies; in socialism, antifascism presumably found its logical continuation and ultimate manifestation. Sustained by this dialogic (or dialectic) relationship between fascism and antifascism, the early antifascist films played a pivotal role in the filmic production of a socialist imaginary: either through the glorification of the communist resistance during the Weimar Republic and Third Reich or through conversion stories that allowed the victims of false consciousness to see the truth of Marxist ideology and socialist reality. In both cases, this revisionist structure, often aided by a series of moralizing flashbacks, allowed DEFA filmmakers to rewrite the past from the perspective of the present and make ordinary East Germans part of the presumably logical unfolding of history.

Yet the antifascist genre, if it can be called that, was anything but stable or uncontested. After its initial codification and canonization in the 1950s, it experienced a final flourishing in the 1960s—that is, the long era dominated by Walter Ulbricht, general secretary of the Central Committee and chairman of the Council of State—when its exemplary stories of resistance were absorbed into the very different registers of the war film and when modernist experimentation released a previously suppressed sense of melancholia that in fact had haunted the genre from the beginning and that is retraceable in the imaginary relations established to, and through, political affects. After all, the substitution of class for race as the primary category of identity formation and the shift from the community to the collective as the ideal model of social organization did not fundamentally alter the affective investment in a political system that remained profoundly hierarchical, authoritarian, and undemocratic and that was to a large degree sustained by the same hatred of bourgeois individualism and love for the totalitarian leader (Hitler, Stalin) shared by fascists and communists alike.[9] By sacrificing personal happiness for the sublime rewards of

political martyrdom and by renouncing heterosexual love for the companion-
ship of all-male groups, the heroes in the antifascist film invited patterns of
identification not dissimilar to those found in the Nazi movement and wartime
propaganda films. By practicing party discipline, ideological rigidity, and a
uniquely communist sexual asceticism, the protagonists may have served as
role models in the struggle against the fascist exploitation of emotions. Yet their
personal pathologies, beginning with their cold rationality and emotional reserve, also represented a return of the repressed, with fascist dispositions now
reappearing in antifascist disguises.

In what ways can antifascism be described as a political affect, and what role
did film play in establishing its aesthetic manifestations? In the East German–
Soviet coproduction *KLK an PTX—Die Rote Kapelle* (*KLK Calling PTZ: The Red
Orchestra*, Horst Brandt, 1971), a committed communist at one point denounces
the bourgeois resistance movement for opposing "fascism on a purely emotional basis." However, scientific Marxism could not prevent antifascism from
being similarly infused with emotions, including growing concerns about its
failure in sustaining socialist subjectivities. The antifascist films established a
master narrative, an imaginary subject position, and an affective model for
public and private identities. Yet as such a political affect, antifascism also organized more complicated processes of identification and projection through
its heroic stories of resistance, struggle, and sacrifice. The fictional confrontation with the enemy, the Nazis, produced predictable feelings of fear, hatred,
and disgust that, behind the familiar antagonistic structure, point to unacknowledged continuities in relationship to power and authority (e.g., in authoritarian personality structures). Similarly, the honorific "antifascist" marked a
position of moral superiority and ideological certainty that nonetheless betrays
a strong attachment to experiences of victimhood—reason enough to take a
closer look at antifascism as political affect and consider its hidden history of
mourning and melancholia.

Described in this way, antifascism provided an affective framework for
working through forgotten or suppressed experiences of persecution and oppression: initially through stories that retell the typical class biographies and
communist martyr legends associated with socialist realism—a style examined
in greater detail below—and the rituals of self-disciplining that were an integral
part of the antifascist struggle, but by the early 1960s also in the form of rising
doubts about the personal sacrifices required in the building of socialism that
contributed to the genre's loss of narrative momentum and sense of psychological stasis. As the "real, existing socialism" failed to live up to the dreams of a
better future, the historical narratives were invaded by more contemporary

references, and the familiar accounts of collective struggles punctuated by scenes of individual pain and suffering. Understanding the revisions of anti-fascism that accompanied the successive waves of liberalization and dogmatization over almost fifty years of GDR culture and society requires that we, in a brief film historical digression, return to its original intentions and conventions after the military and political defeat of the Third Reich.

If the Hollywood anti-Nazi film defined the friend-enemy distinction for postwar cinema in the West, *Bortsy/Kämpfer* (The struggle, Gustav von Wangen-heim, 1936) achieved the same for the antifascist film in the East. Made by Ger-man communists in Soviet exile, this little-known film combined the genre's constitutive elements in almost programmatic fashion: the focus on communist leaders (in this case, Dimitrov) as well as ordinary workers, the insertion of avant-garde techniques (in this case, montage) into socialist realist conventions, and the vacillation between the emancipatory potential of political mobiliza-tion (in this case, for the popular front) and the disciplining effects of political indoctrination. Above all, the film's depiction of the communist resistance in Nazi Germany relied on familiar social stereotypes, binary oppositions, and didactic tones to codify the genre's main affective register as a heroic one—defined by struggles, conflicts, and sacrifices.[10] Following this model, so-called chronicle films (*Chronikfilme*) such as *Die Buntkarierten* (The checkered sheets, Kurt Maetzig, 1949), *Rotation* (Wolfgang Staudte, 1949), and *Lissy* (Konrad Wolf, 1957) featured typical working-class and petit bourgeois characters who make the difficult but necessary transition from apolitical individualism to class consciousness and are rewarded, in the obligatory happy endings, with inclu-sion in the utopian project of socialism. The socialist perspective on German history was directly thematized in *Die heute über 40 sind* (Those who are over forty today, Kurt Jung-Alsen, 1960) and its story of two childhood friends, one the son of a factory owner, who becomes a Nazi sympathizer, decorated officer, and West German industrialist, and the other the son of a factory worker, who becomes a Soviet POW, member of the Free Germany movement, and direc-tor of a people-owned factory.

The gradual shift from the sociopsychology of class inspired by the critical social realism of late Weimar cinema to the ideal-typical representations of class required by socialist realism in the Stalinist mode can be traced exemplarily in the films by Kurt Maetzig and Bulgarian-born Slatan Dudow, the two most prolific practitioners of the antifascist genre during the 1950s. Best known for his collaboration with Bertolt Brecht on *Kuhle Wampe oder: Wem gehört die Welt?* (*Kuhle Wampe or Who Owns the World?*, 1932), the most famous leftist film of the Weimar years, Dudow in his later work relied heavily on character engagement

and the complementary modes of idealization and satirization to instrumental-
ize the antifascist narrative in the ideological confrontations of the cold war. An
unambiguous distribution of sympathies and antipathies allowed him to achieve
perfect affective and ideological alignment, including through the equation of
sexual and political pathology familiar from the Hollywood anti-Nazi films
(e.g., in the depiction of Nazis as effeminate, perverted, or homosexual). Intervening in then-ongoing debates on German unification, *Stärker als die Nacht*
(Stronger than the night, 1952) idealized the communist resistance during the
Weimar Republic and used its legacies to establish a clear link between communism and nationalism, speaking of "our victory for Germany's future."
Meanwhile, the political satire *Der Hauptmann von Köln* (*The Captain of Cologne*,
1956) emphasized the continuities between Third Reich and Federal Republic
and, not unlike Wolfgang Staudte's later *Rosen für den Staatsanwalt* (*Roses for the
Prosecutor*, 1959) in the West, uncovered the infiltration of the political and economic elites by unrepentant Nazis. The statement by one Nazi in *The Captain of
Cologne*, "Comrades, we are back again. . . . We are all back again," was clearly
meant to increase political vigilance against the class enemy and justify so-called
defensive actions such as the building of the Berlin Wall.

By contrast, Maetzig's exploration of the psychological roots and social
consequences of political noninvolvement began with the melodramatic story
of a German Jewish married couple in *Ehe im Schatten* (*Marriage in the Shadows*,
1947) and the chronicle of three generations of a Berlin working-class family in
the previously mentioned *Die Buntkarierten*. Whereas the Jewish protagonists in
the first film are held partly responsible for their racial persecution because of
their bourgeois belief in self-reliance, the working-class protagonists are largely
exonerated as powerless victims of capitalist exploitation and economic crises.
Both films invite empathetic identification with the characters but imply that
postwar audiences must make different choices in their own lives. Maetzig early
on abandoned the critical possibilities of empathy for a more strident critique
of capitalism in *Rat der Götter* (*Council of the Gods*, 1950), a film about the IG Farben
concern responsible for Cyclon B, the poison gas used in Auschwitz. Similarly,
the two-part Thälmann epic — *Ernst Thälmann, Sohn seiner Klasse* (Ernst Thälmann,
son of his class, 1954) and *Ernst Thälmann, Führer seiner Klasse* (Ernst Thälmann,
leader of his class, 1955) — subordinated personal needs and desires entirely to
the grand narrative of the Communist Party and presented the history of
working-class struggles as the prehistory of the GDR.

Seen by millions, the Ernst Thälmann films formalized the filmic conventions and historical explanations against which all later filmmakers formulated
their approach to the antifascist myth. The films celebrated the proletariat as

Günther Simon as the title figure in the two-part *Ernst Thälmann* epic, courtesy DEFA-Stiftung/Heinz Wenzel

Litfass pillar in Leipzig advertising the second part of the *Ernst Thälmann* epic, courtesy SLUB Dresden/ Deutsche Fotothek/Roger & Renate Rössing

the object and subject of history and, through their linear narratives and simple identificatory structures, gave rise to the model GDR citizen out of the legacies of the antifascist resistance. In their idealization of male heroism and extreme cult of personality, however, the films also participated in forms of historical forgetting that would soon haunt the antifascist discourse as a whole.[11] Throughout, Maetzig relied on the classic Marxist analysis of the final years of the Weimar Republic: the control of German politics by international finance capital, the support for the Nazis by German businessmen, and the denunciation of Social Democrats as social fascists. The central conflict is captured in the political alternatives laid out by an anonymous character in *Ernst Thälmann, Führer seiner Klasse*: "The vital question for the German people today is: Reaction or progress? War or peace? Hitler or Thälmann?" Instead of a direct answer, the film presents Thälmann—and, by extension, Ulbricht, who makes a brief appearance in a KPD delegation received by Lenin—as everything that Hitler is not: Thälmann is calm and confident whereas Hitler is choleric, precise, and to the point whereas the Nazi is rhetorically vague, and part of a mass movement whereas his opponent is a puppet in the hands of a few. Above all, the KPD leader has a compelling political program, presented in a 1932 Reichstag speech, that makes antifascism part of the larger project of "social liberation, the fall of capitalism." This "struggle for the liberation of mankind" during his long imprisonment is kept alive with the help of the Thälmann Brigade during the Spanish Civil War and the Soviet Ernst Thälmann Tank Battalion on the battlefields of World War II, a clear allusion to the continued need for military preparedness in the world historical battle between capitalism and communism.

The two-part Thälmann epic is a perfect example of socialist realism, the official style of Soviet film, art, and literature promoted under Stalin and denounced as formulaic and mechanistic by Georg Lukács and other proponents of critical realism. The "historically concrete representation of reality in its historical development," to cite its 1934 definition, required specific formal elements and aesthetic strategies: the heavy reliance on class and gender stereotypes, idealized representations of labor and industry, the cult of masculinity and patriarchy, didactic and propagandistic modes of enunciation, and an overall mood of optimism, heroism, and idealism—all contributing to the production of mentalities that helped to keep in check the deleterious effects of doubt and dispute. Following in that tradition, the political affects referenced by the Thälmann epic remain resolutely unambiguous. Rational argument and self-critique are confirmed as the distinguishing traits of socialist man. Emotions enter the dramatic constellations only to the degree that they make necessary the hardening of the communist leader figure and the strengthening of the revolutionary working class. And the manifestations of longing and desire through which protagonists and spectators are interpellated as postfascist subjects no longer include personal relationships but focus solely on what is both missing and omnipresent in the narrative—socialism as the culmination of history.

As I have argued thus far, the antifascist film established a thematic corpus, social typology, and visual iconography for postfascist socialist culture and society. The fact that DEFA was required to produce a certain number of antifascist films, that the most prestigious ones were released with many print copies, and that their popular reception included aggressive marketing campaigns and obligatory group screenings confirms their relevance to the self-presentation of party and state; such practices also suggest troubling similarities with the propagandistic *Staatsauftragsfilme* (state-commissioned films) made during the Third Reich. Moreover, with the DEFA studio occupying the old Ufa studio in Berlin-Babelsberg and employing many of its former personnel, the filmic medium faced particular challenges in extricating itself from a tradition of mass manipulation—perfected by the Propaganda Ministry during the Third Reich and an integral part of Stalinist cinema since the 1930s—that exploited the possibilities of mechanical reproduction in creating a highly aestheticized version of social reality.

Ideological rigidity invariably produces cracks and fissures in the systems of representation. In the case of the antifascist film, the first signs of a structural tension between political intentions and aesthetic effects can be found in the long history of required cuts or reshoots, tense meetings between production teams and studio officials, behind-closed-doors negotiations with the Ministry of Culture, and last-minute bans and withdrawals from exhibition. Already for the first DEFA production and classic rubble film *Die Mörder sind unter uns* (*The Murderers Are among Us*, Wolfgang Staudte, 1946), the Soviets demanded that the original ending, the killing of the Nazi perpetrator, be replaced with a more conciliatory gesture of moral atonement—an attempt perhaps to leave all political options open in the transitional years of the late 1940s. In *Rotation*, DEFA officials removed a key scene with the father burning his son's Wehrmacht uniform because of its inopportune pacifist message during the beginning of the rearmament race. The focus on the Nazi hangman in *The Axe of Wandsbek* was criticized as counterproductive at a time when the SED leadership demanded more positive heroes; that film became the first official DEFA censorship case. Much later, after the shelving of an entire year's production by the infamous 1965 Eleventh Plenary of the Central Committee of the SED, *Die Russen kommen* (The Russians are coming) was banned in 1968 because of the title's implicit reference to the Soviet invasion of Czechoslovakia and, more generally, the director's suspicious interest in the mass psychology of fascism. Even favored projects and popular successes did not always attract positive reviews, with *Naked among Wolves* denounced for its excessive use of pathos, *The Adventures of Werner Holt* attacked because of its weak main protagonist, and *I Was Nineteen* and *Mama, I'm Alive* criticized for their episodic narrative structures.[12]

The incompatibility of film art and official politics became even more pronounced after the building of the Berlin Wall. During the Ulbricht era (1960–71) and, later, the Honecker era (1971–89), the discourse of antifascism gradually deteriorated into hollow phrases and empty rituals. Paradoxically, its treatment in film, literature, and the visual arts thrived during this period, with filmmakers turning to antifascism as a powerful tool in the critical reassessment of GDR history and identity, evidence of their own conflicted relationships to the party and the state. As the most visible symbol of antifascism's continuing relevance, the Berlin Wall, also known as "the antifascist protective rampart," was initially welcomed by many intellectuals as an instrument of political stabilization and, consequently, a prerequisite for liberalization in artistic matters. Throughout the decade, writers in particular turned to innovative modernist styles to develop a critical perspective on the legacies of fascism and antifascism and to address the contradictions of everyday life under socialism. However, filmmakers' hopes were soon shattered by the shelving of an entire year's production of DEFA films—called *Regalfilme* (shelved films)—by the previously mentioned Eleventh Plenary. Any critical engagement with antifascism was henceforth marked by a double crisis: the crisis of political legitimization in the aftermath of the Eleventh Plenary and the Prague Spring of 1968 and the crisis of filmic representation brought about by the assault on classical narrative cinema by what is known as the international New Waves.

The exposure to artistically innovative films from France, Britain, Poland, and Czechoslovakia inspired DEFA directors to reevaluate their historical and ideological legacies through a cool, modernist aesthetic of alienation. Its characteristics include stark black-and-white cinematography, atonal sound tracks, elliptical editing, fragmented narratives, episodic structures, and symbolically charged mise-en-scènes. These new sensibilities are in full evidence in the highly experimental and visually stunning *Der Fall Gleiwitz* (*The Gleiwitz Case*, Gerhard Klein, 1961). The directors' frequent use of voice-over and their refusal of narrative closure contributed to the impression of a crisis of political legitimization considered troublesome by some in the Ministry of Culture and the SED leadership. Unfortunately, many of these films failed to reach their intended audiences, further proof of DEFA's difficulties in negotiating the competing demands of artistic innovation, popular entertainment, and political education. The return to political and aesthetic orthodoxy demanded by the party in response to such developments and the audience's preference for formulaic genre films proved to be particularly difficult for directors such as Beyer and Carow who believed in the compatibility of socialism and modernism, often seeking inspiration in the work of fellow socialist filmmakers such as Andrei Tarkovsky or Andrzej Wajda but also addressing issues of subjectivity, memory, and history in ways not dissimilar to the directors of the New German Cinema (e.g., Rainer Werner Fassbinder, Volker Schlöndorff).

While Lukács's pronouncements on the nineteenth-century realist novel as the ideal model for critical realism were used during the 1950s formalism debates to dismiss modernist experimentation as decadent, the canonization in the West of modernism as inherently subversive has sometimes distracted from the affirmative function of formal innovation in the cold war context. In the case of DEFA cinema, this means that uncritical reliance on the realism-modernism opposition has allowed scholars to equate artistic experimentation with political dissent. Just as the ideological effects produced by the antifascist classics in the socialist realist mode were never as uncontested and unambiguous as their detractors claimed, modernist sensibilities never implied automatic opposition to the ideological and institutional structures that relied on antifascism as its foundational myth. On the contrary, modernist strategies and techniques could be used to liberate the affective core of antifascism from the ossifications of cinematic illusionism and to redeem the utopia of socialism through aesthetic experiences; to what degree such rescue attempts had system-stabilizing effects remains an unresolved question in the critical assessment of GDR film and literature to this day.[13]

Under these conditions of discursive instability, the convergence of antifascist narrative and war narrative made possible a fundamental realignment in the established binaries of fascist and antifascist and gave rise to the triangulated identificatory patterns that positioned the Germans, in a marked departure from the Hegelian dialectic, as victim, perpetrator, and victor.[14] The war narrative shifted attention from Nazis to Soviets as the main historical agents and brought into sharper relief the role of the Soviet Union in the history of the antifascist resistance and then-ongoing conflicts inside the Eastern Bloc. Accordingly, just as the tanks moving toward Berlin in 1945 in the post-1965 DEFA films can be seen as prefiguring the Soviet tanks appearing on the streets of Berlin in 1953 and of Prague in 1968, the protagonists' preoccupation with party discipline and their hushed references to Moscow can be read to express very contemporary anxieties about the relationship between the SED leadership and the literary and artistic elites, including filmmakers—a reason to continue this historical overview with a brief digression on the World War II film in the East European context.

The representation of World War II until the 1960s had been limited to antiwar films with a humanist message in the style of Kurt Jung-Alsen's *Betrogen bis zum jüngsten Tag (Duped till Doomsday*, 1957) and brief action-filled episodes in many of the antifascist classics mentioned earlier. Shunning the conventional elements of the war film—action, suspense, and violence—allowed a younger generation of filmmakers to explore the everyday realities of war but also to confront the inherent violence of classical narrative and official historiography. The new openness brought a more critical perspective on German-Soviet relations, the myth of communist resistance, the meaning of national identity, and the future of socialism. On the level of narrative, this revisionist process involved a series of significant shifts in focus, tone, and mode of address: a shift in historical time from the Weimar Republic and the Third Reich to the last year of World War II; a shift in settings from densely populated urban centers to vast, empty landscapes on the eastern front; and a shift in protagonists from a cross-section of social classes and generations to the young soldiers who had been socialized into Nazi society and would become the first generation to achieve adulthood in the GDR. Women—marginal characters from the start, with the exception of the idealized proletarian mother—disappeared almost entirely from the scene. Erotic longing and sexual pleasure had never been part of the affective registers of antifascism; now its masculine ethos became even more pronounced. The complications of heterosexual love were replaced by painful confrontations between disillusioned fathers and fanatical sons. These Oedipal conflicts continued in the encounters between Germans and Soviets on the battlefields and framed the self-understanding of East Germans vis-à-vis the Soviets in similarly dependent and resentful terms. Not surprisingly, the critical reception of the Soviet films about World War II ended up being an integral part of this larger process of emotional and political realignment.

Films about the so-called Great Patriot War helped to establish the artistic credentials of postwar Soviet cinema, affirm the power of the Communist Party after the death of Stalin in 1953, and consolidate the leadership role of the Soviet Union throughout the Eastern Bloc.[15] On the one hand, the objectives of national myth-making prevailed, whether in the story of a simple soldier, "a man of unbreakable will" (to quote the closing words), told in the heroic, pathos-laden *Sudba cheloveka* (*Fate of a Man*, Sergei Bondarchuk, 1959) or the glorification of the Red Army in the monumental Soviet–East German coproduction *Befreiung/Osvobozhdenie* (*Liberation*, Yuri Ozerov and Julius Kun, 1969). On the other hand, World War II provided a framework for the critical reassessment of the aesthetic and ideological foundations that buttressed the Stalinist system. Spurred on by the atmosphere of liberalization after Khrushchev's denunciation of Stalin in 1956, a new generation of filmmakers began to experiment with formally innovative styles inspired by German expressionism, Italian neorealism, and French poetic realism and used the implicit critique of socialist realism to pose difficult questions about history, politics, and identity. Mikhail Kalantosov's *Letyat Zhuravli* (*The Cranes Are Flying*, 1957) and Andrei Tarkovsky's *Ivanovo detstvo* (*Ivan's Childhood*, 1962) were received enthusiastically by audiences in East and West Germany but found a more skeptical reception among SED party officials who were concerned about the effects on the collective memory of the war by what they saw as dangerous subjectivism. Similarly, Polish director Andrzej Wajda challenged the official resistance narrative in his famous war trilogy—*Pokolenie* (*A Generation*, 1955), *Kanal* (1957), and *Popiół i diament* (*Ashes and Diamonds*, 1958)—by refusing to separate the history of the communist resistance from the history of the Holocaust. DEFA filmmakers were profoundly influenced by these revisionist accounts, a process that continued throughout the 1970s and is most evident in the resonances, across aesthetic registers, between Wolf's restrained documentary style in *Mama, I'm Alive* and Larisa Shepitko's almost mystical imageries in *Voskhozhdeniye* (*The Ascent*, 1977).

Together the international New Waves and the Soviet war films contributed to a fundamental realignment in the aesthetic and affective economies of the DEFA antifascist film of the 1960s and beyond. If one were to choose one word to describe its unique quality or mood, it would be melancholia. Despite its heroic tone and epic scale, the antifascist narrative had always been troubled by melancholia and its haunting sense of attachment and loss. The explanation is surprisingly simple: historically, the communists did not just fail to stop the Nazi rise to power; they failed to reach large parts of the German working class and lower middle class that, after 1933, gave their support to the Nazi regime and could only in retrospect be recruited to the cause, namely, through the conversion stories supplied by the antifascist films and their literary equivalents. The military defeat of the Third Reich and the founding of the GDR made it possible to rewrite the antifascist narrative from the perspective of communist victory, but under the conditions of "real existing socialism," a lingering sense of loss remained: loss of the infallibility of communist leaders, the inevitability of history, and the invincibility of the collective as the new site of subject formation under socialism.

While historians over the last two decades have worked toward a more nuanced assessment of the role of antifascism in defining collective memory and organizing public life in the GDR, film scholars until recently have clung to a rather normative definition of the antifascist film that reproduces its preoccupation with convention but sheds little light on the contradictory affects organized by its images and stories. Treating it like an established and immutable genre, they have focused on basic story lines, stock characters, typical settings, and recurring motifs while neglecting its profound transformations from the 1950s to the 1960s, that is, the transition from socialist realism to socialist modernism. Reduced to their ideological functions and effects, individual films have been evaluated primarily in relation to their contribution to official historiography, memory culture, and the creation of a socialist heritage. This focus on normative effects has distracted from the self-reflexive qualities of the late antifascist films—their ability to turn semiotic indeterminacy and significatory excess into an instrument of political critique and their heavy reliance on performance and embodiment as alternative sites of subject formation.[16]

The dependence of the early antifascist film on classical narrative and a realist aesthetic and its modernist transformations during the 1960s make clear that the stranglehold of antifascism over the political imagination cannot be explained through ideological analysis alone; the same may be said about the limitations of purely formal readings when confronted with such historically overdetermined subject matter. Here the notion of political affect—and antifascism must be considered a powerful affect—allows us to shed light on the centrality of emotions to the envisioning of the socialist personality. It shifts the locus of analysis from intended meanings to the kind of subject effects found at the intersection of cinema, aesthetics, and politics. To repeat a point made previously, the notion of political affect engages the entire range of filmic means, including the ones most relevant to the third part of this chapter: acting, camerawork, and mise-en-scène. Embedded in the narrative but not reducible to it, affect thus functions both as a transmission belt between politics and history and as a production site for new political subjectivities and identities.

More specifically, the tension between socialist reality and antifascist ideal and the exclusion of anything that might threaten the desired convergence of individual and collective fantasy left indelible traces in the aesthetic and affective registers of the antifascist film and, for reasons already outlined in the introduction, resulted in its strong affinity for melodrama and its suppressed history of melancholy attachments.[17] Especially the validation of individual pain and suffering in the melodramatic mode conflicted with the collective experiences of oppression remembered in the pathos of history and produced the troubling sense of nonidentity—between story and history—at the heart of melancholy antifascism. In his famous essay "Mourning and Melancholia" (1917), Freud defines melancholia as the unwillingness or inability to give up one's narcissistic attachment to a lost object and to complete the required work of mourning. The internalization of the object through a process of narcissistic identification results in an overwhelming sense of dejection and detachment from the world. Applied to the antifascist film, such an understanding of melancholia acknowledges the narcissistic structures that organized political affects in the GDR and culminated in the impossible love of socialism and the Communist Party; its primacy scene, to use another Freudian term, was the double loss of a beloved leader figure—first Hitler, then Stalin.

Of course, the centrality of melancholia to the antifascist film can be read in two ways: as a symptom of the then-contemporary anxieties about the future of socialism, the approach taken in this chapter, and as a working-through of the memories of the Third Reich and World War II. In her study *Film and Memory in East Germany* (2008), literary scholar Anke Pinkert focuses on the latter by reading the antifascist film in relation to trauma, suffering, and loss and by emphasizing "the productive insights that can be gained from defeat." Consequently, the films for her "provide a language, both critical and empathetic, through which a public feeling of 'postwar melancholia' can emerge."[18] Deciphering this language is particularly relevant for a critical assessment of DEFA's contribution to the current debates on German wartime suffering. For Pinkert this contribution is predicated on the rejection of conceptual hierarchies that denounce melancholia as pathological individual grieving and validate mourning as socially engaged memory work. Claiming melancholy for reparative processes and utopian projects, she locates in the antifascist film, and especially Wolf's *I Was Nineteen*, the beginnings of "a radical ethical stance toward the human, a stance that aims at a postmelancholic imagining of a genuine antifascist public in which historical constellations of shared and differentiated losses are recognized and named through a perpetual commitment of German responsibility."[19]

As my analysis has shown thus far, the affective investments of the antifascist film were always contemporary ones; its primary function during the 1960s remained the affirmation of the socialist subject, even if as a subject in crisis. The films of Beyer, Wolf, and, in very different ways, Kunert and Carow make unmistakably clear that the future, not the past, is at stake in their attempts to redeem the discourse of antifascism through its aesthetic revalidation. As a closer look at their films in the next section suggests, the melancholia that Beyer draws upon through the modalities of melodrama and pathos and that Wolf incorporates through his autobiographical voice and documentary style creates the conditions for a critical but affirmative engagement with antifascism and, ultimately, socialism; in Carow, as we have seen, a similar crisis of meaning culminates in a painful confrontation with antifascism in its very absence.

In ways that have been neglected until now, the appeal of the antifascist narrative is inseparable from filmmakers' personal investments in a thus-defined tradition of political resistance. Wolf and Beyer, the two most prominent directors of the 1960s, were passionate antifascists who believed in the public responsibility of artists to engage with difficult and controversial subject matter; both were also loyal, if sometimes difficult, party members. For Wolf the connection was obvious: "No socialism without antifascism," he declared in 1979.[20] The convergence of antifascist and war narrative allowed Beyer and Wolf to remap the emotional landscape of antifascism, forge new affective bonds, and demonstrate its political relevance to the present. Yet the inherent difficulties in representing wartime violence and suffering also allowed them to affirm their own commitments, Beyer by celebrating the leading role of the Communist Party in the antifascist resistance and Wolf by recognizing the Red Army as the driving force in the military defeat of fascism.

These artistic and political choices cannot be understood without some biographical background information. Beyer (1932–2006), who was socialized into GDR society during the early reconstruction period, studied directing at the

Prague Film Academy (FAMU) from 1952 to 1956. Working for the DEFA studio during the last years of his studies, he quickly rose to prominence, with the (in his words) "unplanned trilogy" of *Five Cartridges*, *Naked among Wolves*, and the lesser-known *Königskinder* (*Royal Children*, 1962) hailed as part of a formally innovative socialist cinema. Beyer benefited greatly from the atmosphere of stabilization and liberalization after 1961 until the banning of *Spur der Steine* (*The Trace of Stones*) in 1966 put a temporary end to his film career.[21] The slightly older Wolf (1925–82) grew up in exile in the Soviet Union, was a young soldier in the Red Army during the liberation of Berlin in the spring of 1945, studied directing at the Moscow Institute of Cinematography (VGIK) in the early 1950s, and remained indebted to the Soviet Union in his choice of topics and themes. As president of the Academy of Arts of the GDR since 1965 and head of the Association of Film and Television Workers since 1967, he served as an important mediator between cultural workers and the nomenklatura and always approached filmmaking as part of a larger political project.[22] Experimenting with expressionist and neorealist styles, he started out by retracing the prehistory of fascism in the Weimar Republic: first through the working-class family saga of *Lissy* and then in an adaptation of his father's play about the political failures of the liberal (Jewish) bourgeoisie, *Professor Mamlock* (1961). The latter film, which followed the German-Bulgarian coproduction *Sterne* (*Stars*, 1959), became the first to recognize the centrality of anti-Semitism to the mass appeal of Nazism and, by extension, a Marxist analysis of fascism. Yet as *Leute mit Flügeln* (People with wings, 1960) confirms, Wolf—under pressure—was fully capable of directing straightforward propagandistic works in the accepted socialist realist style.

The convergence of socialism and cinema in their respective oeuvres can be traced back to the making of *Ernst Thälmann, Führer seiner Klasse*, during which Wolf served as Maetzig's directorial assistant and Beyer as an apprentice on the set. In that film, the role of antifascism in forging affective ties to socialism finds telling expression in Ernst Busch's rendition of the Jarama Valley song from the Spanish Civil War, which functions as an important intertext linking their bodies of work in the 1960s: as part of the extradiegetic film score at the beginning and the end of *Five Cartridges* and then reprised in a profoundly moving scene in *I Was Nineteen* when a concentration camp inmate listens to a recording of the song after his release. At the same time, the two directors' aesthetic solutions to the crisis of antifascism can be distinguished through their very different approaches to camerawork and, by extension, filmic reality. Inspired by neorealism but also referencing the stylized look of expressionism, Beyer and his

Jarama Valley song sequence in *I Was Nineteen*

cinematographer, Günter Marcinkowsky, relied heavily on the expressive possibilities of film—extreme close-ups, chiaroscuro lighting, unusual camera angles, and stagelike sets—to codify a positive iconography of antifascism before its subsequent demontage by younger filmmakers.[23] Meanwhile, taking advantage of his experiences in an army propaganda unit, Wolf's cinematographer, Werner Bergmann, in *I Was Nineteen* and *Mama, I'm Alive* experimented with a documentary or newsreel aesthetic, a style that Wolf had learned to appreciate during an early apprenticeship with Joris Ivens in the Netherlands.

Beyer and Wolf, in short, stand for two diametrically opposed tendencies within socialist modernism that assumed special significance in relation to the antifascist narrative. Beyer's position of emotional affirmation and Wolf's strategy of aesthetic reflection can be characterized through a series of discursive oppositions: celebration of the (male) leader versus deconstruction of the myth of (male) agency, confirmation of the power of the collective versus acknowledgment of the complications of identity, embodiment of the antifascist habitus versus retreat to a position of critical detachment, preservation of the pathos of antifascism versus development of a documentary ethos, and reliance on political allegory versus exploration of the visible world. Accordingly, Beyer's emphasis on pathos, melodrama, and the sublime in *Five Cartridges* and *Naked among Wolves* can be described as a defense against the corrosive effects of melancholy, whereas Wolf's focus on physical reality in *I Was Nineteen* and *Mama, I'm Alive* must be interpreted as a sustained reflection on the consequences of historical loss.

To begin with the question of narrative point of view, Beyer privileges the authoritative position of the communist leader and establishes an omniscient perspective from which to present the dramatic events through the lens of

Marxist orthodoxy. However, he can maintain this perspective only by approaching World War II from its other, extraterritorial spaces, the Spanish Civil War and the Buchenwald concentration camp. Enlisting old Comintern positions and popular-front rhetoric, he uses the vast exteriors of the Ebro Valley and the confined interiors of the camp to make a passionate plea for international solidarity that extends from the heated arguments among the communists in the diegesis to the infusion of the entire mise-en-scène with antifascist pathos and what could be called, in a variation of the fascist sublime, the communist sublime.[24] The central concern in both films is the future of the party as embodied by the old German commissar in *Five Cartridges* and the small Polish child in *Naked among Wolves*.

Significantly, the unity and survival of the antifascist brigade in *Five Cartridges* hinges on a cunning deception by Commissar Wittig: the nonexistent secret fascist deployment plan for the Ebro region. Delivered to its destination despite bitter sacrifices and tragic losses, the message hidden in the five cartridges simply states, "Stay together. Then you will live," a revealing commentary on the Communist Party's modus operandi and the mechanisms of externalization that, as in the friend-enemy distinction known from the anti-Nazi film, facilitate the making of socialist subjectivity. The same question of survival dominates discussions among the communists in *Naked among Wolves* about the Polish child and his potential threat to their plans of an armed resurrection, a process controlled once again by the antifascist father/leader figure played by Geschonneck as a stand-in for the party—and the director.

By contrast, Wolf chooses a narrative position, quite literally between the lines, to express both his love for the Soviet Union and his palpable disillusionment with the GDR. His staging of ambivalence relies heavily on autobiographical elements. *I Was Nineteen*'s first-person narrator, Gregor Hecker, is a German-born soldier in the Red Army for whom the country of exile has become his new *Heimat* (homeland), a choice acknowledged by the director in his loving depiction of Russian music, language, and food. Hecker's first words in *I Was Nineteen*, "*Achtung, Achtung*, German soldiers! . . . The war is finally lost. . . . I am a German," foreshadow his encounters with individual Germans—unrepentant officers as well as civilian bystanders—under the conditions of defeat while also allowing for expressions of empathy and understanding. These opening lines not only establish the first-person narrative as a bifurcated one but also reveal Wolf's own strategy as a filmmaker to make the spectator simultaneously look at a defeated Germany through Soviet eyes and witness the effects of these perceptions on a native-born son—an almost paradigmatic re-enactment of ambivalence. This tension is further complicated by his Jewishness, which is alluded to in the documentary footage with a guard from the Sachsen-hausen concentration camp.

The pervasive sense of ambivalence is even more pronounced in *Mama, I'm Alive*. Here four German soldiers desert their units on the eastern front, undergo political reeducation in an Antifa training camp, join the Red Army, and are sent back as German soldiers for reconnaissance missions behind enemy lines. Once again, their Germanness puts them in a position of conflict and contra-diction. Already the film's title, which refers to a note to be delivered to a mother back home, confirms the primary bonds of family and the power of be-longing. The four deserters inadvertently contribute to the death of a Soviet comrade because they are unable to shoot the Wehrmacht soldiers attacking them; as if to prove the futility of their antifascist training, three of the four die on their first military mission.[25]

The filmic reenactment of ambivalence in all four films brings into sharp relief the directors' different aesthetic and political projects. In Beyer, the origi-nal promise of antifascism is preserved through its instant mythification—the myth of the Spanish Civil War in *Five Cartridges* and the myth of the liberation of Buchenwald by communist inmates in *Naked among Wolves*. Even *Royal Chil-dren* uses an old German poem about unrequited love to legitimate the dis-placement of romantic love into the rituals of German-Soviet friendship. How-ever, this transformation of history into myth requires tightly constructed narrative spaces and carefully controlled auditory regimes. As characters turn into allegorical figures, the image loses its connection to physical reality. Its pri-mary purpose from then on is to deny the possibility of loss and ward off the debilitating effects of melancholia. The resultant tension between the physical-ity of the actors' bodies and the sublime body of the Communist Party pro-foundly reconfigures the meaning of antifascism and, in the end, makes it as much an affective state as an ideological position.

The workings of allegory can be reconstructed through an elaborate mon-tage sequence in *Five Cartridges*. Motivated in the narrative through a Russian Brigadist's desperate search for water, the sequence reveals the underlying pattern of displacements, condensations, and substitutions in almost exemplary form. Conceived as a reflection on the power of the Communist Party, the man's hallucination of water starts a series of superimpositions that equates this precious elixir with the party and elevates communism to the source of all life, as evidenced by the transition from individual water drops and glasses of water to young communists marching and singing in a Moscow parade. The produc-tion of empathy via the physical sensation of thirst is translated into alignment and allegiance with the character and his political choices (i.e., his desire for

Montage sequence in *Five Cartridges*     Montage sequence in *Five Cartridges*

communism). No longer contained within the diegesis, the desired affective and ideological convergence finds its ultimate expression in the historical struggle against fascism.

Further insights into the relationship between the politics and affects of embodiment can be found in *Naked among Wolves*, an adaptation of the famous novel by Bruno Apitz.[26] In the same way that *Five Cartridges* presents a model of international solidarity in times of civil war, *Naked among Wolves* offers a testimony to the survival of the party, here personified by the small Polish child, who arrives with a new transport of Jewish prisoners from Auschwitz and is hidden by the communist inmates. The Nazi guards are acutely aware of the child's existence and his symbolic significance. "Once we have the child, we have the party," they maintain and discuss various strategies for using this knowledge to their advantage, especially in light of the advancing American troops. In the confining interiors of the camp, the antifascist heroes can do little more than argue, debate, persuade, and strategize. Again, it is Geschonneck, himself a longtime communist who spent the war years in various concentration camps, who mediates between those want to get rid of the child because he threatens their underground work and those, like the Mueller-Stahl character, for whom the child embodies the utopian promise of socialism. In the end, kindness and compassion triumph over cold reasoning. The child is transferred to another cellblock and the inmates refuse to divulge his whereabouts even under torture—proof that the party can be both powerful and nurturing.

Through the miracle of this "actual living being," depicted in one scene as if he were a religious relic, the communists' love for the party assumes physical form. The child brings together German, Russian, French, and Polish inmates in shared memories of families back home and poignant affirmations of their humanity. His presence forces the members of the cell to practice key aspects of underground work: political analysis and self-critique, complete reliance on others, and willing cooperation within an existing hierarchy. Most importantly, the child functions as a distraction from their cache of weapons and helps them plan their armed insurrection and much-vaunted self-liberation. In the final sequence, the inmates' overjoyed cries of "Comrades, we are free! Free!" and Mueller-Stahl's soothing words to the child—"Now everything is okay. . . . You caused us so much worry. Don't be afraid!"—can be read as both a celebration of the socialist future awaiting them and an apprehensive comment on the coming challenges for the party.

In Beyer, the possibility of social cohesion and individual agency is predicated on, and guaranteed through, the survival of the Communist Party; in accordance with Freud's definition of melancholia, the narcissistic introjections and projections are still intact. By contrast, in Wolf, it is his personal love for the Soviet Union that colors his filmic approach to World War II but also complicates it through his identity as a German and, though rarely addressed, as a Jew. Both *I Was Nineteen* and *Mama, I'm Alive* avoid the moralistic humanism of the antiwar film in the tradition of Bernhard Wicki's West German production *Die Brücke* (*The Bridge*, 1959). Moreover, Wolf's documentary ethics and aesthetics entail both a critique of and an alternative to the hegemonic claims of antifascism as classical realist text. The difficult balancing act between the mere recording of the visible world and its enlistment in a sustained reflection on history, memory, and identity is duplicated in the tension between the conventions of first-person narrative and the withdrawal of personal perspectives from the mise-en-scène. Precisely this vacillation between the "authenticity of autobiography" and "its authenticity-effect," to cite two different interpretations of Wolf's filmic style, opens up a discursive space for emotions—disbelief, disengagement, and disillusionment—previously excluded from the antifascist narrative.[27]

Not surprisingly, the crisis of antifascism is repeatedly thematized through the problem of language and the difficulty of translation. Choosing a discursive approach, Wolf conjures up a melancholy atmosphere through long silences in the dialogue sequences and minimal use of sound in the documentary sequences. Instead of offering identifiable settings, familiar locations, and logical spatiotemporal transitions, he projects his own sense of dislocation into long traveling shots over wide-open landscapes, empty streets, and abandoned dwellings. Sometimes the numbing silence is compensated for through the introduction of music into the diegesis, especially folk songs and political songs that help to restore the lost connection to tradition. At other times, the back and forth between German and Russian language, often without the benefit of subtitles, suggests a complete breakdown in communication and a failure of translatability whose implications extend far beyond these fictional wartime encounters. Even when translations are given, arguments and misunderstandings often follow. For instance, when Gregor in *I Was Nineteen* tells a young German woman about the horrible acts committed by Wehrmacht troops in the Soviet Union, she responds indignantly, "I don't believe it." He translates her answer for a female fellow soldier as "She can't imagine it," which prompts the Russian woman to angrily reply in German, "Scorched earth!" and the German woman to insist, "I didn't do anything. . . . Not me."

As is to be expected, the problem of masculinity plays a key role in staging the crisis of antifascism and reclaiming its legacy through two very different approaches to screen acting and the dynamics of affect and embodiment. Again, this process can be reconstructed through a comparison between Beyer, who uses the war to fortify the antifascist narrative, and Wolf, for whom the war functions as a catalyst in its critical revision. In Beyer, all-male groups led by older authority figures dominate the historical struggle between fascists and antifascists. Traditional masculinity remains their common currency, and their shared strength is based on the rituals of homosocial bonding and the surfeit of hope and trust that keeps them together. A group's effectiveness is measured by the gestures through which individual members acknowledge organizational hierarchies and make the expected sacrifices for the common good. With classical narrative withering away, the desire for unity and strength can henceforth only be preserved through the affective regimes of the body in pain. Erwin Geschonneck, Armin Mueller-Stahl, and Manfred Krug are the actors most closely identified with this ultramasculine phase in the performance of antifascism.[28]

And, indeed, *Five Cartridges* allows for an intimate exploration of the male physiognomy of antifascism: faces marked by hunger and thirst, eyes lined from lack of sleep and fear of death, but also animated by the belief in the righteousness of struggle and the inevitability of victory. By exploring the nuances in their faces and capturing the physicality of their bodies, Beyer creates a rupture between social type and screen persona, between allegorical charge and bodily presence, and between ideological investment and aesthetic surplus. In staging this rupture, he relies heavily on the affective intensities produced by faces in close-up. Composed as part of an elaborate optical screenplay and shot with a deep-focus twenty-eight-millimeter lens, these close-ups serve highly contradictory functions. The camera's detailed attention to the human face evokes a tradition of filmic realism and cinema culture that has a clear socialist genealogy. In particular, it is early film theorist Béla Balázs's reflections on the face as the basis of a new visual language that connect Beyer's apotheosis of international solidarity to earlier reflections on film as the first democratic mass medium.

Armin Mueller-Stahl in *Naked among Wolves*

Erwin Geschonneck in *Five Cartridges*

Accordingly, the physiognomies of the six Brigadists—a Russian, a German, a Pole, a Spaniard, a Bulgarian, and a Frenchman—are absorbed into the composite face of antifascism and literally become one in their desperate search for water. At the same time, the expressive camerawork, lighting, and mise-en-scène claim their faces for a distinctly Christian tradition, an iconographic debt shared with the West German resistance films of the 1950s. From Mueller-Stahl's chapped lips and bloodshot eyes to Krug's scraggly beard and forehead scar, the close-ups repeatedly evoke the iconography of martyrdom, complete with the Christian symbolism first used in *Rotation* and its close-up of a similarly scarred prisoner of the Nazis.

Beyer's expressive "corporeal semantics" culminate in the dramatic death scene that instantiate Wittig as the quintessential antifascist father/leader figure.[29] The shot-reverse shot pattern moves back and forth between close-ups of the dying commissar, played by Geschonneck, the men of the antifascist brigade, and the points of view from which the spectator is supposed to join their unspoken bond. The final superimposition of all faces within one single frame obliterates the difference in the communist body, to cite literary scholar Julia Hell, between the body's corporeality and the metaphysical sublime.[30] The visual presentation of Geschonneck plays with the notion of the king's two bodies, one rooted in his singular physical existence, the other in his function as an embodiment of the community or state. However, his enlistment in such allegorical functions also invites more-troubling comparisons to a famous character actor similarly engaged in the performance of political power: Heinrich George, Geschonneck's uncanny double and the Ufa actor most closely tied to fascist fantasies of the autocratic or populist leader in the Veit Harlan films *Jud Süß* (*Jew Suess*, 1940) and *Kolberg* (1945) as well as numerous other Nazi propaganda films.[31]

Peter Prager, Uwe Zerbe, Eberhard Kirchberg, and Detlef Gieß in *Mama, I'm Alive*

Jaecki Schwarz in *I Was Nineteen*

In Wolf, these strong male leads are replaced by conflicted and indecisive characters—the kind of young men and adolescent boys often found in the classic antiwar film. Their overwhelming sense of disorientation can be seen in the expressionless faces of first-time actors such as Jaecki Schwarz in *I Was Nineteen* and the cast of relative unknowns in *Mama, I'm Alive*. In accordance with Wolf's documentary aesthetics, his actors appear not to perform at all; in fact, many are not even professional actors. Introducing the generation born during the Third Reich and drafted in the last years of the war, these personifications of troubled or immature masculinity facilitate a gradual opening toward the representation of German wartime suffering. The protagonists' youth makes possible a fundamental questioning of old-fashioned notions of character and personality that still inform the expressive aesthetics of Beyer but give way to the more tentative reenactments of postfascist subjectivity in Wolf as well as Kunert and Carow.

Yet what replaces the ethos of sacrifice and the cult of self-denial that in the films of Beyer still presuppose the unity of character, type, and actor in the performance of antifascism? Not wholesale rejection of this foundational myth but open acknowledgment of the highly personal nature of political commitment and its constitutive elements. In Wolf, no established stylistic register seems capable of overcoming the pervasive sense of powerlessness and disbelief; only the principled refusal of stylization promises a formal solution to the underlying dilemma. The loss of confidence in the antifascist narrative is worked out through the recording of everyday moments, the exploration of landscapes in long takes and traveling shots, the use of voice-over and diegetic music as critical commentary, and the inclusion of real settings and documentary sequences. But, above all, it finds expression in the constraints on emotion that haunt the films' main protagonists. Whether working as an interpreter during the surrender of

German troops at Spandau or interviewing the man in charge of the gas ovens at Sachsenhausen, Gregor in *I Was Nineteen* shows almost no emotions. Only when he loses a comrade does he break down and cry, hiding his face from the camera in the film's only moment of intense emotionality. Numbed by the tedium of warfare, the sudden eruptions of violence, and the ubiquity of death, the first-person narrator performs this problem of unrepresentability to quietly subversive effect—perhaps one of the reasons why the film received such a mixed reception in the GDR.

Meanwhile, the aura of melancholia in *I Was Nineteen* points to an affective inhibition or prohibition that prompts one Soviet general to conclude: "You cannot make politics with emotions." However, in *Mama, I'm Alive*, his assertion is ultimately disproved by the Germans' biographical ties to their *Heimat* and the Soviets' legitimate reservations about these improbable political converts. Antifascists by circumstance, the Germans repeatedly question the effectiveness of the Soviets' political reeducation program and remain unconvinced by the blessings of life under socialism. Unlike Gregor in *I Was Nineteen*, who relies on quiet observation but manages to act decisively nonetheless, the four deserters in *Mama, I'm Alive* are paralyzed by their existence between the lines. They not only fail to overcome the gap separating action from reflection, and individual from collective, but they also no longer have access to the symbolic registers and affective investments associated with antifascism, a problem shared by Wolf's young audiences who at the time questioned the film's relevance. Concludes film scholar Larson Powell: "In a sense, the incomprehension of the four antifascists anticipates that of the younger viewers in 1977 who no longer understood the antifascist narrative."[32]

How, then, does Wolf infuse antifascism with new meanings? By making its discursive crisis the subject of competing interpretations and ongoing discussions. "How to account for Goethe and Auschwitz?" wonders Gregor's friend Vadim in *I Was Nineteen*. The German landscape architect, a self-declared representative of inner emigration, explains the irresistibility of the Nazi movement with reference to German culture, more specifically: the Kantian categorical imperative that describes submission to authority as the highest form of duty and, in his view, led to a frenzy of obedience and violence. Evoking the contradictions of German history, a communist concentration camp inmate, meanwhile, resorts to the standard Marxist line when speaking to his Soviet liberators: "Industry paid him [Hitler], the Reichswehr supported him, all those military cliques, they gave him the power." Nine years later, in *Mama, I'm Alive*, such answers no longer satisfy the real and imagined interlocutors in the diegesis and the motion-picture theater. Now the Soviet officer's essay question to his new students, "How did it come to the German catastrophe and what will lead out of it?," cannot be answered simply by having the Germans exchange their gray Wehrmacht uniforms for the olive-drab uniforms of the Red Army. Aware of this problem, another Soviet officer expresses his frustration over the Germans' lack of political commitment and, in response to one soldier who refuses to participate in their first mission, concludes that, obviously, there are "two kinds of Germans, fascists and antifascists" but, even more troubling, there are also "two kinds of antifascists, those who fight and those who build chairs." Perhaps this casual comment was meant to suggest resigned acceptance of the failure of the antifascist narrative, but perhaps it was included to suggest a different politics of everyday life that at once challenges the antifascist myth and extends its values into the practice of everyday life.[33]

As we have seen in this chapter, the history of antifascism was an integral part of the postfascist imaginary in the German Democratic Republic, but what still requires some recognition—partly in preparation for the next chapter—is its continuing relevance to the political imaginary of the German (and European) Left today. Since German unification, these legacies have become ever more contested and elusive. Recent scholarly reassessments of the GDR's state-prescribed antifascism have fundamentally challenged earlier assertions about a strong communist resistance in the Third Reich and highlighted its primary function as an instrument of social control and political legitimation, especially during the freezes and thaws of the 1950s. Antifascism, some scholars now assert, was nothing but a myth; according to intellectual historian Antonia Grunenberg, its imaginary scenarios were strategically marshaled against fascist (or National Socialist) societies as well as bourgeois democracies with promises of an "ideological and aesthetic intensification of social and political reality" under the auspices of one political party.[34] Of course, what such assessments forget or deny is the reality of antifascism as lived experience and political identity for an entire generation of German communists and GDR citizens.

In the same way that the friend-enemy distinction organized through the label "Nazi" (or neo-Nazi) has become a convenient rhetorical device in the increasingly rancorous political debates in the United States, antifascism's polarizing worldview has contributed to its enduring attractiveness to left-leaning and alternative groups, prompting some conservative scholars to call antifascism "the grand delusion of the German Left."[35] Providing a historical model of resistance to nationalism, capitalism, and imperialism, antifascism in the Federal Republic of Germany played a key role during the student movement of the 1960s and the left-wing radicalism of the 1970s. When the GDR was about to disappear as a state, East German writers and intellectuals such as Christa Wolf as late as November 1989 insisted, "We still have time to recover the antifascist and humanist ideals from which we once started."[36] Even today, social activists and leftist politicians from the PDS (Party of Democratic Socialism) use the rhetoric of antifascism to present their struggles against social injustice, economic inequality, and political oppression as part of a longer tradition of resistance that started well before the Third Reich.[37]

Contained within this discursive trajectory and crucial to its continuation despite the end of the GDR and the death of communism are the political affects that, in this chapter, have been approached through the notion of melancholy antifascism. As aesthetic productions, the antifascist films continue to bear witness to this affective history of leftist utopias, including their failures and losses; therein lies their most important contribution to a now-unified history of German cinema. Yet political resistance represents only one category through which to articulate the relationship between fascism and socialism and to measure the relevance of antifascism for emancipatory political movements today. As the next chapter shows, an equally important one is the specter of fascist sexuality that propelled the West German student movement of the 1960s to pursue their project of sexual liberation against the presumably repressive sexual politics of historical fascism and orthodox communism. At the same time, it found expression in a series of highly controversial art films about fascism and sexuality and a short-lived exploitation genre known as Naziploitation produced in postfascist Italy during the 1970s.

# 4

# Between Art and Exploitation

## Fascism and the Politics of Sexuality
## in 1970s Italian Cinema

You herded, feeble creatures, destined for our pleasure.
Don't expect to find here the freedom granted in the outside
world. You are beyond reach of any legality. No one knows
you are here. As far as the world goes, you are already
dead.

Paolo Bonacelli as the Duke in *Salò* (Pier Paolo Pasolini, 1975)

In her influential 1974 essay "Fascinating Fascism," Susan Sontag formulated this chapter's central question in the following way: "Much of the imagery of far-out sex has been placed under the sign of Nazism. Boots, leather, chains, Iron Crosses on gleaming torsos, [and] swastikas . . . have become the secret and most lucrative paraphernalia of eroticism. . . . But why? Why has Nazi Germany, which was a sexually repressive society, become erotic?"[1] Her answer? Because the aestheticization of master-slave relationships derives its rituals, fetishes, and iconographies from what she calls a natural link between fascism and sadomasochism and their shared dependence on the performative staging of sexuality. In the same year, Michel Foucault could barely hide his disgust and contempt when he wondered why the Nazis, those "shabby, pathetic puritanical characters, laughably Victorian old maids, or at best smutty individuals have become the symbol of eroticism." His hypothesis: that the 1970s marked "the beginnings of a re-eroticization of power" but in the realm of politics proper and not, as Sontag seems to suggest, only in sexual practices.[2]

Significantly, both comments on fascism and sexuality were made in response to changing approaches to Nazi imagery in visual media, and film in particular, a change that signaled a fundamental shift from the conventional forms of character engagement suggesting perfect congruence between classical narrative and ideological interpellation to the simultaneously more visual and more visceral effects found in a cinema of weak identifications and unclear investments in the history represented. The specter of "sexy Nazis" or what Christopher Clark, in an appropriately ambiguous phrase, calls "desiring Nazis" also haunts a group of 1970s Italian feature films set during the Third Reich but inextricably linked to the discourses of Fascism (i.e., Italy under Mussolini) and fascism (i.e., as a generic term).[3] These films contributed significantly, and often shockingly, to the project of historical revisionism by confronting fascism's libidinal sources through the lens of sex and violence and by relying on strategies of secularization rather than the formal registers heretofore reserved for such difficult subject matter (Lukácsian) nineteenth-century realism and (Brechtian) early-twentieth-century modernism.[4] As part of a larger shift in historical sensibilities identified by Jean Baudrillard as *mode rétro* (retro style), the art films in that group share a pronounced sense of nostalgia and loss: loss of the certainties of history and ideology but, as I argue, also nostalgia for the dreams of absolute power and total control promised by Nazism but now accessible only through scenarios of erotic domination and submission.[5] Nowhere are the close connections between the loss of ideology as the organizing principle of twentieth-century European history and the loss of classical narrative as the foundation of mainstream cinema more apparent than in the fascist mise-en-scènes staged in the shadow of the international New Waves and that revolutionary moment known as "1968." And no European cinema goes quite as far as the Italian one in compensating for the disappearance of the master narratives offered by cinema and ideology with the denunciatory equation of sexual and political deviancy and its almost compulsive reenactment across the aesthetic divide marked by the famous art films and the infamous exploitation films.

From the perspective of today, Sontag's and Foucault's comments sound strangely dated, a product more of that decade's liberationist fantasies than a qualified engagement with Nazism as a historical phenomenon. But even as our own investment in the fascist imaginary has moved from sex and violence to questions of ethics—with the Nazis now primarily seen as the embodiment of evil—the original questions remain highly relevant, not least for our discussion of political affects: What are we to make of films that, like fascism itself, engage contradictory physical sensations—of pleasure and pain, arousal and disgust—in order to restage the dynamics of sex and death inside the camp as the model of what Giorgio Agamben calls the state of exception?[6] Do these films uncover the sexual nature of political affects mobilized by fascism, or does fascism function primarily as a theatrical mise-en-scène for addressing then-contemporary concerns about the abuses of state power and the threat of bio-politics? Under what conditions is fascism evoked as a sexual *dispositif*, to use another Foucauldian term, and transformed into what comparatist Andrea Slane calls "a metaphor for sexual relations in general"?[7] And as part of which discursive traditions is the sexualization of fascism achieved through the association with (repressed) homosexuality?

Understanding the sexualization of fascism requires us, first of all, to acknowledge the inadequacy of narrative analysis in "making sense" of the films' visual regimes and visceral effects. Instead of focusing on what these films mean, we need to focus on what they do. This can be achieved by expanding the definition of political affects beyond the emotions of the characters in the narrative and the modes of character engagement situating the spectator within the diegesis toward the aesthetic pleasures and cognitive effects gained from the formal and stylistic qualities of film as such. These forms of affective and ideological interpellation confirm the distinction made by cognitive film theorist Carl Plantinga between affects as bodily states—that is, felt physiological responses—and emotions as concern-based construals, with the latter requiring a higher degree of cognitive processing; in fact, the films' shock effects illustrate well what he calls the gatekeeper function of disgust.[8] Their transgressive images are inseparable from the economics of sensation and stimulation shared by what film scholar Linda Williams calls "body genres," including the admixture of arousal and fear (*Angstlust*, in Freud's term) created at the intersection of porn and horror.[9] However, in the larger historical context that makes disgust a particular political reaction formation, the production of powerful affects through sexualized imagery cannot be reduced to sexual terms as the ultimate truth about the subject or a bodily reaction unmediated by culture or politics. Instead, the scenarios of abjection that inform this process of sexualization force us to recognize the centrality of violence to the sexualization of fascism and to consider the particular function of horror and disgust as historically specific strategies of detachment and disengagement. The question is, of course, from what? The answer: from an ideologically based definition of the political of which the Nazis—and, as its generic equivalent, fascism—have become a privileged signifier in mainstream cinema.

As I argue on the following pages, it is the spectacle of what Spanish philosopher Eduardo Subirats calls totalitarian lust that translates the experience of the political into sexualized scenarios but then uses these very scenarios to represent that process as primarily, if not exclusively, sexual.[10] As a result, the coupling of fascism and sexuality becomes a means for acknowledging both the enduring attraction of fascism as a system of total control and the necessity for postfascist societies to contain this threat, namely, by identifying it with deviant sexuality. The sexual politics that take the place of the ideological master narratives of anti-Nazism and antifascism prevalent during World War II and the cold war must therefore be read as an attempt to expand the meaning of the political toward the pleasures of the body and to show the limits of any claims about freedom, equality, and the rule of law through confrontation with democracy's greatest enemy: fascism. In the films discussed in this chapter, Nazism/fascism subsequently comes to stand in for the state of exception described in the introductory quote from *Salò* as the founding moment of any totalitarian regime and perpetuated through its absolute power over life and death.[11]

The 1970s Italian films I discuss highlight the central role of the fascist imaginary in managing the contradictory affects surrounding Nazism, fascism, antifascism, and communism at a particular crisis moment in postwar European democracies. Conceived under the influence of 1968 and its radical politics of desire, the series started with Luchino Visconti's *La caduta degli dei* (*The Damned*, 1969) and inspired several highly controversial films that include Liliana Cavani's *Il portiere di notte* (*The Night Porter*, 1974), Lina Wertmüller's *Pasqualino settebellezze* (*Seven Beauties*, 1975), and, with very different interests outside the purview of this study, Pier Paolo Pasolini's *Salò o le 120 giornate di Sodoma* (*Salò, or the 120 Days of Sodom*, 1975).[12] These well-known filmmakers used the intersection of power and sexuality to highlight postwar Italy's complicated relationship to the fascist *ventennio nero* (i.e., the two black decades, 1922–43) and to confront the return of political violence and fascist tendencies in the unsettling *anni di piombo* (the leaden years of 1973–78). While working in different aesthetic registers, all four directors believed that an uncompromising exploration of power, violence, and sexuality would expose the truth about fascism and, by extension, illuminate the changing terrain of the political after 1968.

The directors' presentist approaches shed important light on the changing status of the Third Reich and the Holocaust as historical referents. Precisely because the films remain haunted by the images of war and genocide, their sexualized imagery ultimately blocks access to historical knowledge and political insight. In the retro style, the representation of history is reduced to a self-referential system of signification, revolving around images of images, that reproduces, on the level of emotions, affects, and sensations, a historically specific crisis of the master narratives: one reason why the contributions by Visconti, Cavani, and Wertmüller (unlike that of Pasolini) have not stood up well to the test of time. Whereas the Hollywood anti-Nazi films served a clear propagandistic purpose during World War II, and the West and East German films about Nazism/fascism played a key role in the ideological divisions of the cold war, the Italian films of the 1970s used the sexualization of power to challenge traditional definitions of democracy as based on free deliberation and rational choice. Furthermore, they relied on the aestheticization of violence to show visual spectacle and spectatorship as essential to the production of political affects in totalitarian and, perhaps, democratic societies as well. Consequently, the filmmakers' decision to focus on the Third Reich represents less an unwillingness to deal with Italian Fascism and its legacies than an acknowledgment that the Nazis had by then already become a ubiquitous media phenomenon—a shifting signifier whose discursive status is thematized in the diegesis through the self-referential use of images (e.g., paintings) and technologies of vision (e.g., cameras, binoculars). The opening sequence of *Seven Beauties*, which features Hitler and Mussolini together in a series of newsreels, directly addresses this interchangeability, with "fascism" henceforth denoting the terror of ideology as such and with "the Nazis" providing the protagonists, costumes, and settings for restaging the historical failure of democracy in the present.

Controversially received, censored, or banned, the films by Visconti, Cavani, Wertmüller, and Pasolini pushed the limits of the acceptable in European art cinema, but similar explorations continued in a short-lived wave of low-budget, low-quality films known as Naziploitation, Nazi porn, or, in Italian, *sadico nazista*. These films appropriated the cultural decadence of *The Damned*, the stylized psychodrama of *The Night Porter*, the grotesque humor of *Seven Beauties*, and the Sadean epistemology of *Salò* for a sensationalist mixture of horror and porn denounced by many critics as Holocaust pornography. Together both groups of films bring into sharp relief the conflicting forces behind the short-lived Italian engagement with "fascinating fascism," and the function of "sexy Nazis" in the global branding of Nazism more generally—reason enough to use the bifurcated perspective of art and exploitation cinema to reconstruct these constellations against the backdrop of 1970s Italian political culture and its preoccupation with history, sexuality, and ideology.

In developing such a contextualized reading, I depart from prevailing approaches in three significant ways. First, instead of maintaining the cordon sanitaire that separates the art films from the Naziploitation films, I read both as part of the same discursive appropriation of fascism, of which its sexualization is only the most visible manifestation. No longer distinguished based on bourgeois criteria of quality and taste, both types of films can be located more productively within a specifically European strategy of product differentiation, shared by the masterworks of auteurist filmmaking and the examples of Eurotrash or Eurosleaze that during the 1970s relied heavily on sexuality as a marker of cultural commodification and an instrument of political critique.[13] Second, instead of using close textual readings to weigh in on the continuing controversy over the films' subversive or exploitative qualities, I emphasize their function as repositories of historically specific thoughts and feelings about politics and sexuality to be located in post-1968 debates about the demise of antifascism, the crisis of communism, and the rise of neofascism. Third, instead of focusing on what are either highly convoluted or barely developed story lines, I examine the films' affective politics through the bodily affects, inscribed in the obligatory scenes of rape, torture, and murder, through which characters as well as spectators are compelled to become part of a highly contradictory discourse about fascism as an experience of sexualized violence and a symptom of sexual degeneracy.

While the convergence of sex and violence was made possible by the dynamics of art and exploitation that haunted European filmmaking in the 1970s, their function as a political fetish—standing in for something (i.e., ideology), the loss of which needs to be disavowed—takes us once more to the beginnings of the fascist imaginary in the Hollywood anti-Nazi film and its representation of sexual violence as a symptom of totalitarian desire. Already a cursory look at a selection of posters confirms that many Poverty Row studios advertised their films through the same lurid scenarios later found in the Naziploitation films; only then, the obligatory SS man's sexual assault on an innocent woman was used to illustrate the threat to American freedom and democracy. As we have seen in chapter 1, Nazi masculinity during the 1940s was frequently depicted as deficient or perverted, for instance, through its association with elite culture, yet its full deviancy assumed center stage only after the rise in the 1960s of Freudo-Marxism as the dominant mode of leftist political analysis and critique.

To further complicate matters in relation to Italian film history, restaging the fascist attractions may have allowed Visconti, Cavani, and Wertmüller to break with the legacies of Italian neorealism, including its postwar claims on the resistance narrative. Yet their sexualized imagery remained very much

under the influence of its main representative, Roberto Rossellini, whose implicit equation of normative heterosexuality and democratic subjectivity produced such problematic figures as the gay Gestapo chief and his lesbian co-
conspirator in *Roma, città aperta* (*Rome, Open City*, 1945) and the Nazi pedophile in
*Germania anno zero* (*Germany Year Zero*, 1948); his *Il generale della Rovere* (*General Della
Rovere*, 1959) addressed the dynamics of Nazism and antifascism in similarly
ambiguous terms. With the simultaneous demise of neorealism and antifascism
as dominant political and aesthetic discourses, the threat of deviancy in the
1970s eventually extended into the entire audiovisual field, resulting in a proliferation of ambiguity and perversity and a crisis of referentiality that infected
all aspects of filmic representation. Whereas the verismo of Rossellini still enlisted melodramatic elements in the identification of a political position clearly
marked as antifascist, the new retro styles no longer offered a space outside the
rituals of domination, subordination, and violence that the fascist imaginary
had become.[14]

   In the larger context of this book, the Italian films of the 1970s represent a
crucial moment in the postfascist imaginary when democratic subjectivity
could no longer be produced through the kinds of political confrontations and
ideological differences that sustained the friend-enemy distinction from the
1940s to the 1960s. As the clearest indicator of this crisis of signification, the defenders of democracy disappear almost entirely from the diegesis; there is no
more "us" versus "them" except in the terms of spectatorship, which means the
terms of abjection. Under these conditions sexuality emerges as a privileged
space for acknowledging the continuing attractions of fascism while controlling
such attractions through their pathologization. Through the association of
sexuality with violence and death, the spectacle of fascism in these films reenacts
what it cannot become under democratic conditions: compelling, overwhelming, and deadly. Accordingly, it is in the dynamic of attraction and revulsion
and the continuous process of abjection that we must locate the political affects
mobilized by Visconti, Cavani, and Wertmüller through their dystopian vision
of a postfascist, post-Marxist, and, from the perspective of contemporary claims
about the end of ideologies, postideological world. The fetishization of Nazi
iconography in the retro style and the equation of political and sexual deviancy
in the figure of the Nazi as (repressed) homosexual play a decisive role in this
almost compulsive process of demarcation and externalization. As in previous
chapters, I will examine these elusive connections in a three-part fashion: a
reconstruction of the discursive constellation marked by the terms Fascism,
Nazism, and fascism in 1970s Italian culture and society, especially in relation
to the politicization of sexuality; an analysis of the sexualization of fascism in

the critically acclaimed art films of Visconti, Cavani, and Wertmüller; and a discussion of the surprisingly similar thematization of sex and violence in exploitation films almost universally reviled as Naziploitation.

Approaching the sexualization of fascism as a historical phenomenon and discursive effect means acknowledging the centrality of the myth of antifascism to postwar Italian politics and society. As in West and East Germany, the heated debates over Fascism and its place in national history, memory, and identity played out against the backdrop of postwar normalization and the Italian equivalent of denazification, *defascistizzazione* (defascisticization).[15] The desired bracketing of Fascism as "a parenthesis in Italian history," to quote influential philosopher Benedetto Croce, was achieved through the myth of the resistance of 1943–45, the equation of resistance with antifascism, and the depiction of Italy as a victim of *nazifascismo*, an impossible concept that captures perfectly the semiotic shifts rehearsed by Visconti, Cavani, and Wertmüller in their films. Conflating these two terms had two contradictory effects. On the one hand, the emergence of fascism as a transhistorical category seemed to confirm leftist paranoia about the rise of neofascism and its promotion of national capitalism as a defense against the emerging neoliberal world order. On the other hand, the retro perspective played into efforts by Renzo De Felice, Italy's leading historian of Fascism, to emphasize the differences between Fascist and Nazi ideology and, in the process, reclaim some positive aspects of Italian Fascism as a broad middle-class movement from what apologists described as its cooptation by the dictatorial Mussolini regime.

Italian studies scholar Claudio Fogu identifies three phases in the changing meaning of Fascism in postwar Italy: from 1946 to 1960, the historicization of resistance as a second *risorgiomento*, that is, the realization of the national unification movement of 1848 under the conditions of modernization; from 1960 to 1974, the ascendancy of Marxist orthodoxy and its equation of antifascism with communism; and from 1974 onward, the disintegration of the Left during a period of civil war, terrorist violence, and political sectarianism. The erosion of antifascism "as the founding ideology of the republic" during the 1970s resulted in a renationalization of the memory of antifascist resistance, with the figure of the communist partisan replaced by the ordinary peasant and soldier, and it undoubtedly contributed to its resurrection—as a return of the repressed—in the Brigate Rossi (Red Brigades) as a self-styled permanent resistance movement.[16] Meanwhile, in the cinema, the effects of sexual liberalization and what film scholar David Forgacs describes as a gradual lifting of restrictions on historical memory, including of the Holocaust, came together in films that profoundly changed the terms of historical representation by redefining the personal and the political based on what he calls "the fascism-perversion equation."[17]

The sexualization of fascism occurred during a decade of civil unrest and political violence, mass strikes and demonstrations, and political kidnappings and assassinations referred to earlier as the traumatic *anni di piombo*. The historical compromise in 1973 between the ruling DC (Democrazia Cristiana, Christian Democrats) and the influential PCI (Partito Comunista Italiano, Italian Communist Party) under Enrico Berlinguer gave the Communists more political influence, especially on the local level, but also contributed to the disintegration of the European Left after the Prague Spring of 1968, a moment that, as shown in chapter 3, resonates deeply in some of the DEFA antifascist films. The challenges to Marxist theories of fascism posed by new social movements, including the women's movement and a variety of autonomous groups, further diminished the PCI's control over the postwar narrative of antifascist resistance and its significance to the management of political affects after the demise of historical Fascism. Meanwhile, neofascist parties such as MSI (Movimento Sociale Italiano, Italian Social Movement) returned to the national stage by aligning themselves with ultraconservative groups, reason for some leftists, including Pasolini, to express grave concerns about the new alliance of neofascism and neocapitalism—what cultural historian Robert Lumley, in anticipation of Agamben's analysis of the state of exception, refers to as Italy's historical states of emergency.[18]

These years of mass mobilization must be seen as a collective effort to at once work through and move beyond the legacies of the *ventennio nero*, but in this volatile mixture of sexual revolution and political violence, Fascism's hatred of democracy and politics of violence returned with a vengeance in the form of leftist terrorism. Like the RAF (Rote Armee Fraktion, Red Army Faction) during the German Autumn of 1977, the Red Brigades carried out a series of bombings, kidnappings, and assassinations, including of DC Prime Minister Aldo Moro in 1978. Left-wing terrorism relied on some of the same arguments that had given rise to the Fascist movement, including the belief in the ethos of radicalism and the possibility of revolution, the justification of violence as a political means (with its attendant disregard for individual lives), and the search for a more authentic mass movement and radical political culture. The crisis of democracy and the assault on the state contributed to a general distrust of ideologies and a subsequent retreat from politics in 1978–80, a period known as the *anni di silenzio* (years of silence). While the old Left became increasingly marginalized, feminist, gay rights, and alternative movements embraced the new politics of subjectivity and, through their hedonistic celebration of alterity as political resistance, affirmed the centrality of individual desire to social change and political life. Looking back at that decade, Wertmüller in 1985 described *Seven Beauties* as a product of this historical moment and its "misjudgments/errors arising out of the logic of violence, the errors arising out of the logic of vitalism," a reference that in her film finds telling embodiment in the figures of the socialist and the anarchist.[19] To what degree the art and exploitation films participated in the attendant process of depoliticization cannot be determined without analyzing the configuration of fascism and sexuality as part of even larger realignments in the sexual *dispositif* itself.

Choosing the 1970s as the point of departure from which to reconstruct this process means to confront the sexual myths of the 1968 generation and to question their heavy reliance on a heady mixture of Marxist theory and Freudian psychoanalysis. In Western Europe, and West Germany in particular, the sexual revolution had been based on two premises: that fascism was the product of a repressive sexual morality and that, in light of the political failures of coming to terms with the Nazi past, a complete break with fascism could be achieved only through a liberated sexuality. The problem of political oppression was thus displaced into that of sexual repression and the possibility of political resistance rearticulated on the level of pleasure, desire, and the imagination.

As historian Dagmar Herzog has convincingly shown, the Nazis were not as repressed sexually as their children wanted them to be, and the rebellious students were much more sexist than their antiauthoritarian posturing and liberationist rhetoric would let us believe.[20] To be sure, scholars have long speculated about the erotic dynamic between the Führer and the masses and pointing to the sexual nature of symbols and rituals as important aspects of Nazi ideology. In the postfascist need for developing further such connections, and to do so primarily for political reasons, we find one explanation for the enlistment of sexual deviancy in the representation of political deviancy. For in advocating sexual liberation as a form of political liberation, the Italian radicals relied heavily on the writings of Wilhelm Reich and Herbert Marcuse, both refugees from Nazi Germany, who focused on sexual repression as a key to understanding the mass appeal of fascism. Two seemingly contradictory lines of argumentation can be traced back to their work in American exile: the equation of democratic subjectivity with heterosexual genital sexuality in Reich and the equation of emancipatory politics with polymorphously perverse eroticism in Marcuse. Whereas Reich's analysis of the homosocial structure of the Nazi party and state served to legitimate the denunciatory equation of fascism and homosexuality, Marcuse's analysis of the reproduction of the structures of political oppression in the bourgeois family lent support to the celebration of sexual transgression as political dissidence.

As is well documented, the enlistment of psychoanalysis in the postwar management of sexual and political deviancy—first in the United States and later in Western Europe—played an important role in the cold war, but in less obvious ways, it also helped to seal the fate of Italian communism, namely, through the ascendancy of Freudo-Marxism. Not surprisingly, the sexualization of the postfascist imaginary and its homophobic undercurrents can be traced back even further: to the involvement of German sociologists and psychologists in research sponsored by OSS (Office of Strategic Services) on the sociopsychology and psychohistory of Nazism, including Hitler's presumably deviant sexuality; to the studies by Adorno and others on the authoritarian personality and its affinities with repressed homosexuality; and to reflections in early Critical Theory on modernism, homoeroticism, and fascism, with Walter Benjamin's analysis of the aestheticization of politics in fascism in the famous "Work of Art" essay now returning to postwar cinema as the aestheticization of politics in the retro style.[21] The implications, in terms of post-1945 cold war thinking and post-1968 leftist melancholy, are clearly spelled out in Adorno's scandalous assertion that "totalitarianism and homosexuality belong together."[22]

Calling desire a key to understanding fascism, literary critic Laura Frost in her compelling analysis of canonical modernist texts from the 1920s and 1930s (F. M. Marinetti, Ezra Pound, D. H. Lawrence) maintains that "antifascist, democratic culture has substantial, unacknowledged libidinal investments in fascism that need to be explored."[23] But if the sexualized imaginary of fascism in early twentieth-century literature was closely linked to the crisis of humanism, individualism, and bourgeois culture, how are we to read the very different post-Holocaust confrontations with fascism as the absolute other of democracy? Moreover, what are we to make of the continuities that link the (homo) sexualization of fascism in the modernist imagination, including its flirtation with authoritarian power, to the more perverted scenarios of cruelty, violence, and self-destruction in the postmodern retro scenarios? In what ways has homo-fascism, to use a term coined by literary scholar Andrew Hewitt, "facilitated the reappropriation of the unimaginable to the terms of the political imaginary, that has served, in other words, to represent the unrepresentable"?[24] If, as Frost and Slane argue, the function of the fascist fantasy is to articulate problems of modern democracies in sexual terms, how are we to interpret the remarkable flourishing of sexualized fantasies of fascist power as pathology

during the 1970s? In what follows I propose that we untangle these relationships by considering violence as the primary scene in the sexualization of fascism and, rather than argue about the films' subversive or exploitative nature,
focus on the ways in which they reproduce the equation of sexual and political
deviancy that came to Italy via German exile scholars in the United States.

The coupling of fascism and sexuality in Italian art cinema produced two
iconic figures that perfectly embody this unsettling equation of political and
sexual deviancy. In 1969, the famously dandyish Helmut Berger in *The Damned*
made a spectacular entrance as Lola Lola from *Der blaue Engel* (*The Blue Angel*,
Josef von Sternberg, 1929). Attired with the fishnet stockings, black corsage, top
hat, and feather boa first featured by Marlene Dietrich in her performance of
Friedrich Hollaender's "Kinder, heut' abend, da such ich mir was aus," Berger
sang of his need for "a man, a real man" and, in this quintessential moment of
gender masquerade and late Weimar decadence, captured the sexual ambiguity, moral depravity, and cold cynicism that has distinguished "sexy Nazis" ever
since. In 1974, an unsettlingly androgynous, topless Charlotte Rampling in *The
Night Porter* dressed up as an SS officer, complete with breeches, suspenders,
and black officer cap to perform another Hollaender song made famous by
Dietrich, "Wenn ich mir was wünschen dürfte." Its tone of melancholy yearning captured perfectly the blurring of boundaries between masculinity and
femininity, heterosexuality and homosexuality, during the hedonistic 1970s, including through a renewed interest in scenarios of domination and submission.

*The Damned* recounts the rise of the Third Reich through the fall of the wealthy
Essenbeck family, loosely modeled on the Krupp steel-producing dynasty and
in full awareness of their own homosexual scandals.[25] Beginning with the 1933
burning of the Reichstag and the 1934 Night of the Long Knives, depicted here
in excessive detail as a homosexual orgy and a political massacre, the story
presents the Nazi infiltration of German society in starkly Oedipal terms. In an
interview, Visconti explained his interest in the Essenbecks through a revealing
analogy that compared the great melodramatic potential of Nazism and the
allegedly minor affective registers of Fascism to that of tragedy versus comedy,
or opera versus operetta.[26] For a filmmaker known for his extravagant opera
productions, the choice was clear: Nazism offered a more thrilling spectacle of
power and desire. In restaging history in melodramatic terms, Visconti relied
heavily on the new perspectives on the Third Reich developed under the influence of Freudo-Marxism; hence the Marxist focus on the alliance of Nazism
with big capital, the use of the Freudian family romance as a key to larger political struggles, and the emphasis on the sexual body as a site of hidden social

Helmut Berger in *The Damned*                    Charlotte Rampling in *The Night Porter*

tensions. At the same time, his nostalgia for the life-world of the aristocracy and his celebration of high culture in the moment of its demise undoubtedly played into the equation of Nazism with modernization and the denunciation of modernism as fascist also found in Pasolini's *Salò*.

All these elements come together in the figure of the highly neurotic Martin von Essenbeck (Helmut Berger), who shares the diagnosis of deficient masculinity with his older rival for the affections of his mother, Sophie (Ingrid Thulin), the social climber Friedrich Bruckner (Dirk Bogarde), and who, under the influence of the cold Nazi bureaucrat Aschenbach (Helmut Griem), eventually overcomes his masochistic tendencies by integrating them into the sadistic practices authenticated by the Nazi state. As in Bernardo Bertolucci's adaptation of the Alberto Moravia novel *Il conformista* (*The Conformist*, 1970), becoming a fascist (or, in his case, a Nazi) means acquiring a self; it means drawing on the surplus of aggression, subservience, and self-loathing associated since Critical Theory with repressed homosexuality. Martin develops this new persona by acting out his sexual perversions: first, by molesting young girls and, in the end, by committing incest with his mother and then forcing her and her new husband to kill themselves with poison. Throughout the protective armor of the SS uniform provides him with a surrogate identity and a fantasy of masculinity. Unlike SA man Konstantin, a petit bourgeois man felled by his lust for power and pretty young men, Martin uses the uniform to disguise his desire for submission and to channel his anger and resentment. With such characteristics, he becomes the model of fascist masculinity for many Italian films and, through the star appeal of Berger, a symbol of the eroticism of the European art film of the decade, reason to look briefly at the conditions of production that made possible the sexualization of fascism in the 1970s.

Visconti and his colleagues developed a self-consciously European cinema of quality entertainment, reminiscent of the Film-Europe movement of the late 1920s, in response to the difficult economic realities after the collapse of the studio system.[27] Their independent production model favored on-location shooting with smaller cameras, fewer light sources, and faster, highly light-sensitive film stock—all crucial to the previously mentioned retro style. Other features included the extensive use of zoom lenses with variable focus as a form of narrative commentary and spatial dislocation, the warm sepia tones and de-saturated color space of then-popular Eastman film stock, and the lush film scores, beautiful costumes, and elaborate set designs used in recreating "Europe" as a fantasy of cultural refinement, political crisis, and sexual licentiousness. Addressing educated, sophisticated, and mature audiences, their films often had to deal with censorship problems, which were then cited as proof of their artistic significance.[28] *The Damned* was released in the United States with an X rating, the feared withdrawal from Italian exhibition of *The Night Porter* resulted in a one-day strike in the film industry, and *Salò* was banned immediately after its scheduled release.

The sexualization of fascism in accordance with the filmic conventions of the retro style is inseparable from its commodification in the making of European art cinema and, as we will see later in the chapter, exploitation cinema. Promoted as a commercially viable alternative to the conventional Hollywood productions and formally innovative New Wave films, the European art film specialized in literary adaptations, biographical films, and historical films that acknowledged sexual desire as a driving force of human behavior and relied on well-known actors to promote a more "enlightened" approach to sexuality and eroticism. *The Damned,* for instance, featured British Dirk Bogarde and Charlotte Rampling, German-speaking Helmut Berger and Helmut Griem, and Swedish actress and Ingmar Bergman muse Ingrid Thulin. Taking full advantage of the inevitable transnational and intertextual effects, *The Night Porter* presented Bogarde and Rampling as the central couple, whereas the soft-core *Salon Kitty* (Tinto Brass, 1976) once again brought together Berger and Thulin. With postsynchronization the norm in Italy, *The Damned* and *Seven Beauties* were dubbed into Italian and German, *The Night Porter* into Italian and English, and *Salò* (like *Salon Kitty* an Italian-French coproduction), dubbed into Italian, French, and German—industry practices that contributed to the transformation of "fascinating fascism" into a multilingual, transnational, and highly profitable European brand.

Using the same production model, Cavani in *The Night Porter* follows the long shadows of fascist power and sexuality into the postwar period, to 1957 Vienna. There former SS officer Maximilian Adolfer (Dirk Bogarde) works as a night porter at the Hotel zur Oper when he recognizes his special "little girl" from the concentration camp in the elegant Lucia Atherton (Charlotte

Rampling), the wife of an American conductor on a European tour.[29] Max is part of a group of ex-Nazis who meet regularly to eliminate evidence implicating them in war crimes, including witnesses who are to be "filed away." Their version of the Freudian talking cure aims at forgetting and repression; to quote one of the members: "We must try to understand whether we are victims of guilt complexes or not and, if so, we must be free of them." Soon Max and Lucia resume their relationship in a *folie à deux* that mimics the performative, consensual dynamics of domination and submission. Their memories of the camp as a transgressive space trigger a series of flashbacks that, even in those introduced from Lucia's perspective, place the woman as the object of desire and the spectacle of suffering. Hounded by the Nazis, the couple retreats to Max's apartment where—trapped, exhausted, and ravenous—they reenact their haunting past before seeking a sacrificial death in the very costumes that defined their relationship in the camp: as SS officer and Max's "little girl."

"Max has imagination," notes one of his Nazi friends, a reference to his sadistic medical experiments and extensive film recordings in the camp. His obsession with visual evidence gives rise to what might be described as an allegory of (fascist) cinema as inherently sadistic, with the analogies between spectatorship and violence a recurring theme in all the films discussed in this chapter, but the relationship between spectatorship and knowledge also draws attention, once again, to the problem of masculinity and, ultimately, of castration as a central preoccupation of the Naziploitation film. Working as a night porter because of "his sense of shame in the light," Max is the personification of (the theory of) the fascist sadist as repressed homosexual. In humiliating, abusing, and torturing Lucia, he punishes the masochistic tendencies within himself and reproduces the heterosexual violence against women in the ritualistic acts prescribed by sadism. His need, quite literally, to shine a light on people and turn them into performers in a fascist fantasy of omnipotence is evident already in his strangely intimate relationship with a gay Nazi dancer, his double not only as a character but also as an actor with a similar gestural style coded as "queer." The connection between the performance of masculinity and what Cavani presents as its narcissistic (i.e., homosexual) origins is developed further in Rampling's appearance as an SS officer—that is, as Max's mirror image—in the "Wenn ich mir was wünschen dürfte" number. Even the Salome reference, with the dead prisoner's head suggesting castration as the symbolic condition shared by Max and Lucia, confirms that the woman, whether under coercion or of her free will, participates in the game of domination and submission only in two disguises: as a little girl or an SS man.

The structural inequality in a relationship inaccurately described by many scholars as sadomasochistic—inaccurate because of the consensual nature of S&M—is established on the level of spectatorial relations. The identification of the narrative perspective with Max's point of view finds telling expression in his aggressive handling of the camera, whereas Lucia's unfocused, empty gaze at no point allows for an alternative point of view. However, if their relationship nonetheless resembles a sadomasochistic game, then it is only because of the spectator's visceral reactions to Max's obvious sadism and more hidden masochism, resulting in a vacillation between empathy with his victim's suffering and contempt for her weakness but also contributing to the highly ambivalent relationship to the perpetrator familiar from the horror genre and its own scenarios of abjection.

More than any other film from the period, *The Night Porter* has raised vexing questions about the function of Nazism in highly sexualized scenarios of domination and submission. At the time of its release, the film was hailed in Italy but attacked in the United States, with critics denouncing it as "political pornography" and "fascist propaganda."[30] Cavani's various comments in interviews at the time only added to the controversy. On the one hand, she recounted stories of Holocaust survivors haunted by their experiences and compelled to relive their traumas in order to conclude, "Lucia and Max show the fundamental face of Nazism, the cold exhibition of a rational violence perpetrated on the individual." On the other, she spoke of her desire simply to "analyze the limits of human nature at the limit of credibility," which for her meant the master-slave dynamics found in all relationships; only during wartime, she elaborated, "the State monopolizes the sadomasochistic energy of its citizens, provokes it, and legalizes it. One may become a victim or an assassin within the law."[31] In the extensive feminist scholarship, early attacks on *The Night Porter* for blurring the boundaries between victim and perpetrator have since given way to effusive praise for Cavani's reevaluation of female masochism as part of a larger critique of patriarchy and heteronormativity. While some scholars have accused *The Night Porter* of reducing "fascism to sadomasochistic theatrics," others have praised its masochistic shattering of the body in the traumatic encounter with the real.[32] However, how Cavani's reduction of fascism to an abstraction, "a figural exploration of forms" and "cold exhibition of a rational violence perpetrated on the individual," achieves such subversive effects without partaking in the commodification of fascism—and, through such symbolic arrangements, the equation of fascism with homosexuality—remains a question yet to be answered.[33]

The controversy over *The Night Porter* continues to this day in sharp disagreements over its representation of female sexuality. Feminist scholars of Italian cinema, most notably Kriss Ravetto in *The Unmaking of Fascist Aesthetics* (2001), tend to read the films of Cavani as well as Wertmüller as an uncompromising exploration of sexual desire and a radical deconstruction of gender binaries. Her close readings show how the films not only reveal sexuality as a performance and masquerade but also interrogate the political function of other gendered binaries (e.g., of pleasure and pain) in the fascist and postfascist imaginary. Intent on undoing the discourse of fascism, *The Night Porter* and *Seven Beauties*, according to Ravetto, frustrate the desire for narratives of redemption and "question the construction of a dialectical narrative as a means of perpetual separation of the subject of history from what is considered abject."[34] By contrast, the so-called neodecadents, among whom she lists Visconti and Bertolucci, allegedly fall back on conventional binaries as they seek to preserve a position of political legitimacy through the othering of evil. In restaging fascism as power in decline, the latter identify its representatives with femininity or homosexuality—a form of othering that, in my view, also informs the contributions of Cavani (and Wertmüller) to the 1970s discourses of politics and sexuality outlined earlier.

Further insights into the alleged deviancy of fascism—and, by extension, the deviancy of ideology tout court—can be found in a film that, at first glance, does not fit into my larger argument because it privileges the Italian perspective and features a man in the position of the victim: *Seven Beauties*. Yet as soon as we see the almost compulsive identification of Italian masculinity with heterosexuality as a direct response to the equation of political and sexual deviancy in the figure of the sadistic Nazi, we can discern the same strategies of rejection, exclusion, and externalization, that is, of abjection—the feeling of horror but also fascination caused, in Julia Kristeva's words, by "what disturbs identity, system, order. What does not respect borders, positions, rules."[35] Once again, this process takes place through the body of a woman: the female camp commandant allegedly inspired by "the bitch of Buchenwald," Ilse Koch, and played in all her terrifying corpulence by Shirley Stoler.[36] Through the spectacle of the grotesque female body, Wertmüller shows the discrepancy between the lofty rhetoric of Nazi ideology and the violence and horror of the camp. Confronted with this embodiment of the monstrous feminine, the typical Italian male is called upon to assert himself: through his machismo and preoccupation with sex, his mother fixation and contempt for women, and his well-developed survival instinct and complete lack of convictions. Pasqualino, played with much gusto by comedian Giancarlo Giannini, is a small-time criminal from Naples who lands in an insane asylum after committing a gruesome murder. Caught raping a female inmate, he is released as a volunteer to the front and eventually captured by the Germans and put in a concentration camp. After the end of the war, he returns home to his prostitute sisters and girlfriend and, as a survival strategy, vows to have a large family. "You are alive," he reminds himself, "yes, I am alive," with his woeful gaze into the camera a tacit recognition of the burden of guilt, complicity, and *maschilismo* that would continue to haunt postfascist Italy.

Modeled on the cunning *furbo* character, the quintessential survivor of the *commedia dell'arte*, Pasqualino embodies the art of accommodation that, according to the film's satirical reenactment of a much-mocked national character trait, allowed the Italians to resist the attractions of ideology and, presumably, never to be real Fascists in the first place. The identification of Nazism with deficient masculinity or its counterpart, monstrous femininity, indirectly confirms the myth of Fascist virility and the uniqueness of *mussolinismo*. As the absolute other of "Italian fascism as a discursive formation whose principal model of articulation is virility," Nazi masculinity can be bracketed as a projection of the social body that has nothing in common with the innate strength, spirit, and vitality of the Italian people.[37] Wertmüller stages this belated victory of the Italian will to life over the Nazi will to power through a series of flashbacks that forever separate the average Italian from the morbid preoccupations of the Third Reich. Relying on the antirealist effects of the grotesque, she advocates a political position associated with anarchism, that is, of insolence, disrespect, and the tone of self-deprecating mockery established by Enzo Jannacci in the opening song addressed to "The ones who say 'Now let's all have a good laugh.' Oh yeah. Oh yeah" and confirmed by Pasqualino in his sarcastic description of life as "a rotten comedy, a lousy farce called living."

All these elements come together in the infamous seduction scene when Pasqualino finds himself alone with the female commandant and is forced to service her sexually. The staging of the scene is a model of stylistic exaggeration: from the ghastly green, red, and blue tones and the deliberate use of props such as boots, whip, stick, and a swastika-adorned carpet to the spatial juxtaposition of Stoler and Hitler (in the photograph) with Venus and Cupid in Bronzino's famous allegorical painting *Venus, Cupid, Folly, and Time* (ca. 1545). Constructed around low-angle points of view that emphasize his diminishment and her enormous size, the entire scene functions as a reenactment of male castration anxiety. Her admonition, "If you don't fuck, you're finished," triggers a flashback sequence in which Pasqualino, first as a young boy and then a grown man, is repeatedly swallowed up by women's fleshiness and insatiable desires.

Shirley Stoler in *Seven Beauties*          Giancarlo Giannini in *Seven Beauties*

To the tune of Zarah Leander's "Ich weiß, es wird einmal ein Wunder gescheh'n," he declares his undying love for the commandant and, after receiving some food, manages to produce the erection necessary for penetration. Her response is more than telling: "Your thirst for life disgusts me," she grumbles and concludes that, faced with such strength of survival, "we [the Nazis] who thought to create a master race are doomed to failure."

In order to understand the superiority of Italian virility celebrated in such scenes, we must take into account the larger intellectual and cultural formation in which sexual deviancy came to stand in for political deviancy; for that reason, we must once again return to the historical context, but this time through the lens of film authorship. All the directors mentioned thus far worked through the complicated relationship of fascism and sexuality in order to affirm or revisit their own political commitments. Predictably, these commitments break down along generational and gender lines and, in the case of Visconti and Pasolini, are troubled by a long history of leftist homophobia. Visconti (1906–76) was a semi-closeted Marxist aristocrat who had been a member of the resistance, and Pasolini (1922–75) a lifelong communist with a complicated relationship to the PCI, having been expelled in 1949 because of homosexual acts. By contrast, Wertmüller (born 1928) openly professed anarchist sympathies, whereas Cavani (born 1933) presented herself as a heretic opposed to all ideologies, including feminism.

Moreover, Visconti and Cavani came to the history of Nazism and Fascism through a long-standing interest in German culture and society. Visconti conceived *The Damned* as part of his German trilogy, the Thomas Mann adaptation *Morte a Venezia* (*Death in Venice*, 1971) and *Ludwig* (1972), about the mad king of Neuschwanstein, with the tension between Eros and Thanatos and the theme of homoeroticism a constitutive element in all three films. Before *The Night Porter*, Cavani in the 1960s had made several documentaries about the Third Reich and women in the resistance for public television; she completed her

German trilogy with *Al di là del bene e del male* (*Beyond Good and Evil*, 1977), about a love triangle involving Friedrich Nietzsche and Lou Andreas-Salomé, and *The Berlin Affair* (1985), about a diplomatic ménage à trois set in the Nazi capital. By contrast, Wertmüller located the question of Fascism within an identifiably Italian context. Working early on as an assistant for Federico Fellini, she set out to expose its historical legacies through the subversive qualities of the theatrical tradition of *commedia dell'arte* and the critical potential of *commedia all'italiana*, that is, film comedy Italian style. Nominated for four Academy Awards, including Best Director, *Seven Beauties* became part of a group of four Wertmüller films starring Giannini, the personification of southern backwardness and political incorrectness, that include the impossibly long-titled *Film d'amore e d'anarchia . . .* (*Love and Anarchy*, 1973).[38]

For the three directors discussed in greater detail here, aestheticization offered an effective strategy for re-creating the fascination of fascism while maintaining critical detachment: through melodrama in the case of Visconti, psychodrama in Cavani, and the grotesque in Wertmüller. To what degree this approach exposed them to fascism's attractions and made them complicit in postmodern denunciations of modernism remains an unresolved question. Visconti, Cavani, and, in very different ways, Pasolini all relied heavily on the discourses of modernism and modernity to articulate the relationship between sexuality and violence and, more specifically, to link fascism to homosexuality. To give a few examples, *The Night Porter* contains a veritable tour de force through the formally innovative and politically contested architecture of New Vienna, including several buildings by Otto Wagner and his students.[39] From the Alexej Jawlensky painting in *The Damned* and the Otto Dix painting in *The Night Porter* to the gallery of modern art (Lyonel Feininger, Ferdinand Leger, Gino Severini, Marcel Duchamp) shown in *Salò*, modernism art is invariably denounced as fascist, a point confirmed in the last film by excerpts from Ezra Pound's *Cantos* and Carl Orff's *Carmina Burana* on the soundtrack. Tracing the genealogy of fascist modernism back to the nineteenth century, *Seven Beauties* meanwhile makes what by now must be considered obligatory musical references to Richard Wagner that include the "Ride of the Valkyries" and the *Liebestod* motif from *Tristan* (i.e., in the "Dreams" song). And time and again, characters can be heard quoting Nietzsche, a tradition that continues even in the Naziploitation films and requires us to consider such intertextual references—and the implicit denunciation of nineteenth-century father figures—in light of the Oedipal scenarios shared by the art and exploitation films.

And indeed, Visconti, Cavani, and Wertmüller rely heavily on Oedipal conflicts in explaining the male characters' sexual and political deviancy, from the mother-son incest in *The Damned* to the mother fixation in *Seven Beauties* to the father-daughter dynamic in *The Night Porter*. Yet since the exercise of power involves more than a sexual game, it might ultimately prove to be more productive to enlist the Marquis de Sade rather than Freud in considering the political significance of aligning fascism so closely with homosexuality as the entry into, or the marker of, a wider range of perversions. After all, all main protagonists are, to use the correct terminology, paraphiliacs: Martin in *The Damned* is a pedophile, and Max in *The Night Porter* is a sadist, as are the concentration camp commandants and female doctors in the Naziploitation films. By contrast, the libertines in *Salò* are partial to sodomy, which, as Pasolini reminds us, is not the same as homosexuality. Violence is the language shared by all, and their need, or desire, to inflict pain and suffering on others finds expression not in the dialogic structure implied by sadomasochism but in the singular exertion of one individual's or group's will over others who are silenced or obliterated in the process. Not surprising given the extensive reception of de Sade's work during the 1970s, via Georges Bataille and Pierre Klossowski, the famous libertine provides the source text for *Salò* and functions as an unacknowledged reference point in the other films. Moreover, his description of private vices as "the anticipatory historiography of public virtues in the totalitarian era" allows us to link the sexualization of power and violence to the crisis of liberal democracy, individual freedom, and the Enlightenment project that, through the specter of "sexy Nazis," haunts the entire series, from *The Damned*'s nostalgia for the aristocracy to Naziploitation's fixation on the camp as a model of the totalitarian state.[40] For, as Gilles Deleuze reminds us in his essay on coldness and cruelty, sadism is inseparable from institutional power: the sadist, after all, does not torture a willing victim.[41] This insight allows us finally to exit the argumentative loop of fascism as sadomasochism as fascism that haunts much of the scholarship on Cavani and focus more specifically on the political affects organized by the spectacle of violence.

The acknowledgment of violence as the *tertium comparationis* of fascism and sexuality is central to the Naziploitation films to be discussed in the final section of this chapter. Known today primarily to aficionados of exploitation cinema, these films fully realize what the art films only allude to, the reduction of fascism to the production of bodies in pain. Their low production values allow us to ignore the barely developed stories and characters and concentrate on the powerful affects produced at the intersection of two body genres, horror and porn. Body genres, to follow the definition by Williams, violate the conventions of classical narrative and its dependence on aesthetic distance in order to produce bodily excess: sex in porn, violence in horror, and emotion in melo-drama. All body genres rely heavily on the bodies of women as "the primary embodiments of pleasure, fear, and pain."[42] The Naziploitation films, in particu-lar, facilitate the encounter of two kinds of bodies: the controlled and control-ling male body and the body of the female other, which invariably means the body in abjection—fleshy, weak, injured, violated, tortured, and dead. Yet in-stead of placing the spectator on both sides of the process of abjection, namely, through sadistic identification with the perpetrators and masochistic identifica-tion with the victims, the Naziploitation films preclude all forms of character engagement and make the entire world of the film the object of revulsion and, ultimately, expulsion from history and narrative. In so doing, the films give rise to a political fantasy about fascism as the abject of ideology itself, a perspective that informs the films by Visconti, Cavani, and Wertmüller but that is acknowl-edged openly only in the debased terms of Naziploitation.

The 1970s were not only formative years for the European art film but also the golden age of exploitation cinema, with Naziploitation violating not one but two taboos: the social taboos regulating the filmic representation of sexual-ity and the ethical and aesthetic taboos surrounding fascism, Nazism, and the Holocaust. In the standard usage of the term, exploitation refers to blatantly commercial films produced with minimum investment for maximum effect. Covering the range from horror and science fiction to underground and soft-core porn, these films are sought out by audiences for their shock value, which means their strong visceral effects. Traditionally identified with bad taste, the category has more recently been reclaimed for an oppositional aesthetics and countercultural sensibility. Film scholars have discovered exploitation as a use-ful category for tracing the conversion of a particular representation into an increasingly devalued signifier of power, sexuality, and violence that started out in the context of art cinema, thus confirming Paul Watson's point that "*all* cin-ema is, to a greater or lesser extent, exploitation cinema."[43] As the most blatant manifestation of a triple crisis—in the Italian film industry, in the modes of historical representation, and in the discourses about fascism, antifascism, and neofascism—this process culminated in a group of films that, stripped of all artis-tic ambition and aesthetic value, display the underlying ideological realign-ments with glaring obviousness.

The majority of Naziploitation films were produced in Italy, the epicenter of exploitation cinema and, together with France and Spain, a main player in European coproductions during the 1970s.[44] Production companies operated outside the old studio system and, like the pretentiously named SEFI (Società Europea Films Internazionali) Cinematografica, approached the subject matter in accordance with the same economic principles of exploitation applied to horror films and spaghetti westerns. The films' low production values are evident in the cheap but gaudy sets and costumes, the unabashedly bad acting, and the many technical flaws (camerawork, lighting, sound). A small group of writers-directors-producers ventured briefly into Naziploitation: Cesare Canevari, the director of *L'ultima orgia dell III Reich* (*Caligula Reincarnated as Hitler/The Gestapo's Last Orgy*, 1976), who also made white slavery films; Luigi Batzella, the director (as Ivan Katansky) of *La bestia in calore* (*SS Hell Camp*, 1977), who started out with *Django* imitations; Sergio Garrone, the director of *Lager SSadis Kastrat Kommandantur* (*SS Experiment Love Camp*, 1976), who specialized in the women-in-prison genre; and Bruno Mattei, the director of *Casa privata per le SS* (*SS Girls*, 1977) and *KZ9 — Lager di sterminio* (*SS Extermination Love Camp*, 1977), who also dabbled in nunsploitation. A true believer in profit maximization, Mattei shot the two last films simultaneously, with some of the same sets and actors; meanwhile, Batzella for *SS Hell Camp* reused entire sequences from an earlier antifascist partisan film, *Quando suona la campana* (*When the Bell Tolls*, 1970).

A product of the deflationary trajectory that started with art films such as *The Damned* and continued with hybrids such as *Salon Kitty*, Naziploitation has been analyzed as "an extreme process of devolution" and "late capitalist recycling."[45] These films constitute what, in Italian, is sometimes called a *filone* (thread) or spinoff, a group of popular films with the same thematic focus, held together by the "centrifugal motion of a larger object that lets loose some of its smaller components or by-products."[46] Thus, if *Salon Kitty* represents a soft-core remake of *The Damned*, *SS Girls* can be described as a hardcore remake of *Salon Kitty*, with the Wallenberg figure returning as the equally neurotic camp commander Schellenberg. *Caligula Reincarnated as Hitler* reproduces the victim-perpetrator dynamic from *The Night Porter*, complete with flashback structure and final *Liebestod* scene. Last but not least, *SS Hell Camp* offers a low-budget version of *Seven Beauties*, with the Stoler character now split into a beautiful female and a grotesque male part. In light of these considerable similarities, the difference between art and exploitation must be located elsewhere, namely, in the latter's unsettling merging of porn and horror, its primary focus on violence, and its turn to revulsion as the most important bodily affect.

Like the art films, the exploitation films (e.g., spaghetti westerns, nunsploitation, sword-and-sandal films, slasher films) were a product of the steady decline of the Italian film industry after the collapse of the studio system in the 1960s.[47] Several factors contributed to this systemic crisis of cinema: growing competition with private television after RAI (Radiotelevisione Italiana) lost its broadcasting monopoly in 1975; a national exhibition circuit dominated by the

Dirk Bogarde and Charlotte Rampling in
*The Night Porter*

Daniela Poggi in *Caligula Reincarnated as Hitler*

Hollywood majors with their big-budget productions and a regional exhibition circuit reserved for smaller exhibition companies and homemade popular genres; and the diminished significance of moviegoing as a national pastime after the introduction of video home recording systems (VHS, Betamax) and, more generally, the continuing diversification of mass media and popular entertainment.

The appearance of more sexually explicit subject matter in motion-picture theaters occurred in response to this increased competition with television and home video, but the simultaneous liberalization of censorship rules and social conventions concerning pornography must be seen as a result of the post-1968 spirit of sexual freedom and antiauthoritarian rebellion. Whereas the educated elites watched *The Night Porter*, *Seven Beauties*, and *Salò* in the new art houses located in the metropolitan centers, enjoying their erotic provocation through the optics of cinephilia, the Naziploitation films openly catered to prurient interests and reached their core audience in the seedy theaters near railroad stations frequented by a largely young, male audience of subproletarians. The degree to which Naziploitation, in a very roundabout way, may also have channeled simmering anger in response to social or racial discrimination can only be surmised through comparison to another exploitation genre, blaxploitation, which in *The Black Gestapo* (Lee Frost, 1975) contributed an American perspective with its references to the black power movement.[48]

Confirming the centrality of Hollywood to the commodification of Nazism, the *Urtext* (i.e., original text) of Naziploitation is in fact an American production, *Ilsa, She Wolf of the SS* (Don Edmonds, 1975). Modeled on *Love Camp 7* (Lee Frost, 1969), the first women-in-prison film set in a Nazi prison camp, *Ilsa, She Wolf of the SS* features buxom blonde bombshell Dyanne Thorne as a concentration camp guard. She performs sadistic medical experiments on female

Poster for *Caligula Reincarnated as Hitler*

Poster for *Ilsa, She Wolf of the SS*

prisoners to prove women's physical superiority while castrating male prisoners who fail to satisfy her insatiable sexual appetites.[49] With her black breeches, tight white shirt, leather boots and gloves, signature SS officer cap, and riding crop and gun holster, Thorne is the embodiment of the dominatrix or phallic woman. Confirming the origins of fascist violence in male castration anxieties, the phallic woman returns in Naziploitation's cruel lesbian wardens and female doctors in the style of SS Doctor Ellen Kratsch (Macha Magall) of *SS Hell Camp*. Unlike the Stoler character in *Seven Beauties*, whose grotesque body evokes the monstrous maternal, Thorne and her more restrained Italian imitators threaten male privilege through their active participation in the subjugation of female prisoners through medical experiments, rape, torture, and murder.

*Ilsa, She Wolf of the SS* also established a convenient model for incorporating extradiegetic references to the Third Reich and Holocaust and, in so doing, "justifying" the use of the Nazis as free-floating signifiers of sexuality and violence. Relying on legitimization strategies known from early sexual hygiene films, Edmonds in the film's preface begins by vouching for its historical accuracy, "The film you are about to see is based upon documented fact" (i.e., the existence of Nazi brothels), and then ends with a truly offensive gesture toward

Holocaust remembrance: "We dedicate this film with the hope that these heinous crimes will never occur again." Such pseudo-arguments stand behind the frequent inclusion in the Italian Naziploitation films of newsreel footage, voice-over commentary, as well as diegetic references to war and resistance and explain Garrone's self-presentation (on the DVD extras of *SS Experiment Love Camp*) as a Holocaust educator providing audiences with a cathartic experience, if not an exorcism of the horrors of the past.[50]

Nonetheless, in the same way that the short-lived popularity of the pornographic Israeli Stalag fiction in the early 1960s coincided with the Eichmann trial, Naziploitation remains inextricably tied to Holocaust memory and more contemporary manifestations of biopolitics, including the post-1968 shift to sexuality as a privileged site for social and political struggles. To repeat a point made earlier, this does not mean that Naziploitation is "about" the Third Reich or the Holocaust. In this exploitative economy of signs and significations, the Holocaust merely provides the liminal condition of referentiality through which the tensions between arousal and fear, pleasure and disgust, and attraction and revulsion are organized and put to maximum effect in the exorcism of past and present Italian traumas. Beginning with the question of gender, it is always women who in Naziploitation are placed in the position of the Jews, a connection made most explicitly in *Caligula Reincarnated as Hitler* and *SS Experiment Love Camp*, where the inmates wear yellow armbands (but without the Star of David). While the division between victim and perpetrator does not follow gendered lines—note the many female doctors—the equation of sexual and political deviancy in the Nazis remains predicated on the image of abjection embodied by their female victims. The obligatory scenes of rape, torture, and murder translate the politics of extermination into sexual terms; under such conditions, anti-semitism and genocide return to filmic representation in the most extreme manifestations of misogyny and sexual hatred.

Based on the numbers format known from hardcore porn, the sex scenes in Naziploitation usually include heterosexual genital, anal, and oral sex, female masturbation and lesbianism, threesomes and orgies, as well as whipping, paddling, suspension, bestiality, and so forth. In a marked departure from conventional porn, all sexual acts are performed under conditions of inequality and coercion; they are always presented as part of, and invariably lead toward, that other scene: the scene of horror, violence, suffering, and death. Moreover, the presentation does not follow the standard sequence of arousal and release, and the prevailing mode of spectatorship is defined less by the desire to look than the terror of visuality itself. For this reason, can we even classify Naziploitation as pornography? As defined by Williams, pornography is "the visual (and sometimes aural) representation of living, moving bodies engaged in explicit, usually unfaked, sexual acts with the primary intent of arousing viewers."[51] While partaking in "the frenzy of the visible" that in hardcore requires the obligatory meat and money shots (i.e., erection and ejaculation), these films offer only simulated intercourse and the kind of gendered scenarios that require full female nudity but leave most of the men dressed at all times.

Whether in the brothel, the laboratory, or the camp, the women are ritualistically subjected to a series of abuses that serve to demonstrate the absolute power of their tormentors. Typically SS officers and their female assistants select a group of young, attractive women who are forced to provide sexual services as a way of advancing the cause of racial science (*Caligula Reincarnated as Hitler*), sustaining the troop's fighting morale (*SS Experiment Love Camp*), and, less frequently, exposing traitors among the military ranks (*SS Girls*). The stories have a predictable pattern: arrival and initiation, examination and selection, followed by medical experiments and various sex and torture scenes. One beautiful woman usually attracts the attention of the male commandant or his female assistant; sometimes a sympathetic doctor or guard rescues her. In the apocalyptic endings, she either suffers a sacrificial death or escapes as the sole survivor, while the camp and its officers vanish in a deadly inferno: a belated indictment of war and genocide that, like the didactic preambles, serves to neutralize the audience's feelings of horror and disgust.

Naziploitation manages the constitutive tension between porn and horror by moving back and forth between two locations: the commandant's villa and the concentration camp. The villa—part plush Victorian boudoir, part medieval hunting lodge—functions as a brothel, with the women portrayed as voluntary participants in the debaucheries. By contrast, the camp, with its laboratory and torture cellar, marks the site where the logical progression from sex to death takes place. While the orgies suggest the primacy of sexual pleasure, the medical experiments reveal power as the ultimate thrill. Inside these hierarchically organized spaces, however, the assertion of normative heterosexuality follows a much more complicated pattern. The inmates, while forced to perform female sexuality in the Nazis' sadistic games, remain unambiguously heterosexual in their illicit camp romances. By contrast, the gendered representation of Nazi power is predicated on the crisis of male heterosexuality, and the cruel treatment of the inmates presented as either a struggle against sexual inadequacy or a manifestation of sexual deviancy. Illustrating the latter point, the female doctors or wardens are beautiful but scarred women whose cold, rational demeanor suggests both lesbianism and feminism. When competing with that special inmate for the commandant's attention, these cartoonish versions of the phallic woman always lose out—their punishment for embodying the threat of castration (i.e., loss of sovereignty) that underlies all scenarios of violence and abuse.

The commandants are usually depicted as fanatical, sadistic, and neurotic men. As in *The Damned* and *The Night Porter*, Nazi masculinity is coded as highly cultured, aristocratic, and narcissistic: in other words, as homosexual. Not only does the men's narcissism prevent them from enjoying the rewards of male power, but their submissive disposition also makes them unable to claim the privileges of true virility reserved for the two mythical figures that remain absent from representation, the resolutely heterosexual Italian fascist and his equally manly counterpart, the antifascist. In their objectification of women, the commandants merely act out what they perceive as the inherent violence of heterosexuality. They rarely participate in their own orgies and prefer the fetishism of Nazi symbols and uniforms and the sublime rewards of classical music or philosophy. In *SS Girls*, Schellenberg experiences his most orgasmic moments playing Bach on his organ and dressing up as a bishop with swastika-adorned miter during a court-martial of disloyal officers. In *SS Experiment Love Camp*, Colonel von Kleiber, who prefers Beethoven, suffers quite literally from the trauma of castration, having lost his testicles to a Russian woman on the eastern front; he later forces a Jewish surgeon among the prisoners to transplant the missing parts from an unsuspecting German soldier. Even the hypermasculinity of Commandant von Starker in *Caligula Reincarnated as Hitler* only hides his masochistic tendencies. Torture for him is an act not of self-assertion but of self-renunciation, which accounts for his extreme sadistic tendencies and his unconscious identification with his female victims—reason enough on the final pages to think of what art historian Silke Wenk calls the pornographization of the Nazi regime not only as an attempt, in her words, to fix the truth of history, but also to displace the political provocation of Nazism into sexualized terms.[52] Described in that way, art and exploitation represent merely different aesthetic strategies for achieving the same highly contradictory effect: direct confrontation with the spectacle of totalitarian lust and denial of its political dimensions through their translation into gendered terms, a process achieved in the affective regimes of abjection.

The division of labor between art and exploitation, which we have established as constitutive of the mode of production in 1970s Italian cinema, found its most telling expression in a film that attempted to partake in both and ended up as a prime example of pornographic kitsch: *Salon Kitty*. Written and directed by Tinto Brass, *Salon Kitty* was the most expensive and ambitious of the dozen Naziploitation films made between 1976 and 1978, right after the Paris Film

The fascist orgy in *Salon Kitty*                    Projections of Hitler in *Salon Kitty*

Festival premiere of *Salò*, and is well suited to summarize the main points made
in this chapter. The film openly cites *The Damned* in its casting of Berger and
Thulin, its story of a dysfunctional aristocratic family, and its heavy reliance
on performative excess. With a cabaret/brothel as the main setting, *Salon Kitty*
also references *Cabaret* (1972), Bob Fosse's famous adaptation of Christopher
Isherwood's *Berlin Stories* and its clichéd images of Weimar sexual decadence
and political crisis in the style of George Grosz and Otto Dix. What distinguishes the 1976 Brass production and all later Naziploitation films is the focus
on sexual violence as the primary means and measure of a dictatorial regime.
The director, best known for his involvement in the infamous *Caligola* (*Caligula*,
1979), spoke openly of his reliance on disgust in generating powerful sensations
and affects: "I am a surgeon. I make an incision, plunge deep, extirpate. The
tumor always turns out to be power. . . . Power is monstrous. Power is the monster."[53] And this monster, Brass seems to suggest, has to be confronted and
exorcised through sexual violence.

   *Salon Kitty* is set in a high-class Berlin brothel frequented by the political,
military, and diplomatic elites and used by the SS for intelligence gathering
during World War II. The main character of Wallenberg (Helmut Berger) is
based on Walter Schellenberg, who was put in charge of the operation by Heydrich.[54] Twenty young women are selected, prepared, and trained for work in
the service of Nazi racial theory; their initiation culminates in an almost clinical
scene of sexual gymnastics that draws heavily on the pseudo-classical imagery
of the cultural film *Wege zu Kraft und Schönheit* (*Ways to Strength and Beauty*, Wilhelm Prager, 1925) and the cult of strength and beauty in Riefenstahl's famous
documentary of the 1936 Olympic Games, *Olympia* (1938). However, Wallenberg's plan to use sexuality as an instrument of political control becomes viable
only after he enlists the services of Madam Kitty (Ingrid Thulin) in turning his
superior racial specimens into high-class prostitutes. The various sexual numbers
that make up the women's second initiation at once evoke the iconography of

the brothel as a utopian space and show its infiltration by the competing fantasy of total control, with the transformation of political subjects into sexual objects completed under the conditions of total surveillance. In the Nazi-run brothel with its sound-recording devices, the pornographic gaze subsequently becomes an extension of the power of the totalitarian state.

The initiation scenes in the training camp and the brothel point to fetishism, and its attendant laws of commodification, as the missing link between the film's parasitic reproduction of fascist aesthetics and the parading of "sexy Nazis" for cheap titillation. The importance of production design in creating this fetishistic scenario is most apparent in the opulent, spectacular art deco sets by Ken Adam, otherwise known for his work on the early James Bond films, and his extensive use of mirrors as symbols of political narcissism in particular. Pushing stylization to the point of campy parody, the figure of Wallenberg realizes his fascist fantasy in a world of great luxury: wood-paneled salons with leather sofas and oriental rugs, vast marbled offices filled with Nazi sculptures and paintings, and ornate Nazi fantasy costumes and paraphernalia. High culture is ubiquitous in the homage to classical music in the diegesis and the film score and the obligatory Nietzschean meditations on power and evil. Notwithstanding the endless displays of female nudity and the romantic subplot involving one of the prostitutes and a German officer, the decidedly queer Wallenberg remains the film's central attraction: vamping it up in front of the mirror, strutting around in his outrageous outfits, and prone to megalomaniac delusions and sadistic excesses. In accordance with the deadly logic of Naziploitation, his political vision of a whore and pimp as the First Couple of the Third Reich reaches its bloody culmination when he is betrayed by his favorite prostitute and killed in a male sauna by his superiors: a fitting ending that once again confirms the triumph of political power over its own sexualized scenarios.

In *Salon Kitty*, this connection finds privileged expression in a bizarre sexual number that functions like an allegory of Naziploitation as a whole. In the eponymous brothel, a high-ranking general uses a prostitute's naked body and face as a projection screen for newsreel footage depicting a Nazi rally. He asks her to place a gigantic pastry phallus between her legs, which he then proceeds to lick and bite off—all while the face of the Führer is projected onto his own, and the voices of the ecstatic masses blend with the screams of the prostitute in the midst of a nervous breakdown. This scene not only corroborates the presumed identity of fascism and pornography but also acknowledges openly the central preoccupation of Naziploitation: the spectacle of male deviancy as reflected in, and deflected through, the sexual humiliation and torture of women.

In the end, neither the kitschy look of *Salon Kitty* nor the graphic style of the lesser-known films can disguise the fact that Naziploitation has little interest in sexual arousal or titillation. Its real turn-on is the power over life and death; its orgasmic discharge comes from the sight of mutilated, violated, and tortured female bodies and the spectacle of male violence that produces them. In other words, the films' main function is revulsion, the affect best suited to expel the specter of fascism from the contemporary constellation. Whereas *The Damned* and *The Night Porter* still place the spectator between sadistic and masochistic subject positions, thereby reproducing the contradictions of power, including its attractions, in the visceral effects of spectatorship, Naziploitation turns both victims and perpetrators into the abject other that needs to be eliminated, expunged, and erased. In so doing, these films mark the endpoint of a chain of displacements that started with Visconti, Cavani, and Wertmüller and gave expression, in the registers of art and exploitation, to the changing affective landscape of fascism, antifascism, communism, and neofascism in post-1968 Italy. This historical moment produced a group of films that located the meaning of the political in the sexual as its most hidden foundation and scandalous manifestation. The concerns about democracy and the state of exception obsessively rehearsed in the setting of the camp may have had its origins in the particular political crises of 1970s Italy. Moreover, the choice of the concentration camp as the primal site of fascist power and violence would not have been possible without growing Holocaust awareness and its contribution to the conceptualization of biopolitics. Yet, with consequences most apparent in the continuing commodification of fascism as a filmic topos, the sexualization of fascism also laid the ground for other strategies of appropriation that have come to dominate the postfascist imaginary since the 1970s. In what ways the affective structures behind the sexualization of fascism continued in the aestheticization of fascism is examined in the next chapter, as are the broader implications for the crisis of democratic subjectivity and the meaning of the political revealed by such enduring attractions.

# 5

## Postpolitical Affects and Intertextual Effects

### On *Moloch* and *Inglourious Basterds*

I am the new avant-garde. I am the new artist, practicing a
new art. And politics is the new art.

Noah Taylor as Hitler in Max (Menno Meyjes, 2002)

$A$ny study on film and fascism eventually has to confront the question of fascist
aesthetics and what Walter Benjamin described as the aestheticization of politics, and any discussion of its function in postfascist cinema must attend to the
almost obsessive reenactment of this aestheticization in textual and intertextual
practices. The cinema of the millennium produced two films that illustrate this
process in almost paradigmatic ways: Aleksandr Sokurov's *Molokh* (*Moloch*,
1999) and Quentin Tarantino's *Inglourious Basterds* (2009).

Both films are indelibly marked by the conditions of filmmaking in the two
countries that were allies during World War II and enemies during the cold
war, conditions—or, rather, their prevailing interpretation—identified with
the prefix "post": postmodernity, posthistory, and postideology. Moreover,
their restagings of fascism remain haunted by the specter of empire and its

decline, *Moloch* by projecting the fall of the Soviet Union onto the Third Reich, and *Inglourious Basterds* by using the Nazi narrative to mourn the death of classical Hollywood. Most importantly, both directors counter the aestheticization of politics in fascism with postmodern strategies of appropriation that guarantee emotional detachment from the fascist spectacle but invite affective engagement with its very conditions of aestheticization. More than in any of the other films discussed in this book, it is consequently the aesthetic that, primarily through intertextual effects, preserves the difference between the emotional and the affective and opens up a space for the unique rewards of filmic self-referentiality.

Of course, the question remains whether the parodistic irreverence in Tarantino serves any other purpose than to affirm the power of film over fascism, and whether the elegiac tone in Sokurov has any other role than to mourn the disappearance of power tout court. My answer in both cases would be a qualified no. Sustained by a self-perpetuating logic of empty signification, fascism in both films functions like a fetish in all three senses of the word: an object with almost supernatural powers (a myth in Lacoue-Labarthe and Nancy's definition) that is then demystified; an object of desire (in Freudian terms) that reveals the condition of lack and disavowal; and an object (in the Marxist sense) that is given commodity status in the context of art cinema and film authorship. The unique forms of spectatorial enjoyment facilitated by such fetishistic self-referentiality are inseparable from what Mouffe calls the postpolitical: forms of engagement with political questions that avoid or dismiss political explanations.[1]

The postpolitical (i.e., as a particular malaise prevalent in Western democracies) is closely related to the equally contested (and perhaps equally limited) term of the postideological, to be understood here with Slavoj Žižek as a contemporary condition in which the political is evacuated of all claims to truth or struggles for change and defined by a purely instrumental view of ideology as mere tools of deception, manipulation, and domination. Under such conditions, symptomatic readings no longer uncover any blind spots in the ideological fantasy. Instead, we must make the filmic simulations of politics and ideology the starting point of any aesthetic interventions. For as Žižek points out, the diagnosis of a postideological world does not relieve us of the necessity of analyzing how ideology continues to structure social reality, including through the notion of postideology, which, in this case, reduces the very embodiment of ideology in the twentieth century—fascism—to a symptom of the crisis of filmic representation and the pleasures of intertextuality.[2] For that reason, it should not surprise us that the postpolitical in the cinema does not do away with representations of conflict and disagreement. On the contrary, through the aestheticization of violence, the specter of antagonism returns to the scene as an intertextual phenomenon, a reference to presumably simpler times defined by clear divisions between enemies and friends. Similarly, the directors' fixation on the physical body of power (i.e., the dictator or his representatives) suggests a strange mixture of relief and dismay about the end of ideology and the crisis of the political that requires further examination.

To understand the removal of the political from the spectacle of fascism, we must return to the diagnosis of fascism as the politicization of the aesthetic. In his famous 1936 essay "The Work of Art in the Age of Its Technological Reproducibility," Benjamin defines the relationship between aesthetics and politics through the two political alternatives available after the Nazi rise to power and concludes that "fascism aestheticizes political life as a means of giving expression to the masses without changing property relations. The inevitable result of this is war. Communism replies by politicizing art."[3] Written in support of the antifascist popular front, his strategic formulation was elevated to leftist dogma after 1968, giving rise both to a politicization of artistic practices in art, literature, and film and a deep suspicion of aesthetic pleasure as a form of political persuasion. With official Nazi art as the most infamous example of such instrumentalization, the only politically responsible approach seemed to be to counter the emotional responses exploited by the fascist sublime with the mental processes initiated by properly political art.[4] But in the same way that the critique of high modernism and its cult of art as secular religion has blurred the boundaries between high and low culture, so recent reassessments of Benjamin's formulation have begun to uncouple the aestheticization of politics from its own fascist/antifascist genealogy. Against the modernist austerity that was to provide protection against the false pleasures mobilized in the name of totalitarian ideologies, a new generation of scholars, first in response to the challenges of Western Marxism, then under the influence of poststructuralist theory, began to take a new look at aesthetic phenomena as a function of antifascist politics and postfascist culture.[5]

Informed by these debates, this chapter uses *Moloch* and *Inglourious Basterds* to consider a third possibility in which the aestheticization of politics in fascism experiences its final demontage in the aestheticization of politics in postfascism—a development already preconfigured in Benjamin's dual articulation of (political) representation and (mechanical) reproducibility. This process, I argue, hinges on an intensification of the intertextual effects that have been a function of the fascist aesthetic from the beginning but are now put into the service of its mournful reenactment and pop-culture parody. The restaging of fascism "as the postmodern equivalent of evil" — that is, a phenomenon in which moral categories have been displaced into aesthetic ones and the underlying binaries (i.e., of good and evil) enlisted in a sustained reflection on representation and signification — shifts the terms of debate once more and confirms the profoundly different meanings ascribed to film, history, and politics in the new millennium.[6]

Nazi aesthetics are above all visual aesthetics, a *Weltanschauung* (literally, view of the world) that, according to Carsten Strathausen, includes a particular perception of self and world that is profoundly cinematic in nature.[7] In blurring the lines between fiction and reality, the fascist aesthetic in many ways anticipated the Baudrillardian hyperreal and the politics of the simulacrum; *Moloch* is a perfect example of what Strathausen calls the appropriation of the Kantian sublime and its return as simulacrum. Similarly, the political and aesthetic project of Nazism politics can be described, in the words of Lutz Koepnick, as an attempt both to claim the autonomy of politics and "to refashion politics as a space of authenticity and existential self-assertion."[8] Yet what happens to this promise of autonomy and authenticity when it is translated into the terms of postmodern intertextuality? And how does the discursive function of such restagings of the fascist aesthetic change in the age of the postpolitical? As noted earlier, scholars tend to equate the postpolitical with two developments: the evacuation of politics of all opposing ideas and practices and the disappearance of all boundaries between political life and entertainment culture. In the same way that it was premature in 1989 to declare the end of history and celebrate liberal democracy as the last form of government, it may be premature now to announce the end of politics and ideology and to diagnose, whether with relief or despair, the ascendancy of a purely managerial understanding of government based on consensus and compromise.

It is as part of such discursive realignments that *Moloch* and *Inglourious Basterds* announce yet another stage in the history of fascism as a floating signifier. For in their artistic resistance both to the fantasies of universal humanism that buttress the postpolitical in the contemporary world and to the conventions of emotional realism that still dominate the fascist imaginary in mainstream cinema, Sokurov and Tarantino give us compelling insights into how such a postpolitical or postideological condition might look or feel. In both films, politics has been extracted from its ideological fantasies. All that remains is a unipolar world in which the place of power is either left empty (*Moloch*) — a uniquely Soviet problematic — or occupied by America in its most mediated form (*Inglourious Basterds*), namely, as Hollywood cinema.

At first glance, *Moloch* and *Inglourious Basterds* seem far too different to warrant a comparative reading. One is a low-budget Russian art film, the other a big-budget Hollywood blockbuster. One was directed by a difficult auteur, the other by a pop-culture icon. One celebrates film as an art form, the other its status as commodity. One conveys a melancholy mood, the other a cool attitude. One presents the past as a series of losses, failures, and catastrophes, the other as an inexhaustible archive of mass-produced sounds and images. Confronted with the problem of historical representation and the future of film, Sokurov and Tarantino take two very different approaches, with the first offering an elegiac contemplation on loss, which still preserves the possibility of redemption through art, and the second proposing a solution to the disappearance of referentiality in the joys of fandom and cinephilia.

Notwithstanding these differences, Sokurov and Tarantino are equally determined to leave behind the formal conventions that bind historical films to the signified—History capitalized—and to benefit from the intertextual relations that reconstitute fascism as an aesthetic and, hence, affective phenomenon. Their approach to narrative is antipsychological, their filmic style antirealist, and their representation of fascism anticonventional, an affront to the defenders of good taste. Both directors reject the false alternatives of empathetic identification and critical detachment that are inscribed in the dichotomy of aestheticization and politicization, relying instead on the affective dissonances produced through postmodern citation and self-referentiality. Furthermore, both cultivate their public personas in response to specific institutional pressures, Sokurov as a (trans)modernist auteur supported by the new financing opportunities available in a transnational European cinema and Tarantino as a postmodernist auteur taking full advantage of the marketing strategies of global Hollywood. Last but not least, both present themselves as apolitical filmmakers, Sokurov at one point insisting that "some things move from aesthetics to ethics and have nothing to do with politics" and Tarantino described by one critic as someone "who as far as I can tell doesn't have a political bone in his body."[9]

Film for Sokurov and Tarantino is not a reflection of reality but a world unto itself. In reconstructing the aesthetic and affective spaces of fascism through textual and intertextual effects, the directors create what postmodern theorist Linda Hutcheon calls historiographic metafiction, "the theoretical awareness of history and fiction as human constructs."[10] Confirming frequently voiced suspicions of a hidden affinity between fascism and postmodernism, with Eric Rentschler describing the Nazi culture industry "a preview of postmodern attractions," their self-reflexive strategies shed new light on the fascination with fascism from the side of aesthetic practices and in relation to the political as a category in crisis.[11] But such a double reading cannot be accomplished through a definition of the politics of representation that fails to take into account the affective nature of aesthetic registers such as elegy, irony, or parody.

Based on the proposition that *Moloch* and *Inglourious Basterds* share key strategies in the aesthetic and affective reenactment of fascism, their unique contribution to the fascist imaginary in postfascist cinema can be approached through a series of questions: Are these films to be read as examples of parody, that is, the production of critical distance through repetition and imitation as difference, or are they little more than pastiche, what Fredric Jameson dismissively describes as "the random cannibalization of all the styles of the past"?[12] If, in the age of the simulacrum, questions of factuality and referentiality have become irrelevant, what is at stake in revisiting the terms and conditions of our historical imaginary? Do these films fundamentally redefine historical representation and political agency, or do they simply displace history and politics into intertextuality? And what is the contribution of their strategies of appropriation, hybridization, and, indeed, bastardization to our understanding of the affective politics shared by film and fascism?[13]

Answering these questions requires us to recognize intertextuality as an affective phenomenon, an engagement with texts and textual effects that has cognitive, emotional, and aesthetic dimensions. Jameson's diagnosis of a "waning of affect in postmodern culture" early on established the link to the condition of the postpolitical.[14] But his formulation might more accurately refer to a waning of emotion—the prerogative of classic narrative—and a corresponding surge in the culturally mediated forms of affect. Denoting the production of textual meaning through explicit references to, or borrowings from, other texts, intertextuality is a key feature of postmodern cinema and its reappropriation of history as a textual construct. In Hutcheon's words, intertextuality in historiographic metafiction "offers a sense of the presence of the past, but a past that can be known only through its texts, its traces—be they literary [or, in this case, filmic] or historical."[15] The ghosts of history and cinema, in short, have become inseparable, if not interchangeable.

In *Moloch* and *Inglourious Basterds*, the centrality of intertextuality as mise en abyme—that is, as infinite mirroring—is openly acknowledged in two scenes featuring a film inside the film, the newsreel of a Wilhelm Furtwängler performance screened for Hitler and his guests in Kehlsteinhaus on the Obersalzberg (in *Moloch*) and the *Nation's Pride* film watched by the assembled Nazi elite in a movie theater in Paris (in *Inglourious Basterds*). Moreover, the genealogy of film

Mélanie Laurent in *Inglourious Basterds*

Yelena Rufanova and Yelena Spiridonova in
*Moloch*

and fascism is referenced through two filmic intertexts: the one directly, the other as a missing link. First, *Moloch* and *Inglourious Basterds* allude to Weimar director Georg Wilhelm Pabst and the mountain film as the model of a fascist aesthetic in which modernity and myth, and technology and nature, are reconciled: Sokurov through his choice of a mountain setting and his heavy debt to German romanticism and Tarantino through his allusions to a Pabst retrospective at the Le Gamaar theater and, by extension, the politics of film aesthetics.

Second, their films must be read in dialogue with the most controversial product of postfascist cinema during the 1970s, Hans-Jürgen Syberberg's eight-hour essay film, *Hitler—Ein Film aus Deutschland* (*Hitler: A Film from Germany*, 1977). The connection between Sokurov and Syberberg is obvious. For both, the Nazi past remains omnipresent through the melancholy fixation on the void occupied by what Syberberg calls the "Hitler in us" and what Sokurov depicts as what might be called the "Hitler for us." Not surprisingly, Susan Sontag, the critic who enthusiastically described *Hitler* as "one of the great works of art of the twentieth century," also hailed Sokurov as "the most ambitious and original filmmaker of his generation working anywhere in the world today."[16] However, Syberberg is also the quintessential postmodernist bricoleur, assembling in *Hitler* a veritable archive of images, sounds, stories, myths, and discourses mobilized by, or projected onto, the Nazis. Accordingly, Syberberg allows us to see self-referentiality in Sokurov and Tarantino as part of a longer project of approaching fascism through its dependence on textual productions and aesthetic traditions. Moreover, his *Hitler* film sheds light on the fundamental difference between the former's defense of metaphysics and the latter's acceptance of its absence, or to phrase it differently: the belief in historical understanding through art and the celebration of textual poaching as cultural literacy.

Based on these introductory comments, this chapter situates the coupling of film and fascism within a longer history of intertextuality and self-referentiality that, in its aesthetic and affective strategies, is essential to the permutations of the fascist imaginary in postfascist cinema. I first consider how *Moloch* and *Inglourious Basterds* simultaneously reconstruct and deconstruct the fascist aesthetic through intertextual effects and affects, thereby entering the highly mediated nature of the fascist life-world but also neutralizing its otherness through the habitus of the postmodern melancholic and parodist, respectively. Situating these films in the larger context of film history and its fantasies about fascist image production, the chapter then briefly considers the surprising number of films about filmmaking in the Third Reich and discusses their fictional reenactments of media politics as an ongoing commentary on the convergence in fascism of illusion and reality and the functioning of intertextuality in postfascist cinema; the representation of moviegoing in the Third Reich as a similarly self-reflective strategy, in this case achieved through the lens of spectatorship, could not be considered because of space limitations.[17]

*Moloch* is the first in Sokurov's tetralogy of films about twentieth-century dictators that includes *Telets* (*Taurus*, 2001), about Vladimir Lenin in the final years of his life; *Solntse* (*The Sun*, 2005), about Emperor Hirohito at the end of World War II; and *Faust* (2011), a filmic reflection on the corrupting effect of power that takes its inspiration from the 1926 classic directed by Friedrich Wilhelm Murnau. Based on a script by Yuri Arabov, the story presents Adolf Hitler, Eva Braun, Joseph and Magda Goebbels, and Martin Bormann during a weekend at the Berghof in the spring of 1942, before the decisive battle of Stalingrad. As in *Taurus* and *The Sun*, the extreme reduction of time and place achieves an almost hypnotic focus on the authoritarian leader as the embodiment of the ultimate truth about power, namely, its inevitability and unrepresentability. With such interests, Sokurov, who in his twenty-year career has made numerous feature films, documentaries, and essay films, including several about artists and composers, stands far removed from the typical concerns of post-perestroika Russian cinema and its heady mixture of social critique, imperial nostalgia, and commercial ambition. His cultural tastes and sensibilities make him a typical product both of nineteenth-century Russian culture, with its great appreciation for Western high culture, and of a well-established affinity in Soviet cinema for existential questions and metaphysical inquiries. The name of his official website, The Island of Sokurov, is a perfect expression of his carefully cultivated persona as an artistic outsider. Nonetheless, his preoccupation with empire cannot be separated from the contradictions of a Soviet/Russian film culture markedly different from the national cinemas of Western Europe and still haunted by what film scholar Nancy Condee calls the imperial trace.[18]

Frequently called the legitimate heir of Andrei Tarkovsky, Sokurov shares the latter's preference for long takes, elaborate camera movements, elliptical editing, and painterly frame compositions and displays a similar interest in dreamlike states, elegiac modes, and melancholy tones. Like Tarkovsky, he builds his minimal narratives around the Aristotelian unity of time, place, and action, focusing all attention on the interface of the physical and the metaphysical unique to the filmic medium. And not unlike Tarkovsky, Sokurov suffered professionally during the late Soviet era, with several films financed but shelved and his work criticized as difficult and self-indulgent. His radical break with official interpretations of fascism is already evident in *Sonata Dlya Gitlera* (Sonata for Hitler, 1989), a short essay film consisting of Nazi and Soviet film footage that, to the sounds of Bach and Penderecki, traces the Hitler dictatorship from its grandiose beginning to its catastrophic end. A clear repudiation of the doctrine of antifascism, the film presents power and oppression as inescapable facts of human existence and impenetrable by a Marxist critique of capitalism. His second filmic confrontation with Hitler offers a more developed version of the same argument.

Coproduced by Lenfilm and Thomas Kufus's Zero Film with significant German financing, *Moloch* (and the other films in the tetralogy) may be dismissed as an idiosyncratic response to the death of communism and the fall of empire. But as noted previously, the film is also a typical product of the new financing schemes available within the project of a transnational Europe. Shown on the international festival circuit, the film won the Best Screenplay Award at Cannes but fared badly at the box office. Many reviewers dismissed *Moloch* as pretentious, bombastic, and reactionary, with some particularly irritated about the implicit equation of fascism and communism in the tradition of cold war theories of totalitarianism; Sokurov's baffling pronouncements in interviews have not always helped matters.[19] Scholars, too, are divided in their critical assessment of his work in general.[20] Paul Schrader includes Sokurov among the representatives of a transcendental style of cinema (e.g., Carl Dreyer, Yasujiro Ozu, Robert Bresson), hailing his work as spiritual, mystical, pure cinema.[21] Amy Levine describes his work in terms of a phantasmatic space that (with Lacan and Deleuze) can be deciphered to reveal illegible political realities.[22] Identifying the director with a modernist tradition, Jameson asks: "Is Sokurov then to be seen as the last modernist, the last great modernist auteur," the creator of "an uncommon and untimely artistic enclave within the global warming of an international postmodern public sphere"?[23] Or do we have to classify him as a postmodernist precisely because of his desire to preserve the physical and the metaphysical, even if only as simulations?

Whether claimed for auteurist, modernist, or poststructuralist readings, Sokurov is very much a product of the contradictions that characterized the transition from Soviet to post-Soviet culture: critical of bourgeois individualism, its myth of freedom and self-determination, but indebted to the canon of Western art and literature; nostalgic for the culture of empire associated with czarist Russia and the Soviet Union but influenced by a uniquely Russian postmodernism and its critique of ideological master narratives.[24] In that sense, Sokurov's practice of what Mikhail Iampolski calls "the dissemination of the aesthetic into the non-aesthetic spheres" translates a shared trait of classical Russian culture and European romanticism into the terms of the postmodern and the postpolitical.[25]

As a mythological figure, *Moloch* refers to "the name of the divinity to which child sacrifices were offered," to use the definition given on the Koch Lorber DVD. Yet the title is also an allusion to two classics of silent cinema featuring Molochs, Giovanni Pastrone's *Cabiria* (1914) and Fritz Lang's *Metropolis* (1927). Partaking equally in mythology and film history, the title poses an obvious question: Who is being sacrificed, to whom, by whom, and why? *Moloch* takes place in the Eagle's Nest during two days in the spring of 1942, a point in the war described by Sokurov (in the 1999 Cannes interview on the DVD) as dramatic but not yet tragic. The story opens with Eva Braun doing calisthenics in the nude. She is waiting for the arrival of Hitler, Bormann, Goebbels, and his wife, Magda. The strange love story of "Adi and Eva" is presented through a series of dinner and after-dinner talks and bedroom and bathroom scenes. Throughout, Hitler is portrayed as a classic hypochondriac, sullen misanthrope, and unabashed misogynist. By contrast, Braun appears as a perfect specimen of Aryan womanhood: blonde, healthy, unaffected, cheerful—and unhappily in love. Conversations among the guests revolve around trivial subject matter: the commercial use of nettles, the advantages of a vegetarian diet, the relationship between climate and ethnicity, and the talents of various German conductors. A picnic on the mountaintop brings further distractions, including from the rivalries among the guests. The arrival of a priest asking Hitler to pardon a deserter briefly interrupts the atmosphere of luxury and boredom. References to the war in the Soviet Union elicit pained silence in Hitler and hushed remarks in the others; the Holocaust is alluded to only once—through a word unknown to the Führer: Auschwitz. The next morning, after a night of carnal relations, he departs with his entourage and leaves behind a dejected Eva Braun.

"My films are about people, not dictators," Sokurov insists in one of his many 1999 Cannes interviews.[26] Asked about the lack of historical context, he explains his approach: "I am not really interested in historical events or the period, I am much more interested in the human being . . . how he changes when he acquires this terrible weapon—politics."[27] It would be pointless to accuse Sokurov of humanizing Hitler with the kind of moralistic arguments leveled against Hirschbiegel and Eichinger in the case of *Downfall*. For Sokurov, the leader is the product of "a feeling . . . that simple people have for this special real person. This feeling is invented, it is transferred to this person, and he is considered a leader." Politics for him is a theater of the powerful, but one in which no one writes his own part: "These people [Hitler and his cohorts], the people of power, turned their lives into theater. Guided by a myth, they conceived and modified their lives, staged real mise en scènes and subordinated their behavior to rituals and ceremonies."[28]

Yet during great crises and catastrophes, this performance quickly turns from dramatic to tragic, to use Sokurov's words. Hitler, when asked about his place in history, harbors no illusions on this point: "If I win, everyone will worship me. And if I lose, even the lowest nobody will use me as a doormat." The film documents this sense of powerlessness in the center of power by having the camera linger on the body of the dictator, revealing the object of transference in all his physical and emotional frailty and confronting the spectator with the structuring void in the fantasy of politics as complete authority and total control. In Sokurov, as in Syberberg, Hitler is introduced as a figure of abjection uncontainable by history or narrative. Where the former locates him within a uniquely German genealogy of romantic yearning, the latter—taking an anthropological perspective—creates what one critic calls "case studies in what happens when a human being assumes the inhuman condition of absolute power."[29]

As noted earlier, Sokurov has been praised as the last representative of a cinema of metaphysical inquiry. Such characterizations underestimate the degree to which the evocation of loss is already predicated on the loss of loss as an authentic experience, an insight acknowledged in his affinity for the grotesque and the absurd. What looks and sounds like transcendence is, in fact, a reenactment of its aesthetic conventions in the cinema; it can therefore be described as postmetaphysical. History marks the point where the fantasies of power by those possessing it make contact with those creating them. By approaching the (fascist) dictatorship through its status as an overdetermined but ultimately empty signifier, *Moloch* frustrates the spectator's desire for simple historical explanations. At the same time, by avoiding the false alternatives posed by the essence and the banality of evil, the film brings us face-to-face with the projections that established the Nazis as a phantasmagoric presence in the cinema and that continue to feed the discourse about fascism as the absolute other. Goebbels cynically explains this process in the film: "If the Führer wasn't the father of the nation, then he could have become a master of paradox in literature." More than fifty years later, Hitler has instead become a master of intertextual effects in film.

The contradictions surrounding Hitler as signifier and signified are brought out through the gap opening up between representation and performance. The lack of psychological interiority focuses all attention on the physicality of his body, his gestures, and his facial expressions, but not in the sense of an actor embodying a historical personality. As a character, Hitler is morose, fretful, and self-involved; he is obsessed with his gastrointestinal problems and dietary regimes. "Don't touch me. I am dying," he implores Eva Braun. Later on, she confronts him with a frank description of his personality: "You don't know how to be alone. Without an audience, you are nothing more than a corpse." Leonid Mozgovoy, a little-known actor cast as Lenin in *Taurus*, plays the role with great restraint: nothing of the comical ranting and raving of the Führer as a madman, and no borrowings from the psychopathology of megalomania. Instead, he uses small hand gestures and awkward movements, suggesting resignation, withdrawal, futility of effort, and existential fatigue. In short, he shows death at work, which also means his own transformation into a floating signifier. Not surprisingly, references to death abound. The priest asking Hitler to pardon a deserter is dismissed with a comment on the paradox that "those who worship a crucifixion do not want to die." Repeatedly the others fantasize about Hitler's death, as does Magda Goebbels when she imagines him not waking up from his nap and Eva Braun as she waits for him in the bathroom with a small revolver in her hand. To his announcement, "We will conquer death," she replies calmly: "Death is death. It cannot be conquered."

However, in the form of intertextuality, film possesses a powerful tool for delaying death, namely, by linking the image of the body of power to other texts and thereby suggesting a line of deferrals, repetitions, and continuations. These intertextual references allow us to reconstruct the intended convergences between aesthetic and affective politics. In Sokurov, this quality is most evident in his reliance on Nazi-era material in the reconstruction of history as audiovisual mise-en-scène. To begin with the choice of place, the setting is Kehlsteinhaus, known in English as Eagle's Nest, which was built as part of the Berghof complex on the Obersalzberg near Berchtesgaden. Most of the exterior and several interior scenes (e.g., the great hall with fireplace, the brass-lined elevator)

Leonid Mosgovoy in *Moloch*          Yelena Rufanova in *Moloch*

were shot on location. Yet the faded colors, the low contrast and soft lighting, and the special lenses and filters, including an anamorphic lens that compresses the image vertically, derealize this mythical place, making the stones, woods, and carpets look more like stage or film sets, faded by the passing of time. Furthermore, the mood of the settings bears the traces of earlier texts, taking the form of imitation or allusion. Eva Braun's recently released home movies from the Berghof, which have the same pastel color hues, are referenced in the Hitler dance scene and establish the model against which Sokurov develops his version of what, in a variation on the fascist sublime, may be called the fascist banal. Meanwhile, the dialogue scenes are modeled on Hitler's *Table Talk* as recorded by Henry Picker, a debt acknowledged in the ubiquitous figure of the silent scribe who doubles as a stand-in for the director.

Throughout, Sokurov mobilizes familiar sounds and images from the archives of fascist attractions. This self-referential method alludes to the metaphysical as a style or habitus but in fact serves highly parodistic purposes. The Russian actors, led by Leonid Mosgovoy (German voice: Peter Fitz) as Hitler and Yelena Rufanova as Eva Braun (German voice: Eva Mattes), speak German throughout, with the visible disconnect between voice and lip movement and the hyperarticulated sound typical of postsynchronization adding to the overall sense of defamiliarization. Similarly associated with Germanness, Wagner pieces such as Siegfried's Funeral March in the credit sequences and Isolde's "Liebestod" aria and other well-known military marches and fanfares (e.g., the Russian song "Von Finnland bis zum Schwarzen Meer" or Franz Liszt's *Préludes* motif from the *Deutsche Wochenschau*) reproduce the soundscapes of dictatorial power familiar from Visconti, Wertmüller, Syberberg, and, not to forget, the early anti-Nazi films. In a key scene mentioned earlier, the self-representation of the Nazi regime is directly thematized in the filmed 1942 performance of Beethoven's "Ode to Joy" by the Berlin Philharmonic under

The riflescope scene in *Moloch*          Kehlsteinhaus in *Moloch*

Furtwängler and its reenactment by Hitler as he imitates the movements of the conductor in front of the screen. The use of Mozart's "Eine kleine Nachtmusik" in the morning-after scene serves more traditionally ironic functions.

Often called painterly, Sokurov's shots are carefully framed, lack spatial depth, and involve little movement by camera and protagonists. In acknowledgment of their formal debt to Russian icons, his images can be described as both iconic and iconographic; the latter quality is evident in the many art historical references—not surprising given the centrality of painting in his earlier work. Allusions to nineteenth-century German romantic painting can be found in the foggy landscapes reminiscent of Caspar David Friedrich, whereas his (simulations of) symbolism and mythology evoke Arnold Böcklin and Franz von Stuck, two of Hitler's favorite painters. In fact, Böcklin's most famous work, *Isle of the Dead*, is a more-than-fitting description of the Eagle's Nest, given its extraterritorial location and morbid atmosphere. Sokurov's approach to figuration as exaggeration is indebted to Goya, another master of the monstrous, whereas his use of light and color betrays the influence of Rembrandt, hailed as the most German of painters during the Third Reich. In the close attention to human flesh and skin—flabby, saggy, wrinkled, bumpy, pallid, gray—as the filmic surface on which the struggle between life and death, and fantasy and reality, takes place, the visual sensibilities of Rembrandt and Goya assume new political relevance.

Most importantly, *Moloch* approaches the spectacle of fascism through its entanglement with various filmic legacies, beginning with German expressionist cinema: the Gothic fantastic of Friedrich Wilhelm Murnau's *Schloß Vogelöd* (*The Haunted Castle*, 1921), the chamber-play dramaturgy of Artur Robison's *Schatten* (*Warning Shadows*, 1923), the spatial metaphors of Fritz Lang's two-part *Die Nibelungen* (1924), and, of course, the mountain film genre in Eva Braun's imitation of Riefenstahl's dance of the sea from Arnold Fanck's *Der heilige Berg* (*The Holy Mountain*, 1926). While it might be difficult to prove direct influences, the countless films about the Third Reich also appear to have served as inspiration. For instance, the looming sense of danger and foreboding is twice alluded to through the point of view associated with a riflescope, a reference to Lang's anti-Nazi film *Manhunt* (1941). Similarly, the preoccupation with physical intimacy recalls the monologues of Hitler's valet and Himmler's masseur in Syberberg's *Hitler* film, and Kehlsteinhaus's claustrophobic exclusivity resembles the Napola school Burg Kaltenborn in Volker Schlöndorff's *Der Unhold* (*The Ogre*, 1996)—two earlier attempts at getting as close as possible to the aesthetics of fascism without reproducing it.

*Moloch* presents Wagnerian music, German romantic painting, and expressionist film as aesthetic manifestations of prefascist tendencies. However, in the privileging of the aesthetic dimension, we can also see the anxiety of influence at work—Sokurov's conscious break with the dominant representation of fascism in Soviet cinema. Three films, each paradigmatic in its own way, haunt the postideological project of *Moloch: Padeniye Berlina* (*The Fall of Berlin*, Mikheil Chiaureli, 1950), the monumental World War II film presented to Stalin on his seventieth birthday but withdrawn from distribution after 1956; Mikhail Romm's *Obyknovennyy fashizm* (*Ordinary Fascism*, 1965), a critically acclaimed documentary/montage/essay film seen by forty million viewers but subject to extensive cuts intended to prevent comparisons between fascism and communism; and the popular television miniseries *Semnadtsat mgnoveniy vesny* (*Seventeen Moments of Spring*, Tatiana Lioznova, 1973), which continues to inspire jokes in contemporary Russia about its legendary Soviet spy turned Nazi operative, Standartenführer Stirlitz.[30]

With a bombastic Shostakovich score, hundreds of extras, elaborate set designs, and monumental battle scenes, *The Fall of Berlin* offers a revisionist account of World War II that begins with the German attack on the Soviet Union and ends with the Soviet conquest of Berlin, including the famous raising of the Soviet flag on the Reichstag. A typical example of the cult of personality that glorified Stalin as the savior of humanity and the protector of peace, *The Fall of Berlin* establishes the Great Patriotic War rather than the October Revolution as the central myth and unifying narrative of Soviet identity. Chiaureli mobilizes standard antifascist arguments in the ideological confrontations of the cold war and, not always bound by historical facts, alludes at one point to a planned US intervention in support of Hitler toward the end of the war. Suggesting at least some familiarity with the Hollywood anti-Nazi film, and Chaplin's *The Great Dictator* in particular, V. Savelyev plays the Führer as a madman, buffoon, and bumbling idiot—the absolute other of Stalin who, at least in this film, arrives godlike in a plane in the defeated German capital, very much like Hitler in

*Triumph of the Will*'s Nuremberg. Sokurov breaks with this Stalinist classic on two levels: in his rejection of the heroic antifascist narrative and its cult of personality and in his opposition to the coupling of film and ideology in the Soviet montage film and socialist realist film.

*Ordinary Fascism*, an even more important intertext for Sokurov, has been called the most influential filmic commentary on the nature of fascism — or, to use the prevalent term, Hitlerism — in Soviet cinema. Like *The Gleiwitz Case*, it includes a rare acknowledgment of fascism's emotional power: in extended reflections on the spectacle of the masses, the rituals of dominance and submission, and the introduction of violence into everyday life. Romm, a professor at the Moscow Institute of Cinematography (VGIK), combined film footage provided by East German archives from the Propaganda Ministry, Hitler's personal archives, and soldiers' home movies with staged scenes and ironic commentary for a sustained reflection on the politics of the fascist spectacle and the urgent need for critical visual analysis. In sixteen chapters, *Ordinary Fascism* attempts to answer the central question: How did fascism happen? Despite its subjective tone, Romm's answers remain in line with Marxist orthodoxy as he cites the strong support for the Nazis by German industrialists, the use of mass psychology to mask a hierarchical class structure, and the cooperation with other fascist movements in Europe. This transnational perspective extends to his closing remarks on the cold war: the alliance between the United States and West Germany, the rise of the United States as an imperialist superpower and, implicitly, successor of the Third Reich, the threat to the Eastern Bloc posed by NATO, and the reemergence of old Nazis and new fascists throughout Europe. Again Sokurov not only rejects the venerated tradition of 1920s leftist montage in which the filmic image is enlisted in a political argument; he adamantly refuses to consider the legacies of fascism in the present, opting instead for the intertextual effects that link the fascist imaginary to the history not of political ideologies but of audiovisual practices.

Last but not least, the hermetic aestheticism of *Moloch* must be approached through its deliberate opposition to the popular antifascism that inspired Nazi espionage stories in the style of the multipart *Shchit i mech* (The shield and the sword, Vladimir Basov, 1968) and that accounts for the enduring cult status of *Seventeen Moments of Spring*. The latter's main protagonist is the ideal New Soviet Man: rational but still soulful, deeply patriotic, committed to the collective, and willing to suppress all individual feelings and desires. Yet with these qualities, Stirlitz/Isayev in fact ends up being the perfect Nazi: the embodiment of duty, service, and commitment to the cause where the real Nazis are corrupt, power-hungry, and weak. Presumably seen by Sokurov, who was twenty-two at the time, *Seventeen Moments of Spring* with its playful reflection on ideological masquerade during the long Brezhnev era marks a peculiar moment in the construction of fascism as the absolute other of communism, offering either a validation of the Communist Party successfully infiltrating a self-defeating Nazi bureaucracy or a veiled commentary on the ineffectiveness of Soviet bureaucracy during a period of military expansion and political stagnation.

If *The Fall of Berlin* used the Nazis to legitimate the cult of personality surrounding Stalin, if *Ordinary Fascism* sought to authenticate the Marxist doctrine of fascism, and if *Seventeen Moments of Spring* promised an ironic apotheosis of the New Soviet Man, where must we locate *Moloch* within this long history of Soviet revisions of film and fascism? The answer: by returning to an intertext (i.e., in the form of documentary footage) shared by *Ordinary Fascism*, *Seventeen Moments of Spring*, and *Moloch*—Furtwängler's 1942 Berlin performance of Beethoven's Ninth Symphony. In the latter, the private screening on the Berghof opens with the *Deutsche Wochenschau* of 11 July 1942 reporting the retreat of Soviet troops and the successful crossing of the Don by the seemingly unstoppable German army. First introduced on the soundtrack as what appears to be nondiegetic sound, the choral finale of the Ninth Symphony celebrating universal brotherhood and tolerance becomes an object of voyeuristic fascination as the camera shows Eva Braun and Magda Goebbels looking through a keyhole and responding with a mixture of amusement and irritation to a scene still hidden from view. Assuming their point of view in the next shot, we are then confronted with the filmic image of Furtwängler conducting and the Führer imitating his movements as a shadow behind the screen. While the women talk about their romantic frustrations, with Braun absentmindedly waving her revolver, Hitler reaches a climax as the screen turns white, he falls back into his seat, and starts a tirade on the state of cinema, concluding, "With the cinematic art form, we cannot compromise ourselves. Better to abolish film." Sokurov could not have said it any better.

*Inglourious Basterds* is both a Jewish revenge fantasy and a fantasy of the cinema's revenge, with the enemy not just the Nazis but our naive assumptions about historical representation. Both perspectives come together in an improbable story that, even as it gestures toward the desire for justice in history, serves primarily the kind of self-referential effects identified earlier as postmodern intertextuality. From the beginning, the tone and mode is performative: "We are going to be doing one thing, and one thing only: killing Nazis," announces Captain Aldo Raine (Brad Pitt) to a group of Jewish recruits before they head off to Germany to spread fear and terror in preparation for the Normandy

Campaign of 1944. Meanwhile, and to summarize the plot, Shosanna Dreyfus (Mélanie Laurent) is the only one in her family to escape the genocidal actions of the infamous "Jew hunter," Colonel Hans Landa (Christoph Waltz). She reappears in Paris as the owner of a movie theater that, at the request of an infatuated German soldier, Frederick Zoller, is chosen for the premiere of a propaganda film about his heroic exploits. In a furious finale, all three groups come together at a gala event attended by the Nazi elite, including Hitler himself: the "basterds," who, with the assistance of movie star Bridget von Hammersmarck, plan to blow up the theater; Shosanna and her black projectionist/lover Marcel, who have filmed an alternate ending for the film and are prepared to burn down the entire place; and Colonel Landa, who, as the embodiment of the typical Nazi villain and dictatorial director, tries to control all players and events until the very end. Shosanna, Zoller, Marcel, and von Hammersmarck die on that fateful evening at the movies, but Landa, too, gets his comeuppance during the planned handover to the Americans when Raines, an even better maker of facts, carves a swastika into his antagonist's forehead, proudly declaring, "This might just be my masterpiece."

Since *Inglourious Basterds* is a Tarantino film, the question automatically arises whether the director might be suggesting the same about his most recent film. Based on a screenplay ten years in the making, with initial plans for an entire series, this international blockbuster was coproduced by the Weinstein Brothers with Studio Babelsberg and, like *Moloch*, made with significant German funding. Shooting took place on the lot of the old Ufa studio in Berlin Babelsberg, with all Nazi parts played by German-speaking actors: Christoph Walz in an Oscar-winning performance, Diane Krüger as Bridget von Hammersmarck, Daniel Brühl as Fredrick Zoller, August Diehl as Major Hellstrom, Til Schweiger as Hugo Stiglitz, and Martin Wuttke as Hitler, drawing on his performance in Heiner Müller's acclaimed 1995 Berliner Ensemble production of Bertolt Brecht's *Der aufhaltsame Aufstieg des Arturo Ui* (*The Resistible Rise of Arturo Ui*). As in *Moloch*, the Germans speak German, with translations in this case provided by Tom Tykwer. Landa also speaks fluent French and Italian, the linguistic equivalent of the Nazis' territorial conquest of Europe. Drawing on familiar American and European stereotypes, Tarantino uses the German actors primarily in the kind of dialogue-driven sequences (e.g., in the farmhouse, the bistro, and the bar) familiar to audiences from *Reservoir Dogs* (1992) and *Pulp Fiction* (1994), whereas the American actors appear in action-driven sequences modeled on his favorite spaghetti westerns and dirty war movies from the 1960s and 1970s.

For many critics Tarantino is the ultimate postmodern filmmaker who uses his well-documented infatuation with popular culture for a self-referential play with images as images, irrespective of their referents.[31] Having acquired his vast knowledge of film history during an early stint as a video-store clerk, he approaches film as the quintessential mixed medium, the conduit not to a physical reality waiting to be redeemed but to a fully mediated world constituted through textuality, intertextuality, and hypermediality.[32] While it may be tempting to treat Tarantino as a unique phenomenon, he is in fact part of a group of Hollywood directors with postmodern sensibilities that includes David Lynch, Tim Burton, and Ethan and Joel Coen; what sets him apart is his affirmative view of the surface character of things and his enthusiastic approach to the logics of cultural consumption. Bastardization is his preferred method for constructing stories and characters and for combining genres and styles. Not surprisingly, the audience's ability to recognize his allusions to obscure works of popular culture constitutes an essential part of the experience of watching a Tarantino film.

Three artistic strategies have informed his work since *Reservoir Dogs* and *Pulp Fiction* and contributed to his cult status as a hipster filmmaker especially among younger (male) fans: his extensive use of filmic self-referentiality in the form of citation, imitation, and parody; his affective affinity for exploitation films, mediocre works, and minor art forms; and his aestheticization or, in the view of detractors, his banalization of violence. Not surprisingly, the critical reception of his films has been divided: exuberant praise for his contribution to postmodern cinema and contemporary media culture, but also condemnation of his filmic style as shallow, narcissistic, puerile, and self-indulgent—an indication to which degree the postmodern still speaks to two very different political sensibilities and cultural mentalities, especially when applied to the fascist imaginary.

Tarantino makes films about films, in this case, films about the Third Reich and the historically overdetermined relationship between film and fascism. His approach is predicated on a postmodern critique of the modernist cult of originality, innovation, and aesthetic transcendence. At the same time, his appropriation of existing works, genres, and styles operates against one of the core assumptions shared by filmic realism and classical narrative, namely, that film either provides access to the real, therein serving critical functions, or that it creates a convincing illusion of reality, therein having affirmative effects. His filmic version of hyperreality confirms Baudrillard's diagnosis of the indistinguishability of reality and fantasy as a central aspect of the postmodern condition. Against the alternatives of modernist disillusionment and willful mass deception, Tarantino insists on the inherent power of disillusioned enjoyment and irreverent appropriation. Drawing primarily on exploitation genres such as blaxploitation, spaghetti westerns, and dirty war movies, he operates outside the high-low culture divide that still haunts traditional notions of film authorship. With his virtuoso command of pop culture references, he addresses an audience familiar with these lowly registers and appreciative of parodistic modes of cultural consumption. Consequently, the aestheticization of violence in *Inglourious Basterds* must be seen not in its referential qualities but in its intertextual effects—a choice many of Tarantino's critics are not prepared to make.

In a film sustained entirely by intertextual effects, the most important question has to be: What is "Operation Kino"? Tarantino is surprisingly clear on this point: "The idea that cinema can bring down the Third Reich is a really juicy metaphor. . . . On the other hand, it's not a metaphor at all. It's the reality of the movie."[33] Accordingly, "Operation Kino" in the diegesis refers to several overlapping projects: the Americans' plan to dynamite the theater during the premiere of *Nation's Pride*, Shosanna's decision to set the theater ablaze with the help of highly flammable nitrate film stock, and, last but not least, the Nazis' intention to use the fantasies provided by the cinema to support a totalitarian regime and its oppressive policies.

However, the larger project entails a more far-reaching reflection on cinema as an audiovisual archive and an instrument of knowledge and power—a dynamic visualized by the round window above the movie marquee, reminiscent of an iris shutter, as the perfect allegory of the cinematic apparatus. As a public space and media technology, the cinema in *Inglourious Basterds* organizes an elaborate framework of references shared by friends as well as enemies; it functions as a form of communication and a method of self-identification and self-construction. Most important for our purposes, the cinema creates a system of affective investments and aesthetic rewards that, by establishing a second-order reality or hyperreality, draws attention to reality—and, by extension, ideology—as a construction. As a result, a position of resistance can be claimed only from the side of the aesthetic.

The introduction of alternate spellings, which marks the shift from *The Inglorious Bastards*, the English title of the original 1978 Italian war film *Quel maledetto treno blindato* directed by Enzo Castellari, to its postmodern reincarnation as *Inglourious Basterds*, captures perfectly the principle of appropriation that situates the films in film history and marks the special place occupied by fascism within that history. To begin with Tarantino's play on names, Aldo Raine is an allusion to 1950s supporting actor Aldo Ray; Hugo Stiglitz and Antonio Margheriti are the names of a 1970s exploitation actor and director, respectively; and

Mélanie Laurent in *Inglourious Basterds*          Mélanie Laurent in *Nation's Pride*

Omer Ulmer pays homage to Edgar Ulmer, the Austrian American director known for low-budget noir films. Aside from a few nods to the Hollywood anti-Nazi film, with Hitler's temper tantrum a repeat performance of Chaplin's *The Great Dictator*, Tarantino borrows heavily from dirty war movies such as *Von Ryan's Express* (Mark Robson, 1965) and *The Dirty Dozen* (Robert Aldrich, 1967). The Italian spaghetti western in the style of *C'era una volta il West* (*Once upon a Time in the West*, Sergio Leone, 1968) provides him with the perfect model of demystification, from its graphic but highly aestheticized depiction of violence to the cool attitude of its group of outcasts, prompting Tarantino to describe the film as "a spaghetti western set in World War II."[34] Divided into five chapters, "Chapter 1: Once upon a Time in Nazi-Occupied France 1941" and "Chapter 2: Inglourious Basterds" openly acknowledge their debt to exploitation cinema, whereas "Chapter 3: German Night in Paris," "Chapter 4: Operation Kino," and "Chapter 5: Revenge of the Giant Face" speak directly to the question of intertextuality and hyperreality, making the cinema itself the agent, the subject, and the scene of action.

As is to be expected, "Operation Kino" involves numerous allusions to German cinema, beginning with the so-called German Night in Paris, a requirement, still explained in the screenplay, that theater owners in occupied France reserve a certain number of nights for German film screenings. Shosanna Dreyfus, now running the Le Gamaar under the assumed name of Emmanuelle Mimieux, first appears to the admiring gaze of Zoller next to a movie marquee, removing the letters of *Die weisse Hölle vom Piz Palü* (*The White Hell of Piz Palü*, Georg Wilhelm Pabst and Arnold Fanck, 1929), with Riefenstahl in a starring role, to advertise a series of films by Max Linder, the famous French silent film star. Colonel Landa's earlier description of Jews as rats refers to the infamous antisemitic propaganda film *Der ewige Jude* (*The Eternal Jew*, Fritz Hippler, 1940), while Shosanna's later self-stylization as "the voice of Jewish vengeance" draws upon a very different lineage. For it is as cat woman, introduced through the lyrics of David Bowie's "Cat People" (Putting Out Fire with Gasoline)" from the eponymous 1982 Paul Schrader horror film (and, by extension, the 1942

Jacques Tourneur of the same title), that she decides to use the opening of *Nation's Pride* to "burn down the cinema on Nazi night!"

With a credit sequence reminiscent of *Triumph of the Will*, *Nation's Pride*, the film within a film directed by Eli Roth (Donny Donowitz in the film), evokes the classical Hollywood war film, with Zoller as an Audie Murphy type, until Shosanna and, with her, a very different resistance narrative take control of the captive audience in the theater.[35] In a perfect example of the Eisensteinian montage of attractions, she cuts from a close-up of the German sniper, defiantly asking, "Who wants to send a message to Germany?" to her own face in close-up answering, "I have a message for Germany: You are all going to die. And I want you to look deep into the face of the Jew who's going to do it." The shot recalls the woman with pince-nez from Sergei Eisenstein's *Bronenosets Potyomkin* (*Battleship Potemkin*, 1925) and establishes a context for other famous Eisenstein citations (e.g., the baby carriage from the Odessa Steps sequence).

Between "German Night in Paris" and "Revenge of the Giant Face," *Inglourious Basterds* relies primarily on film historical references to establish the connection between film and fascism as a given and make it the basis of a new historical hyperreality. The marquee of Le Gamaar features Henri-Georges Clouzot's *Le corbeau* (*The Raven*, 1943), the most famous film produced by the Ufa-affiliated Continental Film under German occupation. Lobby posters advertise his *L'Assassin habite . . . au 21* (*The Murderer Lives at Number 21*, 1942) and the European coproduction *Le domino vert* (The green domino, Alfred Greven, 1935), directed by the future head of Continental. Throughout, Tarantino exhibits a remarkable knowledge of German film history. The name of Wilhelm Wicki, one of the "basterds," alludes to the director of the German antiwar film *Die Brücke* (*The Bridge*, 1959), Bernhard Wicki. Emil Jannings, the acclaimed character actor of German stage and screen—though not, as the film implies, a recipient of the prestigious Iffland ring—attends the premiere of *Nation's Pride* proudly showing off the ring on his finger. Bridget von Hammersmarck is modeled on blonde ingénue Lilian Harvey, whose big hit *Glückskinder* (*Lucky Kids*, 1934) is discussed by the characters and, in the screenplay, actually shown in the theater; von Hammersmarck's fictional oeuvre, advertised on several lobby posters, includes *Fräulein Doktor* (Miss doctor), a reference to the 1937 French Pabst film *Mademoiselle Docteur* (*Street of Shadows*).

To continue with a few more examples, the names mentioned during the game played at La Louisiane—King Kong, Pola Negri, Edgar Wallace, Winnetoo, and Mata Hari—are figures from the imaginary of German popular culture, and the songs played during that sequence include "Ich wollt' ich wär ein Huhn" from the previously mentioned Harvey comedy and Leander's "Davon geht die Welt nicht unter" from the wartime drama *Die große Liebe* (*The Great Love*, Rolf Hansen, 1942). Meanwhile, Shosanna's glamorous outfit in the fifth chapter pays homage both to great Ufa stars such Marlene Dietrich and Zarah Leander and to two Fassbinder divas with a Nazi connection, the Lale Andersen character in *Lili Marleen* (1981) and the Sybille Schmitz–inspired character in *Die Sehnsucht der Veronika Voss* (*Veronika Voss*, 1982). Last but not least, discussions in England about the Nazi film industry focus intensely on Goebbels's desire to develop an alternative, in the words of Lieutenant Hicox, to "the Jewish German intellectual cinema of the twenties" and "the Jewish controlled dogma of Hollywood." In other words, the propaganda minister's ambition according to Hicox is to become the German David O. Selznick. Confirming his expertise, the writings of the British film critic turned secret agent include "Art of the Eyes, Heart, and the Mind: A Study of German Cinema in the Twenties" and a Pabst monograph titled "Twenty-Four Frames da Vinci," with the number alluding to the persistence of vision phenomenon responsible for the illusion of movement in film and with the name of the Italian painter paying homage to the pictorial quality of Pabst's oeuvre.[36]

Just as Sokurov's revisions of Nazism must be evaluated against the filmic legacies and televisual culture of his Soviet youth, Tarantino's dream of Jewish revenge cannot be understood without reference to the founding text of Holocaust remembrance: the influential four-part NBC television miniseries *Holocaust* (Marvin J. Chomsky, 1978), which aired when Tarantino was fifteen and which established the iconography of the Jews as passive victims. Breaking with this filmic tradition, he introduces a beautiful Jewish heroine who, on the day of reckoning, puts on a bright red dress, a dress like the one worn by the young girl in the monochrome scene of Jewish suffering in another famous Holocaust film, *Schindler's List* (Steven Spielberg, 1993). Moreover, rejecting the equation of Jewish masculinity with learnedness in both of these films, Tarantino draws on the alternative iconography of the muscle Jew to celebrate the ruthlessness of the "basterds."

The centrality of intertextuality to the filmic reconstruction of Nazi aesthetics also sheds light on the contradictory affects mobilized by, and projected onto, the main character and dramatic center of the film: Colonel Hans Landa, played brilliantly by Christoph Walz. Tarantino has admitted repeatedly that without the Austrian-born actor, best known for his work on German stage and television, the film could not have been made. With his remarkable linguistic range, Landa is a brilliant conversationalist, using every rhetorical trick to assert his power over his interlocutors. Unlike Mosgovoy's Hitler, he revels in the art of domination; for him, power and desire are identical. "Once upon a time . . . in

Nazi-occupied France": this is how Landa makes his first appearance, like the typical villain in a spaghetti western. But inside the farmhouse, he quickly turns into the caricature of a European gentleman of the old school: gallant in an almost obnoxious way, meticulous to the point of fussiness, courteous with a hint of superiority, and charming with an undertone of aggression. His goal: to find the remaining French Jews hiding in the area and to make the farmer reveal their hiding place. His strategy: to order a glass of milk as a deceptive symbol of his sincerity. First speaking in French, then switching to English, Landa asks: "I have no way of knowing if you are familiar with who I am. Are you aware of my existence?" The farmer's reply—you are "the Jew hunter"—identifies a strategy that Landa uses for all his victims: drawing them in, making them complicit, and having them complete the work of entrapment in a humiliating act of self-incrimination. Three years later, when Landa and Shosanna meet again during preparations for the gala premiere, he asks her to stay behind to discuss security issues. This time he orders a glass of milk for the Jewess, with Tarantino leaving it unclear whether Landa recognizes her and instead using this symbol of innocence to expose his cruelty and malice—traits that find telling expression in the way in which he extinguishes his cigarette in the strudel's cream.

From the beginning, Landa is presented as a monster, separated from the human condition through his lack of affect and empathy. Just as *Moloch*, an ancient Semitic deity, stands for a threat to the divine order, *Monstrum* (Latin for an aberrant occurrence) represents a violation of the natural order; not surprisingly, in light of the connections explored in the previous chapter, some critics have misread Landa's mannerisms as gay. In fact, he fits perfectly the definition of malignant narcissist put forth by two European Jews in American exile: Otto Kernberg in his work on borderline personality disorders in the 1940s, and philosopher Erich Fromm in his treatise *The Heart of Man* (1964). The malignant narcissist stands out through his extreme sense of entitlement, pathological need for attention, and chameleon-like personality; for Fromm, he represents "the quintessence of evil."[37] This description is important not only because it allows us to establish Landa as a psychologically developed character but also because it identifies the mechanisms of emotional detachment for the film as a whole.

The latter is in full evidence in Landa's third appearance (not counting a brief one in La Louisiane) at the movie premiere and in the film's grand finale. He first shows off his language skills in the encounter with the "basterds" and then confronts von Hammersmarck, his hapless Cinderella, with her missing shoe. As in the farmhouse scene, the camera circles around them, creating the spatial equivalent of rhetorical entrapment. The final showdown between the "Jew Hunter" and "Aldo, the Apache" features Landa in full winner mode, with his exclamation in English of "That's a bingo!" adding a gambler's take on the two questions to be decided: the assassination of Hitler, Goebbels, and Göring and his planned rehabilitation as a secret American agent and true democrat. "What shall the history books read?" he asks smugly, only to watch in sheer horror as Raine, at the arranged meeting place, proceeds to add his perspective on history and "give [him] something [he] can't take off," namely, a swastika carved into the Nazi's forehead.

What accounts for Landa's perverse appeal as a character? First, that he claims to possess absolute power, including the power to make his interlocutors confess their guilt and reveal their secrets. Second, and more importantly, he performs the fascist terror as an act of seduction. In a film characterized by the absence of empathetic identification (i.e., sharing emotions with a character) and sympathetic identification (i.e., sharing values with a character), Landa stands for a fundamentally different form of engagement. As the personification of evil, defined here as the absence of empathy, Landa represents the absolute enemy in a narrative cinema until recently built around empathy as its main mechanism of character identification.[38] As he resists such conventional forms of engagement, his version of evil eludes all moral categories and becomes the marker of a very different kind of abjection. In the same way that Hitler in *Moloch* is shockingly ordinary and self-absorbed, his more than willing executioner in *Inglourious Basterds* suffers from a similar and decidedly postmodern ailment: narcissism. Accordingly, intertextuality in this context can be described as a particular affect of detachment from another referent besides history, namely, the political. Whereas Sokurov's Hitler accepts his power with cranky indifference, Tarantino's Landa practices it with theatrical flourish. In foregrounding the element of self-reflexivity on the level of individual pathology (i.e., Hitler and Landa as sociopaths/narcissists) and intertextual productivity, both directors not only refuse to take a political stance but also preempt the possibility of moral judgment through an affective detachment achieved through citation and appropriation. In the end, their films leave us with a much more disturbing scenario: the ascendancy of narcissism as a model for the forms of self-absorption shared by the characters and the texts and intertexts in which they appear—a development that requires a concluding digression on the surprising number of films about filmmaking in the Third Reich and the narcissistic structure of doubling inscribed in their self-referential narratives.

In situating *Moloch* and *Inglourious Basterds* within the larger historical constellation that turned film and fascism into a kind of endless loop, we must begin with two highly allegorical scenes. Often quoted, the first scene reveals the Nazi dream factory at its most cynical and deadly. In 1945 Propaganda Minister Joseph Goebbels spoke at a screening of *Kolberg* in the beleaguered fortress of La Rochelle, urging his audience to consider fascism's desire for a different history in, and of, film. "Gentlemen," he addressed the soldiers and officers in what proved to be a prophetic remark on the longevity of fascist attractions, "in a hundred years' time they will be showing a beautiful color film of the terrible days we are living through. Wouldn't you like to play a part in that film? Hang in there, so that audiences in a hundred years will not jeer and whistle when you appear on the screen."[39] Confirming the Nazis' pathological need for admiring audiences, the second scene from the otherwise unremarkable *The Empty Mirror* (Barry J. Hershey, 1996) shows Hitler watching old party-rally films, wartime newsreels, and home movies from the Berghof. "Everyone who desires adulation will recognize in me the pure manifestation of that dark part of himself," he declares. "I am the perfect reflection of every man with the lust to dominate, who has some bias or prejudice, some unsatisfied craving. Some will condemn me morally, but they cannot escape the power of my image. . . . The essential Hitler has a hold over every human heart."

Separated by more than fifty years of filmmaking, the quote attributed to the real Goebbels and the statement made by a fictional Hitler identify three key elements in the convergence of film and fascism: the belief in fantasy as a generative principle of politics and a founding site of identity; the centrality of affect to the mechanisms of projection and reflection captured in the metaphor of mirroring; and the close collaboration between character and spectator, including of the character as spectator, in the reimagining of politics as performative, spectatorial, and experiential.

The aestheticization of politics was an integral part of Nazi ideology, translating political experiences into aesthetic phenomena and, in turn, using aesthetic experiences to forge new subjectivities and collectivities. However, the reenactment of this process in films about filmmaking relies on this conflation of the political and the aesthetic in order to move from a political critique of fascism to an analysis of its postfascist status as media-produced fantasy. The culture of intimidation, opportunism, and privilege in the Nazi culture industry and the personal and professional motivations of those working within in its hierarchical structures play an important role in these cautionary tales about literature, art, and filmmaking in the Third Reich. Yet it is the doubling effect created by fascism as film that also turns these films into perfect examples of mise en abyme, that is, revealing comments on the vacillation between attraction and revulsion fueling such intertextual productivity. Unlike the better-known films about great artists in the Third Reich, which often end up affirming the high-low culture divide, the films about film actors and directors acknowledge the medium's embeddedness within ideology and, in recognition of film's double status as art and commodity, explore the broader implications in institutional rather than aesthetic terms.[40]

The first films about filmmaking during the Third Reich were made in the GDR as part of early controversies over the role of art and culture in a socialist society. Intent on separating DEFA from Ufa, director Kurt Maetzig drew upon the affective structures of melodrama to distinguish between the victims and the perpetrators in Goebbels's propaganda machine, first by bringing the tragic story of actor Joachim Gottschalk to the screen in *Ehe im Schatten* (*Marriage in the Shadows*, 1947) and then by making the first Veit Harlan trial part of the cold war narrative of *Roman einer jungen Ehe* (*The Story of a Young Couple*, 1952). By contrast, West German productions portrayed film professionals, especially famous female stars, as unwitting participants in the mass deceptions manufactured by the Propaganda Ministry. Two actresses, both of whom committed suicide, came to embody the deadly allure of the Nazi fantasy machine and a feminized mass culture: the popular Renate Müller, whose promising short career was depicted in *Liebling der Götter* (*Sweetheart of the Gods*, Gottfried Reinhardt, 1960), and sultry Sybille Schmitz, whose postwar troubles inspired the previously mentioned *Veronika Voss*. Marking a new stage in coming to terms with German film history, the Marlene Dietrich biopic *Marlene* (Joseph Vilsmaier, 2000) breaks with these critical traditions by cultivating the nostalgic look of heritage and privileging the righteous perspective of exile.

Meanwhile, two very different documentaries on filmmaking during the Third Reich point to a growing desire in the wake of German unification for a simultaneously more immediate and more detached perspective on the Nazi politics of affect. Ray Müller's *Die Macht der Bilder: Leni Riefenstahl* (*The Wonderful, Horrible Life of Leni Riefenstahl*, 1993) presents the most famous director of Nazi cinema as her well-preserved, cantankerous self but, because of the director's obvious fascination with his subject, leaves the contradictions between art and politics unresolved. Meanwhile, Veit Harlan, the director of the most infamous film of the Third Reich, *Jud Süß* (*Jew Suess*, 1940), occupies the emotional center of a highly subjective essay film about the Harlan family by Felix Moeller, *Harlan—Im Schatten von Jud Süß* (*Harlan—In the Shadow of Jew Suess*, 2008), and a controversial German-Austrian production by Oskar Roehler, *Jud Süß—Film ohne Gewissen* (*Jew Suess: Rise and Fall*, 2010), evidence to what degree German cinema remains both haunted by, and indebted to, its own history.[41]

Part of the phenomenon of heritage cinema but markedly different from the retro styles of the 1970s, several European films made since the 1990s use stories set in the film world to revisit the historical conditions that gave rise to fascism as a media-produced fantasy and fantasy-based politics. In all examples, the tension between the critical examination of such a proto-postmodern conception of politics and the parasitic participation in its spectacular effects speaks to a nostalgic engagement with film history informed less by concerns about the corruption of film by politics than the disappearance of classical cinema in the age of audiovisual media (television, computer games, digital technologies). At times, the deliberate blurring of boundaries between the production of moving images and political ideologies is introduced with barely disguised longing for the "golden era of German film" and the kind of social and cultural relevance never regained by cinema after the war. In all cases, the rhetorical strategies are surprisingly similar across national boundaries, beginning with the short-circuiting of illusion and truth through the emphasis on the performativity of (political) identity.

All films include scenes that approach the process of filmmaking through the replacement of reality by fantasy and the complementary move from deception to disillusionment. Modeled on the appearance of a false Hitler on the streets of Warsaw in Lubitsch's famous *To Be or Not to Be*, the classic scene of debunking returns in the little-known German film *Beim nächsten Kuss knall ich ihn nieder* (At the next kiss, I'll shoot him down!, Hans-Christoph Blumenberg, 1996), which starts out with two Nazis greeting each other with the Hitler salute but then reveals them to be Reinhold Schünzel and Conrad Veidt, two exiles playing Nazis in a Hollywood anti-Nazi film. The next three examples feature similar moments of recognition/misrecognition in which actors, directors, and spectators become coconspirators in the reproduction of the fascist fantasy. Thus, the Spanish box-office hit *La nina de tus ojos* (*The Girl of Your Dreams*, Fernando Trueba, 1998) opens on what looks like newsreel footage from a Goebbels speech until the camera pulls back to show the propaganda minister getting pointers on his public performance by film director Herbert Maisch. *The Girl of Your Dreams* recounts the experiences of a group of Spanish actors arriving on the Ufa lot in Babelsberg for the filming of a multilanguage version of *Andalusische Nächte* (*Nights in Andalusia*, Herbert Maisch, 1938), here called *Das Mädchen deiner Träume*.[42] Their approach is one of political noninvolvement: "We're film people, artists. This is not our war," notes one of them. Led by the

Outside the Ufa studios in *The Girl of Your Dreams*        At the Continental studios on the set of *Carnival of Sinners* in *Safe Conduct*

Penelope Cruz character, they nonetheless end up committing small acts of resistance.

Similarly, the French production *Laisser passer* (*Safe Conduct*, Bertrand Tavernier, 2002) fictionalizes the history of the German-owned Continental Film in occupied France to approach the question of resistance and collaboration through the lens of filmmaking.[43] Based on actual people and events, the story juxtaposes the personal and professional choices of two very different men, the assistant director Jean Devaivre, who first works for Maurice Tourneur and then makes films for Continental's Alfred Greven, and the screenwriter Jean Aurenche, who consciously avoids all professional involvement with the Germans. Yet in a suggestive commentary on the deceptiveness of first impressions, it is the committed family man Devaivre who is active in the resistance, whereas the irresponsible Aurenche juggles several mistresses and remains uninterested in the political developments in France.

Taking such lines of inquiry to their logical conclusion, Emir Kusturica in the German-French-Yugoslavian coproduction *Underground* (1995) diagnoses the final victory of film over reality in the aftermath of fascism and antifascism. His controversial treatment of the history of Yugoslavia during and after World War II presents the relationship between mass politics and mass media on, quite literally, two levels: underground, where partisans continue to amass weapons in the erroneous belief that the war is still raging on, and aboveground, where communist apparatchiks invent the official myth of antifascist resistance to consolidate their power base in the new Yugoslavia. When two partisans stumble onto the set of an antifascist war film, they naturally cause pandemonium. The director's instruction to the actors, "Go on acting! Don't interrupt the shot!," illustrates well the cinema's need for the preservation of artificial fantasies of good and evil and the reversal between fantasy and reality on which it is based. Kusturica's "balkanization of history" may also serve as a motto for the two main films discussed in this chapter, which are similarly haunted by the aestheticization of politics under fascism and respond to the disappearance of the real with decidedly postmodern strategies.[44]

Although part of the discourse of the postpolitical that has brought renewed interest in the fascist imaginary, *Inglourious Basterds* and *Moloch* have little in common with the European resistance films discussed in the next chapter. Sokurov and, with very different interests, Tarantino set out to deconstruct fascism through its own means, namely, by reproducing the aestheticization of politics through the intertextual qualities of film. In so doing, they reveal the void at the center of the fascist fantasy. Yet by making film the instrument of its destruction/reconstruction, they also bracket more-traditional definitions of the political that cannot be reduced to aesthetic phenomena and mass cultural practices. Taking a very different approach, the European films about the resistance released in the first decade of the new millennium present historical fiction as unproblematic and unambiguous, with meaningful identities and identifications available even without the false promises of ideology. As becomes clear in the next chapter, the return of politics as history under such conditions is inseparable from nostalgia for the mobilizing force of disagreement as what Jacques Rancière calls the organizing principle of the political.[45]

# 6

# Postfascist Identity Politics

## European Resistance Films
## in the New Millennium

Looking back, it all seemed so simple . . . We were at war.
The Nazis were the enemy. And because good must triumph
over evil, so we would triumph over them.

Cate Blanchett as the title character of *Charlotte Gray*

(Gillian Armstrong, 2001)

Consider the following four scenes, all set in the early 1940s. In Copenhagen, a young man briskly walks down the street toward a middle-aged man identified in the voice-over as a Nazi editor and shoots him in the head execution style. Elsewhere, in broad daylight, a similar scene occurs in Oslo where a young man guns down a German soldier. In Paris, another young man with a cigarette approaches a Nazi officer in a public park, asking him for a light. As soon as the officer responds to his request, he pulls out a gun, shoots him in the stomach, and calmly walks away. And in Amsterdam, a bespectacled young man repeatedly shoots a burly older man—a collaborator—until he falls into a canal, all the while berating him for his use of blasphemous language.

Thure Lindhardt in *Flame & Citron*

Aksel Hennie in *Max Manus*

Robinson Stévenin in *Army of Crime*

Ronald Armbrust in *Black Book*

These scenes are taken from the Danish *Flammen & Citronen* (*Flame & Citron*, Ole Christian Madsen, 2008), the Norwegian *Max Manus* (Joachim Rønning and Espen Sandberg, 2008), the French *L'armée du crime* (*Army of Crime*, Robert Guédiguian, 2009), and the Dutch *Zwartboek* (*Black Book*, Paul Verhoeven, 2006), four recent films about the Danish, Norwegian, French, and Dutch resistance to the Nazi occupation. What distinguishes these films from earlier treatments can be easily summed up: their political justification, emotional validation, and aesthetic celebration of violence. The Nazis in these films may call the resistance fighters terrorists, but for audiences today they are also men (and women) of action, heroes (even if flawed), patriots (even if forgotten), and, in the words of one character from *Max Manus*, "soldiers without a front."[1]

In Schmittian terms, these men can be described as partisans.[2] Partisans, for Schmitt, are distinguished by four characteristics: their irregular status compared to the army and the police, their remarkable physical mobility inside occupied territory, their intense political passion and commitment, and their territorial or, in his words, telluric character. Unlike partisans, who act defensively, terrorists, that other term haunting the popular reception of these films, act offensively from the start. Existing outside the law and embracing violence as a legitimate political means, they challenge the distinction between combatants and noncombatants and complicate the enemy-friend distinction as the foundation of the political. In the films to be discussed, partisans are frequently described as terrorists, with the conceptual slippage among terrorist, partisan, and, to introduce yet another term, freedom fighter, an essential part of this figure's contemporary relevance and appeal.

In what ways do these partisans embody a new kind of democratic subjectivity, and how do they mobilize political affects under conditions described in the previous chapter as the postpolitical? Wherein lies the appeal of such resistance narratives today? My hypothesis: in their revival of the friend-enemy distinction from the war years and their celebration of violence and terror as legitimate political means. Both are introduced precisely to reconnect to the kind of commitments that are no longer readily available through political ideologies or national identities. The fact that heroic stories of resistance to a foreign invader offer reliable emotional returns especially in the cinemas of small nations (e.g., the Scandinavian countries), which are trying to compete with global Hollywood, should not surprise anyone. But the ways these historical reenactments of contemporary politics provide a projection screen for more-recent fears about the demise of the nation-state in an increasingly unified Europe and globalized world are best explored through the emotions associated with, or released through, such moments of excessive violence: the love of freedom, the shame of occupation, the rage against injustice, the desire for revenge, and, last but not least, the pure thrill of violent action.

The domestic reception of these films in mainstream media and online discussion groups allows me to reconstruct the affective and aesthetic economies in the staging of political antagonisms and to analyze the contradictory functions of the resistance narrative in what the last chapter, on *Moloch* and *Inglourious Basterds*, has defined as the age of postideology. Once again, such a contextualized approach requires some introductory comments on the conditions—of cinema, politics, and society—in the European countries where these films were produced, released, and most intensively discussed.

As *Inglourious Basterds* shows, if only in the form of parodistic self-referentiality, violence—the striking back of the oppressed against the oppressor—has become the lingua franca of the day. "Now let's go kill some Nazis" is not just the battle cry of an American soldier with a bad southern accent; in several European films made in the first decade of the new millennium, it also serves as the proud motto of small resistance groups in Denmark, Norway, France, and the Netherlands. In sharp contrast to recent Hollywood films set in the Third Reich—most famously the Stauffenberg resistance drama *Valkyrie* (Bryan Singer, 2008) starring Tom Cruise and the heroic story of the Jewish Bielski partisans in *Defiance* (Edward Zwick, 2008)—these European films do not idealize their protagonists in order to justify violent acts in the face of oppression and persecution.

Unlike recent German films such as *Der neunte Tag* (*The Ninth Day*, Volker Schlöndorff, 2004) and *Sophie Scholl: Die letzten Tage* (*Sophie Scholl: The Final Days*, Marc Rothemund, 2005), they do not draw on a Christian perspective to redefine resistance in ethical or religious terms. And unlike Sokurov and Tarantino, for whom fascism poses primarily an aesthetic challenge to be taken up with the weapons of film, the directors discussed on the following pages present the Nazis—or, rather, what the Nazis have come to signify—as a serious threat that requires a renewed commitment either to the nation-state or other forms of collective identity such as those associated with the elusive category of the people. In short, the recent European resistance films contribute in not-insignificant ways to what Ernesto Laclau calls the return of populist resentment under the conditions of the postpolitical.[3]

Part of a long history of films about the Nazi occupation, collaboration, and resistance, these latest perspectives on the struggle between fascism and democracy are distinguished by a core contradiction: their rejection of the classical resistance narrative with its moral binaries of good and evil and their reintroduction of the friend-enemy distinction as the basis of a decisionist politics of violence. This contradiction plays out in terms that seem to validate nationalism but do so from the perspective of postnationalism or transnationalism, with the prefix "post" announcing the end of the age of nation-states and the prefix "trans" referring to additional layers of economic, social, and political relations beyond the national. Against this backdrop, the acceptance of moral ambiguity and the celebration of the liberating deed give rise to postnational fantasies of home and belonging that find perfect embodiment in the resistance fighter and his contemporary double: the terrorist. Inseparable from the process of European unification and globalization, the films' stories must therefore be read against the backdrop of a number of contradictory phenomena, including nostalgia for the nation from a postnational perspective and the production of fantasies of nation in decidedly transnational contexts. The resultant forms of engagement—not primarily with the characters but with their commitment to civil liberties as the foundation of democracy—can be best examined through the domestic reception of *Flame & Citron*, *Max Manus*, *Army of Crime*, and *Black Book* in a unified Europe defined by two equally important dates, 9 November 1989 (i.e., the fall of the Berlin Wall) and 11 September 2001 (i.e., the 11 September attacks on the United States).

In the cinema and beyond, two factors have contributed to the enlistment of the resistance narrative in contemporary debates on postnationalism, multiculturalism, and globalization. First, the recent wave of European resistance films would be inconceivable without the vast amount of historical scholarship

on the Third Reich and the Holocaust. Since the end of World War II, research on the occupation, collaboration, and resistance in Denmark, Norway,
France, and the Netherlands has produced more-differentiated accounts that
examine both the regimes of terror, violence, and intimidation in everyday life
and the mutually beneficial economic and political relations enjoyed by occupier
and occupied.[4] In the case of France, this has meant addressing the contradictions of a nation divided between fascist sympathies and antifascist activities
and acknowledging the decisive and influential role of the Vichy regime.
Scholars have shown that widespread accommodation to and collaboration
with the Nazi occupation were made possible not only by individual greed, corruption, and opportunism but also by the willing, if not enthusiastic, surrender
of large parts of the population to authoritarian rule out of an intense frustration with parliamentary democracies and a deep-seated antisemitism and anticommunism. Contradicting official narratives according to which the majority
of Frenchmen were part of the resistance movement, studies published since
the 1970s have confirmed the pervasiveness of antisemitism in France and the
Netherlands, two countries with deep involvement in the genocide of European Jewry, and brought to light the activities of indigenous fascist groups especially in the Scandinavian countries.

To come to the second point, the resistance films are unthinkable without
the nostalgia for history that, over the past two decades, has produced heritage
parks, heritage museums, national trusts, and laws for the preservation of national languages and cultures and that can be traced in the so-called heritage
films as its most famous filmic manifestation. Key to the notion of heritage is
the translation of temporal into spatial relations through the focus on set and
costume design and the displacement of questions of historical agency into the
spectacular effects of mise-en-scène. In the films discussed in this chapter, this
usually includes a fetishistic investment in the fashions, hairstyles, and objects
of everyday life (cars, radios, telephones, guns) central to the work of the resistance. Muted color schemes with warm sepia tones, low-contrast lighting, naturalist camera styles, and lush orchestral scores create an atmosphere of both
historicity and pastness that allows for the acting out of very contemporary
longings. Associated with 1980s British cinema during the conservative Thatcher
era, the heritage film as a critical category covers a wide range of genres from
literary adaptations and biopics to period films and costume dramas, offering
idealized versions of Britishness that are most often associated with the Victorian and Edwardian periods. The conservative Pompidou era in France and
the conservative Kohl era in Germany produced similar versions of what Phil
Powrie calls Vichy heritage cinema and what, correspondingly, might be called

Nazi heritage cinema.[5] Heritage films, according to film scholar Andrew Higson, celebrate traditional ways of life based on clear social, national, and ethnic divisions and preserved in the cultural sensibilities of economic and social elites.[6] Less a genre than a historical sensibility, these films represent attempts to come to terms with the loss of empire and the demise of a homogeneous national culture. In what ways they promote an inherently conservative agenda remains a subject of intense debates, given their occasional openness to alternative sexualities and sensibilities.

Introducing action-filled scenes and graphic violence into the heritage film, a genre otherwise known for more contemplative and conversational moods, the resistance films draw upon the look and feel of the 1940s to present decisionism as a viable solution to the pervasive sense of disempowerment and disillusionment shared by wartime Europe and contemporary Europe. Accordingly, the outbursts of violence in the scenes described earlier can be seen as the historical reenactment of a very present-day frustration among many citizens in the Continent's most established liberal democracies with what Žižek calls the deadlocks of postpolitical tolerance; these acts are "the form in which the foreclosed political returns in the post-political universe of pluralist negotiation and consensual regulation."[7] The resultant nostalgia for the will to act and the political legitimacy gained from it find symptomatic expression in the fetishization of violence in all four films. However, the activities of the resistance never rise to the level of what Alain Badiou calls a political event, the kind of irruption or intervention that for him is the founding principle of the political.[8] Despite the inclusion of documentary footage and staged mass scenes, the violence fails to conjure up the collective subject that is the precondition of the political event in Badiou and instead focuses all attention on the individual as the primary site of contemporary identity politics. The attendant shift in the resistance narrative from a Manichean struggle between good and evil toward a more ambiguous moral universe occupied by traitors, informers, and collaborators can be noticed as early as the 1970s in the deconstruction of the myth of French resistance. Then associated with a particular sensibility known as retro style, this revisionist process continued in the discourse of heritage that has informed filmic representations of the Third Reich since the 1990s. In both cases, the selective appropriation of national history by heritage discourse revolves around one central affect: nostalgia. Yet its filmic manifestations are far from homogeneous, and its most recent irruptions decidedly political in tone, especially in the rediscovery of resistance as an essential part of democratic life.

The retro style aimed at a demythologization of the resistance and entailed a critique of official government rhetoric and left-right ideological divides. By contrast, heritage discourse must be associated with a very different project: the remythologization of the resistance through simulations of the national in the age of the transnational. Heritage refers less to a particular look of history, most often achieved through production and costume design, than nostalgia for the kind of commitments and attachments provided by the traditional nation-state, including the antagonisms that define its mechanisms of inclusion and exclusion. In the new millennium, the political quietism shared by 1970s retro style and 1980s heritage style has given way to the contemporary forms of identity politics that are realized through individual acts of resistance and the more hidden resentments channeled through the allegories of war and occupation that are projected onto the most violent period of modern European history.

Establishing this elusive connection between national and postnational imaginaries requires a closer look at audiences, including directors and film critics as stand-ins for the ideal or intended spectator. For that reason, my analysis on the following pages is based on highly contextualized readings that situate the individual films at the intersection of contemporary politics and film history. While the previous chapter focused on intertextual effects to make sense of fascism as an aesthetic phenomenon, this chapter examines the critical reception of films about the anti-Nazi resistance in their respective countries of origin, with reception understood as yet another important mechanism in the naming of real or imagined political enemies and the making of democratic subjectivities. Accordingly, the patterns of reception allow us to reconstruct how domestic audiences, as citizens, experience and interpret films about the resistance within the larger narratives of nation, history, and democracy.

Confirming the power of cinema as a public sphere, critical reviews in national newspapers and interviews with directors, screenwriters, and actors play an important role in identifying preferred and negotiated readings, to use Stuart Hall's well-known distinction, and allow us to reconstruct the horizons of expectation shared by the filmmakers and their audiences. However, it is outside the official channels of reception, namely, in what Hall calls oppositional readings, that we often learn the most about film as a projection screen for more-extreme political fantasies. Following recent trends in reception studies, my analysis includes sources such as online discussion groups with little interest in the films as works of art but an abiding need to give voice to political resentments. As I argue, it is in the crazy rants and paranoid delusions—far removed from the cognitive processes analyzed by theoreticians and the aesthetic judgments passed by reviewers—that we can learn the most about the explosive connection between fascism as filmic fantasy and the crisis of liberal democracy today.

By pitting indigenous populations against foreign invaders and by mobilizing local sensibilities against global forces, the resistance films provide emotionally gratifying answers to the current legitimation crises in European democracies, especially those exploited by populist movements, and the most pressing problems of multiethnic Europe, especially those attributed to Muslim immigration.[9] In offering historical solutions to these problems, all four films focus on violence as a problem and a solution. Yet as I show, they use their politics of violence to very different ends: the celebration of postnational patriotism and love of the "mother country" in *Flame & Citron* and *Max Manus*; the call for leftist class politics and multiethnic solidarity in *Army of Crime*, and the promotion of an American-style identity politics against the backdrop of continuously shifting allegiances in *Black Book*. Part of a postnational Scandinavian heritage cinema, the first two films will be discussed together.

Moreover, these films can be identified with three very different modes of production and forms of reception: two national blockbusters (*Flame & Citron* and *Max Manus*), a domestic failure (*Army of Crime*), and an international success (*Black Book*). While the last film, in typical Hollywood fashion, reduces all events to individual needs and desires, the first three films rely on the old friend-enemy distinction to develop new models for democracy in action: by showing individuals and small groups as effective political actors, by imagining forms of political engagement beyond national, social, or ethnic differences, and by reclaiming the political as a distinct energy uncontainable by the cultural and the social. All four films are indebted to contemporary identity politics and seek to resolve the resultant tension between particularism and universalism—that is, between self-interest and the common good—through recourse to modified versions of the friend-enemy distinction and its performative enactment in repeated acts of graphic violence. And for reasons that require further contextualization in the individual case studies, all films inspired entirely unexpected reactions on the fringes of mainstream reception: anti-Muslim invective in the case of *Flame & Citron* and *Max Manus* and unwarranted speculation about the status of *Black Book* as an anti-American allegory of the Iraq War.

At the time of their release, *Flame & Citron* and *Max Manus* were (and still are) the most expensive and most profitable films ever made in Denmark and Norway, with *Flame & Citron* costing $9 million and *Max Manus* $8 million and with both films making a profit already in the first year of their release. Proudly mentioned in most reviews, these numbers have become an indicator both of the continued economic viability and cultural relevance of national film industries and the desired identity of national cinema and national history.[10] But does such heavy investment in the idea of nation make these films nationalistic, or should we follow political scientist Donald Phillips and differentiate between nationalism as a sense of belonging that is fixed in time and place and a postnational patriotism that remains open to the migration of peoples and ideas and is continuously redefined in accordance with the concerns of the present?[11] Should we be alarmed about the films' nostalgia for nation and homeland, or should we follow film scholar Mette Hjort, who—based on George Orwell's well-known distinction between nationalism's pursuit of power and domination and patriotism's devotion to a particular way of life—concludes that patriotism, "rather than being a symptom of democratic collapse, is a component of the kind of social bond that is the very condition of a well-functioning democracy."[12] The critical reception of *Flame & Citron* and *Max Manus* supports both kinds of readings: a hegemonic one, in which patriotism expresses itself in the fight against dictatorship and occupation but, given its culturalist definition, does not presuppose exclusionary strategies, and an oppositional reading, in which the invasion by the Germans becomes a blueprint for xenophobic fantasies about a new kind of invasion headed by the Muslims as the new Nazis.[13]

Making sense of such presentist readings (or rather, misreadings) requires us to consider the conditions of production and reception that connect *Flame & Citron* and *Max Manus* to the forces of globalization and European unification and the growing nostalgia for nation-based models of identity and belonging. The self-assertion of the cinemas of small nations through stories of national resistance cannot be evaluated outside the contradictions of European filmmaking confronted with the hegemony of global Hollywood, transnational modes of production, and the imperatives of nation branding. Yet new European funding and production schemes do not necessarily translate into international successes or promote cosmopolitan sensibilities. *Flame & Citron* may be a Danish-Czech-German and *Max Manus* a Norwegian-Danish-German coproduction, but in their focus on Danish or Norwegian history both films address themselves primarily to domestic audiences. Avoiding the eclectic or hybrid styles often found in what Hjort calls self-defeating coproductions, each film proved to be enormously successful at home but disappointed in other European markets; the fact that both won numerous awards on the international festival circuit did little to change these differences between domestic and foreign reception.[14] In Denmark, *Flame & Citron* in 2008 grossed $9.210 million, making it the number 1 box office hit of that year, yet *Max Manus* was not even

Danish poster for *Flame & Citron*, courtesy    Norwegian poster for *Max Manus*, courtesy
Nimbus Film                                      Filmkamaratene AS

among the first two hundred films. Meanwhile, in Norway, *Max Manus* in 2008
grossed a remarkable $15.101 million but *Flame & Citron* only $149,776; to offer
a comparison, *Downfall* in 2005 earned a respectable $2.913 million in that
national market.[15]

Confirming the films' overdetermined status as national productions, the
premieres became highly publicized events and were treated as important contributions to official memory culture. Crown Prince Frederik and Crown Princess Mary as well as the last living members of the Danish resistance appeared
among the guests at the gala premiere of *Flame & Citron*. King Harald V and
the sole survivor of the Max Manus group attended the first public screening of
*Max Manus*. In sharp contrast to *Black Book* with its unmistakable Hollywood
provenance, *Flame & Citron* and *Max Manus* were from the beginning regarded
as part of a long national conversation about a resistance movement remembered in scholarly books, individual memoirs, popular myths, and history
museums such as the Museum of Danish Resistance 1940–45 in Copenhagen
and Norway's Resistance (or Norwegian Home Front) Museum in Oslo. (Their
equivalents for the other films are the Dutch Resistance Museum in Amsterdam and numerous regional museums of the French resistance in Lyon, Tou-
louse, Blois, and elsewhere.)

Representative of a group of Scandinavian filmmakers who are no longer bound by overly rigid distinctions between art and entertainment, Ole Christian Madsen, the director of *Flame & Citron*, and Joachim Rønning and Espen Sandberg, the team responsible for *Max Manus*, came to their projects through a long-standing personal fascination with the history of the resistance. In interviews, Madsen, who has been associated with the Dogme 95 group, expressed his desire to refamiliarize Danish audiences with national heroes well known during the 1950s but forgotten, as he claims, because of the pacifism of the 1960s and 1970s. Asked about the seemingly inexhaustible fascination with the war years, he answered: "World War II is such a huge story . . . it's the biggest we've ever had. So there will always be films made about it. But the film's discussion of guerrilla warfare, the whole gray area of such conflict, is quite contemporary. I think whenever there is a war on, there's always more public interest in the subject."[16] Like Madsen, Rønning and Sandberg belong to a younger generation in their thirties and early forties for whom heritage means, above all, action and adventure, as confirmed by their film project *Kon-Tiki* (2012), about Thor Heyerdahl's famous 1947 crossing of the Pacific on a wooden raft. Acutely aware of the importance of historical accuracy, they based their screenplay on two books written by Manus about his experiences during World War II, did extensive research at Norway's Resistance Museum, and interviewed historical witnesses to, in their words, make their exemplary stories of valor and honor relevant for today.

Stylistically, *Flame & Citron* and *Max Manus* can be described as typical examples of heritage cinema and its competing demands of cinematic illusionism, emotional realism, historical authenticity, and political nostalgia. Both productions reference the discourses of nation and homeland that, whether through the association with specific landscapes or lifestyles, have informed Scandinavian film and literature since the beginning of the twentieth century. They borrow elements from Hollywood action adventures, war films, and noir thrillers but also draw on a distinctly European iconography of resistance. Similarly, they address themselves explicitly to domestic audiences but realize their visions of homeland through the transnational modes of financing that allow even small companies to make big-budget films with spectacular settings; the heavy reliance on advanced technologies such as the computer-generated imagery used to show the sinking of the SS *Donau* transport ship in *Max Manus* is a case in point.

At the same time, *Flame & Citron* and *Max Manus* contribute to a different kind of heritage cinema through their disillusionment with traditional nationalism and their nostalgia for new/old forms of political commitment. Both use violence—the experience of violence, the act of violence, and the response to violence—as an energizing device through which to reclaim the affective investments that sustain the idea of nation, beginning with the cult of the hero of the people. Accordingly, *Flame & Citron* offers a fictionalized account of the Holger Danske resistance group, named after the knight of ancient sagas, and two of its leading figures, the flamboyant red-haired Flame (pseud. Bent Faurschou-Hviid) and the rumpled and perennially unshaven Citron (pseud. Jørgen Haagen Schmith), who, in 1943 and 1944, carried out a series of contract killings of Nazi officials and suspected Danish informers. *Max Manus* closely follows the exploits of one resistance fighter from his first arrest by the Germans and escape to England and his return to Norway as a specialist in industrial sabotage who, as a member of Kompani Linge, sank several German Navy ships in 1944 with the help of homemade limpet mines.

Through a montage of newspaper headlines and newsreel footage, the films' opening sequences place the extraordinary stories of these ordinary men within national history. At the same time, the first-person narrative and direct address to the spectator ("you") present the trauma of occupation as an experience shared by protagonists and audiences and, in doing so, establish an emotional matrix for presentist readings. *Flame & Citron* opens on 9 April 1940, the day of the German invasion, with Flame's somber voice setting the mood: "Do you remember when they arrived?" The story of *Max Manus*, following the hero's initiation into warfare during the Finnish-Soviet War, begins in Oslo in June 1940, the month of the Norwegian capitulation. The Danish film introduces the protagonists in the midst of a murderous assignment, giving no further explanations. Meanwhile, the Norwegian film presents resistance as the logical extension of patriotic sentiment. Manus—Aksel Hennie in a refreshingly unsentimental performance—simply acts on what others are thinking: "The government gave up on our defense. . . . We'll build our own army." During a conversation with a British officer, included in all the trailers, he explains his involvement as an act of patriotism: "My country was stolen from me, sir. And I want it back." The films' endings strangely match their different tones and attitudes. Flame and Citron are killed in an apotheosis of violence and buried in a makeshift grave. Manus on liberation day finds himself surrounded by the ghosts of friends who died, experiencing the first signs of survivor guilt in what the closing credits describe as his later bouts with depression and struggle with alcoholism. Acknowledging these personal sacrifices, the credits complete the convergence of individual story and national history promised at the beginning. As we learn, Flame and Citron each received a posthumous state burial and several medals, and Max Manus was given the highest honors bestowed by King Hakoon II.

Between the call to action after the traumatic beginnings and the moment of liberation in the sobering endings, the narratives are constructed around a series of violent acts, shown in often gruesome detail, that maintain spectator interest even in the absence of strong character identifications. Flame and Citron carry out a series of contract killings so brutally efficient that they have earned both characters the honorific "badass" in several online discussion groups.[17] Central to their appeal is the presentation of violence as a performance, that is, not a manifestation of evil (i.e., as in the portrayal of the Nazis). In the opening sequence of *Flame & Citron*, we find Flame getting dressed in front of a mirror, assuming the identity of an assassin. His instructions to himself are clear: "Act with determination. Execute your plan. If you stay calm, no one will suspect a thing. People will only be looking at the deed. . . . I know I am doing the right thing." This performative quality is maintained throughout, with Flame's sartorial elegance and cool demeanor fueling the romance of heroic action and with Citron's scruffy appearance and grumpy look serving as a reminder of the inevitable sacrifices required by life in the resistance.

But what is the right thing? Killing Danes suspected of being traitors but not killing the despised head of the Gestapo? Trusting a mysterious femme fatale or taking orders from a resistance leader later accused of working for both sides? As both men grow increasingly distrustful of their contacts in the underground and uncertain of the righteousness of their mission, individual differences become more apparent. The younger Flame falls for the blonde Ketty, while the more mature Citron loses his wife and daughter to another man. As the cool-headed Flame begins to make mistakes, the more pensive Citron overcomes his initial inhibitions. Yet while the latter is consumed with guilt at the thought of having killed innocent people, the former continues to believe in the necessity of their work. In his words: "The only thing you can do is eliminate them [i.e., the Nazis]. One by one." In their fixation on the violent deed and the decisive act, the two men in the end no longer know who the real enemies are.

The conception of the main characters sparked considerable debate in the Danish press, evidence of the inherent tension between the reclamation of the resistance myth and its reinterpretation through the lens of contemporary anxieties. Unclear whether to think of their actions as justified killings or as senseless murders, some critics denounced Flame and Citron as "maladjusted young men, desperados, if not psychopaths. If they hadn't had the Germans to fight, they might have ended up fighting for something far less noble."[18] Expecting an uplifting story of true heroism, the reviewer in the right-leaning *Jyllands-Posten* was one of several who responded negatively to such moral ambiguity and professed his dissatisfaction with the resultant lack of strong character identifications:

"You are tempted to shrug off both Flame and Citron and say: What concern is that to me!?"[19] However, other critics welcomed such complications as an important commentary on the hurdles to political activism in the age of postideology. To quote a review in the Oslo-based daily *Dagsavisen*: "It becomes increasingly difficult for the pair to separate allies from enemies in this confusing chaos of lies, deceit, and duplicity—and increasingly difficult for us as the audience to determine whether they are brave war heroes or fanatical terrorists. It is one of the movie's strengths that it refuses to give us any simple answers to these dilemmas, and the story has a psychological depth that contradicts the nostalgic war romance."[20]

The male leads themselves did not perceive such ambiguity as an obstacle to character engagement; on the contrary, to them, it allowed for greater critical and emotional complexity. Thus the younger Thure Lindhardt, in an interview with the tabloid *Ekstra Bladet*, defended his character and the message of the film: "It tells us what it means to go to war, and what it means to fight for something you believe in and accept the consequences. I see him not as a psychopath but as someone who believes in justice and who is an idealist."[21] And in an interview with the conservative *Berlinske Tidende*, international screen villain Mads Mikkelsen—Citron in the film—elaborated on the difference between the two title figures:

> Where Flame quickly becomes the lethal killer who never hesitates with the trigger in front of his victims—except on one ill-fated occasion—Citron is a man who is visibly affected by the executions, especially when an innocent child is caught in the crossfire during the attempted assassination of a Gestapo man. . . . I could relate to the situation when it's about close combat and self-defense. But simply liquidating someone from behind must be very, very mind-blowing. I don't think anybody can do that and still be a whole person afterward. When you have crossed that line, I don't think you will walk away without psychological scars.[22]

Unlike *Flame & Citron*, which depicts the evolution of characters as one from certainty to uncertainty, *Max Manus* follows a more affirmative trajectory. It starts with a traumatic flashback to the title figure's first killing of a man during the Finnish-Soviet War, filmed with a handheld camera to give the images a documentary feel, but then proceeds to focus on the making of a national hero. In this film, violence serves as a way of clarifying the differences between friends and enemies and thereby stabilizing the meaning of national identity. The connection between resistance and patriotism is strengthened through the romance between Max and Tikken, with the woman introduced as the healer of the broken man and the heterosexual couple presented as the foundation of national reconstruction after liberation. However, despite all these efforts at closure, even *Max Manus* leaves its audience with a strange sense of foreboding. At their final meeting in prison, the Gestapo man Fehmer asks the hero: "So, do you feel any better? Now that the Big Bad Wolf is behind bars?" The answer, both in the dominant and the oppositional readings of the film, is obviously no.

*Flame & Citron* and *Max Manus* were neither the first Danish or Norwegian films about the resistance nor the first to thematize its problematic role in official memory culture. As early as the 1940s, the possibility of armed resistance in the form of sabotage, assassinations, and other special operations had sparked the filmic imagination. In Denmark, the classic *De røde enge* (*Red Meadows*, Bodil Ipsen, 1945), about a traitor in a resistance group, showed the men's courage and sacrifice in a starkly realist mode. *En dag i oktober* (*A Day in October*, Kenneth Madsen, 1992), about the rescue of the Danish Jews, had already profited from the myth of the resistance by adding a decidedly sentimental touch; offering "a tribute to the human spirit," that film proved moderately successful abroad. Occupation dramas such as *De nøgne træer* (The naked trees, Morten Henriksen, 1991) and *Drengene fra Sankt Petri* (The boys from St. Petri, Søren Kragh-Jacobsen, 1991) were never released in English-subtitled versions, confirming their status as national stories with little international appeal.[23]

Meanwhile, the Norwegian resistance had previously been portrayed in anti-Nazi films such as the British *The Avengers* (Harold French, 1942) and the American *First Comes Courage* (Dorothy Arzner, 1943), with the name of the collaborationist president Vidkun Quisling henceforth serving as a synonym for traitor. The earliest Norwegian war films were made in the 1990s, ushering in a period of historical revisionism. As one of the first to challenge the convenient division between remembering and forgetting, *Knut Hamsun* (Jan Troell, 1996) confronted audiences with an unflattering portrait of the country's most famous writer and infamous collaborator. In the same way that the Hamsun film contributed to the long overdue demontage of a cultural institution, *Max Manus* emphasizes the sacrifices and compromises required of a national hero; therein it resembles the Swedish *God afton, Herr Wallenberg* (*Good Evening, Mr. Wallenberg*, Kjell Grede, 1990) about the Swedish diplomat responsible for the rescue of the Hungarian Jews. Unlike the latter, the recent films present the dynamics of triumph and trauma in the lush appearance of heritage and, in so doing, contribute to the aestheticization of violence found in a similar period piece set in the postwar years, the Swedish *Ondskan* (*Evil*, Mikael Håfström, 2003). And to draw my circles even wider, unlike earlier contributions to the little-known genre of the Nazi zombie film traceable back to 1940s Hollywood, the Norwegian *Død snø* (*Dead Snow*, Tommy Wirkola, 2009) exports the familiar spectacle of blood and gore to a pristine Scandinavian snowscape populated by young, healthy men and women.

The oppositional readings that collapse the historical trauma of Nazi occupation with contemporary fantasies of national self-defense can be approached best through the distinction between "terrorists" and "freedom fighters" frequently made in the Norwegian reception of *Max Manus*. Comparisons to the so-called war on terror appear in many mainstream reviews. Few readers would disagree with the critic for the center-left weekly *Weekendavisen* who wrote: "The film sides with the saboteurs but at the same time is fully aware that the winners write history and decide who the 'terrorists' and who the 'freedom-fighters' are. This current problematic is one of several defining features of the World War II films produced after the millennium."[24] Another commentator added: "It is thought provoking at the present juncture to be reminded that the sabotage our heroes perform is called terrorism by the other side."[25] Treating the Nazi occupation as a measure of civil courage and national pride, a reader writing to the popular tabloid *B.T.* expressed popular sentiment when he asked: "If one imagined a similar occupation again, I wonder if we all would once again be opportunists and traitors? I am afraid we would."[26]

Many references to terrorists and resistance fighters in the mainstream media reflect widespread opposition in the Scandinavian countries to the Iraq war, but some comments also use the resistance narrative to paint a much darker picture of the future of the Nordic and Baltic states under the global regimes of mass migration. Several online discussion groups include anti-immigrant rants, with the Muslims now assigned the place of the Germans and with references to "occupation" assuming entirely different meanings. Thus *Max Manus* prompted the following tirade by one Norwegian contributor: "Yes! It will be a good movie! Too bad that 10 percent of Norway's population doesn't know who these guys are since they don't give a damn about the Norwegian cultural heritage. I am of course thinking of all the Muslims."[27] Similarly, in a Danish right-wing blog, *Flame & Citron* triggers the following paranoid hallucination: "Even a normal trip through town is becoming a surreal experience. Crew-cut Islamofascists [driving around] in large, open Mercedes Benzes and ghostly female coconspirators walking the streets. . . . Sorry to say it, but one automatically thinks of that scene in *Flame & Citron* where the latter has to retreat to a doorway to puke at the sight of Germans marching through the streets. One understands the disgust!"[28] In the actual film, the voice-over comments on Citron's visceral reaction in this way: "He feels sick. A feeling that persists"—to this day, some Scandinavian audiences seem to suggest.

In order to fully comprehend these clearly unintended and unexpected forms of reception, we might want to look at a longer discussion on *Max Manus* in a blog sponsored by *Afterposten*, the largest daily newspaper in Norway. The contributions, by collapsing the *demos* (i.e., a community defined through political processes and negotiations) with the *ethnos* (i.e., a community defined through descent and affiliation), mobilize all the rhetorical devices and strategies necessary to produce an extremely racist, nationalistic reading of the film. Presumably "about" *Max Manus*, the discussion starts out with an analysis of the failure of the Norwegian war effort but soon deteriorates into incoherent ramblings on the lack of political leadership and the threat of foreign infiltration today:

> A: If you look at society today, we are not much better. In Elverum [a Norwegian town] a bus driver is beaten half to death by a gang of immigrants. What do the Norwegian police do? Let them go of course. What we should have done is obvious. But the important question is whether we as a nation have become a bunch of cowards?
>
> B: The "war" we are in now on the other hand, it looks like we don't want to win!!! And we can forget about help from NATO, soon there will probably be a Muslim secretary general. . . . The Nazis came as soldiers, in battleships and military planes. Those who today are occupying Norway come as poor asylum-seekers, as women and children, as "family-immigrants," as imported spouses—not to mention those who "just come" without Norwegian authorities knowing anything at all! Or doing anything to find out . . .
>
> C: But they represent an ideology that surpasses Nazism effortlessly when it comes to racism, antisemitism, Führer worship, belief in one "master race" and everyone else's inferiority (and this time we don't have the advantage of being "Germanic"), violence, oppression, and the absence of rule of law! Today's battle is far more difficult both because we can't easily make out the difference between an enemy and a fellow human being in need and because "our authorities" this time don't want to see the enemy at all! Today the royal family doesn't flee, on the contrary: the king expresses that he is also the Muslims' king. . . . Today the church and priests do not protest; on the contrary: they even open Nidarosdomen [the cathedral of Trontheim] for recitals of the Koran! I wonder what epitaph will be given today's "resistance fighters" fifty to sixty years from now. As always, it is totally dependent on who will be "the victors."[29]

Such comments must be read as a response to the growing Muslim presence in Scandinavian countries and the resulting integration problems experienced by socially and culturally homogeneous societies that until the 1990s were celebrated as models of social democracy and the welfare state and that since then have had to deal with the negative (and positive) effects of globalization and the neoliberal world order. As harbingers of these changes, the migrants, refugees, and asylum seekers who have made these countries their home since the 1960s continue to challenge the foundations of liberal democracy and Western civilization and reveal the limits of European multiculturalism and cosmopolitanism. The 2007 controversy over the Danish Muhammad cartoon confirms the continued commitment to freedom of speech and progressive secularism, but the changes in immigration policies and integration strategies and the rise of the right-wing People's Party in Denmark and the anti-immigrant Progress Party in Norway also indicate a return of the right-wing populisms and *völkisch* ideologies that haunted Denmark and Norway during the 1930s and 1940s. Not surprisingly, the resistance narrative has emerged as one of the privileged sites for the competing affective regimes of postnational patriotism and racist nationalism; that it also lends itself to dreams of international and multiethnic solidarity will become clear in the next case study.

If *Flame & Citron* and *Max Manus* can be described as quasi-official accounts of the Danish and Norwegian resistance, the French *Army of Crime* must be seen as quintessential revisionist history, challenging well-established national myths and patterns of demystification, introducing a marginalized or forgotten group as an important historical agent, and drawing on this other past to shed light on the social and political problems of the present. Directed by Robert Guédiguian, the film claims a legitimate place in history for the communist resistance, as embodied by the so-called Manouchian group led by Armenian worker-poet Missak Manouchian. Its politicized reading of the lessons of history also stands in stark contrast to the concurrent appropriation of the resistance narrative by an apolitical heritage discourse. Not surprisingly, the film was a commercial failure and its critical reception a predictable affair that, more than anything, reflected long-held positions in the postwar approach to the French history of resistance and occupation. But even on such well-trodden ground, the significatory excess produced by the sudden bursts of violence in the film brought into sharp relief one of the most pressing questions in French society today: the meaning of Frenchness in the age of multiethnic societies and fluid national identifications.

The story of *Army of Crime* revolves around a communist resistance group made up of French workers, East European Jews, and Italian and Spanish Brigadists who committed acts of sabotage in Paris in 1943 and early 1944; they were apprehended, convicted, and executed in February 1944. The title

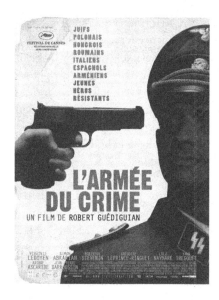

*L'Affiche rouge* poster in *Army of Crime*

French poster for *Army of Crime*, courtesy StudioCanal

references the infamous Nazi poster, the *affiche rouge*, denouncing them as criminals: "Liberators? Liberated by the army of crime!" reads the sarcastic description below their mug shots.[30] The poster's purpose was to depict the communist resistance as a group of foreigners and Jews intent on destroying authentic French culture. Complicating such denunciatory strategies, there have been controversies since the 1980s about whether the PCF (Parti Communiste Français, French Communist Party) sacrificed the Manouchian group to the Nazis in a power struggle with the Gaullists or whether the group was exposed by the anticommunist French secret police, as suggested by the film.

The insistence on forms of political engagement that move beyond an ethnically based definition of Frenchness is part and parcel of the film's narrative strategies and forms of character engagement. The film begins with a Jewish mother's hopeful assertion, "This is France. Nothing can happen to us here. It's the land of human rights." Of course, she is proven wrong by the racial and political persecution that propels her son and his friend to take up arms. By sacrificing their lives, they become role models for audiences today to fight for the universal human rights evoked by the mother. "Died for France" is how the framing story introduces the resistance members on the way to their execution. Moving from 1944 back to 1941, the film brings together two story lines: that of two young men who act out their desire for revenge by killing individual Nazis and that of the older Manouchian—played with quiet intensity by Simon

Abkarian—who recruits them for a new resistance group that is soon carrying out actions throughout Paris. From the outset, violence is presented as essential to the establishment of a dictatorial regime and its inevitable defeat by that elusive but all-powerful force called the people. Manouchian originally opposes participating in violent actions on ethical grounds but eventually learns how to shoot, with Marshal Pétain as a target; it is personal trauma (i.e., the Armenian genocide) that allows him to finally test his new skills on a group of Waffen-SS— with deadly results. Yet unlike his young associates, even in his last letter to his wife he insists, "I feel no hatred for the German people."

An idealist with strong political convictions, director Guédiguian has a German-Armenian background, a long history of involvement with leftist groups, and a highly personal interest in working-class and immigrant culture explored in several earlier feature films set in his hometown, Marseille. His contribution to the return of politicized filmmaking in the French cinema of the 1990s has been recognized in the description of his work as "films of solidarity."[31] If the earlier *Le promeneur du champ du Mars* (*The Last Mitterrand*, 2003) looks back to the Vichy sympathies of the then-last French president, *Army of Crime* introduces the multiethnic group around Manouchian as a model of political activism for contemporary audiences. In an interview with the communist daily *L'Humanité*, Guédiguian spoke openly of his search for "a legend that helps us to live in today's world." He explained, "I wanted to focus on their convictions and show that one can be heroic, even today and even if it does not involve killing or dying. This holds true for all acts of civil disobedience from the directors' movement about ten years ago to protests by undocumented workers, strikes or other acts often defined as illegal."[32] In another interview, Guédiguian discussed his concern that the history of communism and the leftist struggle is being forgotten: "I think the worst thing that's happening to us is that the ties have been broken. In the last twenty to thirty years, there has been a break with five or six generations of struggle and counterculture. Today, people are disoriented. Probably the most serious consequence of the gradual removal of the Communist Party from the French political landscape is the disappearance of a historical alternative that informs class consciousness in towns and factories."[33] The director's desire to intervene in contemporary debates on immigration and to contribute to leftist activism is openly acknowledged in the closing credits: "To relate the commitment of foreigners in the French resistance, I had to alter certain events. That was necessary to recount this modern legend, to help us live here and now."

As expected, the critical reception of *Army of Crime* in the mainstream press was highly politicized. The leftist daily *Libération* was full of praise: "*Army of Crime* is the first fiction film since 1976 dedicated to the story of these 'foreign' communists . . . and it deserves a great deal of credit for having placed the contribution of these 'twenty-three foreigners, and also our brothers,' as Aragon put it, squarely into collective memory."[34] *Le Monde*, the most influential French newspaper, described the film as "a paean to life and the resistance, a highly relevant call for the rights of men, for their right to resist."[35] Some readers took issue with this approach, insisting that "by attempting, for reasons ideological and communitarian, to build a legend and advance a myth, Guédiguian has not paid tribute to the memory of these resistance fighters but instrumentalized their true stories."[36] Others welcomed the explicit comparison to growing conflicts over immigration and multiculturalism and saw the film as a timely reminder of France's multiethnic past; proclaimed one reader: "Yes, immigrants fighting for France!"[37]

Once again, the representation of violence in the film is inseparable from the search for new forms of collective action and social change. To quote one member of the group: "We kill because we are partisans of life. . . . We kill people but we're on the side of life." Unlike *Flame & Citron* and *Max Manus*, *Army of Crime* provides the model for a different kind of life by including moments of private happiness; to quote the reviewer from *Le Monde*: "The character of Manouchian exists to serve the political-ethical project of Guédiguian: he is a man capable of killing while continuing to live and love."[38] In sharp contrast to *Black Box*, violence in *Army of Crime* is never sexualized; on the contrary, the necessity of violence according to the partisans' code of ethics (i.e., violence as a political means) is presented as the guarantor of the sensual eroticism and tender love between Manouchian and his wife. In the French press, the director's nuanced approach to violence inspired frequent comparisons to *Inglourious Basterds*, not surprising given the films' almost simultaneous releases. In the words of one critic: "For Tarantino, the spectacle of violence is the end, the historical context and the identity of the characters ( Jews, Nazis) the means. . . . By contrast, for Guédiguian violence is only a means, problematic but necessary; this is how the people free themselves of their oppressors."[39]

As in the case of *Flame & Citron* and *Max Manus*, several commentators complained about insufficient character engagement. "One doesn't tremble; one doesn't feel thrills. We might blame ourselves for this lack of emotion, even slapping ourselves to force a reaction. But a couple of these blows should be reserved for Guédiguian for not having succeeded at moving us as he should have," concluded one of them.[40] The director's decision to minimize identification—he cites Brechtian defamiliarization as an important inspiration—undoubtedly contributed to such critical reactions. However, the film's lack of emotional resonance, its belated quality, has ultimately much more to do with the steady erosion of the resistance narrative as the foundation of French postwar identity and the model for a uniquely French understanding of culture, politics, and society.

The connection between emotional detachment and depoliticization is fully apparent in the Vichy heritage films that, unlike *Army of Crime*, are no longer concerned with making a political intervention. Well-made middlebrow productions in the 1950s *tradition du qualité*, they offer nostalgic pleasures and retrospective views: Vichy as popular entertainment. Identifying France with a particular culture of everyday life, these films rely on classical narratives, stereotypical characters, opulent sets and beautiful costumes, and, not to forget, famous stars such as Gérard Depardieu, Isabelle Adjani, and Sophie Marceau. More specifically, they use convention, sentiment, and nostalgia as conduit to the affirmation of social and cultural homogeneity as the foundation of national identity. Within such a culturalist understanding of resistance, its political meanings have been evacuated, but its narrative contexts greatly expanded: to the self-referential comments on filmmaking in *Safe Conduct* (already mentioned in chapter 5), the farcical treatment of love and war in *Bon Voyage* (Jean-Paul Rappaneau, 2003), and the sensationalist story of female British Special Operations Executive agents in *Les femmes de l'ombre* (*Female Agents*, Jean-Paul Salomé, 2008). Deprived of their historical referent, these films today rarely invite controversies, usually receive mixed reviews, and fare moderately to poorly at the box office. To give some numbers, *Safe Conduct* grossed only $1.659 million in 2002 domestically, *Bon Voyage* $4.647 million in 2003, and *Female Agents* a surprising $7.710 million in 2008. In the same year, *Valkyrie* in France grossed $5.402 million and *Inglourious Basterds* a whopping $24.978 million.

Earning only a meager $1.135 million in 2009, *Army of Crime* not only refuses to participate in the depoliticization of the resistance as a historical legacy and political concept but also challenges its mythical status in postwar French culture and society—reason to assess its reception as part of the ongoing process of historical revisionism. The complicated history of France during World War II—which includes the German occupation, the collaborationist Vichy regime under Marshal Pétain, the Free France movement led by General de Gaulle in British exile, and a heterogeneous resistance movement consisting of conservative, Catholic, Jewish, and communist groups—had a profound impact on the making of postwar French identity. Called the Vichy syndrome by historian Henry Rousso, the myth of a single France standing behind de Gaulle was established during the Fourth Republic in the 1950s, institutionalized during the Fifth Republic, and repeatedly instrumentalized during the Indochina and

Algerian wars.[41] Suppressing the diversity of the resistance made possible its transformation into an idea of national unity and strength that culminated in what de Gaulle famously called France's *grandeur* (greatness). At the same time, this mythification served to perpetuate the image of an "eternal France" described as simultaneously rural and urban, Catholic and secular, traditional and enlightened, and sustained by the belief in its own glorious history.

Two films established early on the aesthetic and ideological foundations on which postwar conceptions of Frenchness, its heritage or *patrimonoire* (patrimony), became inextricably linked to the years of occupation.[42] René Clement turned filmic realism into an instrument of political critique with *La bataille du rail* (*The Battle of the Rails*, 1945), a fictional treatment, based on real events, of the efforts by French railroad workers to disrupt German troop movements and supply lines. Combining realist and modernist elements, Jean-Pierre Melville, in his adaptation of a famous story by Vercors, staged a haunting encounter between occupier and occupied in *Le silence de la mer* (*The Silence of the Sea*, 1948); Tarantino cited its country-house setting in the first part of *Inglourious Basterds*. Melville also directed *L'armée des ombres* (*Army of Shadows*, 1969), which, despite its melancholy mood and bleak atmosphere, still supports a heroic view of the resistance, including of de Gaulle. Both *Army of Shadows* and *Army of Crime* allude to this modernist masterpiece in their titles and define their very different revisionist projects against its canonical status.

The divisions in the resistance movement between communists and Gaullists were first acknowledged in the French-American coproduction *Paris brûle-t-il?* (*Is Paris Burning?*, Réne Clément, 1966). But it was the deconstruction of the political binaries dominating public debates about Vichy France that brought even greater challenges. Starting the process of demystification, Marcel Ophüls made the critically acclaimed documentary *Le chagrin et le pitié* (*The Sorrow and the Pity*, 1969) about the small town of Clermont-Ferrand during the occupation. Louis Malle, by contrast, explored the contradictions of collaboration through the story of a naive country boy in the highly controversial *Lacombe Lucien* (Louis Malle, 1974). A much greater commercial success, *Au revoir les enfants* (1987), also directed by Malle, became the first film to address French involvement in the Holocaust by recounting the fate of a Jewish boy hiding in a Catholic boarding school. Similarly, the central role of women—and with it, of marriage and family—was finally acknowledged in the true stories of an apolitical female abortionist in *Une affaire de femmes* (*Story of Women*, Claude Chabrol, 1988) and a politically active history teacher in *Lucie Aubrac* (Claude Berri, 1997), two films that forever complicated the depiction of resistance in masculinist terms and of collaboration as female or feminizing.

Read against this rich filmic legacy, the Vichy heritage film must be considered as symptomatic of a deeper crisis of French identity in the age of European unification and globalization—a crisis against which *Army of Crime* mobilizes its activist group of foreigners, immigrants, and exiles and their bold vision of a more inclusive France. This move establishes correspondences between the trauma of Nazi occupation and a very different kind of occupation diagnosed in the provocation of multiculturalism and ethnic and religious diversity, the replacement of the established left-right divide by a political culture organized around scandals and celebrities, and the diminished powers of the Parisian bourgeoisie as arbiters of taste. The pervasive sense of invasion continues in the unresolved problems of decolonization and the visible presence of ethnic minorities in all areas of public life, the increasingly violent clashes in response to growing social and economic inequalities, and the heated debates over religious tolerance and shared cultural norms (e.g., the headscarf debate). To what degree the specter of a homogenized mass culture associated with Americanization also plays a role in nostalgic evocations of wartime France would require further analysis.

During the presidency of center-right Jacques Chirac, Paris in 2005 and 2006 became the center of civil unrest in the *banlieues* led by Franco-Maghrebis from the former colonies and of student-led protests and continuing labor strikes that suggest a return of violence as an expression of populist anger and class resentment anticipated in the very similar looking scenes of exploding cars and burning offices in the anti-Nazi resistance narrative of *Army of Crime*. Of course, this raises the questions: Who, in these analogies, are the resistance fighters, and how is the relationship between past and present established? Guédiguian's answer, as confirmed by the critical reception of his film, involves both the recognition of antagonism as the basis of the political, with the French establishment now in the position of the Nazis, and the call for a revival of old leftist traditions through a broader, more inclusive definition of Frenchness. A very different answer can be found in the third case study of this chapter, the Americanized version of a uniquely European narrative that shifts the site of resistance from collective commitments to individual desires and that articulates its new politics of identity through an exploitative mixture of sex and violence.

Like *Flame & Citron* and *Max Manus*, *Black Book* was (and still is) the most expensive Dutch film ever made, confirming the economic and political profitability of the resistance narrative in contemporary European cinema. After years of difficulties getting financing, the Dutch-German-British coproduction was made for $21 million and grossed $10.508 million in the first year alone.

Waldemar Kobus and Carice van Houten in
*Black Book*

Carice van Houten and Sebastian Koch in
*Black Book*

The premiere on 12 September 2006 in The Hague was a star-studded affair, with Crown Prince Willem-Alexander and Crown Princess Máxima in attendance; extensive media reporting accompanied the film's domestic release. *Black Book* received numerous Dutch film prizes and a nomination for an Oscar for Best Foreign Film but was widely dismissed at the Venice Film Festival. Despite its commercial success, the film garnered decidedly mixed reviews at home and abroad. Taking advantage of new media synergies, Dutch fans had already followed the "making of" on their cell phones, courtesy of Vodafone, and could later read a novelization by Laurens Abbink Spaink written in the first-person narrative of Rachel Stein, the main protagonist. Turning the theatrical run into an educational opportunity, actor Thom Hoffman (cast in a supporting role) re-created the *"Black Book* Experience"—what he called "a fiction about reality back then"—in an exhibition at RAC Hallen in The Hague that combined a historical account of the 1940–45 period with information about the film and its director.[43] An international blockbuster, *Black Book* in 2007 took in an impressive $4.399 million in the United States, where it was marketed as a Holocaust film rather than a Dutch resistance film.

In many ways, *Black Book* represents the exception among recent European resistance films. It is based not on a true story but on true events, to paraphrase Verhoeven; it features a female heroine, privileges the Jewish perspective, and, most importantly, approaches the question of national heritage from the transnational position associated with its Dutch-born Hollywood director.[44] For that reason, its action-driven story of a Dutch Jewish woman trying to survive in the Netherlands under Nazi occupation is well suited to examine the conditions under which an unmistakably American approach to identity politics could be translated into specifically Dutch patterns of reception and exposed to the same kind of overdetermined readings in established newspapers and online discussion groups found for the other three films.

Already a brief plot summary confirms the critics' main points of objection, Verhoeven's sensationalist approach to sex and violence. A singer by profession, Rachel Stein/Ellis de Vries becomes active in a resistance group after losing her parents in an ambush set up by the SS. The largely male group of Dutch patriots, Christians, and one communist is prone to sexist and anti-semitic remarks and includes one member who will later betray them all. During a train ride, Ellis, played by Dutch star Carice van Houten, meets high-ranking Gestapo officer Ludwig Müntze, played by German actor Sebastian Koch. She starts working as a mole in the SS's Sicherheitsdienst (Security Service) head-quarters and begins "sleeping with the enemy," to quote a typical review.[45] Unlike in *Inglourious Basterds*, the Jewish woman actually falls in love with the German officer. Refusing to kill prisoners in a revenge action after a botched escape attempt by the resistance group, Müntze goes into hiding with Ellis be-fore he is court-martialed by the Germans after liberation. Briefly imprisoned by the Dutch, she tracks down and kills the traitor but is exonerated in the end. Throughout, the female lead acts solely based on personal motivations: to re-venge the death of her parents and, later, to escape with her German lover. The fact that she is Jewish and Dutch sets the dramatic events into motion and introduces additional complications. Yet at no point does it become part of her sense of self; as in most Verhoeven films, the female lead is primarily defined through her gender and sexuality.

Like the other resistance films, *Black Book* must be read in dialogue with the few Dutch films about the occupation made since 1945. Unlike *Flame & Citron* and *Max Manus*, it also references the large body of films about the extermina-tion of European Jewry. By adding an improbable framing story, *Black Book* follows other Holocaust films, from *Hitlerjunge Salomon* (*Europa Europa*, Agniezka Holland, 1990) to *Schindler's List*, that similarly locate the telos of Jewish identity in Israel, in this case a kibbutz where Rachel Stein, during the 1956 Suez Crisis, is building a new life under a very different kind of occupation. As a Dutch heroine, the Rachel Stein/Ellis de Vries character recalls Hannie Schaft, the young member of the communist resistance group Raad van Verzet portrayed in *Het meisje met het rode haar* (*The Girl with the Red Hair*, Ben Verbong, 1981). Yet the plucky Jewish woman in *Black Book* can also be seen as a reincarnation of the most famous girl of Holocaust cinema who first appeared on the silver screen in *The Diary of Anne Frank* (George Stevens, 1959). Meanwhile, Verhoe-ven was clearly inspired by *De IJssalon* (*Private Resistance*, Dimitri Frenkel Frank, 1985), which shows the politicization of a young Dutch woman—played, like the Hannie Schaft character, by Renée Soutendijk, a 1980s Carice van Houten—through her complicated relationships with a German Jewish émigré and a "good" German officer played by Bruno Ganz, who may in turn have inspired the Müntze character and Sebastian Koch's interpretation of him. In presenting the history of occupation through the lens of divided identities

(Dutch-Jewish, Dutch-German), Verhoeven closely follows the narrative model established by two recent Dutch World War II films, *De tweeling* (*Twin Sisters*, Ben Sombogaart, 2002), which approaches Dutch-German relations through the motif of doubling, and *Oorlogswinter* (*Winter in Wartime*, Martin Koolhoven, 2008), which takes conflicting family loyalties as an entry point into the self-understanding of a country divided between resistance and collaboration. The sexualization of violence in *Black Book* also pays homage to *The Night Porter* (e.g., in the equation of gun and phallus) and reproduces the male-female power games first used by Verhoeven for pure shock effect in *Basic Instinct* (1992).

The Dutch reception of *Black Book* was inextricably linked to Verhoeven's self-representation as a Dutchman and the public perception of his Dutch-American career.[46] "The prodigal son has returned," writes one reviewer wearily in the online film journal *Totaal*: "His first deed: *Black Book*, a film that, curiously enough, is more 'Hollywood' than all his American productions put together: big, moving, and without too many sharp edges."[47] Almost thirty years earlier, Verhoeven had first explored the subject matter in the wartime drama *Soldaat von Oranje* (*Soldier of Orange*, 1977), based on the memoirs of Erik Hazelhoff Roelfzema, about a group of upper-class men who, frequently clad in tails, experience the occupation primarily as a youthful adventure. Verhoeven's talent for action-driven plots had brought him an invitation to Hollywood, where he made commercially successful action thrillers and science-fiction films before returning to the Netherlands to revisit, once again in collaboration with screenwriter Gerard Soeteman, the history of the resistance. Instead of exploring political attitudes within a particular social milieu, director and screenwriter decided to focus on two outsiders, the good Nazi and the beautiful Jewess, presumably to show the human struggle for survival without moral judgment. Thus, whereas the "soldiers of Orange" are rooted in Dutch culture and society through the bonds of male friendship and class privilege, the main protagonists of *Black Box*, like the characters in Verhoeven's Hollywood films, act as free agents whose actions are based solely on individual self-interest. In a world ruled by greed, lust, suspicion, and betrayal, social classes and structures disappear entirely from view, and political processes are reduced to the visual spectacle of costumes, rituals, and symbols modeled on *Triumph of the Will* and already put on full display in *Starship Troopers* (1997), Verhoeven's fascist science-fiction fantasy.

Almost all Dutch Internet sites dedicated to film, television, and new media (e.g., *Cinema.nl*, *Zi-online.nl*, *FilmLounge.nl*) commented on the absence of clear moral distinctions, with the range of contributions reproducing familiar

European and American positions. Verhoeven's critics expressed their concerns with reference to the film's obligation to historical veracity and aesthetic restraint. Meanwhile, his defenders spoke in the language of identity politics and strong emotions. Some among the latter saw the erosion of the friend-enemy distinction as positive and welcomed the expansion of "the moral gray zone" as an opportunity for multiple identifications: "The roles are not as black and white as in many war films. So there is no real villain or hero, but rather, there is a good side hidden in every villain and vice versa. You even sympathize with the SD boss Muntzen [*sic*]."[48]

Many reviewers were very critical of this approach, with one dismissing such moral relativism as a betrayal of the resistance movement and the personal sacrifices made by its members: "Under the pretext of fiction our guilty conscience is soothed with the idea that everyone was bad in the end anyway. In this way Paul [Verhoeven] sells everyone short who defended the lives of others with great risk to their own lives. Only to end up drawing a parallel with Israel at the end."[49] Another commentator, too, remained unconvinced by overblown claims about the film's critical agenda: "Although the hype would have us believe otherwise, *Black Book* is not an insightful analysis of good and evil, or a challenge to dominant views of the role of the Dutch in World War II. It is much too superficial for that."[50] Yet another critic, writing for a Belgian weekly, mocked the director's pretensions with crudely expressed outrage: "There are an incredible number of bare breasts, for which you could almost forgive Verhoeven for not contributing anything at all to the debate on collaboration and for failing throughout to make a deep impression. . . . World War II as Paul Verhoeven's trashy playground."[51]

At times, the appropriation—and, presumably, Americanization—of the resistance narrative by a representative of global Hollywood inspired scenarios of cultural occupation not dissimilar to those depicted in the film. One way for critics to express their dissatisfaction involved complaining about their indifference toward the characters, a complaint not shared by the one million Dutch viewers who went to see the film in the first year but clearly intended to dismiss the film on the basis of what Hollywood claims to do best: produce strong emotions. The following description of the viewing experience by one critic is fairly typical as it blames Verhoeven's moral relativism for the pervasive lack of character engagement:

> In the first half of the film it becomes clear to the viewer who is "good" and who is "bad." In the second half, it turns out that the characters that were "heroes" in the beginning also have their bad sides, and that some "villains" might be

more heroic than we thought. That may well be very true, but in the moment that it becomes clear that Ellis really is in love with Müntze and even wants to save him, I disengaged. From that moment on, there are no characters left for the viewer to sympathize with, and the story completely loses its dramatic momentum. That's why I was totally apathetic watching the film's last forty-five minutes and kept looking at my watch, counting the seconds until I could leave the theater groaning and moaning.[52]

What accounts for this lack of emotional involvement, or rather, how is the experience of indifference mobilized in what amounts to a European-American disagreement over the role of identity in aligning historical narratives with political affects? The film first introduces the problem of ethnic/religious identity (i.e., the persecution and extermination of the Jews), briefly digresses into the meaning of national identity (i.e., through confrontations between the Germans and the Dutch), and then jettisons both for the story of a doomed heterosexual romance before returning once more to national perspectives in the celebration of liberation in the Netherlands and the work of nation building in Israel. Yet the complete lack of mediation between the personal and the political prevents the spectator from engaging fully on either level; Verhoeven tries to fill this vacuum with bursts of violence that are uncontainable within the narrative but, unlike in the other three films, do not satisfy the kind of nostalgia for the political and its evocations of democracy that find expression in the ongoing negotiation of nationalism and patriotism as two current modes of democratic subjectivity.

Taken together, the absence of clear friend-enemy distinctions and the lack of strong identifications allow us to finally pin down what seemed to be missing in *Black Book*: an emotional commitment to the idea of Dutchness—or Jewishness, for that matter—and, with it, a validation of the resistance on either political or historical grounds. Projecting their own anxieties about globalization onto Verhoeven and his film, many reviewers ended up treating the Nazis on the screen as stand-ins for the presumed excesses of nationalism and militarism in the United States and Israel. Aside from having their own anti-Americanism confirmed in what they saw as Verhoeven's secret attack on America, these displacements allowed some Dutch critics to hold on to the cherished self-image of a country distinguished by its progressive policies, tolerance of difference, and celebration of diversity.

As in the reception of *Flame & Citron* and *Max Manus*, the story of the occupation in *Black Book* has thus functioned as a projection screen for pressing contemporary problems. And once again, the scenarios of occupation have served to reinscribe the complementary roles of occupier and occupied and distract from the fact that the famed Dutch tolerance, in the new millennium, has reached its limits in confrontation with fears about foreign infiltration and manifestations of religious intolerance and ethnic hatred. Accordingly, the Nazi occupation in the film can also be read as a displaced reenactment of what *Black Book* blocks from view: the violence of Islamic fundamentalism that contributed to the 2004 killing of filmmaker Theo van Gogh and the threats against Ayaan Hirsi Ali because of her involvement with his last film, *Submission* (2004). Alternatively, the critics' frustration with *Black Book*'s moral relativism and cynical detachment might be based in their growing awareness of the return of ideology, given the mass appeal of new right-wing populist leaders such as Pim Fortuyn and Geert Wilders, a development perhaps missed by Verhoeven, who left for Hollywood in 1984.

To further complicate matters, the anti-American overtones in the Dutch reception coincided with wide speculations about *Black Book* as an anti-American allegory, a contradiction that, as in the case of *Flame & Citron* and *Max Manus*, can be traced back to the term "terrorist" as an overdetermined marker of conflicting meanings and competing projections. According to Mouffe, terrorism and the responses to terrorism involve a displacement of the political, producing forms of dissent and opposition that find expression in violent actions but are always explained in moral terms (e.g., the just fight, the axis of evil). Thus the adversary or real enemy, a necessary figure at the heart of the political, becomes the absolute enemy.[53] In Schmittian terms, both the partisan and the terrorist are illegal and irregular, but unlike the former, the latter operates systematically and illegitimately in a transnational framework. Collapsing this distinction in order to facilitate presentist readings, references to terrorism accompanied the critical reception of *Black Book* in the Netherlands from the beginning and, in fact, played a key role in early discussions between director and screenwriter. Describing their extensive historical research during preproduction, Verhoeven explained: "It is a term that really was used by the Germans [to describe the members of the Dutch resistance]. . . . Gerard [Soeteman] and I consciously chose the word. What is so interesting is that people used the word back then, but they were referring to the resistance." Adding his voice to the controversy, the author of the novel based on the film, Spaink, insisted on its universal message but, in so doing, inadvertently contributed to such presentist readings: "I think that you have to see *Black Book* as a story that takes place only in World War II. I don't see any critique of the United States. . . . The film reveals how you have to put aside your own goodness to fight evil. . . . That was just as true in World War II as it is in the Iraq War."[54]

Such comments prompted one interviewer of Verhoeven to conclude with the ominous remark that, in the film, "World War II and the war on terror suddenly converge."[55] A few reviewers took issue with what they saw as the director's anti-Bush agenda: "He has the German occupiers consistently call the resistance fighters 'terrorists': a tendentious but oversimplified reference to the present. The freedom fighters of today are the oppressors of tomorrow, says Verhoeven."[56] But even those in agreement with such an approach complained that the implicit comparisons to the Iraq war and the Israeli-Palestinian conflict did not compensate for the film's artistic shortcomings: "Verhoeven does indeed build a bridge between the resistance in World War II and present-day terrorism but chokes on the chasm between European subject matter and American film style."[57]

Reflecting larger developments in contemporary Europe, the four films discussed in this chapter invite presentist readings of occupation and resistance that cannot simply be dismissed as irrelevant or inappropriate. As we have seen, *Flame & Citron*, *Max Manus*, *Army of Crime*, and *Black Book* are inextricably linked to the politics of terror that arrived in Europe in the new millennium. But their function as a projection screen for competing political fantasies is also inseparable from the paradoxes of European film production and heritage culture, that is, the search for new narratives of nation within the terms of the postnational and transnational. This projection of contemporary problems into historical conflicts would not be possible without the disappearance of the "us" versus "them" rhetoric that, during the cold war, provided Western Europeans with a shared ideological topography and distinct national identity. At the same time, the focus on violence as a *tertium datur* (i.e., the element shared by all political actors) remains problematically bound up, namely, as its opposite, with the search for a European democratic habitus, or a set of emotions and beliefs, able to project strength and force without recourse to the rhetoric of evil associated with US military and political hegemony. In mobilizing national, social, and ethnic identities for the production of political affects in the postpolitical age, the films combine the empowerment rhetoric of post-1968 identity politics with the nostalgia for the sense of group solidarity and belonging promised by the nation-state and eternalized in the historical struggles of the anti-Nazi resistance.

According to the most extreme readings and rereadings of the resistance narrative found in some online discussion groups, the current problems of the European nation-state are prefigured in the threat to national sovereignty posed by the Nazis, and the danger emanating from a multiethnic Europe through the equation of Nazis with Muslims as the new occupiers.[58] But even in more mainstream readings encouraged by the directors themselves, the experiences of occupation are often presented as allegories of Americanization and globalization, with the war on terror projected onto (the legacies of) World War II. In both cases, the resistance narratives invite identifications organized around a vague but pervasive sense of threat: to national culture, national unity, and national identity. In these scenarios, the Nazis, who, with the exception of the main villain, remain undistinguished stock characters, act as a leveling—that is, a globalizing—force. The bursts of violence that repeatedly puncture the narratives must therefore be read as symptoms of a deep-seated frustration with the perceived shortcomings of postwar European democracies, their ethos of consensus building and reasoned debate and their increasingly hollow rhetoric of secularism, pacifism, and multiculturalism. The state of exception produced by war and the conditions of emergency that, according to Agamben, allow for a suspension of the rule of law for the common good are, in the end, transformed—or sublated—into a populist fantasy of militancy that, in typical postideological fashion, champions the individual as the embodiment of the people and the most effective weapon against the madness of collectivism, whether in the form of Nazism or, to evoke a recent neologism, Islamofascism.[59]

In the process, democratic subjectivity has been redefined through a momentous shift from ethics to morality that, according to Mouffe, suggests the abandonment of universal standards and norms in favor of an individually felt sense of right and wrong.[60] In the films discussed, this shift is most apparent in the absence of any legitimizing discourses of good and evil such as the ones provided by earlier master narratives of nation and ideology. In what has been described as the age of postnationalism and postideology, it is no longer necessary for the occupied to assert their political legitimacy through moral superiority. Now it is only the act of violence itself that, at least in the cinema, asserts their will to power. Violence, in short, becomes a substitute for belief. It may be the initial problem of the narrative, but it is also the most effective solution. Similarly, in the absence of shared values and beliefs, the characters are left to define their forms of engagement around a uniquely filmic iconography of violence. As a political phenomenon, this belated discovery of violence in national cinemas not known for their interest in action and brutality is indeed noteworthy. It points to a larger crisis of legitimacy caused by the disappearance of forms of political commitment and civic engagement traditionally seen as the foundation of liberal democracies. Violence, by doing away with all ambiguities, offers protagonists and audiences an opportunity to connect to older traditions of engagement while overcoming the pitfalls of quietism and defeatism.

In other words, the representation of violence gives visual and emotional expression to the crises of European democracies that, once again, rely on Nazism and the antagonistic structures engendered by it to work through decidedly contemporary conflicts and contradictions.

Yet how exactly are historical texts and contemporary contexts brought into such close and problematic contact? Returning to the old division between friends and enemies, the new stories of resistance reinscribe the basic principles and processes of the political. On the one side, we have political power *in extremis*, that is, as a dictatorship, restaging the hierarchies between occupiers and occupied in the fascist mass spectacle. On the other, we have resistance fighters who, through the conflation of individual and populist notions of narrative agency, become stand-ins for the people and, within the logic of this strange discursive coupling, of democracy in its truest sense: as the body through which the political assumes form. Affects are central to this process. Identified with traumatic experiences of disempowerment and disenfranchisement, the Nazi occupation provides an affective matrix to which audiences bring contemporary anxieties and frustrations about the perceived disconnect between politicians and the electorate; the helplessness of the nation-state in the face of economic globalization; the weakening of the social-welfare system; the unresolved problems of a multicultural, multiethnic, and multireligious Europe; and the waning popular support for the European Union as an economic, political, and social program. Moreover, in laying bare the (non)functioning of governments, the resistance narrative—in its obsessive focus on Nazi procedures, laws, hierarchies, institutions, and organizations—serves as a permanent reminder of the failure of the nation-state in protecting its citizens then and now. Its affective investments thus always operate on two levels: as a celebration of the power of the people and a critique of the weakness of the elected government. Through this confrontation with its illegitimate double, the Nazi occupation, democracy asserts its foundation on the rule of the people and its dependence on the freedom of the individual as the very embodiment of the people.

How does this confrontation play out in the forms of engagement reconstructed here from the perspective of reception? As all the protagonists learn sooner or later, the Nazis possess the monopoly of violence that finds foremost expression in the power over life and death. They make the laws that control all movements in the public and the private spheres. And they define the identities constructed through the ensuing mechanisms of inclusion and exclusion. In short, their function is to personify the shared origins of subjectivity and subjection. Challenging this system, the members of the resistance become political beings simply through their decision to act—and to act decisively. By acquiring agency, they refuse to acknowledge the legitimacy of the occupying power and demonstrate their resolve to fight that power, if necessary through violent means. Where the heroes of the Hollywood anti-Nazi film and the DEFA anti-fascist film act based on collectively held beliefs, the new resistance narratives are driven by individual reactions and subjective motivations. And unlike the heroes of classic resistance films from the 1940s through the 1960s, their protagonists are for the most part outcasts, loners, and misfits without strong convictions or social ties. This quality makes them ideal projection screens for the growing frustration with parliamentary democracies and political bureaucracies that, in contemporary Europe, has given rise to right-wing, xenophobic populist movements and a renewed fascination with the transformative power of violence. The same quality connects them to the search for very different forms of political engagement that seek to uncouple the postpolitical and the postnational within the neoliberal world order.

The validation of individual self-interest, especially when aligned with populist rage, represents a new stage in the mobilization of the fascist imaginary in the making of political affects. Against the traditional understanding of politics as a process of rational deliberation, the new resistance narratives promote a cult of decisionism and voluntaristic action that makes the acts themselves the foundation of new political concepts. Yet the assertion of one's individual will depends fundamentally on the rhetoric of folk and nation that establishes the meaning of "friend" (i.e., "us") in confrontation with an absolute other. Since the enemies (i.e., "them") rely on violent means to achieve their goals, the defense of the homeland requires a similar commitment to forceful action even without recourse to a particular political ideology or nationalist agenda. As a result, the occupied assert their right to popular sovereignty and take up arms in the name of the people. Their violent actions are the most telling expression of their rejection of traditional forms of nationalism and patriotism; their desire for alternative forms of collective identity based on community, justice, and a sense of belonging; and their search for new scenarios of activism, heroism, and militancy. It is through this strange mixture of postnational patriotism, traditional populism, and contemporary identity politics that the films of the new millennium mobilize the resistance narrative for restagings of the crises of democracy and the nation-state.

With these broader implications, the spectacle of violence in the new millennium takes the place vacated by traditional ideologies, but the nostalgia for political action—that is, for a defense of nation, homeland, and democracy—cannot be understood without recognition of the politics of decisionism that, culminating in the violent acts shared by terrorists, partisans, and resistance fighters, inspired such vastly different readings. Moreover, the meaning of nostalgia cannot be evaluated without a final clarification of its location and direction. Nostalgia, one might ask, for the nation-state? The resistance movement? Political ideologies? Or nostalgia for fascism itself? Much writing on the heritage film is based on the false assumption that nostalgia always entails a yearning for the nation's past and, by extension, a desire to return to an earlier imagined state of unity, harmony, and greatness. Yet nostalgia is equally based on feelings of relief that the past is indeed past and therefore available to other forms of aesthetic appropriation and appreciation. In other words, nostalgia includes the desire to claim unredeemed social and political utopias for the present—even if in full awareness of their impossibility. "Nostalgia is sadness without an object," writes literary scholar Susan Stewart, which makes it as much about the feelings associated with the object—in this case, political beliefs and commitments—as about the object itself.[61]

Accordingly, in *Flame & Citron* and *Max Manus*, the resistance narrative establishes the terms through which to imagine new forms of postnational patriotism founded on the love of country and the desire for community. *Army of Crime* presents the historical resistance as a model of political activism based on both class-consciousness and ethnic and religious diversity. And in *Black Book*, the resistance narrative converges with American-style forms of identity politics while inviting anti-American readings of contemporary wars and occupations. In the mainstream media, these films inspired critical readings that combined nostalgia for nation and heritage with concerns about the state of European democracies and the proliferation of political violence. On the political fringes, the Nazi occupation provided a convenient projection screen for new forms of racism and xenophobia directed especially against Muslim minorities. In all cases, the patterns of reception remain haunted by the conflation of resistance fighter and terrorist that found its most compelling and troubling expression in the spectacle of political violence. The paradoxes of the postpolitical age sought an outlet in the search for legitimate agonistic forms of expression in order to prevent the irruption of such antagonisms in terrorism. By responding to these conflicting demands, *Flame & Citron*, *Max Manus*, *Army of Crime*, and *Black Book* confirm the enduring relevance of the fascist imaginary in the new millennium. How the same dynamics of the postpolitical and postnational played out in the Berlin Republic is the subject of the final chapter.

# 7

## Entombing the Nazi Past

### On *Downfall* and Historicism

> I feel no sympathy. . . . I repeat, I feel no sympathy.
>
> Ulrich Matthes as Joseph Goebbels to one of the generals

> Compassion is a primal sin.
>
> Bruno Ganz as Adolf Hitler to his dinner guests

In July 2008 a new branch of Madame Tussauds opened on Berlin's famous Unter den Linden, displaying among its motley group of politicians, celebrities, and historical personalities a wax figure of Adolf Hitler. But instead of the youthful Führer from the London branch, visitors were confronted with the defeated old man from the last days in the bunker. Controversies had surrounded the Hitler figure from the start, with politicians denouncing the exhibition as a Nazi Disneyland and protesting the frivolous display of this personification of evil in such close proximity to two famous monuments to Germany's troubled past, the Brandenburg Gate and the Holocaust Memorial. On opening day, a man ripped off the figure's head, making it, in the words of one commentator, the only successful assassination attempt on Hitler. The figure was quickly repaired and, despite the usual uproar in the media, Madame Tussauds announced that it had no intentions of removing the offending display.[1]

The wax figure could just as well have been taken from *Der Untergang* (*Downfall*, 2004) or been modeled on its famous Hitler performer, Bruno Ganz. Media mogul Bernd Eichinger, the most influential and successful German film producer of the postwar period, made the film in collaboration with leading Hitler biographer Joachim Fest and emerging director Oliver Hirschbiegel. *Downfall*, for which Eichinger also wrote the screenplay, uses the last days of the war as a lens through which to explain the Third Reich and commit its legacies to history once and for all. The heavy reliance on the staging conventions of the wax cabinet, a precinematic popular diversion, is not coincidental; neither are the attendant strategies of historicization. Both the blockbuster film and the wax cabinet share an approach to history grounded in nineteenth-century historicism, especially its belief in the distinctness of all historical periods and its insistence on showing history "as it really was" (Leopold von Ranke), that is, without judgment, falsification, or embellishment.[2]

In both settings, history is re-created through a naturalistic mise-en-scène that keeps the spectators at a safe distance and creates the illusion of objectivity and authenticity. Furthermore, both media rely on a premodern aesthetic of simulation and are profoundly aware of the constructed nature of history and its heavy dependence on audiovisual media. Once again, at the beginning of the twenty-first century, film and fascism join forces, but this time in the service of an almost obsessive fixation on history and memory in literature, art, architecture, and museum culture; an emphatic rejection of the politics of nationalism in favor of what the previous chapter calls postnational patriotism; and a conscious opposition to ideology as a driving force in history and an instrument of political analysis and critique.[3]

Enlisting familiar illusionist methods in the making of what might be called a postnational, postpolitical approach to fascism, *Downfall*'s historicist sensibilities open up a space for new conceptions of German history and identity developed within contemporary media society and event culture yet modeled on the historicism of the nineteenth century. Not only is everything presented as historically specific; everything is explained historically. With such particularism comes an uncritical acceptance of the world as given, closed to alternative visions but fully available to historical understanding through the lens of mimetic representation. The historicist mentality embodied by the Hitler of *Downfall* and Madame Tussauds appeared first after the founding of the Wilhelmine Empire in 1871 and, once again, after German unification in 1990. However, in today's cinematic version of the wax cabinet, the displacement of politics into history takes place within a globalized culture industry that reduces the national to a defensive strategy, retrograde aesthetic, and nostalgic phenomenon.

And today, it is the identification with Germans as victims, and with German history as a series of crises, traumas, and failures—in short, downfalls—that redefines national identity as a performative category in tightly orchestrated media practices and public events.

As a perfect example of *Eventkino* (to cite RTL [Radio Télévision Luxembourg] programming)—a form of commercial cinema sustained more by hyperbolic patterns of reception, promotional materials, and product tie-ins than by the artistic quality of the work itself—*Downfall* must be situated within the expanded field of historical culture defined by mass publishing, academic research, audiovisual practices, and new digital media. It is a field defined by important anniversaries, museum exhibitions, commemorative sites, and public debates and dominated by audiovisual practices and multimedia effects. The synergies among the institutions of traditional high culture, including book publishing, an image-driven and scandal-obsessed political culture, and a profit-oriented global entertainment culture are nowhere more pronounced than in the historical films that since 1989 have provided the Berlin Republic with an affective framework for the rearticulation of history, nation, and heritage beyond the familiar historical arguments and legitimating narratives.

Using *Downfall* as a case study, this final chapter seeks to move beyond the evaluative binaries—conservative versus progressive, subversive versus affirmative—often used to dismiss historicization as problematic on aesthetic and political grounds and to approach the phenomenon through a series of deceptively simple questions: What does historicization in filmic and audiovisual media look like? How does it work, and what does it achieve? In what ways does it move from the postwar discourses of coming to terms with the past toward a very different understanding of German history, namely, as part of a "natural history of destruction" replete with national crises, disasters, and catastrophes and continuously rewritten through the public rituals of forgetting and remembering?[4] And to turn to the central concerns of this book, in what ways does historicization neutralize the political affects that informed East and West German analyses of fascism and enlist the Nazi past in the very different affective regimes of postnational patriotism?[5]

This is not the place to engage with the extensive and often self-serving debates in German mass media, and among historians of modern Germany, about the implications of a historicization and normalization of the Nazi past, that is, its integration into the broader streams of German and European history. German unification, the fall of communism, and the inevitable passing of time have profoundly changed the way in which the fascist imaginary is mobilized and utilized in the cinema, with the history of the Third Reich assuming yet another set of functions in the age of what some have called, rather prematurely, posthistory. The disappearance of the West German habitus of guilt and shame, a process to be explained in generational terms, and the concurrent disintegration of the master narratives of antifascism and anticommunism have produced a deep crisis in the established notions of German history and identity. The clearest indicator in filmic and literary practices is the emphatic rejection of an older *Gesinnungsästhetik* (aesthetics of conscience) that privileges political and ethical over aesthetic considerations and uses literary and filmic practices to work through political problems. One outcome, measurable in filmmakers' choices and audiences' tastes, has been a diversification of affective registers, including humor, satire, grotesque, and a marked preference for the nostalgic or antiquarian pleasures of historicism. A parallel shift in the forms of character engagement—from the Nazis' demonization to their humanization—has been an integral part of this complicated process.

But what does normalization in this context actually mean? How does it alter the conditions of memory and commemoration? And how does it change the relationship between past and present that has been constitutive of the fascist imaginary until this point? Here, historian Gavril Rosenfeld offers a useful distinction between normalization as descriptive (i.e., a result of the passing of generations) and prescriptive (i.e., as a goal to be actively pursued) that allows us to avoid the empty polemics surrounding *Downfall* and similar films. He also proposes to distinguish among three different modes of historicization: to relativize the past in order to downplay its unique aspects, to universalize the past and make it part of broader forces and developments, and to aestheticize the past through visual and narrative strategies that neutralize its moral dimensions.[6] The Eichinger production combines all these discursive effects, which accounts for its overdetermined status in public debates and goes a long way toward explaining its artistic mediocrity, a distinction, however, that will have little relevance to my discussion. For while the film, in its formal approach to historicization, is very much a product of the postpolitical as analyzed by Mouffe and others, the debates generated by the film must be seen as a compelling demonstration of the strength and vibrancy of democratic culture that has developed in the Federal Republic since 1945. Seen less as a text than as a producer of contexts, *Downfall* can therefore be more productively compared to an earlier media event that made an even greater intervention into the public sphere: the American television series *Holocaust*.

*Downfall* is only the most famous and most controversial in a group of recent German films and television dramas that approach the Third Reich as a distinct historical period, an important part of postfascist identity construction, and profitable subject matter in the domestic and international marketing of fascist imaginaries. In initiating yet another phase in the seemingly interminable process of coming to terms with the past, these films have reconfigured basic elements of the Third Reich narrative: from the focus on ordinary Germans back to the political and military leadership, from confrontation with the victims of the Nazi regime to validation of German wartime suffering, and from testimonies to individual resistance to rationales for its difficulty or impossibility.[7]

Dismissed as either a German version of the heritage film—Nazi heritage films, to use the equivalent term to Vichy heritage films—or an example of what its most outspoken German critics call *historytainment*, these productions have been accused of depoliticizing the Nazi past through their melodramatic or sentimental treatments, their preoccupation with historical authenticity at the expense of critical analysis, and their heavy reliance on personalization and psychologization.[8] Approaching the question of nation from a postideological perspective, they have contributed to a momentous shift from the postwar project of coming to terms with the past to the very different postunification discourses of history, memory, and heritage culture.

In the process, political ideologies have been replaced by national identity as a consumable good. With the nation reduced to one site of identity formation among others, its difficult history can subsequently be experienced without shame—characteristics that have played a key role in the domestic reception of recent German films and television dramas about the Nazi past. As a historical metaphor and a marker of trauma, "downfall" in this larger context, then, refers to the almost compulsive reenactment of the final days as a process of distancing, of closing off, in short, of musealization. The fixation on the apocalyptic ending serves to prove that this period is finally, irrevocably, over. As a thus-defined performance of incomprehensible otherness, the Nazi past can be purged of the rhetoric of collective guilt and integrated into the heterogeneous narratives that today constitute German identity within other European constructions of the postnational.

The recent German films about the Third Reich differ fundamentally from the European resistance films, with the celebration of political violence reserved for the revolutionary chic of 1970s terrorism in films like *Die Stille nach dem Schuss* (*The Legend of Rita*, Volker Schlöndorff, 2000), *Baader* (Christopher Roth, 2002), and *Der Baader Meinhof Komplex* (*The Baader Meinhof Complex*, Uli Edel, 2008), another kind of heritage indeed. Given the dearth of innovative directors working in historical genres—film authorship continues to be associated with contemporary sensibilities—the Nazi heritage films also have little in common with the aesthetic provocations of *Moloch* and *Inglourious Basterds*. While sharing its historicist aesthetic with heritage culture as a whole, *Downfall* must be distinguished from more conventional fare for a simple reason: the fundamental difference between historical films featuring historical figures and fictional scenarios set against the backdrop of historical events. In the claustrophobic spaces of the bunker, there is no room for the real or imagined German-Jewish love stories introduced elsewhere to suggest the possibility of post-Holocaust reconciliation. Instead the focus on the political and military elites at the moment of their self-destruction promotes an attitude of disengagement that is necessary for the witnessing of their "downfall" and consequently makes possible the liberation of the present from the burdens of the past.

Relying on a historicist sensibility and engaging antiquarian perspectives, *Downfall* requires neither identification with the main characters nor understanding for their personal and political choices. Yet through its status as a media event, the film provides a mechanism of emotional detachment that, paradoxically, facilitates the self-recognition of contemporary German audiences as victims of their own history. Significantly, the affective investments organized by the film are not located within the diegesis but arise instead from the audience's relationship to the Nazi past and its political significance today. This fundamental tension between detachment from the historical event and attachment to its legacies produces the attitudes, mentalities, and sensibilities often associated with historicization; it also marks the end of the project of post-fascism and its haunting effects and therefore needs to be distinguished from the political project of New German Cinema and the critical self-reflexivity of 1970s retro styles.[9]

In the following pages, this complicated process will be traced on three levels: the visual and narrative elements that align the film with a historicist aesthetic, the intertextual references that link it to other filmic representations of Hitler and the Nazi past, and the critical debates that make historicization part of a new event-based political culture. By focusing on a single film, rather than the ensembles presented in previous chapters, I use the book's final chapter to bring together various critical approaches—the focus on production and reception, considerations of genre and authorship, and the role of actors and performance—for the analysis of an important film that, in my view, announces yet another paradigm shift in the postfascist imaginary, this time associated with the inevitable process of historicization and what has become known as a normalization of the Nazi past. Whether the latter is to be described as the product of successful postwar democratization, a troubling depoliticization of history, or a new understanding of political engagement remains to be seen; what is obvious already is that affects play a key role in the ongoing negotiation of history and politics.

The question of historicization, first raised in the *Historikerstreit* (historians' debate) of the 1980s, has always hinged on two issues: the relationship between historical narrative and its political function, and the relationship between historicization and normalization of the Nazi past.[10] The rejection of the theories of fascism developed in the context of ideology critique and the return to a Hitler-centric historiography have been an integral part of this process; so has the growing attention to affects as an essential part of history and memory. Meanwhile, the modernist and postmodernist styles that have complicated filmic representations of the Third Reich since the 1960s have given way to the combinations of classical narrative, emotional realism, and historical verisimilitude that found a particularly fertile ground in German mainstream cinema and television.

Taking, in the words of Hirschbiegel, "a new approach to history," *Downfall* uses a highly conventional narrative, familiar characters, naturalist acting styles, and television-like camerawork and production design to achieve the desired historicist effects.[11] The constitutive elements of such an undertaking come from the filmic and audiovisual archives of fascism and the long history of Hitler performances cataloged in the appropriately named *Hitler Filmography*.[12] Based on such an imaginary movie catalog, Eichinger and Hirschbiegel introduce stock characters such as the Hitler Youth member confronting the betrayal of his ideals, the Prussian general torn between his oath of loyalty and love of country, the brave army doctor saving lives in the midst of carnage, and the naive young woman placed at the center of history through no choice of her own. Familiar from myriad other films about the Nazi past, standard scenes include extravagant official ceremonies, dance-on-the-volcano debaucheries, infighting among the leadership, excessive brutality and violence, and plenty of senseless orders, mad confessions, and last-minute suicides by members of Hitler's inner circle. Once again the emotional universe of National Socialism is re-created through the dichotomies of fanaticism and opportunism, cynicism and idealism, and grandiosity and subservience routinely enlisted to account for Hitler's uncanny power over his followers. It is from this repository of pre-existing images and stories that the film builds its historicist dream world and offers up its dramatic reenactments as historical facts.

In the cinema, historical reconstruction is usually achieved through formal strategies that deny the constructed nature of the fictional world and promote mimesis and empathy as conduits to knowledge and understanding. Using the last ten days as a lens through which to make sense of the entire Third Reich, the film opens with the official celebrations on 20 April 1945—Hitler's fifty-sixth birthday—and ends with his suicide, together with Eva Braun, on 30 April and the unconditional surrender of the German army on 2 May 1945. Bracketed by these dates, the events unfold seemingly without agency or causality, except for the hidden forces alluded to by the Spenglerian rise and fall in the film's title. Through the bunker as the primary setting, the events are literally contained within an unrepeatable past. With all elements aligned toward their inevitable demise, history proceeds in the form of negative teleology, unencumbered by competing points of view and alternative interpretations. Individuals rather than universal principles or abstract ideas determine its course. Detailed description and complete immersion in facts take the place of the theoretical concepts that distinguish the analysis of fascism in the East German antifascist films of the 1950s and 1960s and the sociopsychology of authoritarianism in the West German films of the 1970s and 1980s. Critical reflections on historical agency and causality give way to a preoccupation with unmediated visibility as the foundation of historical reality that in *Downfall* promises to grant access to the hidden truth of Nazism.

All these developments come together in a pivotal scene that consists of a series of shots/countershots and lasts little more than a minute: Hitler's abdication of power. This moment occurs after a tense meeting with the generals that the Führer cuts short with the fateful words: "It is over. The war is lost. . . . Do whatever you like." The scene opens with a medium shot of the bunker's occupants standing in the hallway, their backs to the camera, staring at the door from which such unimaginable pronouncements emanate. Suddenly the door opens, and the men and women create a passageway for Hitler as he moves toward the camera. Cut to a medium shot of Hitler walking slowly past Traudl Junge, his secretary, and two other staff members. Cut to a medium shot of the generals watching Hitler pass through the hallway. Cut to a medium shot of the officers seeing him reach the door and turn around to address the two women. Cut to a close-up of Junge listening to his plan for her escape from Berlin. Cut to a medium shot of Hitler and Eva Braun, with him declaring: "Everything is lost." Cut to Junge's face in close-up, with the camera moving in on her eyes as she hears him repeat: "Hopelessly lost." Cut to Hitler and Braun, who takes his hands and declares: "You know I'll stay with you. I won't let you send me away." Cut to Hitler kissing her on the mouth while the others look away in embarrassment. Cut to a medium shot of the officers, generals, and secretaries, all made uncomfortable by this unexpectedly intimate scene. Cut to a medium

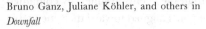

Bruno Ganz, Juliane Köhler, and others in
*Downfall*

Alexandra Maria Lara in *Downfall*

Ulrich Mühe in *Downfall*

Thomas Kretschmann and others in *Downfall*

shot of the couple still kissing, and then another close-up of Junge's face as she declares: "My Führer, I am staying too." Cut to a medium shot of Hitler and Braun retreating to his private quarters. Cut to the generals standing frozen in a medium shot, with Goebbels rushing toward the camera and then, followed by the panning camera, exiting on the left. Cut to a close-up of Goebbels entering the bathroom and looking into the mirror. Cut to a medium shot of one of the officers asking, "What now?"

What happens in this scene? At the moment that the Nazi dream of world domination is invaded by the bitter realities of war, a new fantasy takes over the film, the fantasy of politics as a series of individual decisions and personal relationships. The sudden power vacuum caused by the abdication of the Führer has to be compensated for through the production of intimacy, but it is an intimacy that is uncomfortable and almost repulsive. Hitler's concern for the welfare of Junge and his public displays of affection for Braun announce nothing less than his psychological withdrawal from Germany and the emergence of the surrogate figure of "Hitler as a human being." At the moment that the political actors, quite literally, lose their script, the relationship of historical agency to spectatorship and performance becomes glaringly apparent, a moment acknowledged by the minister of propaganda as he rehearses his new tragic persona in the bathroom mirror.

Significantly, the collapse of the Nazi power structure is presented through a series of spectatorial relationships: of the bunker inhabitants looking expectantly at the Führer and then averting their eyes from the man, but also of Hitler taking in the sight of his subordinates standing motionless and silent. The only character shown in close-up is Junge, with her rosy complexion and dewy eyes the embodiment of goodness and innocence. Functioning like a blank screen, her face captures the entire range of emotions present at the scene: shock, disbelief, helplessness, bewilderment, and fear, but also blind love and utter dependency. This kind of psychologization has profound implications for the patterns of affective engagement and disengagement during the remainder of the film. Producing distance precisely through the lack of a clear narrative point of view, the film approaches historical events exactly as the participants experience them: as primal scenes of powerlessness. Not surprisingly, the suggestion by one general that they should "end the spectacle" fails to result in any decisive action. In a world where only "the Führer is the Führer"—to quote a particularly absurd but very revealing explanation for the pervasive sense of paralysis—disengagement becomes the only appropriate mode for responding to the forces of doom, and that holds true for the historical figures in the film as well as the contemporary spectators watching them.

In this context, Fest's declaration, "I have always approached Hitler like a scientist studying a strange reptile under the microscope," can be read both as a protection against stylistic excess and as a prescription for the emotional detachment required for historicization.[13] The introduction of an eyewitness supports his underlying claims to historical authenticity and instant medialization. In fact, framing devices are a frequent feature of the historical novel, where they usually serve to legitimize the truthfulness of a story that seems to tell itself. In this case, the eighty-one-year-old Junge from *Im toten Winkel* (*Blind Spot: Hitler's Secretary*, 2002), the acclaimed film portrait by André Heller, provides the appropriate tone of guilt and regret to justify the spectator's subsequent immersion in what Eichinger and Hirschbiegel depict as the incomprehensible tragedy of German history. In choosing a naive young woman, *Downfall* offers access to the center of power without demanding responsibility for any decisions. As a stand-in for the spectator, the Junge figure reconciles knowledge of the historical facts with the blamelessness of the passive observer; she is also the only character who openly speaks about her feelings. Anticipating this emotional strategy of disengagement in the linguistic shift between first- and

Traudl Junge from *Blind Spot: Hitler's Secretary* in     Alexandra Maria Lara in *Downfall*
*Downfall*

third-person singular, she confesses in the opening sequence: "I have the feeling that I should be angry with this child, this childish young thing, or I
shouldn't forgive her for not realizing the horrors, the monster, before it was
too late, for not realizing what she was getting into. . . . And yet, it is very hard
to forgive myself for doing it."

Through the vacillation between guilt and innocence, Traudl Junge and, to
a lesser degree, Albert Speer provide a privileged perspective on the hermeti-
cally sealed world of the bunker and a model of positive self-identification for
contemporary German audiences. Her double appearance as a young woman
in the fictional world and as an old woman in the documentary sequences allows
the discharge of her and our shame into the mediated spaces of public debate
and cultural life. The wrinkled face of the real Junge not only serves as a convenient marker of time but also defines the historical distance from which later
generations, perhaps as young as Junge when she became Hitler's secretary,
are to view the events depicted on the screen. As a consequence, National Socialism is demarcated, separated, and externalized and becomes, in the words
of Junge, "the dream from which we want to awaken but can't." Describing
this process in psychological terms, journalist Jens Jessen argues that the film,
through the presence of Junge, "organizes an enormous emotional detachment
[*Absetzbewegung*] for the spectator. It looks at Hitler's world as if it were an absolute other, a completely sunken world. . . . To the spectator, the Germany in
which Hitler was possible seems entirely gone."[14] But precisely this sense of
puzzlement, Jessen concludes, is never translated into real understanding, the
kind of understanding that requires the acknowledgment of history as a site of
contestation and involves recognition of its political uses and abuses.

To a large degree, historicization depends on visual registers and spectatorial effects, but in *Downfall*, it is neither a realist nor a modernist aesthetic that

deconstructs the historical process by making visible the underlying social and political forces.[15] Infusing the antiquarian attention to detail with the glossy surface of simulation, the film insists on the accessibility of the past and the representability of history. The mechanisms of power are re-created through the arrangement of discrete scenes into a colorful panorama of history. Based on this additive principle, the film consists almost entirely of close-ups and medium shots whose composition, lighting, and depth of field betray years of work in television by cinematographer Rainer Klausmann. The grayish and greenish tones in the bunker scenes, evocative of the *Feldgrau* of Wehrmacht uniforms, add historical patina through a technical process known as desaturation, which depletes the color scheme to suggest the passing of time. By contrast, the intense reds and blues of the battle scenes add a much-needed sense of drama, with the ubiquitous fires a convenient symbol of the conflagration and purification of history. Throughout, the static camerawork adds to the tableau-like quality of the images and heightens the pervasive sense of confinement and powerlessness. The lighting of the bunker achieves a separation of figure and ground that shares with blue screen technology a similar disregard for the integrity of the filmic image and the contingencies of narrative space. Even the addition of more-subjective point-of-view shots (e.g., in the opening sequence with Junge) achieves no clear narrative point of view, reason enough to take a closer look at production design as a key element of historical reconstruction.

The world of historicism is a world of props, costumes, and set pieces. Part *Titanic* and part *Big Brother, Downfall* restages the last days of the Third Reich as a series of carefully composed interiors and exteriors. Having established his reputation for claustrophobic settings with the psycho thriller *Das Experiment* (*The Experiment*, 2001), Hirschbiegel, in close collaboration with production designer Bernd Lepel, relies heavily on the spatial order of the proscenium stage to separate the spectators from the catastrophic events depicted in the diegesis. As in the battle panoramas of the precinematic era, historical reality is evoked through typical objects and settings that give the past a material basis and, rather ironically, a manageable scale. Despite its epic length of 155 minutes, *Downfall* feels small, static, lifeless, and self-contained, a long series of tableaux vivants that strives toward the monumental but produces only miniatures. Even the street battles and bombing raids cannot distract from the film's heavy debt to the 1920s chamber-play film, with the bunker meticulously reconstructed according to historical records and furnished with the greatest attention to detail. From the floral-patterned yellow sofa in Eva Braun's private salon and the ornate red carpet in the hallway to the Bauhaus-style lamps in the staff quarters and the monogrammed tableware in the dining room, the film re-creates the scene of the crime, as it were, without revealing much about the protagonists, their motives, or their attitudes.

Animating these living pictures with competent performances, the actors complete the transformation of the past into a consumable spectacle. The dependence of history on performativity is acknowledged openly when Speer says to Hitler: "You must be on the stage when the curtain falls." Once again, the prevailing approach is naturalistic, with any theatrical excess or psychological depth contained within a historicist preoccupation with costumes, poses, and gestures. Bruno Ganz, who prepared for the role by studying newsreels and photographs, received special praise for reproducing Hitler's mannerisms with great precision and for portraying the Führer as a "human being."[16] In interviews, many of the leading actors spoke proudly of their striving toward highest authenticity. However, authenticity in the historicist universe means a conception of character outside any social factors or political explanations. Precisely this mechanical approach to acting, in combination with the static camerawork and mise-en-scène, prevents audiences from gaining access to the inner world of the characters and what they represent. Trapped within the politics-as-performance metaphor, the historical personalities disappear behind the screen personas of the leading stars of German cinema. This constitutive tension in the historicist performance between the fetishization of authenticity and the dramatic techniques of imitation accounts for the lack of character development noted, with much indignation, by Wim Wenders: "I didn't see Hitler at all. Or Goebbels and his wife. All of them remained altogether invisible."[17]

By giving the audience only Bruno Ganz, Ulrich Matthes, and Corinna Harfouch, *Downfall* effectively blocks access to the functioning of power in the Third Reich and reduces its main representatives to figures from a house of wax: history displayed for the cheap thrills and therapeutic needs of later generations. Even the occasional gestures toward melodrama—Hitler's tears, Junge's sobbing, and Magda Goebbels's cries—fail to illuminate the socio-psychological foundations of Nazism and the enduring appeal of "fascinating fascism." "Compassion is a primal sin," remarks Hitler during his last supper. Accordingly, the film may provide us with brief moments of empathy, necessary to facilitate character engagement even with the monsters of history, to allude to Noël Carroll's analysis of the horror film, but with the exception of the Junge figure, such temporary alignments never turn into more-enduring allegiances. In the same way that Hitler trained himself not to feel compassion, the film allows his audience both to detach from the spectacle of Nazi rule in the moment of its decline and to reject the burden of historical guilt and shame taken on by the survivors (metaphorically speaking) from the bunker. As a result, audiences are finally able to confront this period of German history with the same mixture of curious detachment and spectacular enthrallment experienced by the visitors of the battle dioramas and wax cabinets of the late nineteenth century and the heritage parks and history museums of the early twenty-first century. Whatever is lacking in relationship to the characters is more than compensated for by the affective politics of historicization that make the audience detach from the Nazi past and accept its legacies as an integral part of their national heritage. Guilt replaced by acceptance: this indeed is the ultimate goal.

Historicization, as the historians' debate has shown, means the application of new research questions, comparative perspectives, and interpretative methods to established fields of inquiry. Contributing to the process, scholars since the 1980s have insisted on the singularity of the Holocaust and the specificity of National Socialism but have also paid closer attention to local and regional differences and the continuities with pre-1933 and post-1945 Germany. They have approached these questions with an acute awareness of the centrality of the Nazi past to the self-presentation of the Federal Republic and, today, the Berlin Republic. But as the generation of historical witnesses passes away and the Nazi past joins the German postwar division in defining collective memory and national heritage, historicization becomes increasingly dependent on medialization and its particular modes of representation. In film and television but also in print media, this revisionist project is most apparent in the German-Jewish stories of reconciliation; in the focus on Germans as victims and innocent bystanders; and in what appears to be the widespread desire for a less problematic relationship to German history.

While unique in its status as a blockbuster and media event, *Downfall* was not the first postunification film to approach the Nazi past through the lens of historicization and its spectatorial and emotional rewards. In fact, it belongs to the larger constellation of conventional genre cinema, postnational patriotism, and political conservatism that after German unification gave rise to what film scholar Eric Rentschler describes as a "cinema of consensus" but that, as chapter 6 shows, cannot be called a strictly German phenomenon.[18] But while the look of history is surprisingly similar across national boundaries, with *Flame & Citron* even shot on the Babelsberg studio lot, the stories and narrative points of view are not. In contrast to the nostalgia for the friend-enemy distinction that fuels the celebration of violence in the latter, many Nazi heritage films rely on the power of love to distinguish "us" (i.e., the Germans) from "them" (i.e., the

Nazis) and to reclaim a positive meaning of German identity from the country's haunted past.

To mention only a few examples, the loving sacrifices of German women on behalf of their Jewish partners in *Comedian Harmonists* (*The Harmonists*, Joseph Vilsmaier, 1997), *Aimée & Jaguar* (Max Färberböck, 1999), *Leo und Claire* (*Leo & Claire*, Joseph Vilsmaier, 2001), *Nirgendwo in Afrika* (*Nowhere in Africa*, Caroline Link, 2001), and *Rosenstrasse* (Margarethe von Trotta, 2003) affirm private life as the true locus of political resistance and historical agency. In other films, the idealism of youth inspires compelling stories of seduction and betrayal in the style of *Napola* (*Before the Fall*, Dennis Gansel, 2003) but also attests to, as do *Der neunte Tag* (*The Ninth Day*, Volker Schlöndorff, 2004) and *Sophie Scholl: Die letzten Tage* (*Sophie Scholl: The Final Days*, Marc Rothemund, 2005), the power of religious faith.[19] Confirming the international marketability of these films, the Academy Award nominations over the last two decades have repeatedly included German-language films about the Third Reich: *Das schreckliche Mädchen* (*The Nasty Girl*, Michael Verhoeven) in 1990, *Schtonk!* (Helmut Dietl) in 1992, *Downfall* in 2004, and *Sophie Scholl: The Final Days* in 2006; *Nowhere in Africa* received the Oscar for Best Foreign Language Film in 2003, and *Die Fälscher* (*The Counterfeiters*, Stefan Rudowitzky, 2006) in 2008.

The Nazi heritage films market the Nazi past—and its increasingly exotic spectacles of political power and ideology—to an international audience, but the most significant work of historicization is currently taking place on German television. This shift to television as the privileged medium for big-budget productions and important media events partly accounts for the significant differences in the international and national reception of *Downfall* and shows the historicist project as one specifically aimed at German audiences. Since the early 1990s, journalist Guido Knopp has produced numerous multipart documentaries for ZDF (Second German Television) in the style of *Hitlers Helfer* (*Hitler's Generals*, 1996), *Hitlers Frauen* (*Hitler's Women*, 2001), and so forth. More recently, television has become the preferred venue for big-budget, multipart miniseries dominated by a small group of directors. The unabated fascination with Hitler's inner circle inspired Holocaust comedies in the vein of Kai Wessel's *Goebbels und Geduldig* (Goebbels and Geduldig, 2001) and gave rise to television plays such as Jo Baier's *Stauffenberg* (2004) and miniseries such as Heinrich Breloer's three-part *Speer und er* (*Speer and Hitler: The Devil's Architect*, 2005). Last but not least, Hans-Christoph Blumenberg's docudrama *Die letzte Schlacht* (The last battle, 2005), Baier's controversial *Dresden: Der Film* (2006), and Wessel's *Die Flucht* (*March of Millions*, 2007) transformed the experience of World War II and the expulsion from the East into melodramatic scenes of German wartime suffering and sparked intense debates about the political affects mobilized by large-scale productions that feature Germans as the victims of history.[20]

Notwithstanding its unique status as an international blockbuster, *Downfall* must be located within these two larger developments in the medialization of the Third Reich: the emergence of nationally specific forms of heritage cinema distinct from 1970s retro styles and the unabated popularity of historical docudramas and miniseries on television. Whereas the films tend to privilege stories of ordinary Germans living in extraordinary times, most television productions seem to favor the epic scales of history, with individuals, whether famous or not, presented as part of larger social conflicts and national traumas. In a peculiar reversal of media hierarchies, with film traditionally regarded as the preferred medium for *grand récits*, German film companies since the early 1990s have complied with the conventions of nation branding on global markets, which includes acknowledgment of the German as perpetrator and victim, whereas television has successfully managed to reconcile the competing demands of information and entertainment in the hybrid form of *historytainment* and its more one-sided address to a domestic audience looking for validation of German suffering and victimhood.

Central to both media contexts is nostalgia for the nation in the postnational age; the Nazi past, in this new spirit of postnational patriotism, is no longer a burden but a heritage, invested with all the sentiments, attachments, and beliefs that the term suggests. In the moment that the Third Reich can be disengaged from ideology critique and become subject to historicization, the meaning of politics becomes available to renegotiation as well. Thus, in sharp contrast to the West and East German films that, whether through the discourse of antifascism, the analysis of authoritarian society, or the critique of patriarchy and masculinity, took a clear political position vis-à-vis the events depicted on the screen, the films produced since unification openly reject overt political readings and rewrite history as biography, including that of Hitler. The result is a highly contradictory mixture of political affects and effects: rejection of the fanaticism that distinguishes past and present ideologues but also nostalgia for the power of conviction that sustains identities; opposition to the core assumptions of nationalism but also continued fascination with German history as a "negative" mark of distinction; and denunciation of the politicization of the aesthetic but also an aestheticized engagement with the fascist mass spectacle as media event.

In many of the examples listed earlier, the narratives are constructed around average people who at once become the victims of history and the agents of its overcoming. Yet the symbolic flight from the Nazi past—captured in *Downfall*'s closing image of a woman and child escaping from a sunken world destroyed by ideology—requires a fundamental rearticulation of politics as a private experience. Accordingly, political resistance is found, above all, in the pursuit of individual happiness, an approach that, once again, stands in marked opposition to the obligatory sacrifices for the collective in the East German antifascist films and the equation of the personal and the political by the representatives of New German Cinema. Rejecting what film scholar Thomas Elsaesser calls their "brooding obsession with Germany's own unredeemed and irredeemable past as a nation," the new generation of filmmakers exhibits what might be described as intense curiosity.[21] In ways crucially important for the larger questions addressed in this book, political passions and convictions are rejected as suspect and dangerous, forever linked to the fascist imaginary, and replaced by the personal commitments formed around such presumably universal categories as love, hope, trust, and faith. Private virtue instead of public morality, familial conflicts instead of political struggles, affect and empathy instead of critical analysis—these, then, are the postpolitical coordinates of historicization.

How do concepts like nostalgia and heritage help us understand the particular affective investments mobilized by, and projected onto, *Downfall*? Only by highlighting the difference between the epic scale and sweeping spectacle of historicization and the affinity of heritage in the German context for the aesthetics and sentimentality of genre painting. German film scholars have repeatedly turned to concepts developed in other national cinemas to analyze a series of shifts in historical representation while maintaining the evaluative binaries (e.g., critical vs. affirmative) associated with the socially critical and formally innovative art cinema modeled by New German Cinema. Perhaps inspired by the French retro films, Rob Reimer coined the term "Nazi-retro film" to describe the tension between reflection and retrospection as constitutive of West German cinema since the 1950s.[22] Since then, Lutz Koepnick and others have appropriated the term "heritage film" from British cinema to diagnose the noticeable paradigm shift between films made before and after 1989 and to examine their contribution to the postunification search for a national heritage. Like the British heritage films made during the conservative Thatcher era, their German equivalents have been described as a product of the social conservatism, economic neoliberalism, and historical revisionism of the Kohl era and analyzed (i.e., usually dismissed) as symptomatic of a *konservative Wende* (conservative turn) that continues to this day. Part of the normalization of German history and cinema, *The Harmonists*, *Aimée & Jaguar*, *Nowhere in Africa*, and similar productions according to Koepnick satisfy populist sentiments and popular traditions by providing "sweeping historical melodramas that reproduce the national past, including that of the Nazi period, as a course of nostalgic pleasures and positive identifications."[23]

What separates the Nazi heritage films from their British precursors, most scholars seem to agree, is the absence of the aesthetic qualities that deconstruct the meaning and function of history and that, especially in the form of post-heritage cinema, open up a space for self-reflexive experiments with generic conventions and alternative histories of gender, sexuality, and ethnicity.[24] Instead of the subversive mixture of irony, melancholy, and hedonism found in the critically acclaimed Merchant-Ivory productions, Joseph Vilsmaier (Koepnick's main example) and Eichinger and Hirschbiegel, for that matter, produce little more than naturalist-milieu studies weighed down by their sentimental tone and melodramatic flourish, reason for Mattias Frey to propose expanding post-unification historical imaginaries beyond the Third Reich and World War II to consider the broader implications of what he calls "retrovision." Given his exclusive focus on textual analysis, however, such an intervention only partly addresses the problem.[25]

In the end, it might be more productive to focus not on what the films mean—or fail to mean according to their critics—but on how they contribute to the changing public debate on Nazism. As the reception of *Downfall* confirms, the filmic representation of the Third Reich in the German context remains haunted by the presence of the referent and the attendant representational taboos. Sufficiently removed in time to be historicized but too close to be mythologized, these representations cannot fall back on an established iconography of imperial power and approach the archives of historical characters, stories, and settings as a source of aesthetic and other pleasures. As a result, heritage in the German context remains inextricably tied to, and problematically defined by, the failure of nation, hence its greater success in the nostalgic reenactments of local and regional culture found in the recent *Heimatfilme* (homeland films). What Koepnick calls the heritage films' "semantic inventories of banal nationalism" and what he dismisses as a "chimera of national normalcy" may very well describe some forms of nostalgia for the nation haunting the postnational imaginary of the Berlin Republic.[26] However, they function in fundamentally different ways from the triumphs and defeats of empire in the British heritage films. For the same reasons, the distinction proposed by Richard Dyer that "history is a discipline of enquiry into the past; heritage is an attitude towards the legacy of the past" may be accurate in describing two types of emotional engagement.[27] When applied to actual films, however, it only serves to justify old binaries (e.g., high art/leftist/critical vs. popular culture/ conservative/affirmative) that reveal more about enduring critical orthodoxies than their new political function within contemporary debates about nationalism and postnationalism.

In the search for generic precursors, aesthetic influences, and intertextual effects, we might be better served by situating *Downfall* and other recent German films about the Nazi past within West German film history and the critical examination of Nazism and its legacies beginning with the Young German Cinema of the early 1960s. In other words, the film's historicist approach must be evaluated within the history both of postwar films about the period and the aesthetically mediated emotions that, as we see in chapter 2, make them an integral part of the political culture of the Federal Republic and its continuing attempts to re-envision Germanness beyond or outside nationalism. As these films reject, revise, and replace earlier representational models, they not only integrate the Nazi past into the history of the cold war and the German division but also formulate their postideological project with acute awareness of the highly mediated nature of these legacies. To begin with an obvious intertext, *Downfall* may be described as a remake of Eichinger's first international blockbuster, *Das Boot* (*The Boat*, Wolfgang Petersen, 1981), which re-creates the claustrophobic interiors of the submarine in the underground world of the bunker but shifts the location from the periphery to the center of the Third Reich and replaces the figure of the heroic leader (i.e., the captain) with the weak leader abandoning his people. By focusing on interpersonal dynamics as the basis of the Nazis' power, Eichinger in both cases sets out to illustrate Fest's central thesis, formulated in the latter's journalistic and scholarly writings, about the unique emotional connections that made Hitler the voice of the Germans and that allegedly dissolved with his death.

One of several films to use the last days in the bunker as a lens through which to explain the Nazi dictatorship, *Downfall* can furthermore be described as a deliberate departure from the political moralism and existential humanism that informed the official stance of "never again" in Georg Wilhelm Pabst's *Der letzte Akt* (*The Last Ten Days*, 1955) and postwar cinema in general.[28] Eichinger's approach also announced a radical break with the formal experiments of New German Cinema, including the surfeit of reflexivity in one of his own productions, Hans-Jürgen Syberberg's *Hitler—Ein Film aus Deutschland* (*Hitler: A Film from Germany*, 1977). The preference for the claustrophobic mise-en-scènes shared with reality television and its own brand of banality, obscenity, and the grotesque found first expression in Christoph Schlingensief's *100 Jahre Adolf Hitler: Die letzte Stunde im Führerbunker* (100 years of Adolf Hitler, 1989), a sort of

*Downfall* without the good intensions (or pretensions). Treating performativity as a key to historical understanding, Hitler actor Ganz meanwhile completed the equation of National Socialism with Hitler's physical and psychological frailty that already informed Armin Mueller-Stahl's portrayal of the hundred-and-three-year-old man in his directorial debut, *Gespräch mit der Bestie (Conversation with the Beast*, 1991). The most recent manifestation of what, evoking Marx, can only be called the return of history as farce, Dani Levy's *Mein Führer: Die wirklich wahrste Wahrheit über Adolf Hitler (My Führer*, 2007) with comedian Helge Schneider in the title role, suggests that in the ongoing process of historicization, German-speaking filmmakers have finally taken possession of the entire range of generic choices, aesthetic means, and critical registers available within the postfascist imaginary.

Any discussion of the intertextual effects organized by *Downfall* must take into account the performance of Nazism by its major and minor players, beginning with Swiss-born Bruno Ganz in the role of Hitler. While Ganz's stature as one of the great actors of the German-speaking stage and his international fame as the antihero of the New German Cinema and, later, the European art film, works against any facile equation of actor, character, and historical figure, his association since the 2000 Peter Stein production with Goethe's Faust as the embodiment of the tragic hero was bound to further essentialize the implied struggle between knowledge and power. In fact, the Faust intertext imbues Hitler, his aging, frail body ravaged by Parkinson's disease, with an aura of tragic mortality. In casting the other inhabitants of the bunker, Eichinger brought together a group of leading actors from stage and screen, including Corinna Harfouch as Magda Goebbels, Heino Ferch as Albert Speer, and Juliane Köhler as Eva Braun. With the exception of newcomer Alexandra Maria Lara, "the German Kate Winslet, the survivor of Eichinger's *Titanic*," all of them had already participated in the ongoing revisions of German history initiated by *The Harmonists, Aimée & Jaguar, Rosenstrasse*, and *The Ninth Day*.[29]

In fact, these actors have become identified with a uniquely German physiognomy, a physiognomy marked as German through its association with an extremely nationalistic period of German history and its deviation from the normative standards of beauty, glamour, and sex appeal established by contemporary Hollywood stars. Eichinger's assertion that "history is made by individuals" thus finds confirmation in the corollary that historical films are made by stars. The function of these national stars as German actors and public figures, in turn, demonstrates that awareness of the performativity of history is entirely compatible with nostalgic reenactments of national character and individualized conceptions of historical agency and political subjectivity.

The integrative qualities of this star-based physiognomy of the Third Reich are especially pronounced whenever actors are cast on both sides of the German-Jewish dynamics of victim and perpetrator and appear utterly convincing as members of the Nazi regime and the resistance movement. Blurring the boundaries between individual films, the composite figures produced through such an intertextual conception of role, performance, and star persona establish Germanness as an integrative category beyond the old binaries of self and other and allow for a performative reenactment of history through the identificatory structure of the star system. Profiting from the resultant intertextual effects, Ulrich Matthes's hollow-cheeked portrayal of the propaganda minister in *Downfall* thus references his appearance in the same year as a Catholic priest on furlough from the Dachau concentration camp in *The Ninth Day*. As Magda Goebbels, Corinna Harfouch performs Aryan womanhood with the same intensity as the famous German actress who, in *Die Schauspielerin* (*The Actress*, Siegfried Kühn, 1988), converts to Judaism in order to live and die with her Jewish lover. Juliane Köhler's interpretation of the Eva Braun character combines aspects of the clueless Aryan *Hausfrau* in love with a Jewish woman from *Aimée & Jaguar* and the resourceful German Jewish wife and mother in the émigré story of *Nowhere in Africa*, whereas Heino Ferch, the romantic lead of many relationship comedies from the 1990s, approaches the part of Albert Speer with the same masculine composure that distinguishes his earlier appearance as an SS officer in Schlöndorff's *Der Unhold* (*The Ogre*, 1996) and one of the Jewish members of the famous a cappella singing group in *The Harmonists*. Ulrich Noethen, first seen as the second Jewish member of the Comedian Harmonists, returns in *Downfall* as Heinrich Himmler, but only after having been cast in two other films about the rise of National Socialism, as a fanatical Nazi in *Viehjud Levi* (*Jew-Boy Levi*, 1999) and the Jewish writer Kurt Tucholsky in *Gripsholm* (Xavier Koller, 2000).

Historicization is a process of visual and narrative reconstruction, a reworking of images and feelings that needs the release of its affective investments into social interactions and cultural practices in order to realize its full meaning. This revisionist process shares with the historical celebrations, anniversaries, and monuments of the late nineteenth century a fundamental dependence on *Öffentlichkeit* (public sphere or publicity) in producing a new historical consciousness and a different understanding of political affect. In the Berlin Republic, historicization has taken place primarily as a generational project, propelled forward by the opposition to the legacies of the 1968 generation shared by their historical antagonists, the conservative elites, and their postideological children and grandchildren. But it has also occurred as part of the seismic shifts in the contemporary media landscape: from the clear hierarchies between film and television toward a wider range of overlapping distribution systems and forms of reception (DVD, Internet); from top-down models of historical knowledge, political commentary, and cultural critique to interactive, rhizomic, and occasionally viral strategies of historical revisionism; and from a public sphere dominated by literary critics and the feuilleton toward a much more heterogeneous, decentered system that includes the official culture of commemoration and a decidedly populist approach to the politics of history and memory.

In audiovisual media, this means moving beyond the identity politics of postmemory—to use a term coined by Marianne Hirsch—so central to the generational mourning work of women filmmakers such as Helma Sanders-Brahms and Margarethe von Trotta, and integrating the traumas of the past into more-affirmative accounts of German history.[30] Instead of deconstructing classical narrative through the complicated entanglements of the personal and the political, historicization relies heavily on the participatory aspects of multimedia events in order to turn the Nazi past into an easily consumable object of *historytainment*. Historicization allows those growing up in postunification Germany to reject what many regard as the self-righteous habitus of coming to terms with the past in the tradition of Heinrich Böll, Günter Grass, and the 1968 generation and to develop their own uses of German history through the public rituals and political affects associated with postnational patriotism. Once again, the purpose is to move beyond the high-culture/low-culture divides (Adorno vs. Knopp, *Shoah* vs. *Holocaust*) that still define the "proper" ways of commemoration and remembrance and to identify, without aesthetic or political judgment, the conditions under which the historicization of the Nazi past is de facto taking place; the critical reception of *Downfall* is very revealing in this regard.

*Downfall* benefited greatly from the new alliances between contemporary media culture and postideological political culture that consolidated around the sixtieth anniversary of the end of World War II in 2005. As the best-known product of that moment, the film participates in a momentous shift in the historical imagination from the Holocaust as the telos of Nazi ideology to a self-consciously German history written from the perspective of World War II. This shift has made possible a growing recognition of German wartime suffering and a new emphasis on Germans as victims rather than only as perpetrators. These complicated constellations of history, memory, and trauma were first explored in W. G. Sebald's influential essay *On the Natural History of Destruction* (1999) and Günter Grass's novel *Crabwalk* (2002), whereas the presentation of history as catastrophe found its most controversial expression in Jörg Friedrich's *The Fire: The Bombing of Germany, 1940–1945* (2002). In the same way that *Downfall* took part in the media frenzy around the commemoration of World War II, it contributed to the equally important history of forgetting that erupted in controversial public pronouncements about "the innocence of being born late" (Helmut Kohl) and "Auschwitz as a moral cudgel [*Moralkeule*]" (Martin Walser).[31]

In the case of the Eichinger-Hirschbiegel production, balancing the demands of remembering and forgetting meant mobilizing all forces in the literary and postliterary public sphere to get the maximum return on the considerable investments in financial and political capital. The cost of the film production, which at $15 million was very high by German standards, required that every phase, from preproduction (e.g., screenplay rewrites, casting decisions) to postproduction (e.g., advertising, marketing), be fully aligned with the symbolic economy of event culture. Personifying the contemporary auteur as event manager, Eichinger made sure that the film attracted the widest possible audience, received the greatest media coverage, and became the most important media event of the year. Aiming for maximum synergies, he relied on two well-known source texts, a historical account of the last days in the bunker by Fest and an autobiographical account by Junge. The republication of Junge's *Bis zur letzten Stunde* (*Until the Final Hour*) in 2004 gave additional credence to her film appearance as a historical witness, with the interview scenes at the beginning and end taken from the previously mentioned Heller documentary.[32] Even Fest's historical sketch for *Downfall* was reprinted together with the screenplay to produce the obligatory "book to the film," thus continuing "the recycling mechanisms of Führer marketing" that earlier had led to the film adaptation of his own Hitler biography in *Hitler—Eine Karriere* (*Hitler: A Career*, 1977).[33]

When *Downfall* opened on 16 September 2004, it entered the domestic market with a record number of four hundred prints; 750,000 people saw the film during the first week after its opening. A luxury edition of the DVD, complete with interviews and scenes from the set, was released in March 2005. And a three-hour, two-part television version—the director's cut, in Hirschbiegel's words—was shown on ARD (First German Television Network) on 19 and 20 October 2005, reaching more than 20 percent of the television audience.[34] From the beginning, the film generated two fundamentally different but equally intense responses, which in turn became an integral part of its status as a media phenomenon. Audiences were either deeply moved or felt bored and indifferent, a division that found telling expression in the public statements by two directors from the old New German Cinema. On the one side, there was

Schlöndorff sharing at the international premiere in Toronto that "he rarely ha[d] been so moved and agitated," asserting, "*Downfall* will divide film history in a before and after."[35] On the other side, his colleague Wenders expressed puzzlement about his complete lack of an emotional response. "This couldn't have been it! Something must be missing!" he declared incredulously.[36]

Within the circular reasoning that characterized much of the critical reception of *Downfall*, the seemingly endless discussions about Hitler, World War II, and to a lesser degree National Socialism became irrefutable proof of the film's artistic qualities, and the increasing willingness in public debate to acknowledge German suffering a clear indication of its political relevance. Prior to its official release, several articles and interviews appeared in the country's major newspapers, assessing the significance of what was inaccurately referred to as the first German film about Hitler. The countless interviews given by Eichinger and his collaborators were meant to answer the usual complaints about a banalization of the Nazi past while supporting calls for a normalization of German history. After the premiere, the media responded with a steady stream of reviews, interviews, polemics, editorials, and critical essays, confirming what chapter 6 examines as a major function of the fascist imaginary in postpolitical culture, namely, to redefine nation and nationalism in contemporary Europe. On morning radio and late-night television, in daily newspapers from the sensationalist *Bild* to the conservative *Welt*, and in the special displays of large book chains and the customer comment sections of Amazon.de, *Downfall* was instantly treated as the media event it was intended to become. The official website for *Downfall* (http://www.untergang.film.de) catered equally to film fans' demand for drama and suspense and history buffs' interest in authentic detail. Acknowledging the need for further didactic instructions, the website (now defunct) even included materials for the classroom, complete with discussion guidelines for high school teachers.[37]

The German reception of *Downfall*, while still dependent on the traditional venues for film criticism, realigned the categories of evaluation with the new realities of event culture. Performative rather than substantive, these debates were ultimately about the meaning of history, politics, and ideology in postunification Germany.[38] On the feuilleton pages of the *Frankfurter Allgemeine Zeitung*, the *Süddeutsche Zeitung*, *Der Spiegel*, and *Die Zeit*, the nation's leading critics offered responses ranging from grave concern and aesthetic repulsion to feigned indifference and tentative praise. Following highly politicized patterns established in the old Federal Republic, *Downfall*'s aesthetics of historical reconstruction was often equated with a conservative agenda and the film viciously attacked for what it does not do.[39] Predictably, many reviewers complained about the conventional style of a big production that, like *Das Boot* twenty-three years earlier, reduced World War II to a historical spectacle. Some extolled the skilled performance of the actors, especially Ganz, while complaining about Hirschbiegel's uninspired direction. Others found the film to be disappointing, a sort of oversized television play, but recognized the filmmakers for overcoming the so-called Hitler taboo—even if this entailed little more than a banal version of Arendt's banality of evil thesis.[40] Much of the discussion focused on the legitimacy of portraying Hitler as a human being without ever clarifying the significance of such a representation for a new understanding of the Nazi past. Even *Bild* asked: "Should it be allowed to depict Hitler as a human being?"[41] According to a survey commissioned by the weekly magazine *Der Stern*, 69 percent of Germans approved of Eichinger's decision to approach the routine equation of Hitler with evil and madness from the side of his humanity. Throughout, two tendencies can be identified: relative indifference to aesthetic criteria in the evaluation of the film and intense attention to its status in the shifting terrain of postfascist cinema. Central to the latter position are the emotions, attitudes, and dispositions validated by the film—by the film not as film but as the signifier of a different approach to the Nazi past.

Encouraging such symptomatic readings, the filmmakers themselves identified their project with a self-consciously German perspective and long-overdue generational shift. Eichinger set the tone when he declared prior to the film's release that some "subjects are so specific that a nation must be able to give them artistic expression."[42] In a later interview with Frank Schirrmacher, editor of the *Frankfurter Allgemeine Zeitung*, he confessed to working through his own traumas as a West German eager to leave behind the politically correct, overly moralistic, and oppressively egalitarian culture established by the 1968 generation of *Gutmenschen* (literally, "good human beings") and to return to the more conservative view of "history made by individuals."[43] In that desire, he was joined by former DEFA actress Harfouch, who admitted that "this film has brought us some sort of emotional-intellectual peace . . . because after the film, I am now able to compare the two systems [i.e., the Third Reich and the German Democratic Republic]."[44] Mockingly, critic Diedrich Diederichsen described that interview as yet another scene from the bunker and, by extension, contemporary media culture, concluding, "The head of the entertainment industry and the head of the feuilleton, joined by the great actress. . . . It is a meeting of power-hungry people."[45]

As is to be expected, the filmmakers' direct appeal to German audiences prompted angry protests as well as passionate endorsements. Historians took the lead, including former chancellor Helmut Kohl, who declared that "the film had to be made."[46] Those assembled at the Forty-Fifth Historians' Convention in Kiel wavered between praise for the film's historical accuracy and concern about its conventional narrative, but overall, they, too, professed to having been moved.[47] Meanwhile, the "Political Psychology" section of the Professional Organization of German Psychologists denounced *Downfall* as psychologically manipulative, intent on weakening "the cognitive ability to distinguish between reality and its reconstruction."[48] Subject to the rituals of German *Streitkultur*, a culture invigorated by controversy, the film elicited the most provocative statements from members of the cultural establishment. Theater producer Peter Zadek aimed for maximum shock value when he compared the three million Germans who went to see the film to the three million Germans who had voted for Hitler in 1933.[49] Choosing a more serious tone, Wenders declared the film's lack of a clear narrative perspective (*Erzählhaltung*) and position (*Standpunkt*) politically and aesthetically suspect; hence his conclusion in a much discussed editorial that "*Downfall* serves neither the uppercase nor lowercase *G* of *Geschichte* [in the sense of large histories and small stories]. Above all, the film has no opinion, neither of fascism nor of Hitler."[50]

Attesting to the very different conventions and expectations governing the postliterary public sphere, much of the controversy surrounding *Downfall* took place outside the refined world of the feuilleton and the academy. The heated debates about what it means to make a German film about the German past quickly moved from morning radio and late-night television to new digital formats such as Internet discussion boards and the personal weblogs of cinephiles, history buffs, and neo-Nazis, where fantasies of nation and national identity are kept alive in global contexts and virtual communities. On the discussion board connected to the official film website maintained by Constantin Film, participants pondered questions such as "How important is the film for Germany?" and "How will it be perceived abroad?" When not quibbling over minor historical details, most participants seemed to agree on several key issues: that it was high time for Germans to take control of their own history; that Germans, while no longer guilty, are still responsible for the crimes of the past; and, a particularly frequent comment, that Germans have as much right to feel patriotic as the people of other nations.[51]

In the first months after the film's release, many contributors speculated anxiously about the film's reception in the United States and, in a sort of preemptive strike, accused Americans of being completely ignorant of German history, prone to equate all Germans with Nazis, and guilty of the same militaristic aggression as the Nazis.[52] Ironically, it is in the transnational, virtual communities of the World Wide Web that "Germanness" continues to function as a category of identity construction, with the equation of "German" and "Nazi" a driving force behind the seemingly inexhaustible fascination with this particular period of German history. It is also the World Wide Web, as an integral part of contemporary event culture, that aligns historicization with the virtual identities in which Germanness amounts to little more than a voluntary or temporary identity performance, unencumbered by the constraints of social reality or political ideology. In this context, referring to *Downfall* as a German film, made by German filmmakers, about a German topic, and with a new take on German history means constructing a fiction of nation from a postnational perspective. To ascribe to it a particular political position (e.g., conservative, nationalist, right wing) would mean ignoring the fundamental changes in the global media networks and European political imaginaries since 1989.

In order to fully understand *Downfall*'s function as a catalyst for old arguments and new attitudes, it is necessary to account for the growing significance of event culture and its specific function as a surrogate public sphere and a laboratory of publicly consumed emotions. *Events*, to use the German neologism, are the products of a contemporary media society characterized, on the one hand, by an accelerated consumption of culture and knowledge and, on the other, by a predominance of mediated forms of communication and sociability. Organized by a new breed of event managers and cultural impresarios, these events often take place outside established institutions such as art museums, exhibition centers, concert halls, and public libraries. As media events, they are not identified with a particular work or place but refer instead to the discursive and affective space created by the high-profile release of a film like *Downfall* or a book like Daniel Jonah Goldhagen's *Hitlers willige Vollstrecker* (*Hitler's Willing Executioners*, 1996). These forms of engagement are a constitutive part of the work and often overshadow it in terms of artistic or scholarly relevance.

On the most basic level, event culture provides the kind of experiences of community and belonging that constitute what sociologist Gerhard Schulze calls *Erlebnisgesellschaft*, a society held together by commercially produced and socially based experiences; therein it closely resembles the late nineteenth-century culture of national anniversaries, pageants, and ceremonies.[53] According to Schulze, this new experience-based society produces a profoundly different relationship between self and world in which the world is expected to adjust to the narcissistic needs and hedonistic desires of the self. Often evoked in critical writings on contemporary museum culture, cultural tourism, and the heritage industry, the emotionally charged category of *Erlebnis* suggests a cultural experience that remains short-lived and does not enter into the fabric of tradition.

Its emotional qualities do not automatically give rise to aesthetic experiences or critical insights. Thus, in the same way that *Erlebnis* does not necessarily translate into *Erfahrung*, defined (in accordance with Benjamin's distinction between both terms) as something meaningfully experienced, an *Erlebnis*-driven event remains dependent on the cultural commodities and media productions that give rise to it in the first place.

Described in this way, *Downfall* aims at an *Erlebnis*-based understanding of the Third Reich. It generates its strongest affects on the periphery of the diegesis, in the interspace between film spectatorship and historical consciousness. Whereas the world of the diegesis produces emotional detachment, the world in which the film is consumed generates an intense emotional involvement with the past, namely, in the relationships established through film spectatorship and public reception. Like all historical films, *Downfall* reconstructs the past through invention, alteration, condensation, and other established narrative strategies. Through its status as a media event, the Eichinger production also creates a discursive space in which audiences become consumers of Germany's difficult history: they take possession of it through the imaginary experience of "we Germans" and "our history." In other words, emotional reactions are generated not through immersion in the fictional world of the bunker but through the overdetermined meaning of this setting and its protagonists in relation to early postwar discourses of coming to terms with the past and the very different configurations of history, memory, and spectacle in contemporary entertainment culture. These mediated experiences serve as the shared reference point for the virtual communities involved in the making of a postpolitical approach to German history and a postnational definition of German identity. Both take an active part in the normalization of the German past and use this process to reinscribe democratic subjectivity through the emotions and affects generated in the continuing engagement with history in its various mediated forms.

To understand the continuing fixation on *Downfall*, it might be useful to draw on the medical metaphors that recognize the connection between the body politic and the physical bodies on, and in front of, the screen and to acknowledge the unconscious processes and ritualistic acts that contribute to the making of political affects. Comparing the German preoccupation with the Third Reich in film, literature, and popular culture of the 1970s to a homeopathic process, German scholar Eric Santner, for instance, likens these representations to small doses of poison that are introduced into an ailing body to achieve a cure.[54] Alternatively, the postfascist imaginary could be described as a form of immunization whose purpose is to protect the healthy body of democratic subjectivity against dangerous political infections. In the age of digital culture,

Haven't they ever heard of Fair Use? Title 17, U.S.C., Section 107?

*Downfall* on YouTube

German poster for *Downfall*, courtesy Constantin Film

the notion of the viral perhaps captures best the logics of production and reproduction behind the fascist imaginary that made possible the YouTube transformation of Hitler from *Downfall* into a so-called Hitler meme. The viral, after all, not only offers the most appropriate metaphor for contemporary media culture, given its incredible speed of circulation and proliferation, but also serves as a telling model of the decentered appearance of affects, emotions, and other mass mobilizations in the organization of public life and political speech.

In lieu of a conclusion to this chapter and the book, we might therefore want to end with a strange media phenomenon that takes us back to Foucault's diagnosis cited in the introduction about fascism's usefulness as a floating signifier: the proliferation of parodies of *Downfall* on the video-sharing website YouTube. Since 2006 they have taken on an almost viral afterlife, confirming the principle of remixing and remastering that has been part of the fascist imaginary from the beginning and pointing to the centrality of appropriation as the generative and formative principle of the fascist imaginary in postfascist cinema. It is in this spirit of appropriation that the central scene from *Downfall*—the "It is over. The war is lost" scene analyzed earlier—continues in more than a hundred parodies that add different English subtitles to the original German dialogues. Eichinger and Hirschbiegel have expressed their amusement over the clips, but Constantin Film since 2010 has been sending Digital Millennium Copyright Act takedown notices to YouTube charging copyright violations.

Almost all the parodies involve crises of leadership and experiences of defeat. The pleasure of seeing Hitler ranting and raving over some perceived slight or temporary setback can best be described with the German word *Schadenfreude*, the joy over someone else's misfortune. These new versions either refer to the battle of competing media technologies and information systems (e.g., Xbox Live, Broadband, Blu-Ray, iPad) or they focus on political rivalries (e.g., the 2008 US presidential election) and economic crises (e.g., the 2007–10 housing bubble and global economic recession).

All these scenarios revolve around two central points made throughout this book, the historically developed relationship between film and fascism as one of mutual instrumentalization and the remarkable availability of the quintessential modern dictatorship to appropriation in ever changing texts, contexts, and intertexts. Thus, in one clip, the generals tell Hitler that he has become a phenomenon on the Internet, to which he responds indignantly: "Six million views! Every one at my expense! . . . I am a goddam meme."[55] And indeed, his presence has become so ubiquitous, so viral, and so parasitic that Hitler himself seems to have lost interest: "How many times do we have to see that damn *Downfall* clip? Just stop—please just stop."[56] In light of the endless reproducibility of Nazi images and stories, it may be time to conclude this examination of the affective dynamics linking fascism and democracy as well. Filmmakers will continue to make films about fascism in the broadest sense in order to address problems of modern democracy, and this study has attempted to offer new insights into this complicated and contradictory process. Moreover, in focusing on the connection between affective and ideological interpellation, the seven chapters have presented models for how to analyze the political function of historical films and, even more important, how to think about feelings, emotions, and affects in relation both to film as a work of art and to cinema as a public sphere.

# Notes

## Introduction

1. Nigel Andrews, quoted by Saul Friedländer, *Reflections of Nazism: An Essay on Kitsch and Death*, trans. Thomas Weyr (Bloomington: Indiana University Press, 1993), 16.

2. Boyd Farrow, "How Hitler Conquered Hollywood: Why Are Today's Film-Makers So Desperate to Confront Nazism?," *Guardian*, 5 February 1999, http://www.guardian.co.uk/film/1999/feb/05/features4. The phenomenon was addressed in Piotr Uklanski's controversial "The Nazis" photo installation in the "Mirroring Evil" exhibit at the Jewish Museum in New York in 1998, which included 164 photographs of actors playing Nazis; see the book of the same name published by Scalo in 1999.

3. Colin Covert, "Nazi Overload, Heavy-Handed Treatment Doom *Defiance*," *Wichita Eagle*, 16 January 2009, http://www.kansas.com/entertainment/v-print/story/665035.html; and Neil Cohen, "Reel Thoughts: Nazis, Nazis Everywhere!," *Movie Dearest*, 28 December 2008, http://tinyurl.com/722qfj9.

4. On the terms "fascism" and "Nazism": The first one represents the broader generic term, encompassing both the historical phenomenon of European dictatorships in the interwar years and its various and highly contested postwar meanings as a political regime, ideology, and mentality. "Nazism" refers to the Third Reich specifically, and "Fascism" rather than "fascism" to Italy under Mussolini.

5. Requiring at least a cursory acknowledgment, the ubiquitous presence of Nazis as iconic figures in American popular culture since the 1960s can be seen in the Nazi-ruled planet in *Star Trek*'s 1968 "Patterns of Force" episode and Hitler and Eva Braun pretending to commit suicide in the fourth season of Fox's animated series *Family Guy*; the captured Nazi officer on the album cover of Thelonious Monk's *Underground Monk* (1968) and the fascist aesthetic in Michael Jackson's 1995 HIStory video; the evocation of the Nazi past in postmodern novels such as Thomas Pynchon's *Gravity's Rainbow* (1974) and Don De Lillo's *Running Dog* (1978); the Riefenstahl aesthetic in Bruce Weber's advertising campaign for Calvin Klein during the 1980s and the toy tableaux staged in David Levinthal's controversial *Mein Kampf* (1993–94) art installation; the figure of the "Soup Nazi" from the 116th episode of the NBC television series *Seinfeld* (1995) and the

infamous "Feminazis" evoked since the 1990s by conservative radio talk-show host Rush Limbaugh; the regular appearance of Nazi villains in international blockbusters such as *Raiders of the Lost Ark* (Steven Spielberg, 1981) as well as low-budget productions such as *Hard Rock Zombies* (Krishna Shah, 1985) and *Surf Nazis Must Die* (Peter George, 1987); and in genres ranging from musicals such as *The Producers*, made twice, in 1968 by Mel Brooks with Zero Mostel and Gene Wilder, and in 2005 by Susan Stroman with Mathew Broderick and Nathan Lane, to science-fiction films like *Barb Wire* (David Hogan, 1996), *Starship Troopers* (Paul Verhoeven, 1997), and *Iron Sky* (Timo Vuorensola, 2012). On this puzzling history of a fascinating fascination, see Florentine Strzelczyk, "Fascism and Family Entertainment," *Quarterly Review for Film and Video* 25.3 (2008): 196–211; and "Our Future—Our Past: Fascism, Postmodernism, and *Starship Troopers* (1997)," *Modernism/ modernity* 15.1 (2008): 87–99. On comparable developments in German popular culture and mainstream cinema, see Georg Seeßlen, *Tanz den Adolf Hitler: Faschismus in der populären Kultur* (Berlin: Klaus Bittermann, 2002); and Dietrich Kuhlbrodt, *Deutsches Film- wunder: Nazis immer besser* (Hamburg: Konkret Literatur, 2006).

6. My phrasing is inspired by Brian Massumi's definition of affect "as an ability to affect and be affected" in his foreword to Gilles Deuleuze and Félix Guattari, *A Thousand Plateaus*, trans. Brian Massumi (Minneapolis: University of Minnesota Press, 1987), xvii.

7. Robert Burgoyne, *The Hollywood Historical Film* (London: Wiley-Blackwell, 2008), 11.

8. Robert Rosenstone, *Visions of the Past: The Challenge of Film to Our Idea of History* (Cambridge, MA: Harvard University Press, 1998), 45–79; Robert Rosenstone, *History on Film/Film on History* (London: Longman, 2006). For an anthology that addresses broader theoretical questions, see Marcia Landy, ed., *The Historical Film: History and Memory in the Media* (New Brunswick, NJ: Rutgers University Press, 2001).

9. Michel Foucault, "Powers and Strategies," in *Power/Knowledge: Selected Interviews and Other Writings, 1972–77*, ed. Colin Gordon (New York: Pantheon, 1980), 139.

10. Jean Baudrillard, "History: A Retro Scenario," in *Simulacra and Simulation*, trans. Sheila Faria Glaser (Ann Arbor: University of Michigan Press, 2008), 43.

11. Ernesto Laclau, "Politics and the Limits of Modernity," in *Postmodernism: A Reader*, ed. Thomas Docherty (New York: Columbia University Press, 1993), 335.

12. See Anton Kaes, *From "Heimat" to "Hitler": The Return of History as Film* (Cambridge, MA: Harvard University Press, 1989). For the broader implications, see also his "History and Film: Public Memory in the Age of Electronic Dissemination," *History and Memory* 2 (1990): 111–29.

13. Hans Magnus Enzensberger, "Über die Schwierigkeiten, ein Inländer zu sein," in *Deutschland, Deutschland unter anderem: Äußerungen zur Politik* (Frankfurt am Main: Suhrkamp, 1968), 12. All translations from non-English sources are mine.

14. A historical survey of the term "fascism" and its political afterlife can be found in Walter Lacquer, *Fascism: Past, Present, Future* (Oxford: Oxford University Press, 1996). For a polemic against its inflationary uses, see A. James Gregor, *The Search for Neofascism: The Use and Abuse of Social Science* (Cambridge: Cambridge University Press, 2006), 1–29.

On contemporary manifestations and critical reassessments of fascism, see Angelica Fenner and Eric Weitz, eds., *Fascism and Neo-Fascism: Critical Writings on the Radical Right in Europe* (New York: Palgrave, 2004), especially the overview given by Andrew Hewitt, "Ideological Positions in the Fascism Debate," 19–42.

15. Ann Cvetkovich, *An Archive of Feelings: Trauma, Sexuality, and Lesbian Public Cultures* (Durham, NC: Duke University Press, 2003).

16. Carl Schmitt, *The Concept of the Political*, trans. and introduction by George Schwab, foreword by Tracy B. Strong, with notes by Leo Strauss (Chicago: University of Chicago Press, 2007), 26.

17. Carl Schmitt, *Theory of the Partisan: Intermediate Commentary on the Concept of the Political*, trans. G. L. Ulmen (New York: Telos, 2006), 85–95.

18. Susan Sontag, "Fascinating Fascism," in *Under the Sign of Saturn* (New York: Farrar, Straus & Giroux, 1980), 73–105.

19. Philippe Lacoue-Labarthe and Jean-Luc Nancy, "The Nazi Myth," trans. Brian Holmes, *Critical Inquiry* 16 (1990): 292. Mythic thinking is also central to the definition of fascism by Roger Griffin in *The Nature of Fascism* (London: Routledge, 1993).

20. Andrea Slane, *A Not So Foreign Affair: Fascism, Sexuality, and the Cultural Rhetoric of American Democracy* (Durham, NC: Duke University Press, 2001), 1–20.

21. Jacques Rancière, *Hatred of Democracy*, trans. Steve Corcoran (London: Verso, 2009), 7. It is interesting to note that Rancière (and, to some degree, Badiou) has explored some of his ideas about representation, modernity, and politics through the history of film; see his *Film Fables*, trans. Emiliano Battista (Oxford: Berg, 2006). On film and history in particular, see his "Die Geschichtlichkeit des Films," in *Die Gegenwart der Vergangenheit: Dokumentarfilm, Fernsehen und Geschichte*, ed. Eva Hohenberger and Judith Keilbach, trans. Stefan Barmann (Berlin: Vorwerk, 2003), 230–46.

22. On this problematic, see Chantal Mouffe, *The Democratic Paradox* (London: Verso, 2000). For an analysis of the broader implications for our understanding of signification and intentionality, see Walter Benn Michaels, *The Shape of the Signifier: 1967 to the End of History* (Princeton, NJ: Princeton University Press, 2004).

23. Claude Lefort, *Democracy and Political Theory*, trans. David Macey (Minneapolis: University of Minnesota Press, 1989), 11–17. See also Claude Lefort, *The Political Forms of Modern Society: Democracy, Bureaucracy, Totalitarianism* (Cambridge, MA: MIT Press, 1986).

24. On the distinction between politics (*die Politik, la politique*) and the political (*das Politische, le politique*) in political theory, see Oliver Marchart, *Post-Foundational Political Thought: Political Difference in Nancy, Lefort, Badiou and Laclau* (Edinburgh: Edinburgh University Press, 2007), 35–60; and Thomas Bedorf and Kurt Röttgers, eds., *Das Politische und die Politik* (Frankfurt am Main: Suhrkamp, 2010), 13–39.

25. Chantal Mouffe, "Politics and Passions: The Stakes of Democracy," *Ethical Perspectives* 7.2–3 (2000): 148–49. For an analysis of political discourse and its underpinnings (e.g., the privileging of rationality), see also William E. Connolly, *The Terms of Political Discourse* (Princeton, NJ: Princeton University Press, 1993).

26. Alain Badiou, "A Speculative Disquisition on the Concept of Democracy," in *Metapolitics*, trans. and introduction by Jason Barker (London: Verso, 2005), 78.

27. Miriam Hansen, "The Mass Production of the Senses: Classical Cinema as Vernacular Modernism," *Modernism/modernity* 6.2 (1999): 59–77.

28. Joseph Goebbels in a 1933 interview with *Lichtbild-Bühne*, quoted in David Welch, *Propaganda and the German Cinema, 1933–1945* (London: I. B. Tauris, 2006), 63. The comment was made in response to the problems with Nazi movement films such as *Hans Westmar* (Franz Wenzler, 1933) and *S.A.-Mann Brand* (Franz Seitz, 1933).

29. The terms in parentheses are taken from Ann Cvetkovich, "Public Feelings," *South Atlantic Quarterly* 106.3 (2007): 459–68; Kathleen Stewart, *Ordinary Affects* (Durham, NC: Duke University Press, 2007); and Lauren Berlant, *The Female Complaint: On the Unfinished Business of Sentimentality in American Culture* (Durham, NC: Duke University Press, 2008).

30. See Carl Plantinga, "Emotion and Affect," in *The Routledge Companion to Philosophy and Film*, ed. Paisley Livingston and Carl Plantinga (London: Routledge, 2009), 86. Noël Carroll likewise distinguishes between emotions and affects, with affect as the broader term comprising unconscious responses and emotion designating "a narrower subclass of affect, namely, what might be even more accurately called cognitive emotions (i.e., affects that include cognitive elements)." See his "Film, Emotion, and Genre," in *Engaging the Moving Image* (New Haven, CT: Yale University Press, 2003), 60. For an introduction to the work on affect and emotion in cognitive film theory, see Murray Smith, *Engaging Characters: Fiction, Emotion, and the Cinema* (Oxford: Clarendon, 1995); Greg M. Smith, *Film Structure and the Emotion System* (Cambridge: Cambridge University Press, 2003); and Carl Plantinga, *Moving Viewers: American Film and the Spectator's Experience* (Berkeley: University of California Press, 2009). Cognitive approaches to film and emotion have been anthologized in Carl Plantinga and Greg M. Smith, eds., *Passionate Views: Film, Cognition, and Emotion* (Baltimore: Johns Hopkins University Press, 1999).

31. For two representative anthologies, see Patricia Tiniceto Clough, with Jean Halley, *The Affective Turn: Theorizing the Social* (Durham, NC: Duke University Press, 2006); and Melissa Gregg and Gregory Seigworth, eds., *The Affect Theory Reader* (Durham, NC: Duke University Press, 2010). For a German contribution, see Michaela Ott, *Affizierung: Zu einer ästhetisch-epistemischen Figur* (Munich: edition text + kritik, 2010). For an example of affect theory in film studies, see Marco Abel, *Violent Affect: Literature, Cinema, and Critique after Representation* (Lincoln: University of Nebraska Press, 2007). Other disciplines tend to use affect synonymously with emotion and are usually more specific in their findings and less theoretically obtuse. On affect in relation to historical reenactment, see Vanessa Agnew, "History's Affective Turn: Historical Reenactment and Its Work in the Present," *Rethinking History* 11.3 (2007): 299–312. On affect in relation to memory, see Alison Landsberg, "Memory, Empathy, and the Politics of Identification," *International Journal for Politics, Culture, and Society* 22 (2009): 221–29. For a compelling critique of affect theory, see Ruth Leys, "The Turn to Affect: A Critique" (lecture at the John

Hope Franklin Humanities Institute at Duke University, Durham, NC, 25 January 2011).

32. Eric Shouse, "Feeling, Emotion, Affect," *M/C Journal* 8.6 (2005), http://journal.media-culture.org.au/0512/03-shouse.php.

33. See John Protovi, *Political Affect: Connecting the Social and the Somatic* (Minneapolis: University of Minnesota Press, 2009), a Deleuzian reading of body politic, political cognition, and political affect in contemporary American culture.

34. Brian Massumi, "The Autonomy of Affect," in *Parables for the Virtual: Movement, Affect, Sensation* (Durham, NC: Duke University Press, 2002), 40, 42.

35. Louis Althusser, "Ideology and Ideological State Apparatuses," in *Lenin and Philosophy and Other Essays*, trans. Ben Brewster (New York: Review Press, 1971), 169.

36. See Giorgio Agamben, *State of Exception*, trans. Kevin Attell (Chicago: University of Chicago Press, 2005), 1.

37. Linda Williams, "Melodrama Revised," in *Refiguring American Film Genres*, ed. Nick Browne (Berkeley: University of California Press, 1998), 42–88.

38. Peter Brooks, *The Melodramatic Imagination: Balzac, Henry James, Melodrama, and the Mode of Excess* (New Haven, CT: Yale University Press, 1995), 15.

39. For non-English-language film titles, when a film is mentioned for the first time, the original title will be given (together with the name of the director and year of release), with the US release title or, if not available, an English translation in parentheses; thereafter, only English titles will be used.

40. Fredric Jameson, *The Political Unconscious* (Ithaca, NY: Cornell University Press 1981), 9.

41. Siegfried Kracauer, *From Caligari to Hitler: A Psychological History of the German Film*, ed. and introduction by Leonardo Quaresima (Princeton, NJ: Princeton University Press, 2004), 3–11.

42. Georg Seeßlen, "Faschismus, Krieg und Holocaust im deutschen Nachkriegsfilm," in *apropos: Film 2000—Das Jahrbuch der DEFA-Stiftung* (Berlin: Das Neue Berlin, 2000), 268.

43. The existing monographs and anthologies on the topic either deal with West German films (e.g., Robert and Carol Reimer) or offer a West-East German comparison (e.g., Detlef Kannapin). Several studies focus on a particular period (e.g., Wolfgang Becker and Norbert Schöll on postwar cinema; Anton Kaes on New German Cinema; Margrit Frölich, Christian Schneider, and Karsten Visarius on postunification cinema); all remain within the discursive paradigm of coming to terms with the past and its emphasis on national history, memory, and identity. For full bibliographical references for these works, see chapters 2, 3, and 7. The most recent study published in German, Sonja M. Schulz's *Der Nationalsozialismus im Film: Von "Triumph des Willens" bis "Inglourious Basterds"* (Berlin: Bertz, 2012), provides a broad overview that includes films made in the Third Reich.

44. See the recent anthologies by Rainer Rother and Karin Herbst-Meßlinger,

eds., *Hitler darstellen: Zur Entwicklung und Bedeutung einer filmischen Figur* (Munich: edition text + kritik, 2008); and Karolin Machtans and Martin Ruehl, eds., *Hitler–Films from Germany: Myth, Memory, and History in German Cinema and Television since 1945* (London: Palgrave, 2012).

45. The political legacies of the Third Reich have inspired spy thrillers, action adventures, and political dramas such as *The Spy Who Came in from the Cold* (Martin Ritt, 1965) on Nazism and communism; *The Quiller Memorandum* (Michael Anderson, 1966) on neo-Nazi groups in West Berlin; *The Odessa File* (Robert Neame, 1974) on Nazis in West German society; *Marathon Man* (John Schlesinger, 1976) on Nazis in international business; and *La question humaine* (*Heartbeat Detector*, Nicolas Klotz, 2007) on Nazism and global capitalism. German films tend to approach these issues through their cold war and postunification manifestations: *Der Hauptmann von Köln* (*The Captain from Cologne*, Slatan Dudow, 1956) on Nazis in West German politics and industry; *Rosen für den Staatsanwalt* (*Roses for the Prosecutor*, Wolfgang Staudte, 1959) on Nazis in the West German legal system; *Die Spur des Bernsteinzimmers* (*The Mystery of the Amber Room*, Roland Gräf, 1992) about Nazi criminals in postunification Germany; and *Schtonk!* (Helmut Dietl, 1992) about the Hitler diaries scandal. Many films set after 1945 measure the aftereffects of Nazism/fascism either through intergenerational conflicts involving the children of victims and perpetrators or through the appearance of neo-Nazi sympathizers among disenfranchised social groups. The first include *Nicht versöhnt* (*Not Reconciled*, Jean-Marie Straub and Danièle Huillet, 1965), *Deutschland, bleiche Mutter* (*Germany, Pale Mother*, Helma Sanders-Brahms, 1980), *Crawlspace* (David Schmoeller, 1986), *Music Box* (Costa-Gavras, 1989), *Apt Pupil* (Bryan Singer, 1998), and *Meschugge* (*The Giraffe*, Dani Levy, 1998); the latter can be found in the bleak scenarios of contemporary life shared by *American History X* (Tony Kaye, 1998) and *Rossiya 88* (*Russia 88*, Pavel Bardin, 2009). For a study that explores the legacies of fascism through the Freudian family romance, see Susan Linville, *Feminism, Film, Fascism: Women's Autobiographical Film in Postwar Germany* (Austin: University of Texas Press, 1998).

46. Good examples for the affinities between fascist imaginary and exploitation cinema are *She Demons* (Richard E. Cunha, 1958), *They Saved Hitler's Brain* (David Bradley, 1963), *Flesh Feast* (Brad F. Grinter, 1970), *The Boys from Brazil* (Franklin J. Schaffner, 1978), *The Lucifer Complex* (Kenneth Hartford, 1978), and *Hitler's Daughter* (James A. Contner, 1990). Two more-serious German film dramas, *Gespräch mit der Bestie* (*Conversation with the Beast*, Armin Mueller-Stahl, 1996) and *Nichts als die Wahrheit* (*After the Truth*, Roland Suso Richter, 1999), also thematize the biological longevity of Nazism through its old but seemingly immortal Mengele and Hitler figures. To this list of biopolitical horror films we may even want to add *Made in Israel* (Ari Folman, 2001), a grotesque Israeli comedy that brings together several assassins in their hunt for the last living Nazi in Israel; my thanks to Ofer Ashkenazi for the reference.

47. See Eric Rentschler, *Haunted by Hitler: The Return of the Nazi Undead* (Cambridge, MA: Harvard University Press, forthcoming).

48. For a book that covers some of the same films from a Holocaust perspective, see Laurence Baron, *Projecting the Holocaust into the Present* (Lanham, MD: Rowman & Little-field, 2005).

## Chapter 1. Democracy in Action

1. Klaus Mann, "What's Wrong with Anti-Nazi Films?," *Decision* 2.2 (1941): 27–35; reprinted in *New German Critique* 89 (2003): 174. For a different interpretation, see Wolf-gang Gersch, "Antifaschistische Filmarbeit deutscher Emigranten," *Filmwissenschaftliche Beiträge* 16.1 (1975): 59.

2. See the films listed under "Hollywood Antinazifilm" at http://www.cine-holocaust.de. The only alternative to the dominance of Hollywood anti-Nazi imaginary and its ideological underpinnings can be found in the cinemas of the Eastern Bloc countries, especially the antifascist films discussed in chapter 3. On the role of Hollywood in establishing an almost universally valid Nazi iconography, see Moshe Zimmermann, "Wie sieht ein Nazi aus? Hollywoods 'Drittes Reich' im Film," *SBR-Schriften, Stiftung Bibliothek des Ruhrgebiets* (2004): 15–44.

3. On the artistic transfers between Hollywood and Babelsberg, see Lutz Koep-nick, *The Dark Mirror: German Cinema between Hitler and Hollywood* (Berkeley: University of California Press, 2002).

4. Scott Spector, "Was the Third Reich Movie-Made? Interdisciplinarity and the Reframing of 'Ideology,'" *American Historical Review* 106.2 (2001): 460–84.

5. Jan-Christopher Horak, *Anti-Nazi Filme der deutschsprachigen Emigration von Holly-wood, 1939–45* (Münster: MAkS, 1985), 91. For a comprehensive history, see Anthony Heilbut, *Exiled in Paradise: German Refugee Artists and Intellectuals in America from the 1930s to the Present* (Berkeley: University of California Press, 1997).

6. Horak, *Anti-Nazi Filme*, 343–44.

7. Examples include the well-known Michael Powell/Emeric Pressburger productions *Contraband* (Michael Powell, 1940), *Pastor Hall* (Roy Boulting, 1940), and *The 49th Parallel* (Michael Powell, 1941), as well as *Night Train to Munich* (Carol Reed, 1940), *Pimpernel Smith* (Leslie Howard, 1941), and *The Goose Steps Out* (Will Hay, 1942). On German-speaking émigrés in Britain, see Tobias Hochscherf, "'You Call Us "Germans," You Call Us "Brothers"—But We Are Not Your Brothers!': British Anti-Nazi Films and German-Speaking Émigrés," in *Destination London: German-Speaking Émigrés and British Cinema, 1925–1950*, ed. Tim Bergfelder and Christian Cargnelli (New York: Berghahn, 2008), 181–94. On British wartime cinema in general, see Anthony Aldgate and Jeffrey Richards, eds., *Britain Can Take It: British Cinema in the Second World War* (Edinburgh: Edinburgh University Press, 1994); and Robert Murphy, *British Cinema and the Second World War* (London: Continuum, 2000).

8. On these Hitler performances, see Ronny Loewy, "Konstrukte des Bösen in den Filmstudios von Los Angeles: Hitler als Figur in Hollywood," in *Hitler darstellen: Zur*

*Entwicklung und Bedeutung einer filmischen Figur*, ed. Rainer Rother and Karin Herbst-Meßlinger (Munich: edition text + kritik, 2008), 34–41. The counterpart of Bobby Watson in East German and Soviet cinema was Fritz Diez, who ended up playing the Führer a total of seven times, relying on the same elements of madness and buffoonery.

9. On the "Mickey-Maus Staffel," see J. P. Storm and M. Dreßler, *Im Reiche der Micky Maus: Walt Disney in Deutschland, 1927–1945* (Berlin: Henschel, 1991), 142–45.

10. On this point, see Jörn Glasenapp, "Indifferenz oder Propaganda? Überlegungen zu Hollywoods verspäteter Antwort auf die Judenverfolgung im 'Dritten Reich,'" in *Die Shoah im Bild*, ed. Sven Kramer (Munich: edition text + kritik, 2003), 31–49.

11. Richard Dyer, "The Role of Stereotypes," in *The Matter of Images: Essays on Representation* (London: Routledge, 1993), 16.

12. Siegfried Kracauer, "National Types as Hollywood Presents Them," *Public Opinion Quarterly* 13.1 (1949): 53–72. According to Inken Heeb, 75 percent of all feature films produced in Hollywood since 1946 associate Germans with Nazism, World War II, and the Holocaust; see *Deutschlandbilder im amerikanischen Spielfilm, 1946 bis 1993* (Stuttgart: ibidem-Verlag, 1997).

13. On the connection between normative notions of masculinity and their mobilization in political ideologies, see George Mosse, *The Image of Man: The Creation of Modern Masculinity* (Oxford: Oxford University Press, 1996); and the chapter titled "Nazism, Psychology, and the Making of Democratic Subjects," in Slane, *Not So Foreign Affair*, 111–37. On the postwar years, see also Robert J. Corber, *In the Name of National Security: Hitchcock, Homophobia, and the Political Construction of Gender in Postwar America* (Durham, NC: Duke University Press, 1993).

14. Interestingly, the few Soviet anti-Nazi films made during the 1940s are similar to the Hollywood anti-Nazi films in the use of national stereotypes, the reliance on generic conventions, and the preference for sociopsychological explanations. Especially the association of Nazism with lewdness and debauchery, both markers of upper-class decadence, follows the pattern established by Veidt as the quintessential Prussian officer while ignoring the traditional Marxist critique of fascism as a petit bourgeois movement. One of the most successful early films with an antifascist theme, *Podvig razvedchika* (*Secret Agent*, Boris Barnet, 1947), also known as *Exploits of an Intelligence Officer*, uses the device of class masquerade to stage the German-Russian confrontation. Played by the critically acclaimed Pavel Kadochnikov, a Soviet agent poses as a German businessman in the Ukraine to establish contacts with high-ranking Nazi officers. Warmhearted, caring, and nurturing among his comrades and with an easy casualness symbolized by typical Russian clothes (collarless shirts, soft caps), he turns into the exact opposite in his German business persona: the cold and calculating Mr. Eckert, with his elegant suit, bow tie, monocle, and cigarette dangling from his mouth almost undistinguishable from Veidt's officers in the Hollywood anti-Nazi film.

15. On *Tomorrow the World!*, see Jennifer Fay, "Germany Is a Boy in Trouble," *Cultural Critique* 64 (2006): 196–234.

16. On *Hitler's Children*, see Slane, *Not So Foreign Affair*, 42–70. Compare the contemporary review by Bosley Crowther, *"Hitler's Children*, Fictionalized Version of 'Education for Death,' Makes Its Appearance at the Paramount Theatre," *New York Times*, 25 February 1943.

17. On German-American film relations, see Markus Spieker, *Hollywood unterm Hakenkreuz: Der amerikanische Spielfilm im Dritten Reich* (Trier: Wissenschaftlicher Verlag, 1999); and Sabine Hake, "The Foreign and the Familiar: On German-American Film Relations, 1933–1940," in *Popular Cinema of the Third Reich* (Austin: University of Texas Press, 2000), 128–48.

18. George W. Herald, "Sex Is a Nazi Weapon," *American Mercury* 54 (June 1942): 662–63.

19. Klaus Mann, "What's Wrong with Anti-Nazi Films?," 177.

20. Harold Lasswell, *Propaganda Technique in World War I* (1927; repr., Cambridge, MA: MIT Press, 1971), 221 and 222.

21. On the limits of wartime propaganda, see Paul Lazarsfeld and Robert K. Merton, "Studies in Radio and Film Propaganda," *Transactions of the New York Academy of Science* 6.2 (1943): 58–75.

22. Siegfried Kracauer, "Propaganda and the Nazi War Film," in *From Caligari to Hitler*, 208. Kracauer's work for the Rockefeller Foundation and Adorno's work in the Princeton Office of Radio Research contributed significantly to the prevailing theories of Nazism during and after the war.

23. For discussions of *Confessions of a Nazi Spy*, see Horak, *Anti-Nazi Filme*, 106–33; Michael E. Birdwell, *Celluloid Soldiers: The Warner Bros. Campaign against Nazism* (New York: New York University Press, 2000), 57–86; Saverino Giovacchini, *Hollywood Modernism: Film and Politics in the Age of the New Deal* (Philadelphia: Temple University Press, 2001), 93–107; and David Welky, *The Moguls and the Dictators: Hollywood and the Coming of World War II* (Baltimore: Johns Hopkins University Press, 2008), 116–32.

24. Jack Warner, press information for *Confessions of a Nazi Spy*, 15 (LOC file CL 8823). Warner is referring to William Wellman's *Public Enemy* (1931).

25. The Production Code has been reprinted in Frank Miller, *Censored Hollywood: Sex, Sin, and Violence on Screen* (Atlanta: Turner, 1994), 295–97.

26. For a case study on the film's international reception, see Daniel Marranghello, "A Note on Political Censorship in Costa Rica: The Banning of *Confessions of a Nazi Spy* in 1939," *Historical Journal of Film, Radio and Television* 11.2 (1991): 185–86.

27. On the Warner studio during World War II, see Birdwell, *Celluloid Soldiers*, as well as Martin Kaplin and Johanna Blakley, eds., *Warner's War: Politics, Pop Culture & Propaganda in Wartime Hollywood* (Los Angeles: Norman Lear Center, USC, 2004).

28. For other contemporary reviews, see David Woolf, "Fact into Film in *Confession of a Nazi Spy*," *Films* 1.1 (1939); and Manfred George, "Anti-Nazi Filme: Ein Beitrag zur Entwicklung der Hollywooder Filmarbeit," *Aufbau*, 23 August 1940.

29. On the Bund and similar groups, see Sander A. Diamond, *The Nazi Movement in the United States, 1924–1941* (Ithaca, NY: Cornell University Press, 1974), 179–269. On the

American debates on Nazism, including its depiction as gangsterism in the anti-Nazi film, see Michaela Hoenicke Moore, *Know Your Enemy: The American Debate on Nazism, 1933–1945* (Cambridge: Cambridge University Press, 2010).

30. On Hollywood and politics during the 1930s and 1940s, see Larry Ceplair and Steven Englund, *The Inquisition in Hollywood: Politics in the Film Community, 1930–60* (Carbondale: University of Illinois Press, 2003). Valuable insights into the interaction between Hollywood and Washington during World War II can be found in Clayton R. Koppes and Gregory D. Black, *Hollywood Goes to War: How Profit, Politics, and Propaganda Shaped World War II Movies* (Berkeley: University of California Press, 1990).

31. See the 1942 "Government Information Manual for the Motion Picture Industry," reprinted in *Historical Journal of Film, Radio, and Television* 3.2 (1983): 171.

32. Walter Wanger, "The Role of Movies in Morale," *American Journal of Sociology* 47.3 (1941): 378–83.

33. Michael Denning, *The Cultural Front: The Laboring of American Culture in the Twentieth Century* (London: Verso, 1997).

34. Max Horkheimer, "The Jews and Europe," in *Critical Theory and Society: A Reader*, ed. Stephen Eric Bronner and Douglas McKay Kellner (London: Routledge, 1989), 78.

35. Giovacchini, *Hollywood Modernism*, 108–9.

36. Thomas Doherty, *Projections of War: Hollywood, American Culture, and World War II* (New York: Columbia University Press, 1993), 5. On the anti-Nazi film in a larger political context, see his *Dictators, Democracy, and American Public Culture: Envisioning the Totalitarian Enemy, 1920s–1950s* (Chapel Hill: University of North Carolina Press, 2002), 188–218.

37. Dana Polan, *Power and Paranoia: History, Narrative, and the American Cinema, 1940–1950* (New York: Columbia University Press, 1985), 8 and 9.

38. Ibid., 12–13.

39. Giovacchini, *Hollywood Modernism*, 50.

40. Not surprisingly, these films are the ones that have attracted the most critical attention. See Gerd Gemünden, "Brecht in Hollywood: *Hangmen Also Die* and the Anti-Nazi Film," *TDR: The Drama Review* 43.4 (1999): 65–76; and Gerd Gemünden, "Space Out of Joint: Ernst Lubitsch's *To Be or Not to Be*," *New German Critique* 89 (2003): 59–80.

41. See Katrin Sieg, *Ethnic Drag: Performing Race, Nation, and Sexuality in West Germany* (Ann Arbor: University of Michigan Press, 2002).

42. Walter Slezak, quoted by Horak, *Anti-Nazi Filme*, xiii.

43. See Emil Ludwig, *How to Treat the Germans* (New York: Willard, 1943); and Thomas Mann, "Germany and the Germans," in *Death in Venice, Tonio Kröger, and Other Writings*, ed. Frederick A. Lubich (New York: Continuum, 1999), 317–18.

44. Lion Feuchtwanger, quoted in Giovacchini, *Hollywood Modernism*, 159. For additional documents, see the 1943 Writers' Congress Papers in the UCLA Archives. On these debates, compare Marjorie Lamberti, "German Antifascists in America and the Public Debate on 'What Should Be Done with Germany after Hitler,' 1941–45," *Central European History* 40.2 (2007): 279–305.

45. Franz Neumann, *Behemoth: The Structure and Practice of National Socialism* (New York: Oxford University Press, 1942), 476. For the other references in this paragraph, see Emil Lederer, *State of the Masses: The Threat of a Classless Society* (New York: W. W. Norton, 1940); Karl Mannheim, *Man and Society in an Age of Reconstruction* (London: Kegan, Paul, 1940); and Max Horkheimer and Theodor W. Adorno, *Dialectic of Enlightenment: Philosophical Fragments*, ed. Gunzelin Schmid Noerr, trans. Edmund Jephcott (Stanford, CA: Stanford University Press, 2002).

46. For references, see Margaret Mead, "These Things We Can Do," in *And Keep Your Powder Dry: An Anthropologist Looks at America*, introduction by Hervé Varenne (New York: Berghahn Books, 2000), 159–66; Richard M. Brickner, *Is Germany Incurable?* (New York: J. B. Lippincott, 1943); and Theodor W. Adorno et al., *The Authoritarian Personality* (New York: Harper & Row, 1950).

47. Smith, *Engaging Characters*, 6.

48. Ibid., 6.

49. Ibid., 201.

50. Noël Carroll, "Toward a Theory of Film Suspense," *Persistence of Vision* 1 (1986): 76.

51. Doherty, *Projections of War*, 169.

52. To cite another example of the gradual slippage from Nazi to communist as the enemy of democracy, the story for *The Whip Hand* (William Cameron Menzies, 1951) originally involved Nazis plotting bacteriological warfare in rural Minnesota but was then changed to focus on communists at the request of RKO head Howard Hughes.

53. Chantal Mouffe, *On the Political* (London: Routledge, 2005), 5.

54. Georgi Dimitrov, "The Fascist Offensive and the Task of the Communist International in the Struggle of the Working Class against Fascism," speech at the Seventh World Congress of the Communist International in 1935, reprinted in *Against Fascism and War* (New York: International, 1986), 36.

55. Halford E. Luccock, "Disguised Fascism Seen as a Menace," *New York Times*, 12 September 1938. The argument is repeated almost verbatim by Katherine Hepburn in *Keeper of the Flame* (George Cukor, 1942) in a rare filmic contribution to the debate on homegrown fascism.

56. Clifford Kirkpatrick, *Nazi Germany: Its Women and Family Life* (Indianapolis: Bobbs-Merrill, 1938), 21. For a recent analysis of America allegedly on the verge of fascism, see Naomi Wolf's list of "ten steps to fascism" in *The End of America: Letter of Warning to a Young Patriot* (White River Junction, VT: Chelsea Green, 2007).

## Chapter 2. Resistance to the Resistance

1. On *Vergangenheitsbewältigung* in postwar West German cinema, see Jürgen Berger, Hans-Peter Reichmann, and Rudolf Worschech, eds., *Zwischen gestern und morgen: Westdeutscher Nachkriegsfilm, 1946–1962* (Frankfurt am Main: Deutsches Filmmuseum, 1989). On the representation of the Third Reich and the Holocaust, see Wolfgang Becker and

266 Notes to pages 67–69

Norbert Schöll, *In jenen Tagen . . . Wie der deutsche Nachkriegsfilm die Vergangenheit bewältigte* (Opladen: Leske + Budrich, 1995); Christoph Classen, *Bilder der Vergangenheit: Die Zeit des Nationalsozialismus im Fernsehen der Bundesrepublik Deutschland 1955–1965* (Cologne: Böhlau, 1999); and Claudia Dillmann and Ronny Loewy, eds., *Die Vergangenheit in der Gegenwart: Konfrontationen mit den Folgen des Holocaust im deutschen Nachkriegsfilm* (Frankfurt am Main: Deutsches Filminstitut, 2001).

2. The standard accounts in English are Heide Fehrenbach, *Cinema in Democratizing Germany: Reconstructing National Identity after Hitler* (Chapel Hill: University of North Carolina Press, 1995); Jennifer Fay, *Theaters of Occupation: Hollywood and the Reeducation of Postwar Germany* (Minneapolis: University of Minnesota Press, 2008); and Cora Sol Goldstein, *Capturing the Germany Eye: American Visual Propaganda in Occupied Germany* (Chicago: University of Chicago Press, 2009). On the politics of denazification, see Tom Bower, *The Pledge Betrayed: America and Britain and the Denazification of Postwar Germany* (Garden City, NY: Doubleday, 1982). On the importance of the Western alliance and the rhetoric of Western civilization to the postwar settlement, see Patrick Thaddeus Jackson, *Civilizing the Enemy: German Reconstruction and the Invention of the West* (Ann Arbor: University of Michigan Press, 2006). On denazification and postwar democratization in the Hollywood rubble films, see my "Erziehung zur Demokratie: Trümmerfilme *made in Hollywood*," in *Träume in Trümmern: Filmproduktion und Propaganda im Europa der Nachkriegszeit, 1945–60*, ed. Johannes Roschlau (Munich: edition text + kritik, 2010), 85–95.

3. On the Adenauer era, see Robert G. Moeller, ed., *West Germany under Construction: Politics, Society and Culture in the Adenauer Era* (Ann Arbor: University of Michigan Press, 1997); and John S. Brady et al., eds., *The Postwar Transformation of Germany: Democracy, Prosperity, and Nationhood* (Ann Arbor: University of Michigan Press, 1999).

4. On the concept of totalitarianism, see Hannah Arendt's classic 1951 study *The Origins of Totalitarianism* (New York: Harcourt, Brace & Jovanovich, 1973) and a critical reassessment of the term by Michael Geyer and Sheila Fitzpatrick, eds., *Beyond Totalitarianism: Stalinism and Nazism Compared* (Cambridge: Cambridge University Press, 2008), 1–40.

5. Jeffrey Herf, *Divided Memory: The Nazi Past in the Two Germanys* (Cambridge, MA: Harvard University Press, 1997), 201.

6. Frank Biess, "Survivors of Totalitarianism: Returning POWs and the Reconstruction of Masculine Citizenship in West Germany, 1945–1955," in *The Miracle Years: A Cultural History of West Germany, 1949–1968*, ed. Hanna Schissler (Princeton, NJ: Princeton University Press, 2000), 376–408. On the centrality of anticommunism to West German identity, see also Eric D. Weitz, "The Ever-Present Other: Communism in the Making of West Germany," in Schissler, *Miracle Years*, 219–32.

7. Smith, *Engaging Characters*, 102.

8. Raya Morag, *Defeated Masculinity: Post-Traumatic Cinema in the Aftermath of War* (Brussels: Peter Lang, 2009), 17–30. On gender in Adenauer cinema, see Hester Baer, *Dismantling the Dream Factory: Gender, German Cinema and the Postwar Quest for a New Film Language* (New York: Berghahn, 2009).

9. Gilles Deleuze, *Cinema 1: The Movement-Image*, trans. Hughes Tomlinson and Barbara Habberjam (Minneapolis: University of Minnesota Press, 2006).

10. *"Canaris*: Erdachte Verschwörung," *Der Spiegel*, 23 June 1954, 31.

11. Europa Filmverleih, press release, quoted in Claudia Dillmann and Ronny Loewy, eds., *2 x 20. Juli—die Doppelverfilmung von 1955* (Frankfurt am Main: Deutsches Filminstitut, 2004), 15.

12. *The Devil's General* was released in a 120-minute screen version and reduced to 115 minutes in the most recent German DVD version. The original length of *Canaris* was 112 minutes, while the German DVD version is only 108 minutes long. *It Happened on July 20th* has been cut from 79 to 73 minutes and *The Plot to Assassinate Hitler* from 97 to 94 minutes. Based on rereleases in the 1960s and 1970s, West German television versions of these films also vary greatly in length. On these television broadcasts, see Wulf Kansteiner, "Nazis, Viewers, and Statistics: Television History, Television Audience Research, and Collective Memory in West Germany," *Journal of Contemporary History* 39.4 (2004): 575–98. On censorship in the Adenauer era in general, see Stephan Buchloh, *"Pervers, jugendgefährdend, staatsfeindlich": Zensur in der Ära Adenauer als Spiegel des gesellschaftlichen Klimas* (Munich: Campus, 2002).

13. On the West German war film, see Robert G. Moeller, *War Stories: The Search for a Usable Past in the Federal Republic of Germany* (Berkeley: University of California Press, 2001), 123–70; and Bärbel Westermann, *Nationale Identität im Spielfilm der fünfziger Jahre* (Frankfurt am Main: Peter Lang, 1990), 30–95.

14. Letter by Artur Brauner, 8 February 1955, Artur Brauner Archiv, Deutsches Filminstitut, Frankfurt am Main.

15. On Hasse as a gay actor, see the exhibition mounted by Schwules Museum Berlin in 2003, "Ein kapitaler Spätentwickler: Hommages an O. E. Hasse zum 100. Geburtstag und 25. Todestag." Hasse frequently collaborated with Weidenmann, whose preference for all-male settings in the wartime propaganda film *Junge Adler* (*Young Eagles*, 1944) continued in the platonic friendships of older men with younger men in popular television series such as *Derrick* (1975–98) and *Der Alte* (The old one, 1977–99).

16. Review of *Canaris*, *Film-Echo*, 1 January 1955.

17. On the use of newsreel footage in *Canaris*, see Becker and Schöll, *In jenen Tagen*, 175–80.

18. See Erica Carter, "Men in Cardigans: *Canaris* (1954) and the 1950s West German Good Soldier," in *War-Torn Tales: Representing Gender and World War II in Literature and Film*, ed. Danielle Hipkins and Gill Plain (New York: Peter Lang, 2007), 195–222. On a very different reading of postwar notions of heroism that focuses on the figure of the *Schlappschwanz* (literally, "limp dick"), see Jennifer Kapczynski, "Armchair Warriors: Heroic Postures in the West German War Film," in *Screening War: Perspectives on German Suffering*, ed. Paul Cooke and Marc Silberman (Rochester, NY: Camden House, 2010), 17–35.

19. Carter, "Men in Cardigans," 220.

20. Helmut Lethen, *Cool Conduct: The Culture of Distance in Weimar Germany*, trans. Don Reneau (Berkeley: University of California Press, 2002).

21. Ulrike Weckel, "Eingeschränkte Vieldeutigkeit: Die Verfilmung von Carl Zuck-mayers Theatererfolg *Des Teufels General* (1955)," *WerkstattGeschichte* 13 (2005): 89–101. See also the discussion of the *Mitläufer* (fellow traveler) in Ulrike Weckel, "The *Mitläufer* in Two German Postwar Films," *History & Memory* 15.2 (2003): 64–93.

22. Aside from the museum catalog edited by Dillmann and Loewy, see Drehli Robnik, *Geschichtsästhetik und Affektpolitik: Stauffenberg und der 20. Juli im Film, 1948–2008* (Vienna: Turia + Kant, 2009), which also discusses the television drama *Stauffenberg* (Jo Baier, 2004), with Sebastian Koch in the title role, the Tom Cruise vehicle *Valkyrie* (Bryn Singer, 2005), and an earlier English-language production with a decidedly muscular lead, Brad Davis, in the television drama *The Plot to Kill Hitler* (Lawrence Schiller, 1990). On the resistance myth in general, see Bill Niven, *Facing the Nazi Past: United Germany and the Legacy of the Third Reich* (London: Routledge, 2002), 62–94. On the Stauffenberg myth in a historical context, see also Bill Niven, "The Figure of the Soldier as Resister: Ger-man Film and the Difficult Legacy of Claus Schenck Graf von Stauffenberg," *Journal of War and Culture Studies* 2.2 (2009): 181–93.

23. For a useful overview, especially in relation to literature and literary debates, see Stephen Brockmann, *German Literature at the Zero Hour* (Rochester, NY: Camden House, 2004).

24. On coming to terms with the past as a West German discourse, see Ulrich Brochhagen, *Nach Nürnberg: Vergangenheitsbewältigung und Westintegration in der Ära Adenauer* (Hamburg: Junius, 1994); Peter Reichel, *Vergangenheitsbewältigung in Deutschland: Die Ausein-andersetzung mit der NS-Diktator von 1945 bis heute* (Munich: H. C. Beck, 2001); and Peter Reichel, *Erfundene Erinnerung: Weltkrieg und Judenmord in Film und Theater* (Munich: Hanser, 2004), 71–82.

25. Friedrich Meinecke, *The German Catastrophe: Reflections and Recollections* (Cambridge, MA: Harvard University Press, 1950). Originally published as *Die deutsche Katastrophe: Betrachtungen und Erinnerungen* (Wiesbaden: E. Brockhaus, 1946).

26. Helmuth Plessner, *Die verspätete Nation: Über die politische Verführbarkeit bürgerlichen Geistes* (Frankfurt am Main: Suhrkamp, 1982), completed in 1935 and first published in 1959.

27. Karl Jaspers, *The Question of German Guilt*, trans. E. B. Ashton, introduction by Joseph W. Koterski (New York: Fordham University Press, 2000). Originally published as *Die Schuldfrage* (Heidelberg: Lambert Schneider, 1946).

28. Dolf Sternberger, *Der Begriff des Politischen* (Frankfurt am Main: Insel, 1961).

29. Wolfgang Abendroth, *Gesammelte Schriften*, vol. 2, *1949–55*, ed. Michael Buck-miller, Joachim Perels, and Uli Schöler (Hanover: Offizin, 2008).

30. Theodor W. Adorno, *Can One Live after Auschwitz? A Philosophical Reader*, ed. Rolf Tiedemann, trans. Rodney Livingstone (Stanford, CA: Stanford University Press, 2003), 4. Evidence of his debt to psychoanalysis, Adorno uses the term *Aufarbeitung* (working through) instead of *Bewältigung* (coming to terms with).

31. Alexander and Margarete Mitscherlich, *The Inability to Mourn: Principles of Collec-tive Behavior*, trans. Beverly Plaszek, preface by Robert Jay Lifton (New York: Random House, 1975). Originally published as *Die Unfähigkeit zu trauern* (Munich: Piper, 1967).

32. Aleida Assmann, *Der lange Schatten der Vergangenheit: Erinnerungskultur und Geschichts-politik* (Munich: C. H. Beck, 2006).

33. Michael Geyer, "Cold War Angst: The Case of West-German Opposition to Rearmament and Nuclear Weapons," in *The Miracle Years: A Cultural History of West Germany, 1949–1968*, ed. Hanna Schissler (Princeton, NJ: Princeton University Press, 2001), 376–408.

34. Becker and Schöll, *In jenen Tagen*, 23–24 and 181–82.

35. For two comparative analyses in the German context, see Joachim Schmitt-Sasse, ed., *Widergänger: Faschismus und Antifaschismus im Film* (Münster: MAkS, 1993); and Detlef Kannapin, *Dialektik der Bilder: Der Umgang mit NS-Vergangenheit im deutschen Spielfilm; Eine vergleichende Studie zur Bedeutung des Films für die politische Kultur in Deutschland, 1945–1989/90* (Berlin: Dietz, 2005). On the contribution of feature films to the divided history of postwar Germany, see Irmgard Wilharm, "Der Quellenwert von Filmen für die doppelte deutsche Nachkriegsgeschichte," in *DEFA-Film als nationales Kulturerbe?*, ed. Klaus Finke (Berlin: Vistas, 2001), 81–92. For the divisions of postwar cinema in general, see John Davidson and Sabine Hake, eds., *Framing the Fifties: Cinema in a Divided Germany* (New York: Berghahn, 2007).

## Chapter 3. Melancholy Antifascism

1. The standard works on the antifascist film in German are Detlef Kannapin, *Antifaschismus im Film der DDR: DEFA-Spielfilme, 1945 bis 1955/56* (Cologne: Papy-Rossa, 1997); and Anne Barnert, *Die Antifaschismusthematik der DEFA: Eine kultur- und filmhistorische Analyse* (Marburg: Schüren, 2008). English-language analyses can be found in Barton Byg, "The Anti-Fascist Tradition and GDR Film," in *Proceedings, Purdue University Fifth Annual Conference on Film* (West Lafayette, IN: Purdue University Press, 1980), 115–24; Christiane Mückenberger, "The Anti-Fascist Past in DEFA Films," in *DEFA: East German Cinema, 1946–1992*, ed. Seán Allan and John Sanford (New York: Berghahn, 1999), 56–76; and Daniela Berghahn, "Liars and Traitors: Unheroic Resistance in Antifascist DEFA Films," in *Millennial Essays on Film and Other German Studies*, ed. Daniela Berghahn and Alan Bance (Oxford: Peter Lang, 2002), 23–40. For a survey of DEFA films with an antifascist theme published in the GDR, see also *Das Thema "Antifaschismus" in Filmen der DDR für Kino und Fernsehen, 1946–1984* (Berlin: Verband der Film- und Fernsehschaffenden, 1985).

2. Raymond Williams, *Marxism and Literature* (Oxford: Oxford University Press, 1978), 132.

3. *Mama, I'm Alive*, though strictly not part of the 1960s modernism paradigm, is included in this group because of its significance to Wolf's contribution to the antifascist film and World War II film.

4. The best surveys of DEFA cinema can be found in Ralf Schenk, ed., *Das zweite Leben der Filmstadt Babelsberg: DEFA Spielfilme, 1946–1992* (Berlin: Henschel, 1994); Allan and Sanford, *DEFA*; Helmut Pflügl, ed., *Der geteilte Himmel I: Höhepunkte des DEFA-Kinos 1946–1992* (Vienna: Filmarchiv Austria, 2001); and Daniela Berghahn, *Hollywood behind*

*the Wall: The Cinema of East Germany* (Manchester: Manchester University Press, 2005). For a reading of DEFA cinema that emphasizes its political functions but reduces its aesthetic positions to ideological effects, see Klaus Finke, *Politik und Film in der DDR*, 2 vols. (Oldenburg: BIS-Verlag, 2007).

5. Aside from the coproductions mentioned earlier, these include the East German–Czech *Jahrgang 21/Ročník 21* (Born in 1921, Václav Gajer, 1958), and *Schüsse in Marienbad/ Výstřely v Mariánských Lázních* (Shots in Marienbad, Ivo Toman, 1974), the East German–Polish *Begegnung im Zwielicht/Spotkania w mroku* (Encounter in the twilight, Wanda Jakuboska and Ralf Kirsten, 1960), and the East German–Bulgarian *Amboss oder Hammer sein/Nakovalnja ili čuk* (Hammer or anvil, 1972) about the Reichstag fire trial of Georgi Dimitrov. DEFA coproductions with the Soviet Union continued until the 1980s, with *Alexander der Kleine/Aleksandr malenkiy* (*Little Alexander*, Vladimir Fokin, 1982) and the two-part *Der Sieg/Pobeda* (Victory, Jevgeni Matveyjev, 1985) the best-known films about World War II and its aftermath. On the role of coproductions in establishing the discourse of antifascism in a transnational context, see Mariana Ivanova, "DEFA and East European Cinema: Co-Productions, Transnational Exchange and Artistic Collaborations" (PhD diss., University of Texas, 2011).

6. On GDR memory culture, see Thomas C. Fox, *Stated Memory: East Germany and the Holocaust* (Rochester, NY: Camden House, 1999); and Martin Sabrow, ed., *Geschichte als Herrschaftsdiskurs: Der Umgang mit der Vergangenheit in der DDR* (Cologne: Böhlau, 2000), especially Thomas Heimann, "Erinnerung als Wandlung: Kriegsbilder im frühen DDR-Film," 37–86. On the GDR dictatorship in general, see Alf Lüdtke, ed., *Herrschaft als soziale Praxis: Historische und sozial-anthropologische Studien* (Göttingen: Vanderhoeck & Ruprecht, 1991); Richard Bessel and Ralph Jessen, eds., *Die Grenzen der Diktatur: Staat und Gesellschaft in der DDR* (Göttingen: Vanderhoeck & Ruprecht, 1996); Konrad Jarausch, ed., *Dictatorship as Experience: Toward a Socio-Cultural History of the GDR* (New York: Berghahn, 1999); Thomas Lindenberger, ed., *Herrschaft und Eigen-Sinn in der Diktatur* (Cologne: Böhlau, 1999); and Corey Ross, *The East German Dictatorship: Problems and Perspectives in the Interpretation of the GDR* (London: Arnold, 2002).

7. Georgi Dimitrov, "The Fascist Offensive and the Task of the Communist International in the Struggle of the Working Class against Fascism," speech at the Seventh World Congress of the Communist International in 1935, reprinted in *Against Fascism and War* (New York: International, 1986), 2.

8. On the conditions of filmmaking during these years, see Thomas Heimann, *DEFA, Künstler und SED-Kulturpolitik: Verständnis von Kulturpolitik und Filmproduktion in der SBZ/DDR, 1945 bis 1959* (Berlin: VISTAS, 1994).

9. On this point, see Gareth Pritchard, *The Making of the GDR, 1945–53: From Antifascism to Stalinism* (Manchester: Manchester University Press, 2004).

10. See Katrin Morlok, "Gustav von Wangenheims Kämpfer (Borzy) als Beispiel," in *Filme für die Volksfront: Erwin Piscator, Gustav von Wangenheim, Friedrich Wolf—antifaschistische Filmemacher im sowjetischen Exil*, ed. Rainhard May and Hendrik Jackson (Berlin: Stattkino, 2001), 134–63. For a critical reassessment from the period, see Gersch, "Antifaschistische Filmarbeit deutscher Emigranten," 40–62.

11. On this point, see Russell Lemmons, "'Great Truths and Minor Truths': Kurt Maetzig's Ernst Thälmann Films, the Antifascism Myth, and the Politics of Biography in the German Democratic Republic," in Davidson and Hake, *Framing the Fifties*, 74–90.

12. Reviews are reprinted in Lissi Zilinski et al., eds., *Spielfilme der DEFA im Spiegel der Kritik* (Berlin: Henschel, 1970); and Rolf Richter, ed., *DEFA-Spielfilm-Regisseure und ihre Kritiker*, 2 vols. (Berlin: Henschel, 1983).

13. On the insulating effect of aesthetic utopias, see the important article by Wolfgang Emmerich, "Affirmation-Utopie-Melancholie: Versuch einer Bilanz von vierzig Jahren DDR-Literatur," *German Studies Review* 14.2 (1991): 325–44. On the unwillingness to address Stalinism as loss, compare Patricia Herminghouse, "Confronting the 'Blank Spots of History': GDR Culture and the Legacy of 'Stalinism,'" *German Studies Review* 14.2 (1991): 345–65.

14. For recent anthologies on German wartime suffering, see Ursula Heulenkamp, ed., *Schuld und Sühne? Kriegserlebnis und Kriegsdeutung in deutschen Medien der Nachkriegszeit (1945–1961)* (Amsterdam: Rodopi, 2001), esp. Wolfgang Mühl-Benninghaus, "Vergeßt es nie! Schuld sind sie! Zu Kriegsdeutungen in den audiovisuellen Medien beider deutschen Staaten in den vierziger und fünfziger Jahren," 742–57; Bill Niven, ed., *Germans as Victims: Remembering the Past in Contemporary Germany* (New York: Palgrave, 2006); Helmut Schmitz, ed., *A Nation of Victims? Representations of German Wartime Suffering from 1945 to the Present* (Amsterdam: Rodopi, 2007); and Cooke and Silberman, *Screening War*.

15. The Soviet perspective on antifascist films and World War II films was presented in the leading GDR film journal, *Filmwissenschaftliche Beiträge* (16.1 [1975]), by L. Muratow, "Der internationale Film im Kampf gegen den Faschismus," 7–39; and Juri Chanjutin, "Warum werden Filme über den Krieg gedreht," 63.

16. In his study on embodiment in DEFA cinema, Stefan Zahlmann examines the heightened significance of the body in reenacting the contradictions of history, memory, and identity. See Stefan Zahlmann, *Körper und Konflikt in der filmischen Erinnerungskultur der BRD und DDR* (Berlin: Berlin-Verlag, 2001); and Stefan Zahlmann, "Die besten Jahre? DDR-Erinnerungskultur in Spielfilmen der DEFA," in *Vom kollektiven Gedächnis zur Individualisierung der Erinnerung*, ed. Clemens Wischermann (Stuttgart: Metzler, 2002), 65–88.

17. On melodrama and pathos as distinguishing marks of the DEFA studio style, see Detlef Kannapin, "Gibt es eine spezifische DEFA-Ästhetik? Anmerkungen zum Wandel der künstlerischen Formen im DEFA Spielfilm," in *apropos: Film 2000—Das Jahrbuch der DEFA-Stiftung* (Berlin: Das Neue Berlin, 2000), 142–64.

18. Anke Pinkert, *Film and Memory in East Germany* (Bloomington: Indiana University Press, 2008), 3.

19. Ibid., 178.

20. Konrad Wolf, "Kein Sozialismus ohne Antifaschismus," *Sinn und Form* 31.4 (1979): 730–42; reprinted from "Kunst im Kampf gegen Faschismus gestern und heute," speech before the Academy of Arts of the GDR, *Sonntag* 33.20 (1979): 8–9.

21. Frank Beyer, *Wenn der Wind sich dreht: Meine Filme, mein Leben* (Munich: Econ, 2002), 91. On Beyer, see Ralf Schenk, ed., *Regie: Frank Beyer* (Berlin: Edition Hentrich,

1993). On the shooting of the film, see Frank Beyer, "*Fünf Patronenhülsen*: Aus der Werkstatt des Regisseurs," *Filmwissenschaftliche Mitteilungen*, supplement to *Deutsche Filmkunst* 1 (1961): 3. Anecdotal reminiscences about the shooting of his antifascist trilogy can be found in Beyer, *Meine Filme, mein Leben*, 91–119. On the myth of the Spanish Civil War in the GDR, see Josie McLellan, *Antifascism and Memory in East Germany: Remembering the International Brigades, 1945–1989* (New York: Oxford University Press, 2004); and Arnold Kramer, "The Cult of the Spanish Civil War in East Germany," *Journal of Contemporary History* 39.4 (2004): 531–60.

22. On history and identity in Wolf, see Marc Silberman, "Remembering History: The Filmmaker Konrad Wolf," *New German Critique* 49 (1990): 163–91; and Gertrud Koch, "On the Disappearance of the Dead among the Living: The Holocaust and the Confusion of Identities in the Films of Konrad Wolf," *New German Critique* 60 (1993): 57–75. On the antifascist film and its affinities with the *Gegenwartsfilm*, see Barton Byg, "From Anti-Fascism to *Gegenwartsfilm*: Konrad Wolf," in *Studies in GDR Culture and Society 5: Selected Papers from the Tenth New Hampshire Symposium on the German Democratic Republic* (Lanham, MD: University Press of America, 1985), 115–24. For a historical biography that sheds light on the three subject positions—German, Soviet, and Jewish—that inform Wolf's engagement with antifascism, see the biography by Wolfgang Jacobsen and Rolf Aurich, *Der Sonnensucher Konrad Wolf* (Berlin: Aufbau, 2005).

23. Here it would be interesting to compare *Five Cartridges* to *Le quattro giornate di Napoli* (*The Four Days of Naples*, Nanny Loy, 1962) and its neorealist depiction of the populist uprising of the citizens of Naples against the German occupiers in 1943.

24. The term is inspired by Slavoj Žižek, "The Fetish of the Party," in *The Universal Exception* (London: Continuum, 2006), 67–93.

25. The absorption of the antifascist narrative into the war narrative is even more evident in two World War II films from that decade, *Meine Stunde Null* (*My Zero Hour*, Joachim Hasler, 1970), about a German soldier captured by the Soviets and working with them to end the war, and the German-Soviet coproduction *Ich will euch sehen* (I want to see you, János Veiczi, 1978), about a German soldier-turned-partisan.

26. On the novel and its film and television adaptations, see Thomas Heimann, *Bilder von Buchenwald: Die Visualisierung des Antifaschismus in der DDR (1945–1990)* (Cologne: Böhlau, 2005), 71–104.

27. Marc Silberman, "The Authenticity of Autobiography," *German Cinema: Texts in Context* (Detroit: Wayne State University Press, 2000), 145–61; and Thomas Elsaesser and Michael Wedel, "Defining DEFA's Historical Imaginary: The Films of Konrad Wolf," *New German Critique* 82 (2001): 19.

28. On DEFA stars and the performance of masculinity, see Claudia Fellmer, "The Communist Who Rarely Plays a Communist: The Case of DEFA Star Erwin Geschonneck," in *Millennial Essays on Film and Other German Studies*, ed. Daniela Berghahn and Alan Bance (Oxford: Peter Lang, 2002), 41–62. On the crisis of masculinity in early DEFA film, compare Anke Pinkert, "Can Melodrama Cure? War Trauma and the Crisis of Masculinity in Early DEFA Film," *Seminar* 44.1 (2008): 118–36.

29. The term "corporeal semantics" is taken from Horst Ruthrof, *Semantics and the Body: Meaning from Frege to the Postmodern* (Toronto: University of Toronto Press, 1997).

30. Julia Hell, *Post-Fascist Fantasies: Psychoanalysis, History, and the Literature of East Germany* (Durham, NC: Duke University Press, 1997), 67. For a comparative reading of *Five Cartridges*, see Stefan Soldovieri, "German Suffering in Spain: Cold War Visions of the Spanish Civil War in *Fünf Patronenhülsen* (1960) and *Solange du lebst* (1955)," *Cinémas: Revue d'études cinématographiques* 18.1 (2007): 53-69.

31. On the king's two bodies, see Ernst Kantorowicz, *The King's Two Bodies: A Study in Medieval Political Theology* (Princeton, NJ: Princeton University Press, 1954). For a reading that applies these ideas to socialist realism, see Claude Lefort, "The Image of the Body and Totalitarianism," in *Political Forms of Modern Society*, 292-306.

32. Larson Powell, "Mama, ich lebe: Konrad Wolf's Intermedial Parable of Antifascism," in *Edinburgh German Yearbook*, vol. 3, *Contested Legacies: Constructions of Cultural Heritage in the GDR* (Rochester, NY: Camden House, 2009), 71. For a more conventional reading that emphasizes the difficulties of memory as the foundation of socialist identity, see Knut Hickethier, "*Mama, ich lebe* (1977): Erinnerung als Identitätssuche," *Beiträge zur Film- und Fernsehwissenschaft* 31.29 (1990): 168-82.

33. The DEFA antifascist films produced during the Honecker era after 1971 privileged the existential questions of guilt, hope, and personal responsibility first explored by Beyer in his Jurek Becker adaptation *Jakob der Lügner* (*Jacob, the Liar*, 1974) and in *Der Aufenthalt* (*The Turning Point*, 1983) as part of a larger critique of 1950s and 1960s orthodoxy. The similarities with the West German films of the 1970s and their conception of the personal as the political are confirmed by a comparison between Ralf Kirsten's *Ich zwing dich zu leben* (*I'll Force You to Live*, 1978) and Helma Sanders-Brahms's *Deutschland, bleiche Mutter* (*Germany, Pale Mother*, 1980). In contrast to the strong feminist voices in New German Cinema, the belated introduction of female perspectives in *Die Verlobte* (*The Fiancée*, 1980) and *Die Schauspielerin* (*The Actress*, 1988) became possible in the East only after the demise of any totalizing claims to historical agency associated with antifascism. On this point, see Daniela Berghahn, "Resistance of the Heart: Female Suffering and Victimhood in DEFA Antifascist Films," in *Screening War*, 165-86.

34. Antonia Grunenberg, *Antifaschismus, ein deutscher Mythos* (Reinbek: Rowohlt, 1993), 11.

35. Manfred Agethen, Eckhard Jesse, and Ehrhart Neubert, eds., *Der missbrauchte Antifaschismus: DDR-Staatsdoktrin und Lebenslüge der deutschen Linken* (Freiburg: Herder, 2002); see in particular the contribution by Anne Kober, "Antifaschismus im DEFA-Film: Ein Fallbeispiel; *Rat der Götter*," 202-20. For a very different approach, see Robert Erlinghagen, *Die Diskussion um den Begriff des Antifaschismus seit 1989/90* (Berlin: Argument, 1997).

36. Christa Wolf, "Für unser Land," in *Im Dialog: Aktuelle Texte* (Frankfurt am Main: Luchterhand, 1990), 170-71.

37. For postunification assessments of antifascism, see Konrad Jarausch, "The Failure of East German Antifascism: Some Ironies of History as Politics," *German Studies*

*Review* 14.1 (1991): 87–102; and for a scathing critique, see Dan Diner, "On the Ideology of Antifascism," *New German Critique* 67 (1996): 123–32.

## Chapter 4. Between Art and Exploitation

1. Sontag, "Fascinating Fascism," 102 and 104.

2. Michel Foucault, "Film and Popular Memory," in *Foucault Live Interviews, 1966–1984*, ed. Sylvère Lotringer, trans. Martin Jordin (New York: Semiotext(e), 1996), 127. Foucault's analysis of the retro mode was prompted by Louis Malle's *Lacombe Lucien* (1974), one of the first post-Gaullist films about collaboration in Vichy France. On its controversial reception, see Richard Golsan, "Collaboration and Context: *Lacombe Lucien*, the *Mode Rétro*, and the Vichy Syndrome," in *Identity Papers: Contested Nationhood in Twentieth-Century France*, ed. Steven Ungar and Tom Conley (Minneapolis: University of Minnesota Press, 1996), 139–55.

3. I borrow this phrase from the title of Christopher Clark's book project (mentioned on his 2010 Rutgers University Department of German website) titled "Desiring Nazis: Fascism and Sexuality in Contemporary German Culture."

4. For an example of the high stakes involved in the choice of an appropriate aesthetic register, see Berel Lang's argument in *Act and Idea in the Nazi Genocide* (Chicago: University of Chicago Press, 1990) against nineteenth-century realism and, by extension, the classic realist text in cinema as an appropriate form for representing the Holocaust.

5. See Baudrillard, "History: A Retro Scenario," 43–47. Similarly, Saul Friedländer characterized the new discourse on Nazism as an attempt simultaneously to understand and experience fascism's uncanny power over emotions, images, and phantasms. The films of the 1970s, he explained, thrive on "an aesthetic frisson, created by the opposition between the harmony of kitsch . . . and the constant evocation of themes of death and destruction," through which the contradictions of modernity are projected onto what he described as the basic modalities of power, namely, those of submission and domination. See *Reflections of Nazism*, 18.

6. Agamben, *State of Exception*. The term "biopolitics" first appears in Michel Foucault, "The Birth of Biopolitics," in *Ethics, Subjectivity, and Truth*, ed. Paul Rabinow (New York: New Press, 2006), 73–80. On the sexual *dispositif*, see also Michel Foucault, *History of Sexuality: An Introduction*, trans. Robert Hurley (New York: Vintage, 1990), 1:75–132, translated there as "deployment."

7. Andrea Slane, "Sexy Nazis and Daddy's Girls: Fascism and Sexuality in Film and Video since the 1970s," in *War, Violence, and the Modern Condition*, ed. Bernd Hüppauf (Berlin: de Gruyter, 1997), 154.

8. Plantinga, *Moving Viewers*, 57.

9. The term is introduced by Linda Williams, "Film Bodies: Gender, Genre, and Excess," in *Film Genre Reader II*, ed. Barry Keith Grant (Austin: University of Texas Press, 1995), 141–59.

10. On the significance of *Salò* (and, by extension, some of the other films included

in this chapter) for contemporary representations of torture and the spectacle of totalitarian power, see Eduardo Subirats, "Totalitarian Lust: From *Salò* to Abu Ghraib," trans. Christopher Britt Arredondo, *South Central Review* 24.1 (2007): 174–82.

11. The term was introduced by Carl Schmitt in his Weimar legal writings on dictatorship to describe the suspension of law by the sovereign and has since been taken up by Agamben in *State of Exception*.

12. Because of its very different aesthetic and political project, *Salò* is not discussed in this chapter but is referenced whenever relevant for the larger discourse on fascism and sexuality.

13. Researching the Italian reception of Naziploitation is difficult, given the lack of film reviews or exhibition data. In the United States, many of the films have been re-released on DVDs (in cut and uncut versions) and seem to enjoy a cult following among aficionados of sleaze and horror, a phenomenon that has nothing to do with the historical context in which they were produced. In Italy, France, Spain, and Great Britain, these DVDs are available as US imports (e.g., through amazon.uk, amazon.fr, and amazon.it). On their rerelease on Exploitation Digital, see Graeme Krautheim, "Desecration Repackaged: Holocaust Exploitation and the Marketing of Novelty," *Cinephile* 5.1 (2009): 4–11. With the exception of *Salon Kitty*, none of these DVDs can be purchased in Germany, and it is unclear whether the films, including the Italian–West German coproductions, ever had theatrical releases in West Germany. I am grateful to Marcus Stiglegger for clarifying some of these issues for me.

14. In the cinema, the association of fascism with the homosocial or homosexual continues in recent films such as the British production *Bent* (Sean Mathias, 1996) and the German *Napola—Elite für den Führer* (*Before the Fall*, Dennis Gansel, 2004); the role of fascism in gay porn is evident in *The Raspberry Reich* (Bruce LaBruce, 2004). Films about neo-Nazi groups in the United States such as *American History X* (Tony Kaye, 1998) and *The Believer* (Henry Bean, 2001) similarly associate fascism with (the crisis of) white masculinity and the power of homosocial bonding.

15. As noted already in the introduction, I capitalize Fascism when referring to the period in Italian history marked by Mussolini's rule and use lower case when evoking the broader cultural and political imaginaries outlined in the introduction.

16. Claudio Fogu, "*Italiani brava gente*: The Legacy of Fascist Historical Culture on Italian Politics of Memory," in *The Politics of Memory in Postwar Europe*, ed. Richard New Lebow, Wulf Kansteiner, and Claudio Fogu (Durham, NC: Duke University Press, 2006), 157.

17. David Forgacs, "Days of Sodom: The Fascism Perversion Equation in Films of the 1960s and 1970s," in *Italian Fascism: History, Memory and Representation*, ed. R. J. B. Bosworth and Patrizia Dogliani (London: Palgrave, 1999), 216–36. On the larger historical continuities, see David Forgacs, "Post War Italian Culture: Renewal or Legacy of the Past?," in *Reconstructing the Past: Representations of the Fascist Era in Post-War European Culture*, ed. Graham Bartram, Maurice Slawinski, and David Steel (Keele, Staffordshire: Keele University Press, 1996), 49–66.

18. On Italy during the 1960s and 1970s, see Robert Lumley, *States of Emergency: Cultures of Revolt in Italy from 1968 to 1978* (London: Verso, 1990), 271–336; and, more generally, Paul Ginsborg, *A History of Contemporary Italy: Society and Politics, 1943–1988* (London: Penguin, 1990), 348–405. Both terms, "state of emergency" and "state of exception," are translations of the German *Ausnahmezustand*.

19. Lina Wertmüller, interview with Gertrud Koch and Heide Schlüpmann, "Der Mensch in Unordnung," *Frauen und Film* 39 (1985): 83.

20. See Dagmar Herzog, *Sex after Fascism: Memory and Morality in Twentieth-Century Germany* (Princeton, NJ: Princeton University Press, 2005).

21. For references, see Wilhelm Reich, *The Mass Psychology of Fascism*, trans. Victor R. Carfagno (New York: Farrar, Strauss & Giroux, 1970); Herbert Marcuse, *Eros and Civilization: A Philosophical Inquiry into Freud* (Boston: Beacon, 1966); Adorno et al., *Authoritarian Personality*; and Walter Benjamin, *The Work of Art in the Age of Its Technological Reproducibility, and Other Writings on Media*, ed. Michael W. Jennings, Brigid Doherty, and Thomas Y. Levin, trans. Edmund Jephcott et al. (Cambridge, MA: Belknap Press of Harvard University Press, 2008), 19–55. On the so-called sexual secrets of fascism as hypothesized in relation to Hitler, see Ron Rosenbaum, *Explaining Hitler* (New York: Random House, 1998), esp. 99–152.

22. Theodor W. Adorno, *Minima Moralia: Reflections from Damaged Life*, trans. E. F. N. Jephcott (London: New Left Books, 1974), 46.

23. Laura Frost, *Sex Drives: Fantasies of Fascism in Literary Modernism* (Ithaca, NY: Cornell University Press, 2003), 15. For an excellent analysis of "Nazism, Psychology, and the Making of Democratic Subjects" in the American context, see Slane, *Not So Foreign Affair*, 109–37.

24. Andrew Hewitt, *Political Inversions: Homosexuality, Fascism, and the Modernist Imaginary* (Stanford, CA: Stanford University Press, 1996), 1. For a comparative perspective, see Erin G. Carlston, *Thinking Fascism: Sapphic Modernism and Fascist Modernity* (Stanford, CA: Stanford University Press, 1998).

25. On *The Damned*, see Henry Bacon, *Visconti: Explorations of Beauty and Decay* (Cambridge: Cambridge University Press, 1998), 144–55; and Michel Boujut, ed., *"Les Damnés", un film de Luchino Visconti," Avant Scène Cinéma* 501 (2001): 1–142. For a biographical account that sheds light on Visconti's cultural tastes and political commitments, see Gaia Servadio, *Luchino Visconti: A Biography* (New York: Franklin Watts, 1983). On the German trilogy in particular, see Claretta Micheletti Tonetti, *Luchino Visconto* (New York: Twayne, 1997), 127–65. On Visconti's politics, see Michèle Lagny, "Visconti, la revue cinéma et l'utopie communiste en Italie (1945–1975)," in *Caméra politique: Cinéma et Stalinisme*, ed. Kristian Feigelson (Saint Etienne: Sorbonne Nouvelle, 2005), 209–17.

26. Quoted in Alfons Arns, "'Germania comme patria dell'angoscia': Die Physiognomie des Nazismus in Luchino Viscontis *La Caduta degli dei* (*Götterdämmerung*)," in Schmitt-Sasse, *Widergänger*, 229.

27. For an introduction to postwar Italian cinema, see Peter Bondanella, *Italian Cinema: From Neorealism to the Present* (New York: Continuum, 2001), 275–383.

28. In fact, the sexualization of fascism cannot be understood outside the financially beneficial alliance of European art cinema and soft porn during the 1970s that also produced the *Emmanuelle* (1974) series with Sylvia Kristel and *Histoire d'O* (*The Story of O*, 1975), both directed by Just Jaeckin, and inspired artistically ambitious works such as Ken Russell's D. H. Lawrence adaptation, *Women in Love* (1969) and Bernardo Bertolucci's *Ultima tango a Parigi* (*Last Tango in Paris*, 1973).

29. On *The Night Porter*'s misrepresentation of history and failure at Holocaust memoralization, see Rebecca Scherr, "The Uses of Memory and the Abuses of Fiction: Sexuality in Holocaust Fiction and Memoir," *Other Voices: The (e)Journal of Cultural Criticism* 2.1 (2000), http://www.othervoices.org/2.1/scherr/sexuality.html. Sexuality as a subversive force is discussed in Laura Pietropaolo, "Sexuality as Exorcism in Liliana Cavani's *Night Porter*," in *Donna: Women in Italian Culture*, ed. Ada Testaferri (Ottawa: Dovehouse, 1989), 71–79; and Lisa Patti, "Fascinating Fashion: Visual Pleasure in *Il portiere di notte*," *Forum Italicum* 40.1 (2006): 118–32. For the very different response of a Soviet film critic who, during a visit to Paris, saw *The Night Porter*, see Sergej Jutkewitsch, "Retro, Porno und Faschismus," trans. Robert Wieland, *Filmwissenschaftliche Beiträge* 16.2 (1975): 219–31.

30. Andrew Sarris, "The Nasty Nazis: History or Mythology," *Village Voice*, 17 October 1974, 77; and Henry Giroux, "The Challenge of Neo Fascist Culture," *Cinéaste* 6.4 (1975): 31.

31. Liliana Cavani, interview by Claire Clouzot, quoted by Gaetana Marrone, *The Gaze and the Labyrinth: The Cinema of Liliana Cavani* (Princeton, NJ: Princeton University Press, 2000), 82 and 90.

32. The references are, in that order, to Naomi Greene, *Pier Paolo Pasolini: Cinema as Heresy* (Princeton, NJ: Princeton University Press, 1990), 202; Kriss Ravetto, *The Unmaking of Fascist Aesthetics* (Minneapolis: University of Minnesota Press, 2001), 46; and Eugenie Brinkema, "Pleasure in/and Perversity: Plaisagir in Liliana Cavani's *Il portiere di notte*," *Dalhousie Review* 84.3 (2004): 419–39. For an appreciative reading of *The Night Porter*, see also Teresa de Lauretis, "Cavani's *The Night Porter*: A Woman's Film?," *Film Quarterly* 30 (1976–77): 35–38.

33. Marrone, *Gaze and the Labyrinth*, 105 and 198.

34. Ravetto, *Unmaking of Fascist Aesthetics*, 19.

35. Julia Kristeva, *Powers of Horror: An Essay on Abjection*, trans. Leon S. Roudiez (New York: Columbia University Press, 1982), 4.

36. For critical readings of *Seven Beauties*, see Richard Astle, "*Seven Beauties*: Survival, Lina Style," *Jump Cut: A Review of Contemporary Media* 15 (1977): 22–23; Ralph Tutt, "*Seven Beauties* and the Beast: Bettelheim, Wertmüller, and the Uses of Enchantment," *Literature Film Quarterly* 17.3 (1989): 193–201; Mariani Umberto, "The 'Anti-Feminism' of Lina Wertmüller," *Annual of Foreign Films and Literature* 2 (1996): 103–14; and Josette Déléas, "Lina Wertmüller: The Grotesque in *Seven Beauties*," in *Women Filmmakers: Refocusing*, ed. Jacqueline Levitin, Judith Plessis, and Valérie Raoul (Vancouver: University of British Columbia Press, 2002), 151–66.

37. Barbara Spackman, *Fascist Virilities: Rhetoric, Ideology, and Social Fantasy in Italy* (Minneapolis: University of Minnesota Press, 1996), ix. Even the sympathetic depiction of the antifascist as homosexual in *Una gionata particolare* (*A Special Day*, Ettore Scola, 1977) confirms this problematic coupling of Fascism and masculinity.

38. For surveys of Wertmüller's early career, see Wolfgang Jacobsen et al., eds., *Lina Wertmüller* (Munich: Hanser, 1988); and Grace Russo Bullaro, *Man in Disorder: The Cinema of Lina Wertmüller in the 1970s* (Leicester: Troubador, 2007).

39. To give a few examples of the highly symbolic function of modern architecture in *The Night Porter*, the main setting is the 1899 Medallionhaus on Linke Wienzeile built by Otto Wagner, one of the leading figures of the Vienna Secession. The old Nazis attend a funeral at the Zentralfriedhof in the Feuerhalle Simmering, built in 1922 by Clemens Holzmeister as Austria's first crematorium, and Max and Lucia's imprisonment takes place in Karl-Marx-Hof, the famous public housing estate built in the late 1920s by Wagner student Karl Ehn and a hotbed of political resistance during the 1934 Austrian civil war preceding the *Anschluss* (annexation).

40. Horkheimer and Adorno, *Dialectic of Enlightenment*, 93.

41. See Gilles Deleuze, "Coldness and Cruelty," in *Masochism* (New York: Zone Books, 1989), 37–46.

42. Williams, "Film Bodies," 143. For a similar argument in the context of horror, see Carol J. Clover, *Men, Women, and Chain Saws: Gender in the Modern Horror Film* (Princeton, NJ: Princeton University Press, 1992). On the tension between porn and horror, compare Carolyn J. Dean, "Empathy, Pornography, and Suffering," *differences: A Journal of Feminist Cultural Studies* 14.1 (2003): 88–124.

43. Paul Watson, "There Is No Accounting for Taste: Exploitation Cinema and the Limits of Film Theory," in *Trash Aesthetics: Popular Culture and Its Audience*, ed. Deborah Cartmell, I. Q. Hunter, Heidi Kaye, and Imelda Whelehan (London: Pluto Press, 1997), 82. On exploitation cinema, see Eric Schaefer, *"Bold! Daring! Shocking! True!": A History of Exploitation Films, 1919–1959* (Durham, NC: Duke University Press, 1999); Joan Hawkins, *Cutting Edge: Art Horror and the Horrific Avant-Garde* (Minneapolis: University of Minnesota Press, 2000), especially her discussion of sleaze mania, Euro trash, and high art (3–32); and Jeffrey Sconce, ed., *Sleaze Artists: Cinema at the Margins of Taste, Style, and Politics* (Durham, NC: Duke University Press, 2007).

44. Significantly, both Spain and France are countries with a fascist past of their own. In France, Eurocine produced *Train spécial pour SS* (*Hitler's Last Train*, Alain Payet, 1977), *Helga, la louve de Stilberg* (*Helga, She Wolf of Spilberg*, Alain Garnier alias Patrice Rohm, 1977), and *Elsa Fräulein SS* (Mark Stern, 1977). The prolific Jesus (or Jess) Franco directed (often under a pseudonym) a series of Nazi-themed women-in-prison films, including the Spanish-German coproduction *Greta, Haus ohne Männer* (*Ilsa, the Wicked Warden*, 1977) with Dyanne Thorne, and the French production *Convoi de filles* (*SS Nazi Convoy*, 1978). More concerned with horror, the Nazi zombie films made by Franco also fall into this broader context. My thanks to Jill Robbins for drawing my attention to his films.

45. Omaytra Cruz, "Tits, Ass, and Swastikas: Three Steps toward a Fatal Film

Theory," in *Necromonicon: Book Two*, ed. Andy Black (London: Creation Books, 1998), 95; and Mikel J. Koven, "'The Film You Are About to See Is Based on Documented Fact': Italian Nazi Sexploitation Cinema," in *Alternative Europe: Eurotrash and Exploitation Cinema since 1945*, ed. Ernest Mathijs and Xavie Mendik (London: Wallflower, 2004), 24.

46. Tamao Nakahara, "Bawdy Tales and Veils: The Exploitation of Sex in Post War Italian Cinema (1949–1979)" (PhD diss., University of California at Berkeley, 2005), 18. The dissertation deals with nunsploitation.

47. Other examples of Italian exploitation cinema include the sword-and-sandal films about ancient Greco-Roman history and mythology known as *peblum*; the horror and slasher films of Dario Argento and Mario Bava, sometimes referred as *giallo* (yellow) because of their debt to pulp fiction; the *mondo* documentary films with their sensational-ized accounts of cruelty, murder, death, and bizarre tribal rituals on foreign continents; and a unique Italian variant of the women-in-prison genre, the nunsploitation films with their deliberate attacks on religion and the Catholic Church. For a reference guide listing productions by year, see Adrian Luther Smith, ed., *Delirium Guide to Italian Exploitation Cinema, 1975–1979* (London: Media Publications, 1997).

48. The sexualized iconography of Naziploitation continued throughout the 1980s, for instance, in the nightclub scene in the mystery thriller *The Formula* (John G. Avidsen, 1980), where SS regalia-wearing strippers gyrate in front of projected images of Nazism, World War II, and the Holocaust. The ways in which Naziploitation sets out to pro-voke, if only in the form of postmodern citation, is openly acknowledged in *Werewolf Women of the SS*, the fake movie trailer included in Quentin Tarantino and Robert Rodriguez's homage to B pictures appropriately called *Grindhouse* (2007). For an anthology on Naziploitation that approaches the genre as a transnational and multimedial phe-nomenon, see Daniel H. Magilow, Elizabeth Bridges, and Kristin T. Vander Lugt, eds., *Naziploitation! The History, Aesthetics and Politics of the Nazi Image in Low-Brow Film and Culture* (New York: Continuum, 2012).

49. Lynn Rappaport, "Holocaust Pornography: Profaning the Sacred in *Ilsa, She Wolf of the SS*," *Shofar* 22.1 (2003): 53–79; see also Jean Pierre Geuens, "Pornography and the Holocaust: The Last Transgression," *Film Criticism* 20.1–2 (1995–96): 114–30. Speaking of Naziploitation in general, Geuens maintains that "the films fail to break through the cultural defenses, the *cordons sanitaires*, that society erects to protect us from being soiled by the stench and the excrescence of the camps" (127).

50. On horror as a framework for thinking about the Holocaust, see Caroline Joan Picart and David A. Frank, *Frames of Evil: The Holocaust as Horror in American Film*, fore-word by Dominick LaCapra, introduction by Edward J. Ingrebretsen (Carbondale: Southern Illinois University Press, 2006); and, more generally, Joshua Hirsch, *Film, Trauma, and the Holocaust* (Philadelphia: Temple University Press, 2004); and Adam Lowen-stein, *Shocking Representation: Historical Trauma, National Cinema, and the Modern Horror Film* (New York: Columbia University Press, 2005). The centrality of gender and femininity to the discourses of abjection is examined in Barbara Creed, *The Monstrous Feminine: Film, Feminism, Psychoanalysis* (London: Routledge, 1993).

51. Linda Williams, *Hard Core: Power, Pleasure, and the "Frenzy of the Visible"* (Berkeley: University of California Press, 1999), 30.

52. Silke Wenk defines pornographization as specific rhetorical moves that sexualize both victims and perpetrators and, through the focus on sexuality, attempt to fix the truth of history, often through a reinscription of traditional gender binaries and a feminization of fascism. See Silke Wenk, "Rhetoriken der Pornografisierung: Rahmungen des Blicks auf die NS Verbrechen," in *Gedächtnis und Geschlecht: Deutungsmuster in Darstellungen des nationalsozialistischen Genozids*, ed. Insa Eschenbach, Sigrid Jacobeit, and Silke Wenk (Frankfurt am Main: Campus, 2002), 269–94.

53. Quoted by Marcus Stiglegger, *Sadiconazista: Faschismus und Sexualität im Film* (St. Augustin: Gardez! Verlag, 1999), 132–33 and 137.

54. It might be interesting to compare Berger's performance of Nazi sexual pathology in *The Damned* and *Salon Kitty* with that of Peter O'Toole as the sadistic general in *The Night of the Generals* (Anatole Litvak, 1967).

### Chapter 5. Postpolitical Affects and Intertextual Effects

1. On this point, see Mouffe, *On the Political*; and Jacques Rancière, *On the Shores of Politics*, trans. Liz Heron (London: Verso, 2007).

2. Slavoj Žižek, *The Sublime Object of Ideology* (London: Verso, 1989), 28–30.

3. Benjamin, *Work of Art*, 42.

4. For a general introduction to the question of Nazi aesthetics, see Frederick Spotts, *Hitler and the Power of Aesthetics* (New York: Overlook, 2009).

5. For scholarship on Benjamin's notion of fascist aesthetics, see Ansgar Hillach, "The Aesthetics of Politics: Walter Benjamin's 'Theories of German Fascism,'" *New German Critique* 17 (1979): 99–119; Martin Jay, "The Aesthetic Ideology; or, What Does It Mean to Aestheticize Politics?," *Cultural Critique* 21 (1992): 41–61; Lutz Koepnick, "Fascist Aesthetics Revisited," *Modernism/modernity* 6.1 (1999): 51–73; and Brett Wheeler, "Modernist Reenchantments I: From Liberalism to Aestheticized Politics," *German Quarterly* 74.3 (2001): 223–37; and "Modernist Reenchantments II: From Aestheticized Politics to the Artwork," *German Quarterly* 75.2 (2002): 113–17. Compare Jonathan Simons, "Aestheticization of Politics: Benjamin, Fascism, and Communism" (paper presented at the annual meeting of the National Communications Association, Chicago, November 2009), http://www.allacademic.com/meta/p364905_index.html.

6. Spackman, *Fascist Virilities*, x.

7. Carsten Strathausen, "Nazi Aesthetics," *Culture, Theory and Critique* 42.1 (1999): 15.

8. Lutz Koepnick, *Walter Benjamin and the Aesthetics of Power* (Lincoln: University of Nebraska Press, 1999), 3.

9. Aleksandr Sokurov, interview by Nikkolai Kudin, "Stand Up and Be Counted," http://tinyurl.com/7hojl5b; Patrick Goldstein, "*Inglourious Basterds*: Is Quentin Tarantino Trivializing the Holocaust?," *Los Angeles Times*, 27 January 2010, http://tinyurl.com/y8eaflc.

10. Linda Hutcheon, *A Poetics of Postmodernism: History, Theory, Fiction* (London: Routledge, 1988), 5; on the broader political implications, see also her *Politics of Postmodernism* (London: Routledge, 1989). Not surprisingly, Sokurov as well as Tarantino have inspired hypertheoretical readings, the former in Diane Arnaud, *Le cinema de Sokourov: Figures d'enfermement* (Paris: Édition diffusion, 2005), and the latter in Fred Bottig and Scott Wilson, *The Tarantinian Ethics* (London: Sage, 2001), and Richard Green and K. Silem Mohammad, eds., *Tarantino and Philosophy* (Peru, IL: Open Court, 2007).

11. Eric Rentschler, *The Ministry of Illusion: Nazi Cinema and Its Afterlife* (Cambridge, MA: Harvard University Press, 1996), 223.

12. Fredric Jameson, *Postmodernism, or the Cultural Logic of Late Capitalism* (Durham, NC: Duke University Press, 1991), 18. My definition of parody is indebted to Linda Hutcheon, *A Theory of Parody: The Teachings of Twentieth-Century Art Forms* (Urbana: University of Illinois Press, 2000), 6.

13. I adopt the term "bastardization" from Georg Seeßlen, *Quentin Tarantino gegen die Nazis: Alles über "Inglourious Basterds"* (Berlin: Bertz + Fischer, 2009), 13–15.

14. Jameson, *Postmodernism*, 11.

15. Hutcheon, *Poetics of Postmodernism*, 125.

16. Susan Sontag, press release for *Russian Ark*, 2002.

17. The examples are numerous: Alfred Naujocks enjoying Paul Hörbinger in *Der Fall Gleiwitz* (*The Gleiwitz Case*, Gerhard Klein, 1961), Arnold Clasen showing *Regine* (Erich Waschnek, 1935) in *Dein unbekannter Bruder* (*Your Unknown Brother*, Ulrich Weiß, 1982), Standartenführer Stirlitz enduring Marika Rökk in *Semnadtsat mgnoveniy vesny* (*Seventeen Moments of Spring*, Tatiana Lioznova, 1973), Maria and Pauline crying over Zarah Leander in *Heimat, eine deutsche Chronik* (*Heimat: A Chronicle of Germany 1*, Edgar Reitz, 1984), Isabelle Adjani watching herself on the screen in Nazi-occupied France in *Bon Voyage* (Jean-Paul Rappeneau, 2003), and so forth.

18. Nancy Condee, *The Imperial Trace: Recent Russian Cinema* (Oxford: Oxford University Press, 2009), 3–48.

19. Benjamin Halligan, "The Elusive Hitler: A Dialogue on Sokurov's *Moloch*," *Central Europe Review* 2.3 (2000), http://www.ce-review.org/00/3/kinoeye3_halligan .html. On the popularity of historical films in Russian cinema, see David Gillespie, "Reconfiguring the Past: The Return of History in Recent Russian Film," *New Cinemas: Journal of Contemporary Film* 1.1 (2002): 14–23; and David Gillespie, "Alexander Sokurov and the Russian Soul," *Studies in European Cinema* 1.1 (2004): 57–65.

20. For critical assessments of Sokurov, see Dragan Kujudzic, "After 'After': The 'Arkive' Fever of Alexander Sokurov," *Quarterly Review of Film and Video* 21.3 (2004): 219–39; and Thorsten Bolz-Bornstein, "On the Blurring of Lines: Some Thoughts about Alexander Sokurov," *Cinetext*, 12 September 2002, http://cinetext.philo.at/magazine/ bornstein/sokurov.html. See also the chapter on Sokurov in Thorsten Bolz-Bornstein, *Films and Dreams: Tarkovsky, Bergman, Sokurov, Kubrick, and Wong Kar-wei* (Lanham, MD: Lexington Books, 2007), 31–36. Extensive scholarship on Sokurov can be found in France, including a special issue of *CinémAction* 133 (2009), edited by François Albera and

Michel Estève. The first English-language anthology is Birgit Beumers and Nancy Condee, eds., *The Cinema of Alexander Sokurov* (London: I. B. Tauris, 2011), which includes discussions of *Moloch*.

21. Sokurov, interview by Paul Schrader, "The History of an Artist's Soul Is a Very Sad History," *Film Comment* (November–December 1997): 20–35. See also Schrader's *Transcendental Style in Film: Ozu, Bresson, Dreyer* (Berkeley: University of California Press, 1977). For a postmodern reading of such constructions, see Thomas Elsaesser, "Postmodernism as Mourning Work," *Screen* 42.2 (2001): 201.

22. Amy Levine, "Phantasmatic Cinema: Delinkage and Disarticulation in Michelangelo Antonioni, Bela Tarr, Jean-Luc Godard and Alexander Sokurov" (PhD diss., University of Minnesota, 2009), esp. 210–58.

23. Fredric Jameson, "History and Elegy in Sokurov," *Critical Inquiry* 33 (2006): 10 and 11. The same issue of *Critical Inquiry* includes an interview with Sokurov conducted by Jeremi Szaniawski (13–27). Another possibility would be to identify Sokurov with transmodernism; this is the approach taken by Jeremi Szaniavskim in "Modernism/Postmodernism/Transmodernism: New Adventures in Cinematic Canon Building," in *Reading without Maps: Cultural Landmarks in a Post-Canonical Age*, ed. Christophe Den Tandt (Brussels: Peter Lang, 2005), 355–78.

24. For an insightful analysis of this moment, see Mikhail Epstein, *After the Future: The Paradoxes of Postmodernism and Contemporary Russian Culture* (Amherst: University of Massachusetts Press, 1995).

25. Mikhail Iampolski, "Representation, Mimicry, Death: The Latest Films of Alexander Sokurov," in *Russia on Reels: The Russian Idea in Post-Soviet Cinema*, ed. Birgit Beumers (London: I. B. Tauris, 1999), 143.

26. Sokurov, quoted by Nick Holdsworth, "My Films Are about People, Not Dictators," *Telegraph*, 18 February 2005, http://tinyurl.com/bmqa5w6. Interestingly, *Moloch* inspired a postcolonial version in the French-Haitian production *Moloch tropical* (Raoul Peck, 2009).

27. Quoted in Stefan Steinberg, "Aesthetic Choices: Aleksandr Sokurov's *The Sun*," *World Socialist Web*, 20 November 2009, http://www.wsws.org/articles/2009/nov2009/soku-n20.shtml.

28. Sokurov, quoted on the website of the Cannes Film Festival 1999, http://www.filmfestivals.com/cannes99/html/seloff9.htm.

29. Dennis Lim, "Taking a Man, Then Removing His Myth," *New York Times*, 15 November 2009.

30. My thanks to Lida Oukaderova and Mila Ganeva for sharing their memories and insisting that I take a closer look at the series.

31. The writings on *Inglourious Basterds*, and Tarantino in general, are either trivia-based (i.e., by fans for fans) or, especially in the German context, hypertheoretical. For recent monographs that include *Inglourious Basterds*, see Aaron Barlow, *Quentin Tarantino: Life at the Extremes* (New York: Praeger, 2010), 139–54; Tarantino's screenplay for the film has been published as *Inglourious Basterds: A Screenplay* (New York: Little, Brown, 2009).

32. M. Keith Booker, *Postmodern Hollywood: What's New in Film and Why It Makes Us Feel So Strange* (New York: Praeger, 2007). See also Carl Boggs and Tom Pollard, "Postmodern Cinema and Hollywood Culture in an Age of Corporate Colonization," *International Journal of Inclusive Democracy* 7.1 (2001): 159–81.

33. Quoted by Glenn Whipp, "Quentin Tarantino's *Basterds* Is a Glorious Mash-Up," *Los Angeles Times*, 16 August 2009.

34. Quentin Tarantino, quoted by Assaf Uni, "The Holocaust, Tarantino Style: Jews Scalping Nazis," *Haaretz*, 7 October 2008, http://tinyurl.com/cue9fyv.

35. The references are to the most-decorated American World War II hero turned actor whose story was fictionalized in *To Hell and Back* (Jesse Hibbs, 1955) and to the sniper film *Enemy at the Gates* (Jean-Jacques Annaud, 2001).

36. A good discussion of hyperreality in *Inglourious Basterds* can be found in Kristen Coates, "Hyperreality in *Inglourious Basterds*: Tarantino's Interwoven Cinematic World in 1940s Cinema," *Film Stage*, 26 June 2010, http://tinyurl.com/c9gtlz7.

37. Erich Fromm, *The Heart of Man: Its Genius for Good and Evil* (New York: Harper & Row, 1964); and Erich Fromm, *The Anatomy of Human Destructiveness* (New York: Henry Holt, 1973), esp. chap. 13 on Hitler as a case study of malignant aggression and necrophilia, 411–80.

38. Gustave Gilbert, the US Army psychologist studying Nazi leaders during the 1945 Nuremberg trials, was the first to offer this definition of evil. Evidence of the urgency of addressing the question of evil, two scholars with a Marxist history have tried to make sense of its existence without resorting to religious categories; see Alain Badiou, *Ethics: An Essay on the Understanding of Evil*, trans. and introduction by Peter Hallward (London: Verso, 2001); and Terry Eagleton, *Evil* (New Haven, CT: Yale University Press, 2010).

39. Joseph Goebbels, quoted in Erwin Leiser, *Nazi Cinema*, trans. Gertrud Mander and David Wilson (New York: Macmillan, 1975), 132.

40. The opposite approach can be found in the films of Hungarian István Szabó. Whether dealing with the actor Gustav Gründgens in *Mephisto* (1981) or the conductor Wilhelm Furtwängler in *Taking Sides* (2001), his historical biopics may bemoan the corruption of the creative process by political power and personal ambition, but in their affirmation of the artist as romantic genius they also validate clear distinctions between art and politics. In line with the more recent preference for a psychologization of history and politics, television miniseries such as *Klemperer—Ein Leben in Deutschland* (Klemperer—a life in Germany, Kai Wessel, 1999), about the writer of the famous wartime diaries, and *Speer und er* (*Speer and Hitler: The Devil's Architect*, Heinrich Breloer, 2005), about the master builder of Germania, explore the effects of compliance or resistance on the individual and his sense of personal and artistic integrity. A rare exploration of the aesthetics and erotics of fascism from a woman's perspective can be found in *Die Hitlerkantate* (*Hitler Cantata*, Jutta Brückner, 2006).

41. An earlier television drama, *Jud Süss—Ein Film als Verbrechen?* (Jew Suess—A film as crime?, Horst Königstein, 2001), with Axel Milbert as Veit Harlan, served as preparation for *Speer and I*, for which Königstein, together with Breloer, wrote the screenplay.

42. On *Nights in Andalusia* and *The Girl of Your Dreams*, see Daniel Otto, "Andalusische Nächte in Babelsberg: Mehrsprachenversionen aus Gründen der Staatsraison," in *Babylon in FilmEuropa: Mehrsprachen-Versionen der 1930er Jahre*, ed. Jan Distelmeyer (Munich: edition text + kritik, 2006), 157–74.

43. On *Safe Conduct*, see Diane Afoumado, "*Safe Conduct*: A Tribute to the French Film Industry during the Second World War," in *Repicturing the Second World War: Representations on Film and Television*, ed. and introduction by Michael Paris (New York: Palgrave Macmillan, 2008), 70–82. Tavernier was accused of condoning political opportunism through his positive portrayal of Aurenche and sued by Devaivre for not fully acknowledging his contribution in the credits. See Geoffrey McNab, "Don't Mention the War," *Guardian*, 23 October 2002.

44. Luisa Rivi, "*Underground* and the Balkanization of History," in *European Cinema after 1989: Cultural Identity and Transnational Production* (New York: Palgrave Macmillan, 2007), 91–108.

45. See Jacques Rancière, *Disagreement: Politics and Philosophy*, trans. Julie Rose (Minneapolis: University of Minnesota Press, 1999).

## Chapter 6. Postfascist Identity Politics

1. The rediscovery of the 1930s and 1940s as the golden era of resistance by oppressed ethnic and national groups is a transnational phenomenon not limited to Europe and even extends to East Asia, as can be seen in *Lust, Caution* (Ang Lee, 2007), about the Chinese resistance to the Japanese occupation of Shanghai in 1942, and *John Rabe* (Florian Gallenberger, 2009), about the German businessmen protecting the Chinese population against Japanese atrocities during the Nanking massacre in 1937. The new Jewish resistance narratives, whether in the historical format offered by *Defiance* (Edward Zwick, 2008) or the contemporary perspective taken by *The Debt* (Assaf Bernstein, 2007) and the 2010 Hollywood remake directed by John Madden, are part of such transnational trends.

2. Schmitt, *Theory of the Partisan*, 14–22.

3. See Ernesto Laclau, *On Populist Reason* (London: Verso, 2005).

4. For France, see David Schoenbrun, *Soldiers of the Night: The Story of the French Resistance* (New York: Dutton, 1980). A tribute to the Danish resistance can be found in John Oram Thomas, *Giant Killers: The Story of the Danish Resistance Movement, 1940–45* (London: M. Joseph, 1975), including on Flammen and Citronen (226–44). On Norway, see Tore Gjelsvik, *Norwegian Resistance, 1940–1945*, trans. Thomas Kingston Derry (Montreal: McGill-Queens University Press, 1979). For the Netherlands, consult Gerhard Hirschfeld, *Nazi Rule and Dutch Collaboration: The Netherlands under German Occupation, 1940–45*, trans. Louise Willmot (Oxford: Berg, 1988).

5. Phil Powrie, "Heritage, History, and 'New Realism,'" in *French Cinema in the 1990s: Continuity and Difference*, ed. Phil Powrie (Oxford: Oxford University Press, 1999), 1–21.

6. See Andrew Higson, *English Heritage, English Cinema: Costume Drama since 1980* (Oxford: Oxford University Press, 2003), especially his discussion of the heritage film debate (46–85). For a critique of the term and its undertheorized application, see Claire Monk, "The British Heritage Film Debate Revisited," in *British Historical Cinema: The History, Heritage, and Costume Film*, ed. Claire Monk and Amy Sargeant (London: Routledge, 2002), 176–98.

7. Slavoj Žižek, "Carl Schmitt in the Age of Post-Politics," in *The Challenge of Carl Schmitt*, ed. Chantal Mouffe (London: Verso, 1999), 35.

8. See Alain Badiou, *Being and Event* (London: Continuum, 2006).

9. For introductions to the problematic in the European context, see Alec C. Hargreaves, *Multi-Ethnic France: Immigration, Politics, Culture and Society*, 2nd ed. (London: Routledge, 2007); Ian Buruma, *Murder in Amsterdam: Liberal Europe, Islam, and the Limits of Tolerance* (London: Penguin, 2007); and Göram Larsson, ed., *Islam in the Nordic and Baltic Countries* (London: Routledge, 2009). In Scandinavia, Muslims constitute 3–5 percent of the population; in France, the number is 8–10 percent, and in the Netherlands approximately 6 percent, with the vast majority living in cities. The violent potential of right-wing nationalism and Christian fundamentalism found tragic expression in the terroristic attacks of 22 July 2011 in and near Oslo, the deadliest events in Norway since World War II.

10. For overviews of contemporary Scandinavia cinema, see Gunnar Iverson, Astrid Soderbergh Widding, and Tytti Soila, *Nordic National Cinemas* (London: Routledge, 1998); and Andrew K. Nestingen and Trevor Glen Elkington, eds., *Transnational Cinema in a Global North: Nordic Cinema in Transition* (Detroit: Wayne State University Press, 2005).

11. Donald G. Phillips, *Post-National Patriotism and the Feasibility of Post-National Community in United Germany* (Westport, CT: Praeger, 2000), 21–22. The possibility of post-national patriotism was first discussed by Arjun Appadurai in "Patriotism and Its Futures," *Public Culture* 3.5 (1993): 411–29. For a useful introduction to the paradoxes, see Ulf Hedetoft and Mette Hjort, eds., *The Postnational Self: Belonging and Identity* (Minneapolis: University of Minnesota Press, 2002). On the role of affect in forging democratic commitments, see Patchen Markell, "Making Affect Safe for Democracy? On 'Constitutional Patriotism,'" *Political Theory* 28.1 (2000): 38–63. On the implications for democracy, see also Jürgen Habermas, "The Postnational Constellation and the Future of Democracy," in *Postnational Constellations: Political Essays*, ed. and introduction by Max Pensky (Cambridge, MA: MIT Press, 2001), 58–112.

12. Mette Hjort, *Small Nation, Global Cinema: The New Danish Cinema* (Minneapolis: University of Minnesota Press, 2005), 131.

13. The same displacement can be found in the discursive constellations that, according to Leslie Adelson, make the Turks assume the place of the Jews in contemporary German debates about culture and identity; see Leslie Adelson, *The Turkish Turn in Contemporary German Literature* (New York: Palgrave, 2005), 1–30; my thanks to Larson Powell for drawing my attention to this connection.

14. Mette Hjort, "From Epiphanic Culture to Circulation: The Dynamics of Globalization in Nordic Cinema," in Nestingen and Elkington, *Transnational Cinema in a Global North*, 199.

15. The numbers are taken from http://boxofficemojo.com/.

16. Ole Christian Madsen, interview by Guy Lodge, *incontention*, 7 August 2009, http://www.incontention.com/2009/08/07/interview-flame-citron-director-ole-christian-madsen/.

17. There are many reasons to assume that these discussion groups are dominated by young men; their penchant for graphic violence on the screen is inseparable from the popularity of first-person shooter video games with a World War II focus such as *Commando: Behind Enemy Lines, Day of Defeat: Source, Wolfenstein 3 D, Company of Heroes, Battlefield 1942*, and others.

18. Per Jul Carlson, "Frihedskæmperen Max Manus. Glade gutter i krig," 18 February 2010, http://tinyurl.com/c54wrhf. The source is the website of Danish public radio.

19. Johs. H. Christensen, "Gangster-besættelse," *Jyllands-Posten*, 28 March 2008.

20. Espen Svenningsen Rambøl, *Dagsavisen*, 2 October 2008, http://www.dagsavisen.no/kultur/filmer/article371606.ece.

21. Thure Lindhardt, interview by Maja Skov Vang, "Ingen popstar: Jeg er en medløber," *Ekstra Bladet*, 26 March 2008. Interestingly, in 1997, *Ekstra Bladet* ran a series on "The Foreigners" that reported on alleged abuses of the welfare system by refugees and asylum seekers.

22. Mads Mikkelsen, interview by Kristian Lindberg, "Jeg er ikke i dette job for at overgå mig selv," *Berlingske Tidende*, Magasin, 16 March 2008.

23. On the occupation in Danish cinema, see Ebbe Villadsen, "The German Occupation as a Subject in Danish Film," *Scandinavica: An International Journal of Scandinavian Studies* 39.1 (2000): 25–46.

24. Bo Green Jensen, "Modstandskamp: Dø om så det gælder," *Weekendavisen*, 8 January 2010.

25. Einar Guldvog Staalesen, *NRF*, 17 December 2008, http://www.nrk.no/nyheter/kultur/1.6358788. The NRF is the Norwegian Broadcasting Corporation.

26. Kim Sternberg, "Debat: Besættelse; Kun få gjorde modstand," *B.T.*, 30 March 2008.

27. Discussion of *Max Manus*, YouTube, May 2010, http://www.youtube.com/comment_servlet?all_comments&v=ooH8L3KRWvc (web page no longer available).

28. TB, comment, "Børn sælger sex, det gør de jo," *Snaphanen*, 15 September 2008, http://tinyurl.com/77xq530.

29. Internet discussion in response to Erling Fossens's "Resistance Glorified," 13 December 2008, http://tinyurl.com/6uqlsej.

30. An earlier version, *L'affiche rouge*, was filmed by Frank Cassenti in 1976.

31. Powrie, "Heritage, History, and 'New Realism,'" 15.

32. Robert Guédiguian, interview by Michel Guilloux, *l'Humanité*, 8 September 2009, http://www.humanite.fr/node/19488. The directors' movement refers to the

1997 call for civil disobedience signed by many filmmakers in support of undocumented immigrants.

33. Guédiguian, interview by Martin Hoszik, *Seenin.co.uk*, 23 September 2009, http://tinyurl.com/lva6qy.

34. Marc Semo, "Les sacrifiés de l'affiche rouge," *Libération*, 16 September 2009. The poet Louis Aragon wrote a poem called "L'affiche rouge."

35. "Le regard juste de Guédiguian sur *L'armée du crime*: Un beau film sur le groupe de resistants etrangers fusilles au mont Valerien en 1944," *Le Monde*, 5 September 2009.

36. Op-ed, "*L'armée du crime* de Robert Guédiguian, ou la légende au mépris de l'histoire," *Le Monde*, 15 November 2009.

37. Traversay, *Télérama* forum, *L'armée du crime*, 15 September 2009, http://tinyurl.com/787wsyl. On this point, compare *Les hommes libres* (Free Men, Ismaël Ferroukhi, 2011).

38. "*L'armée du crime*: L'affiche rouge, histoires de sang et sens de l'histoire," *Le Monde*, 15 September 2009.

39. Mehdi Benallal, "*L'armée du crime* face aux *Batârds sans gloire*: Deux films 'anti-nazis'," *Le Monde diplomatique*, 27 September 2009, http://blog.mondediplo.net/2009-09-27-L-armee-du-crime-face-aux-batards-sans-gloire.

40. Cécile Mury and Pierre Murat, review of *L'armée du crime*, *Télérama* 3114, 18 September 2009, http://www.telerama.fr/cinema/l-armee-du-crime,46983.php.

41. Henry Rousso, *The Vichy Syndrome: History and Memory in France since 1944*, trans. Arthur Goldhammer (Cambridge, MA: Harvard University Press, 1991).

42. For an overview of the representation of occupation, collaboration, and resistance in French cinema, see Guy Austin, *Contemporary French Cinema: An Introduction* (Manchester: Manchester University Press, 1996), especially the chapter on heritage, 142–70; Naomi Greene, *Landscapes of Loss: The National Past in Postwar French Cinema* (Princeton, NJ: Princeton University Press, 1999); Richard J. Golsan, "The Legacy of World War II in France: Mapping the Discourses of Memory," in Lebow, Kansteiner, and Fogu, *Politics of Memory in Postwar Europe*, 73–101; and Leah D. Hewitt, *Remembering the Occupation in French Film: National Identity in Postwar Europe* (New York: Palgrave Macmillan, 2008).

43. "Acteur Thom Hoffman laat mensen Zwartboek beleven," *Dagblad van het Noorden*, 4 May 2006, http://tinyurl.com/824lfyl.

44. According to Verhoeven and Soeteman, the main characters are composites of historical figures, and the eponymous black book, listing the names of traitors and collaborators, actually existed.

45. For examples, see Linda Ruth Williams, "Sleeping with the Enemy," *Sight and Sound* 17.2 (2007): 18–20; and Julia M. Klein, "Sleeping with the Enemy in Verhoeven's *Black Book*," *Chronicle of Higher Education* 53.32 (2007): 89. Often cast as a Nazi, Koch had earlier appeared as Rudolf Höss in *Amen* (Costa-Gavras, 2002) and the title figures in the television dramas *Stauffenberg* and *Speer and Hitler*; van Houten was subsequently cast as Nina von Stauffenberg in *Valkyrie*.

46. On Verhoeven, see Rob van Scheers, *Paul Verhoeven*, trans. Aletta Stevens (London: Faber & Faber, 1997), especially the chapter on *Soldier of Orange*, 107–22. For an

introduction to Dutch cinema, see Ernest Mathijs, ed., *The Cinema of the Low Countries* (London: Wallflower, 2004), including its chapter on *Soldier of Orange*, 141–48. A brief discussion on the representation of the resistance can be found in Cornelia Ganitta, "Jenseits von Gut und Böse: Das Thema Widerstand im niederländischen Film," *epd Film* 24.5 (2007): 12–13.

47. Ruben Heijloo, review of *Zwartboek*, *Film Totaal*, 9 September 2006, http://www.filmtotaal.nl/recensie.php?id=7723.

48. Anonymous review of *Zwartboek*, *NOS*, 4 September 2006, http://headlines.nos .nl/forum.php/list_messages/4108.

49. "Als we allemaal slecht zijn," *FilmLounge.nl*, 6 August 2007, http://www .filmlounge.nl/films/9078_zwartboek.html?t=recensies-kritieken.

50. Anonymous review of *Zwartboek*, *GeenComentaar.nl*, 20 September 2006, http:// www.geencommentaar.nl/index.php/2006/09/20/recensie_zwartboek.

51. Eric Stockman, review of *Zwartboek*, *Humo.be*, 2 December 2006, http://www .humo.be/tws/film-reviews/3473/paul-verhoeven-zwartboek.html.

52. Martin Kooistra, review of *Zwartboek*, *Prikstok.nl*, 30 September 2006, http:// www.prikstok.nl/index.php?go=films&filmid=22.

53. Mouffe, *On the Political*, 64–89.

54. Laura van Baars, "De 'verboeking' van *Zwartboek*," *NRC Handelsblad*, 15 September 2006, http://www.nrc.nl/media/article1723846.ece/De_verboeking_van_ Zwartboek.

55. Ronald Ockhuysen, "Altijd op zoek naar de confrontatie: Interview met Paul Verhoeven over *Zwartboek*," *Cinema.nl*, 14 September 2006, http://www.cinema.nl/ artikelen/2157703/altijd-op-zoek-naar-de-confrontatie (web page no longer available).

56. Dana Linsen, "*Zwartboek* walst grijs verleden uit," *NRC Handelsblad*, 13 September 2006, http://www.nrc.nl/film/article1723131.ece/Zwartboek.

57. Jeroen Vormeer, review of *Zwartboek*, *Xi-online.nl*, 22 August 2007, http://www .xi-online.nl/film/zwartboek/.

58. On this problematic, see Erik Oddvar Eriksen, Christian Joerges, and Florian Rödl, eds., *Law, Democracy and Solidarity in a Post-National Union* (London: Routledge, 2008).

59. Agamben, *State of Exception*.

60. Chantal Mouffe, "Which Ethics for Democracy?," in *The Turn to Ethics*, ed. Marjorie B. Garber, Beatrice Hanssen, and Rebecca L. Walkowitz (New York: Routledge, 2000), 85–94.

61. Susan Stewart, *On Longing: Narratives of the Miniature, the Gigantic, the Souvenir, the Collection* (Durham, NC: Duke University Press, 1993), 23.

## Chapter 7. Entombing the Nazi Past

1. See Catherine Hickley, "Wax Hitler, Head Repaired, to Return to Madame Tussauds Berlin," *Bloomberg*, 7 July 2008, http://tinyurl.com/7j6gkem. The appearance

of Nazi figures and symbols on the streets of contemporary Berlin has been a recurring feature of news reporting about the changing attitudes brought about by the historicization of the Nazi past; a recent occasion was the adornment of the Admiralspalast with red banners featuring swastika-like pretzels for the 2009 German premiere of the Broadway musical *The Producers: Springtime for Hitler*. The normalization of the relationship to Hitler was also in full evidence in the 2010 exhibition *Hitler and the Germans* organized by the German Historical Museum in Berlin.

2.  Historicism (*Historismus*) in this context combines two meanings, both equally relevant to the understanding of *Downfall* (and neither one to be confused with the kind of contextualizing textual readings of history associated with Anglo-American New Historicism). In the first sense, *Historismus* refers to a tradition in nineteenth-century German historical thought, analyzed by Ernst Troeltsch and Friedrich Meinecke, that emphasizes the historicity of social and cultural phenomena and the uniqueness of all historical periods. In the second sense, *Historismus* refers to the eclectic architectural styles of the Wilhelmine Empire and the self-reflexive styles of postmodernist architecture; both aspects, the alliance of architecture with power and the aesthetics of simulation, can be found in *Downfall*'s approach to production design. Alexander Ruoff briefly discusses the *Wertfreiheit* of historicism in "Die Renaissance des Historismus in der Populärkultur: Über den Kinofilm *Der Untergang*," in *Filmri:ss: Studien über "Der Untergang,"* ed. Willi Bischof (Münster: Unrast, 2005), 69–78.

3.  On the new *Geschichtsgefühl*, to cite the 122/123 (2004) issue of *Ästhetik und Kommunikation*, see the discussion by Johannes von Moltke in "Sympathy for the Devil: Cinema, History, and the Politics of Emotion," *New German Critique* 102 (2007): 17–43; and, in a broader context, Roel Vande Winkel, "Hitler's *Downfall*, a Film from Germany (*Der Untergang*, 2004)," in *Perspectives on European Film and History*, ed. Leen Engelen and Roel Vande Winkel (Gent: Academia Press, 2007), 183–219. On the emotionalization and privalization of history, see also the various contributions on *Downfall* in *Das Böse im Blick: Die Gegenwart des Nationalsozialismus im Film*, ed. Margrit Frölich, Christian Schneider, and Karsten Visarius (Munich: edition text + kritik, 2007).

4.  The reference is to W. G. Sebald, *On the Natural History of Destruction*, trans. Anthea Bell (London: Hamish Hamilton, 2003). On the film's apocalyptical aspects, see Jean-Charles Margotton, "Le dimension apocalyptique dans le film *Der Untergang (La Chute)*," *Cahiers d'études germaniques* 51 (2006): 91–102.

5.  For the main works on the history of *Vergangenheitsbewältigung*, see Aleida Assmann and Ute Frevert, *Geschichtsvergessenheit, Geschichtsversessenheit: Vom Umgang mit deutschen Vergangenheiten nach 1945* (Stuttgart: Metzler, 1999); Eike Wenzel, *Gedächnisraum Film: Die Arbeit an der deutschen Geschichte seit den sechziger Jahren* (Stuttgart: Metzler, 2001); Reichel, *Vergangenheitsbewältigung in Deutschland*; Reichel, *Erfundene Erinnerung*; Siobhan Kattago, *Ambiguous Memory: The Nazi Past and German National Identity* (Westport, CT: Praeger, 2001); Alon Confino, *Germany as Culture of Remembrance: Promises and Limits of Writing History* (Chapel Hill: University of North Carolina Press, 2006); and Wulf Kansteiner, *In Pursuit of German Memory: History, Television, and Politics after Auschwitz* (Columbus: Ohio University

Press, 2006). On the contemporary discourse of memory and commemoration, see Niven, *Facing the Nazi Past*. For a reading of the historicization of Nazism that takes into account the collapse of socialism as its political alternative, see Konrad H. Jarausch and Michael Geyer, *Shattered Past: Reconstructing German Histories* (Princeton, NJ: Princeton University Press, 2002). On the presence of these discourses in everyday life, see Norbert Frei, *1945 und wir: Das Dritte Reich im Bewusstsein der Deutschen* (Munich: C. H. Beck, 2005), esp. "Die Gegenwart der Vergangenheit"; and Hannes Heer, *"Hitler war's": Die Befreiung der Deutschen von ihrer Vergangenheit* (Berlin: Aufbau, 2005).

6. Gavril Rosenfeld, *The World Hitler Never Made: Alternate History and the Memory of Nazism* (Ann Arbor: University of Michigan Press, 2005), 257.

7. On the connection to the debate on wartime suffering, see Paul Cooke, *"Der Untergang* (2004): Victims, Perpetrators, and the Continuing Fascination of Fascism," in Schmitz, *Nation of Victims?*, 247–61; and Paul Cooke, "The Continually Suffering Nation? Cinematic Representations of German Victimhood," in Niven, *Germans as Victims*, 76–92. For a useful overview of memory work in postunification cinema, see Daniela Berghahn, "Post-1990 Screen Memories: How East and West German Cinema Remembers the Third Reich and the Holocaust," *German Life and Letters* 59.2 (2006): 294–308. On *Downfall* and the rewriting of the war narrative, see Tony Barta, *"Downfall* and Other Endings: German Film and Hitler's War after Sixty Years," in Paris, *Repicturing the Second World War*, 192–204; and Elisabeth Kimmer, "More War Stories: *Stalingrad* and *Downfall*," in *The Collapse of the Conventional: German Film and Its Politics at the Turn of the Twenty-First Century*, ed. Jaimey Fisher and Brad Prager (Detroit: Wayne State University Press, 2010), 81–108.

8. In the debate on *Downfall*, these points have been made by Joachim Güntner, *Neue Züricher Zeitung Online*, 17 September 2004, http://www.nzz.ch/2004/09/17/fe/page-article9V2MS.html.

9. For a reading on the nostalgia film that emphasizes the continuities, compare Fredric Jameson, "Postmodernism and Consumer Society," in *The Cultural Turn: Selected Writings on the Postmodern, 1983–1998* (New York: Verso, 1998), 1–20.

10. On the historians' debate, see Peter Baldwin, ed., *Reworking the Past: Hitler, the Holocaust, and the Historians' Debate* (Boston: Beacon Press, 1990), especially the contributions by Martin Broszat, "A Plea for the Historicization of National Socialism," 77–87, and Saul Friedländer, "Some Reflections on the Historicization of National Socialism," 88–101, as well as their exchange of letters in "A Controversy about the Historicization of National Socialism," 102–32. For a discussion of the underlying issues at stake, see Jürgen Habermas, "Concerning the Public Use of History," *New German Critique* 44 (1988): 40–50; his more recent take on the same problematic can be found in "On the Public Use of History," in Pensky, *Postnational Constellations*, 26–37. For a historical assessment of the debate on coming to terms with the past, see the chapter titled "A Usable Past? Museums, Memory, and Identity," in Charles M. Maier, *The Unmasterable Past: History, Holocaust, and German National Identity* (Cambridge, MA: Harvard University Press, 1997), 121–72; for an excellent discussion of the differences between East and West, see Kattago, *Ambiguous Memory*.

11. Oliver Hirschbiegel, interview by Anke Westphal, *Berliner Zeitung*, 11 September 2004.

12. See Charles P. Mitchell, *The Hitler Filmography: Worldwide Feature Film and Television Miniseries Portrayals, 1940 through 2000* (Jefferson, NC: McFarland, 2002). Interestingly, the author in the same year also published *The Devil on Screen: Feature Films Worldwide, 1913 through 2000* (Jefferson, NC: McFarland, 2002). On the representation of Hitler in postwar German cinema, see Alexandra Hissen, "Die Darstellung von Adolf Hitler im deutschsprachigen Spielfilm nach 1945" (PhD diss., University of Trier, 2009).

13. Joachim C. Fest, interview by Christoph Amend, *Die Zeit* 42 (2004).

14. Jens Jessen, "Stilles Ende eines Irren unter Tage," *Die Zeit* 36 (2004).

15. On the question of realist representation and performance, see Christine Haase, "Ready for His Close-up? On the Success and Failure of Representing Hitler in *Der Untergang*," *Studies in European Cinema* 3.3 (2005): 189–99; and Steffen Hantke, "Hitler as Actor, Actors as Hitler: High Concept, Casting, and Star Performance in *Der Untergang* and *Mein Führer*," *Cinephile* 5.1 (2009): 19–28.

16. Bruno Ganz, interview by Andreas Kilb, *Frankfurter Allgemeine, Sonntagszeitung* 28, 21 September 2003.

17. Wim Wenders, "PResident Evil oder Das einheimische Böse," *Neue deutsche Literatur* 52.8 (2004): 58. For a very similar response to Syberberg's *Hitler*, see Wim Wenders, "That's Entertainment: Hitler (1977)," in *West German Filmmakers on Film: Visions and Voices*, ed. Eric Rentschler (New York: Holmes & Meier, 1988), 126–31.

18. See Eric Rentschler, "From New German Cinema to the Post-Wall Cinema of Consensus," in *Cinema and Nation*, ed. Mette Hjort and Scott MacKenzie (London: Routledge, 2000), 260–77.

19. As the difference between *Sophie Scholl* and an earlier adaptation, *Die weisse Rose* (*The White Rose*, Michael Verhoeven, 1982) shows, religious faith has taken the place of political ideology in offering a place of moral certainty and personal agency. The role of the church continues to be examined critically in coproductions such as the Canadian-German-American *Bonhoeffer: Agent of Grace* (Eric Till, 2000), about the Protestant pastor Dietrich Bonhoeffer, and the French-German-Romanian *Amen* (Costa-Gavras, 2002) about the less-than-honorable role of the Vatican, as seen from the perspective of an idealistic priest. Confirming the growing relevance of faith-based narratives, *Truth & Treason* (Matt Whitacker, 2012), a Utah-based film production, uses the story of German Mormon Helmut Hübener to assert the identity of church and faith. The broader turn to ethical questions can also be noted in such diverse films as the British-German production *Good* (Vicente Amorin, 2008), about the political opportunism of a highly educated man who knew better, and *The Reader* (Stephen Daldry, 2008), about the corruption of an uneducated woman who, out of shame about her illiteracy, chose not to know.

20. Teamworx, which produced the last two films, describe themselves as a "market leader in event productions." The company specializes in staging German history as a series of political crises (e.g., the 2001 production *Der Tunnel*, about the building of a tunnel under the Berlin Wall, and the 2005 production *Die Luftbrücke*, about the Berlin airlift) and natural disasters (e.g., the 2006 production *Die Sturmflut* [Storm tide], about

the Hamburg flood of 1962). For a comparative reading of recent television trends, see Tobias Ebbrecht, "Docudramatizing History on TV: German and British Docudrama and Historical Event Television in the Memorial Year 2005," *European Journal of Cultural Studies* 10 (2007): 35–53.

21. Thomas Elsaesser, *New German Cinema: A History* (New Brunswick, NJ: Rutgers University Press, 1989), 239.

22. See Robert C. and Carol J. Reimer, *Nazi-Retro Film: How German Narrative Cinema Remembers the Past* (New York: Twayne, 1992), 1–13.

23. Lutz Koepnick, "'Amerika gibt's überhaupt nicht': Notes on the German Heritage Film," in *German Pop Culture: How American Is It?*, ed. Agnes Müller (Ann Arbor: University of Michigan Press, 2004), 192. See an earlier version of the argument in Lutz Koepnick, "Reframing the Past: Heritage Cinema and Holocaust in the 1990s," *New German Critique* 87 (2002): 47–82.

24. See Claire Monk, "Sexuality and Heritage," *Sight and Sound* 5.20 (1995): 32–34. Confirming the fundamentally different aesthetic and critical project associated with British heritage and post-heritage films, even *Aimée & Jaguar*'s lesbian love story or *Before the Fall*'s homosocial friendship function in highly conventional ways and lack the queer sensibility that distinguishes the best examples of the British films. Similarly, German filmmakers seem entirely untouched by the postmodern sensibilities found in a neo-noir rubble film like *The Good German* (Steven Soderbergh, 2006).

25. See Mattias Frey, *Historical Films in Postwall Germany: A Cinema of Retrospection* (New York: Berghahn, forthcoming), esp. the introduction.

26. Koepnick, "'Amerika gibt's überhaupt nicht,'" 198 and 197.

27. Richard Dyer, "Nice Young Men Who Sell Antiques: Gay Men in Heritage Cinema," in *Film/Literature/Heritage: A Sight and Sound Reader*, ed. Ginette Vincendeau (London: British Film Institute, 2001), 44.

28. The two other English-language bunker films are *Hitler: The Last Ten Days* (1973) with Alec Guinness and *The Bunker* (1981) with Anthony Hopkins; all three closely follow the account given by Hugh Trevor-Roper in *The Last Days of Hitler* (1947). A comparative analysis of the performances by Guinness, Hopkins, and Ganz would reveal an increasing emphasis on Hitler's madness, that is, on Nazism as pathology. Expanding the intertextual references to comics, Walter Moers's famous cartoon *Adolf: Der Bonker* (Adolf: The bunker, 2006) and the video clip *Adolf, die Nazisau—ich hock in meinem Bonker* (Adolf, the Nazi pig—I am sitting in my bunker) can be seen as a politically incorrect spoof of *Downfall* and earlier bunker films.

29. Rüdiger Suchsland, "Geburt einer Nation in der Illusionsmaschine: Vor dem Filmstart von Bernd Eichingers *Der Untergang*," *Telepolis*, 7 September 2004, http://www.telepolis.de/r4/artikel/18/18274/1.html.

30. Marianne Hirsch, *Family Frames: Family, Photography, and Postmemory* (Cambridge, MA: Harvard University Press, 1997).

31. The references are to Helmut Kohl's speech before the Israeli Knesset on 24 January 1984 and Martin Walser's acceptance speech of the Friedenspreis des Deutschen Buchhandels on 11 October 1998.

32. Traudl Junge, *Bis zur letzten Stunde: Hitlers Sekretärin erzählt ihr Leben*, written with Melissa Müller (Berlin: List, 2004). The book was first published in 2002, the year Junge passed away. An English translation appeared the following year: *Until the Final Hour: Hitler's Last Secretary*, ed. Melissa Müller, trans. Anthea Bell (London: Weidenfeld & Nicolson, 2003).

33. Reinhard Mohr, "Soll man Hitler etwa als Elefant zeigen?," *Spiegel Online*, 24 September 2004, http://www.spiegel.de/kultur/gesellschaft/0,1518,319650,00.html.

34. Regarding a famous example of blockbuster marketing that shares *Downfall*'s aesthetics of catastrophe, see Gaylyn Studlar and Kevin S. Sandler, eds., *Titanic: Anatomy of a Blockbuster* (New Brunswick, NJ: Rutgers University Press, 1999).

35. Jordan Mejias, "*Untergang* im Ausland: So muß es gewesen sein," *Frankfurter Allgemeine Zeitung*, 16 September 2004.

36. Wenders, "PResident Evil oder Das einheimische Böse," 58.

37. See the *Materialien für den Unterricht* prepared by Kulturfiliale Gillner and Conrad, with authors Karin Springer and Dr. Bernhard Springer; a PDF version is available on the web. The film's official German website has been taken down; its official English-language website http://www.downfallthefilm.com is still available.

38. On the German reception of *Downfall*, see John Bendix, "Facing Hitler: German Responses to *Downfall*," *German Politics and Society* 25.1 (2007): 70–89. For a very conventional reading of the film, see, in the same volume, Jürgen Pelzer, "'The Facts behind the Guilt'? Background and Implicit Intentions in *Downfall*," 90–101.

39. For example, see Daniel Kothenschulte, "Hitler—eine Barriere: Oliver Hirschbiegels und Bernd Eichingers Film *Der Untergang* versucht die Rekonstruktion und scheitert an der Erfindung," *Frankfurter Rundschau Online*, 14 September 2004, http://www.fraktuell.de/ressorts/kultur_und_medien/feuilleton/?cnt=503722 (web page no longer available).

40. Hannah Arendt, *Eichmann in Jerusalem: A Report on the Banality of Evil* (London: Penguin, 1994).

41. "Darf man Hitler als Mensch zeigen?," *Bild*, 16 September 2004.

42. Marian Blasberg and Jörg Hunke, "Hitler ist greifbarer geworden: Bernd Eichinger über sein Bild des Despoten und wie die Deutschen ihre Geschichte aufarbeiten sollten," *Frankfurter Rundschau* (Magazine), 11 September 2004. In the interviews included on the Constantin Film DVD, Hirschbiegel speaks about his "historical mission" as a German and a filmmaker, and Thomas Kretschmer sees much value in "Germans telling such films."

43. Frank Schirrmacher, "Hitler spielen," interview with Bernd Eichinger and Corinna Harfouch, *Frankfurter Allgemeine Sonntagszeitung*, 22 August 2004.

44. Ibid.

45. Diedrich Diederichsen, "Der Chef brüllt wieder so," *taz*, 15 September 2004.

46. Quoted in "Kohl lobt *Der Untergang*," *netzzeitung*, 17 September 2004, http://www.netzeitung.de/entertainment/movie/305430.html.

47. Sven Felix Kellerhoff, "'Es menschelt nicht': Die deutschen Historiker sahen *Der Untergang*," *Die Welt*, 17 September 2004. On a typical reading of the film that reflects

the preconceptions of the discipline, see Michael Wildt, "*Der Untergang*: Ein Film inszeniert sich als Quelle," *Zeithistorische Forschungen / Studies in Contemporary History* 2.1 (2005), http:// www.zeithistorische-forschungen.de/16126041-Wildt-1-2005.

48. "BRD-Psychologen halten den Film *Der Untergang* von Oliver Hirschbiegel für ein Machwerk," *Junge Welt*, 11 November 2004.

49. Peter Zadek, "Wer hat Angst vor Adolf Hitler?," *Cicero* 12 (2004), http://www .cicero.de/97.php?item=358&ress_id=7.

50. Wim Wenders, "'Tja, dann wolln wir mal': Warum darf man Hitler in *Der Untergang* nicht sterben sehen? Kritische Anmerkungen zu einem Film ohne Haltung," *Die Zeit* 44 (2004).

51. *Diskussionsforum* at http://www.untergang.film.de (website no longer available).

52. On the difficulty and necessity of distinguishing between national and international reception, see David Bathrick, "Whose Hi/Story Is It? The U.S. Reception of *Downfall*," *New German Critique* 102 (2007): 1–16.

53. See Gerhard Schulze, *Die Erlebnisgesellschaft: Kultursoziologie der Gegenwart* (Frankfurt am Main: Campus, 1992).

54. Eric Santner, *Stranded Objects: Memory, Mourning, and Film in Postwar Germany* (Ithaca, NY: Cornell University Press, 1990), 21–24.

55. "Adolf Hitler Is a Meme," http://tinyurl.com/742d8om. "Meme" refers to potentially viral cultural concepts and ideas that spread through the Internet, and it is not coincidental that the man responsible for the historical convergence of film and fascism returns in such a hyper-replicated mode in the digital subculture. On this phenomenon, see Virginia Heffernan, "The Hitler Meme," *New York Times Magazine*, 24 October 2008, 20–22. On these proliferating *Downfall* parodies and the attendant debates on fair use and scholarship in the critical commons, see Alex Lewitt, "Memes as Mechanisms: How Digital Subculture Informs the Real World," 2 February 2010, http://tinyurl.com/ 6wt85q6. On the broader cultural context, see Sonja M. Schultz, "Der Diktator im Internet," in *Hitler darstellen: Zur Entwicklung und Bedeutung einer filmischen Figur*, ed. Rainer Rother and Karin Herbst-Meßlinger (Munich: edition text + kritik, 2008), 86–100.

56. "That Damn Downfall Clip," http://www.youtube.com/watch?v= C7dkK6r2mHU (web page no longer available).

# Index of Names

# Index of Films

*Films are listed under original-language title. Page numbers in italics indicate illustrations.*

## WISCONSIN FILM STUDIES